...te student at Balliol College, Oxford, where he received a DPhil in Irish history in 2003. His first book, *The Fenian Ideal and Irish Nationalism, 1882–1916*, was published in 2006. He writes for the London Review of Books and teaches history at the University of Southampton.

ALSO BY MATTHEW KELLY

The Fenian Ideal and Irish Nationalism, 1882–1916

MATTHEW KELLY

Finding Poland

From Tavistock to Hruzdowa and Back Again

VINTAGE BOOKS
London

Published by Vintage 2011

2 4 6 8 10 9 7 5 3 1

First published in Great Britain in 2010 by
Jonathan Cape

Vintage
Random House, 20 Vauxhall Bridge Road,
London SW1V 2SA

www.vintage-books.co.uk

Addresses for companies within The Random House Group Limited can be
found at: www.randomhouse.co.uk/offices.htm

The Random House Group Limited Reg. No. 954009

A CIP catalogue record for this book
is available from the British Library

ISBN 9780099515999

The Random House Group Limited supports The Forest Stewardship Council®
(FSC®), the leading international forest certification organisation. All our titles
that are printed on Greenpeace approved FSC® certified paper carry the FSC®
logo. Our paper procurement policy can be found at:
www.randomhouse.co.uk/environment

Printed and bound in Great Britain by
CPI Bookmarque, Croydon, CR0 4TD

To Nana and Arfer

Nana's Map

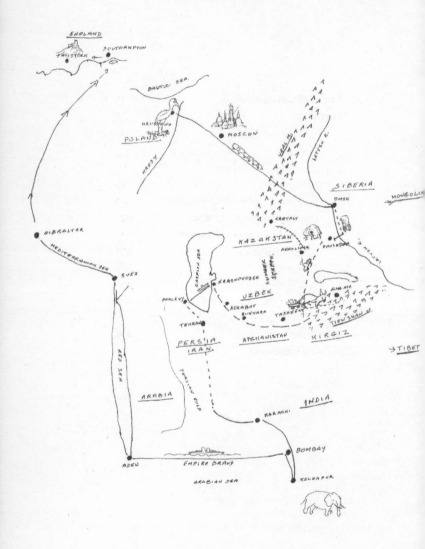

Contents

List of Illustrations

Foreword

Between Memory and History

The past is gone. All we have is the present and the histories we can construct from the different traces left by the past. It would be impossible to provide a comprehensive taxonomy of the great variety of historians involved in these reconstructions. A classifying endeavour might begin by identifying the academics, the popularisers, the memoirists, the mythologists, the yarn-spinners. But it could be extended to include almost everybody, for at one time or another we can all be found shaping what we think we know of the past into narratives that explain the present. And these narratives very often embed notions of progress or decline as determined by present-day feelings of optimism or pessimism, hope or despair, gratitude or regret, centredness or marginality. The past has no shape or meaning; it gains both as we turn it into history.

Academic historians – and by profession I'm an academic historian – have, in theory, a developed alertness to the imposition of these 'narrative tropes' on our understanding of the past. In the loosest sense, I've been trained and inducted into a profession that lives by strict rules and proce-dures, opaque though they are. Historians know when they are reading academic history. The signs are immediately evident in the critical vocabulary, the cautious tone, the unemotive language, the literary tech-niques deployed to distance the reader from the subject, the close reading of archival sources, the presence of footnotes and bibliographies. It is even evident in the layout of the page, the austerities of the typeface and, all too often, the disparity between a seductive cover and dry content. More fundamentally, these trappings are underpinned by two basic attitudes of mind. First, a questioning attitude towards what we think we know about the past and a tendency to question or problematise received wisdoms. Second, the disciplining and sometimes troubling thought that in the past the future – our present – was one of any number of possibilities. A deep scepticism – as opposed to cynicism – properly characterises my caste, for all its individual and collective expertise. We aim for objectivity and detachment, though we know this can only ever be an aspiration; we allow ourselves the privilege of moral judgement and yet accept that how we are situated in time and place renders such judgements subjective; we know that our conclusions can only ever be provisional. We transgress our caste rules when we forget that the historians of the future will ask different questions of the pasts we write about; they will stand on our shoulders while at the same time finding us naïve, methodologically unsophisticated and transparently partisan.

At their most caste-bound professional historians write monographs. Diligently researched, tightly focused, and clearly positioned in relation to active historical debates, monographs are published by academic presses in relatively small print runs and sold at high prices. They are primarily purchased by libraries, read by specialists and the occasional enthusiast. The greatest historians in any given subject area are often unfamiliar to the general reader. They are those who through a succession of research-driven publications have changed the way their peers think about a particular period or historical problem. The monograph is everything the general reader does not seek in a history book but, done well, it will win a historian the esteem of his or her peers.

This book is not a monograph. Instead, it embodies in quick succession and sometimes simultaneously a range of historical personalities. Critical use is made of primary sources, much testimony and unverifiable memory is reproduced, autobiography is used to frame the story and first-person impressions to soften the narrative. Attempts are made to historicise memories but the memories themselves, often fragmentary, are presented as they were presented to me. Historical debates are introduced if pertinent and, where necessary, I've happily deferred to the expertise of others. Photographs warm the text: where the words that cross the page particularise, the accumulation of lines across a face universalise.

Much of the first half of the book could not have been written without the monograph literature produced by a new generation of historians of the Soviet Union and Central Europe. Readers intrigued by the themes I've touched on should turn to highly readable cited works by Kate Brown, Katherine Jolluck, Terry Martin, Timothy Snyder and Lynne Viola, as well as those of long-established scholars like Norman Davies, Jan T. Gross, Tadeusz Piotrowski, Antony Polonsky and the late Keith Sword, pioneer of the study of the Polish community in Britain. Later sections are more strongly rooted in primary sources, those pieces of paper bequeathed to the present by the past. Some of these can be found in public archives, others have sat undisturbed for many years in a house in Devon. Where there is no call number there is no endnote. Parts of this book were only possible because my grandmother, to me always Nana, was willing to write down her memories. Photocopies of her originals, written in clear capital letters and more extensive than I ever presumed to expect, came to me through the post at timely intervals. These chapters of autobiography, staccato and episodic, but replete with startling images and suffused with great warmth, have found their way into my text. Shrouded in a more formal prose, I hope shifts in register and obvious changes in content will alert the reader to their presence. I try not to think of how much time went into writing these, but I'm very grateful. I'm equally grateful to Nana for the absolute trust with which yellowing piles of letters, albums of photographs, and little plastic boxes of military insignia and other memorabilia have been placed at my disposal. Nothing, to my knowledge, has been withheld and nothing of what follows has been read by a member of my family before publication. When I tried to express my gratitude for this uninhibited access, it was shrugged off as though it were odd to think it should be otherwise.

This book will not be the last word on the subject. Aspects of the story cry out for further investigation and some parts will only be understood properly when graduate students with the necessary Russian, Polish and English language skills make them their PhD topics. More than this, there will be Poles, whose experiences ran parallel to those of my protagonists, who will be dissatisfied by what they read here. It will not tally with their perception of the first half of the twentieth century. In particular, I have read many heartbreaking accounts of the premature deaths of children, parents and grandparents, often buried in unmarked graves somewhere in Russia or Soviet Asia, or in cemeteries in some corner of the British Empire. Each family's experience deserves its own book, but it cannot be this one. For, though shadowed by the millions who died under Stalinism and Nazism, this is primarily an account of a nuclear family which survived and went on to live a relatively ordinary post-war life. The story I tell cannot but be marked by this fact. I'm reluctant to make clichéd remarks about this testifying to their human spirit for I reject the implication that those who died somehow lacked this nebulous quality. Instead, I end this foreword on a different note. This book stars two sisters, Danusia and Wanda Ryżewskie.* They appear as the authors of letters written long ago and as voices in the present. Danusia is Nana and her present-day voice is here attributed to Nana. Had the author of this book been one of Wanda's grandchildren a different perspective would have shaped its tone and content. The sisters Ryżewskie may be a charming combination, but if heroes must be found among the Poles deported to the Soviet Union in 1940–1, it is not the children or even the soldiers we should salute first, but the mothers who selflessly dedicated themselves to ensuring, insofar as they could, that their children survived.

---

* Polish surnames have masculine and feminine forms. In this case Ryżewski is masculine and Ryżewska feminine. The plural form is Ryżewscy and Ryżewskie, respectively.

I

Trains

Childhood journeys, when time stretched longer, distances seemed greater and expectations were more intense, become deeply etched in the memory. They help build our mental hinterland, broadening our empirical and emotional frame of reference. When triggered by external associations and unexpectedly recalled, such memories can be powerfully affecting, generating a gamut of emotion. The journey that I remember with most pleasure and which, to this day, still excites me, is from London to Devon. I had grandparents in both places and a great-grandmother in Devon. When I was a small child we lived for a short time in Belvedere in Kent. Each year we journeyed to Haye Down Farm, a few miles north of the west Devon town of Tavistock, to stay with Babcia, our great-grandmother, an elderly Polish woman.

As a seven- or eight-year-old, 'Paddington' was one of the most evocative words in the English language, and to this day it is freighted with a mass of associations and images. The incomprehensible echoing voice of the station announcer, the deep growl and high-pitched whistling of a stinking Intercity 125 as it hauled its mighty weight out of the station, and the griminess that left black smudges on clean hands. No railway station could be mightier. I knew nothing of King's Cross, Euston or Waterloo, but I could not imagine choosing to travel from one of these lesser stations if Paddington was an option. That blue and yellow livery of the Intercity 125, long gone from British high-speed trains, now seems redolent of a bygone age, of the last gasp of industrial Britain.

Preparing for this journey involved all the pleasures of organising my favourite things, ritualistically laying them out on the bed, selecting one item, setting aside another, until some kind of aesthetic and functional balance was achieved. I picked up my parents' suggestions and turned them into points of high principle. 'Wear something comfortable for the journey,' Mum once said, giving us a stronger sense of personal control over our dress than was really the case. Thereafter it seemed to me that tracksuit bottoms and a loose T-shirt were the only clothes for travelling, and making sure they were clean and ready became essential preparation for any long journey. Books also loomed large in my preparations. I read avidly, gorging myself on the dozens of slightly old-fashioned children's adventure stories I picked up at school jumble sales for five or ten pence. Planning my reading was a pre-holiday delight, something I have yet to grow out of.

I knew all about the Intercity 125, about how the diesel engine turned a generator that powered the electric engines that turned the wheels. I vaguely recognised that this was a British way around the enormous expense of modernising the railways, of not electrifying the tracks, which had happened in Japan and France. The Japanese *Shinkansen*, the 'bullet train', was the stuff of fantasy; it was soon to be joined in my imagination by the French TGV. It was difficult to believe that their system was quite so superior to ours and as I parroted vital facts to my parents about the performance of the 125 (most importantly that it was called a 125 because this was its cruising speed in em pee aitch) my excitement was always slightly tempered by the knowledge that it could be so much better. Television adverts sowed further doubts. 'We're getting there,' British Rail told us, humbled by Thatcherite invective.

Following a journey of distracted reading and unquenched desires related to the buffet car, we'd arrive at Plymouth. Passing through Exeter St David's was a highlight, and this was entirely determined by the sonorous syllables of the station name. It gave me the idea of Exeter as a sprawling metropolis, the Gotham of the South-West rather than a busy cathedral city. At Plymouth, we took a taxi to the bus station. There, in that musty building, dark, low-ceilinged and utterly municipal, peppered with drunks and mums struggling with shopping, we'd wait for the bus to Tavistock. All subsequent efforts to modernise the bus station seem doomed to failure. It is one corner of England that will be forever 1979.

From the upper deck, obsessively sliding my ticket in and out of a join in the back of the seat in front, I'd watch the landscape gradually transform almost in tandem with the shift from day to dusk. Wheezing through the rush-hour traffic, the bus took us beyond the post-war dinge of Plymouth and we were soon skirting the south-western edges of Dartmoor. Urbanites might find the thought of a double-decker bus crossing open moorland incongruous but this is a common sight in the West Country. The Transmoor Link, which during the summer connects

Exeter to Plymouth via Dartmoor, is one of *the* great bus routes. As the Routemaster appears in the distance it seems plaintively isolated, transported from its natural habitat, but as it rattles along, one notices the chatty burr of the Devonian accents, the old women clutching chrome fittings, the earthy tint to the floor and the freshness of the air coming in through the open windows. Travelling north from Plymouth we could see, beyond unfenced roads, sheep, gorse and scatterings of rocks pointing through the scraggy grass, all intimations of the open expanse of the high moor beyond.

Forty minutes later we were in Tavistock. To this day, entering this small market town never fails to give me an extraordinary feeling of well-being. Now, I'm more likely to be driving down from London and on reaching Exeter I find the B3212, which crosses the moor, an irresistible alternative to the sensible A30, the dual carriageway that skirts the moors to the north. The B3212 ascends steadily from the dairy country of the valleys to the harsher, unenclosed lands of the higher reaches, where the sky opens up, the wind blows stronger, and Dartmoor's tough little ponies gather at the roadside and sheep sprawl between bouts of intense grazing. From Princetown, the bleak home of Dartmoor Prison, the road descends steeply into Tavistock, reversing the earlier transition from dairy to sheep farming, from green to yellow. My maternal grandmother, Nana, now lives there with Arfer, whom she married in the mid-1970s after being widowed in the 1960s. Dominated by its magnificent town hall and famous for its pannier market – one of *the* joys of childhood holidays – Tavistock is proud to be the birthplace of Sir Francis Drake and got rich as a stannary town, one of the transport hubs of the Devon tin mining industry. Despite the recent downturn, the town is thriving with new apartment blocks having been squeezed in everywhere and housing estates encroaching on the surrounding country. There is, unfortunately, no better description for Tavvy than 'bustling'.

From Tavistock, Mum always liked us to take Johnny Bassett's taxi. He'd been driving her and her sister to Haye Down Farm for years and I now understand that for Mum to be driven by Johnny, to chat about local affairs, to hear Johnny comment on how recently he'd seen Babcia, gave her experiences of this place a feeling of continuity, strengthening her sense of belonging here. In some ways these journeys saw her coming into her inheritance, developing an adult relationship with the place she had always travelled to in August: she was bringing to 'the Farm' her husband and children – the latter multiplying with impressive rapidity. And in this book of journeys, we should remember how even the shortest acquire significance. Only someone intimate with the facts of Mum's life could begin to understand her exuberance. Dad, I think, took this combination of nostalgia and possession with good humour and years later, after a protracted and messy divorce, had surprisingly benign memories of those Polish women who never stopped talking or filling his glass. 'Another bottle for the road, Jim?' was one his favourite faux quotations.

We four, myself, Hannah, who is seventeen months younger than me, and Sam and Laura, who long after it was appropriate would still be referred to as 'the little ones', got into the back of the taxi. Sam would have been cupped into Dad's arm, the rest of us bony hip to bony hip. Mum would sit in the front with Johnny, of whom I have no memory, but apparently he had a booming voice and I imagine his taxi smelt of cigarette smoke because everything then did. He would take us northwards out of the town; rapidly ascending, we passed under Tavistock's awesome viaduct, the lit streets giving way to country lanes canopied by overhanging trees. First we headed towards Brentor, the tiny village famous for the little granite church which had been planted on top of a tor in the thirteenth century, one of the many steep Dartmoor hills crowned with an outcrop of granite that provide epic 360-degree views. Following a left-hand turn for Chilaton, we would head a mile or two west to 'the Farm'. It now feels like an ancestral home, lost, as they must always be, to financial misfortune. How easily our experiences can be made to fit such narrative *topos*. In the back of the taxi things were quiet. Sam had been carried sleeping from the bus; Laura was collapsed across Dad's spare leg. Hannah and I were expectantly alert, the excitement heightening as through the dense foliage the evening light flickered a darkening blue as though – as I remember it now – we were in a film.

Babcia would run down the garden path, arms outstretched, her old-fashioned apron tightly binding her solid, round body. I, the fastest and oldest, would be the first to grapple with the ancient gate and a second or two later was swung round, covered in kisses and incomprehensible endearments. I thought all this impossibly athletic for someone who seemed the archetype of old age, but I easily overestimated my own size and weight. When Babcia died on Boxing Day in 1983, aged eighty, I thought this extraordinarily old and had alarming intimations of my own mortality when I began to discover that friends had grandparents and great-grandparents alive and well into their nineties.

Of these times at Haye Down, it's the meals I remember most. They would begin with soup, which seemed an incredibly refined way of commencing a meal. Also refined, it seemed to me, were the white tablecloth, the carefully laid out cutlery, the condiments, the glasses, the soup tureen and the candles. None of this was evidence of wealth or an urge to be ostentatious; it was simply how a meal ought to be presented, ought to be worked through. I've no memory of there being much conversation. Mum and Babcia probably got to work in Polish, Dad would have made some inroads into something strong. We children ate with tremendous reverence and reserve, awed by the immaculate but heavily laden table, and not entirely sure of the proper way to go about getting the last of the soup from the bowl. We knew that to drink from the bowls, while acceptable at home, was incorrect here. Tentatively, we tipped the bowl away, scooping the last of the speckled purple liquid from the bowls, adult in their wide rims, shallowness and faded green trim.

The soup varied and often was heartily stocked with rice, but I like to remember it as borscht, the delicious sweet-sour beetroot soup found throughout Eastern Europe and Russia. An old cliché says there are as many different versions as there are Polish – or Russian, or Lithuanian, or Ukrainian – housewives. Other foods included *pierogi*, Polish dumplings boiled in a pan of water and stuffed with pork, or, if served as a dessert, with fruit. Another firm favourite was *gołąbki*, cabbage leaves tightly bound around meat, mushrooms and rice, and boiled, preferably the day before eating. These dishes would be accompanied by bean or beetroot salads. It was hearty stuff. No one goes hungry in a Polish household and Polish food, we were convinced, was proper food. When we played outside, Babcia would bring a great treat, *kogiel-mogiel*, a simple mixture of raw egg yolk and lots of sugar, which she spooned into our mouths out of a teacup.

The Polish food freighted with most significance was torte. A Polish torte bears little resemblance to the light, frozen pudding cake that masquerades under the same name in British supermarkets. The real thing is a formidably rich cake that to get right takes considerable skill, experience and time. It is dense with nuts, coffee cream and chocolate, and is a Christmas essential. And when pronounced with a Polish accent, the word *torte* itself has a much richer, rounder sound than the clipped English pronunciation, the 'r' almost giving it a second syllable. Torte is also, unquestionably, an adult treat and, as a child, I didn't quite share the buzz of excitement that came a couple of hours after Christmas lunch when it was due to be served. Like beautiful flowers, beer, or the *Antiques Roadshow*, torte is one of those adult things children just don't get. And to me, working through even a very modest slice seemed something of a duty; to the assembled grandparents, aunts and uncles, who had taken an interest in the torte's existence from the moment of their arrival, it was as though a very rare Burgundy had been recklessly uncorked. For just as taking Johnny Bassett's taxi was more than a convenient way of travelling the four miles from Tavistock to 'the Farm', the cultish enthusiasm with which the torte was eaten was only tenuously connected to its taste. After Babcia's death eating Polish food ceased to be unselfconscious and routine. No longer was it merely a formidably effective way of satisfying an appetite, it was now an assertion of difference. That stack of dishes deposited by the sink, each fingertip-smeared with chocolate, were the used Communion plates of an auto-exotic ritual of belonging.

I remember the houseflies. They, like the ticking clock, were another thing that marked this household as unfamilar. Bluebottles slid proprietarily across the hand-washed tablecloth, glinting in their green and purple 'Barbarella' suits, their complicated structures precise against the starched white. Or they buzzed around with great speed and agility, occasionally settling, with the gentlest touch, on bare forearms. Our attempts to swat them came to nothing and I think we'd have been shocked by the mess of a successful killing. Perhaps what was most strange about the flies was Babcia seeming unaware of their presence.

Somewhere about the house, sensibly keeping a low profile, was Kicia, Babcia's cat. She was striped black and silver and, in contrast to our cats, the long-suffering Bugsy and Pixie, was reluctant to be mauled by our sharp little hands. A small scratch seemed a low price to be paid for our ham-fisted attempts to win her round. Kicia would outlive Babcia, retiring to Nana's and Arfer's house, where, though much-loved, she never quite gave up her independent ways. She seemed peculiarly Polish, despite her authentic Devonian origins.

There was little Devonian about Babcia. She looked every bit the Eastern European peasant woman. She was small, round and robust, with the square practical hands that can be seen in my mother and aunt but are less marked in their children. She had been widowed some twenty years previously and could only speak Polish, which she constantly spoke to herself. She owned a small cottage and some eighty acres, part of which was woodland. The rest was a portion of a large field and unmarked sections were owned by various neighbours, some of whom were Polish. The cottage was built from brick, wood and corrugated iron, and was kept warm with a wood-fired range, which Mum coveted more than any other inanimate object. The room adjacent to the kitchen was at once a bathroom, an intermediary wood store (the main one was in an outside building), and the loo. The bath was a steel tub which had to be filled with hot water heated on the range. At least one old bath, upturned, lay discarded outside the cottage. The loo was a bucket which was regularly emptied; a smaller version was provided in our bedroom because we couldn't reach the door handle. The floor of this utility area, I think, was earthen, covered by a few planks of wood; the rest of the cottage was tiled. 'The Farm' had ceased to be 'working' after Babcia's husband died in the 1960s, the decade before we were born, and in her old age Babcia was involved in a protracted dispute with a local dairy farmer ('tricky Dickie'), who claimed rights to graze cattle on her land. I remember her distress one morning when the cattle broke through the fence and into her vegetable garden. After Nana inherited the farm she faced successive court appearances and fines for taking down fences Dickie had put up. It was the kind of dispute that easily sours relations between rural neighbours.

The Ryżewscy had been in the area since the late 1940s and Babcia was well known locally, not least for her insistence on walking the four miles into Tavistock to do her shopping. Sometimes she might be offered a lift by a passing motorist, and perhaps she expected no less, but the walk itself was a natural part of rural life and certainly not something a woman in her seventies should baulk at. She kept chickens, and she happily broke their necks and plucked them when necessary. Each year Mum would be presented with a 'bird' to be carried back to London, a small pool of blood collecting in the bottom of its carrier bag. Babcia grew fruit, blackcurrants and gooseberries in particular, which she made into jams and puddings – both flavours seemed horribly adult to us children, tutored as we were in the apple and banana. Out in Babcia's garden, Hannah and I would pick gooseberries from the bush. With our teeth we could peel the skins back from the aperture made by the stalk and then bite the fruits in half, thrilled by the sharp taste and dissolving into mild hysteria as we caught the look of excited revulsion in each other's eyes. Jars of gooseberry jam sat in cupboards for months at home. We'd pull off the rubber band, letting it scrunch the greaseproof paper covering into a small tepee, then involuntarily shiver as we swallowed lumps of sharply flavoured sugared fruit.

Babcia's wood was damp, mossy and lichen-covered, with plenty of fallen branches and bramble patches nestled in the carpet of decaying leaves. She still chopped wood, losing an index finger to the axe at some point, and over dinner that stump fascinated me. She also went mushrooming early in the morning, beating the birds at their own game. Ordinary things like the delivery of milk seemed special. It came in plastic pouches, another exotic feature of country life, and was left by the side of the road, buried in fallen leaves. I'd go to collect it, weaving my way through the wood to the rotten gate, almost spongy with damp and luridly green. Wiping off the leaves clinging to the wet plastic, I loved the feeling of the chilled liquid moving around inside the bag.

Much of the garden area was by this point massively overgrown, a thicket of brambles, tall grass, dried yellow by the sun, and the occasional gorse bush, which thrive in west Devon. In the heat of midsummer everything became crisp and yellow, and I remember the buzz of flies in the haze and lifting feet high to bring them down with a satisfying crackle into tall, dry grass. We would have huge bonfires, which I, in my nascent machismo, considered my particular demesne, always identifying at an early stage in the proceedings a useful stick that would act as poker and symbol of my authority. We baked potatoes in the embers of the fire and crunched our way through their charcoal-covered skins.

That fire stick might, in some unconscious way, have been related to my favourite object in that house: my great-grandfather Rafał's army truncheon. It was a heavy, dense piece of wood, painted black and flawlessly smooth, with a broken leather strap.* He had been a captain in the Polish army, I would say with unconcealed pride to friends at school. 'Captain' meant a lot to schoolboys, it evoked Kirk or Hook, but it also meant the Second World War. It seems strange to remember how conscious we were of that war, despite its distance in time. We were at the tail end of the post-war dispensation. The wartime gener-ation was only just beginning to relinquish its political pre-eminence, handing the baton on to the baby boomers. And although our teachers were generally too young to have served in the war, the *Beano*esque idea that the teacher could be diverted from chemistry to wartime reminiscences about his shrapnel wounds had a kitschy, anachronistic currency. I remember looking up 'captain' in the encyclopaedia and being disappointed to discover the relative lowliness of the rank. I was also annoyed by a friend who knew the Polish army had faced German tanks on horseback and hadn't stood a chance. This, I had already decided, was the romantic way to go. I had, perhaps, picked up in a diluted form what the Polish Nobel Laureate Czesław Miłosz, when talking about the relationship between identity and enmity, described as those 'hereditary encumbrances which endure, not in the blood but in words'.[1]

Retrospectively, these summer holidays are identifiably idyllic, but at the time I don't think we could fathom this solitary old woman living in the woods in such primitive conditions. Jetting off to Portugal or Spain, I slowly came to realise, represented a shorter journey than taking the train to Devon. There was, very obviously, something different, alien, about Babcia. It was not just the language or the food that set her apart, but our vague sense of the peculiar means by which she came to be there. As I hit adolescence and began to devote a great deal of time to pondering the mechanics of human reproduction, the old woman in the woods, now dead, began to take on even greater

---

* I have since learnt that it was an ordinary policeman's truncheon that Babcia kept to protect herself at night.

significance. I knew enough to understand that my existence depended on the chance meeting of my parents at teachers' training college in London. At some point I grasped that had my parents met a day later the whole progress of their relationship would have been that tiny bit different, meaning their first squealing product couldn't have been me. Becoming conscious of this element of chance was perplexing enough, but I soon realised that the Polish and Irish dimension of my family story added a further mind-boggling layer of fluke to my conception. My grandmother being taken to Siberia by the Russians had somehow determined my very existence. And it is not entirely flippant to suggest that the origins of this book lie in the disquiet provoked by this adolescent narcissism which, as I write, still has the capacity to unsettle me.

History, then, had made me in a way that seemed to differentiate me from my classmates. I found their Englishness, not in terms of behaviour but as an idea of familial descent, genuinely baffling. It seemed to possess a kind of bland grandeur, a purity that one would never choose to have. And though outwardly there is nothing to distinguish me from an English person of my generation, class and educational background, I have always taken a quiet pride in my hyphenated background, regarding it, against more rational judgement, as carrying some kind of significance. Despite this, I'd never describe myself as Irish-Polish, and it is somewhat paradoxical that this stems from an English reticence about showing off, about making oneself exceptional. Whereas in the United States a hyphenated identity is legitimising, providing evidence that one's achievements stem from hard work rather than hereditary good fortune, in Britain being able to slide in unobtrusively, learning the language, the accents and the attitudes of the social elite is the way to get ahead.

Consequently, Nana, with her thick Polish accent and Polonised-English, can still be asked about when she arrived and whether she likes it here. She is white, she's doesn't fit into familiar narratives of emigration, people find it difficult to place her. In England, in contrast to black or Asian Britons, she will always be 'an alien', as her papers were stamped when she arrived here in 1947. Despite having spent her whole adult life here, she is convinced that as she gets older her English is deteriorating. Maybe, just as memories of childhood retain a vividness with which, as we age, few adult memories can compete, she is somehow reverting to a more deeply ingrained, atavistic Polishness.

As a child, I was conscious of our difference through other markers.

One day I discovered that I was the only (nominal) Catholic in the class. Doubtless my teacher put this down to my Irish surname, an accurate enough surmise, but this only tells half the story – the less unusual half. My mum's Christian name was another oddity. Schoolchildren are fascinated by their and their friends' parents' names, though I perhaps more so than others for I was always surprised when friends did not seem to know what their parents were called. 'What!' they would exclaim. 'Your mum's name's Nazi?' No, I insisted, frustrated by their ignorance, it's Narcy, it's Polish, it's short for Narcyza, it's a flower.

But why had this come to be? Why did we have these beetrooty summer holidays? I knew it had something to do with the Russians and when Nana had been in Siberia during the Second World War. I knew she had travelled on a train and the toilet had been a hole in the floor. I later discovered other things. We were from near Kraków, which I knew was an important Polish city. I would later be disappointed to find where Nana had actually grown up was now in Belarus. The importance I'd attached to this Polishness seemed undermined by this. Thanks to school history, however, I began to develop a more historically sophisticated outlook, realising that neither borders nor populations were permanent, but it was still far from clear why Nana had experienced what she had. As I got older and my questions became more probing, her stories of being deported began to dry up. I pompously told myself that this was because she recognised that I had grasped how nasty the transportation was and I was not to be fobbed off with jolly stories of exotic experiences. I was wrong about this.

As my interest has become more focused and serious, as I have become more direct about my desire to know and the possible use to which her information might be put, Nana has proved extremely fluent, the memories flowing, studded with unexpected detail and vibrancy, the information rapidly accumulating. Without realising it, I had underestimated not only how much she remembered, how much of her childhood could be recalled, but how much she knew of a more general, historical nature. Later conversations triggered rushing memories and though I wish I'd taped our first discussions, that initial feeling of spontaneity was never lost. And although she was given a Dictaphone, she found talking to it difficult, preferring the natural flow of conversation; the questions and the attention of another person strengthening the lived reality of those years. There is, I am sure, a therapeutic element to these conversations, as there also is to Nana's gathering together and ordering of materials. She has photos, some of which are reproduced in this book; she has official documents, including her identity papers; and, most precious of all, she has a long series of letters from the 1930s detailing the family's history, her father's Company diary from when he was in Soviet Asia in 1942–3, and the many letters the family exchanged through a long period of wartime separation.

Nana has this readiness to talk in common with many of the Poles I've met who shared her experiences, and this seems new. Partly it is related to the revelations of the 1990s, when the Soviet archives began to be opened up. But also it's because they're conscious of their mortality, that they are aged grandparents whose stories might be lost with them. Many of the accounts that have proved central to the writing of this book are addressed to grandchildren. It seems the deportees, now elderly pensioners, often find it easier to talk to their grandchildren, particularly as they become young adults, than to their own children. Recently I talked to two daughters of transportees, both middle-aged women, one British, one American, both close to their mothers, both involved in survivors' organisations, both with an encyclopaedic knowledge of their parents' experiences. I mentioned, with intentional casualness, that I'd been struck by the matter-of-factness with which some of the survivors, particularly the women, spoke about their ordeal. They seemed a tough bunch, I ventured. Recognition flashed between the two women, registering a moment of mutual sympathy.

I've sensed on a few occasions this guardedness from the children of the transportees, a slight intimation of the toughness of their upbringings, a toughness born of the trains and the camps. For it seems the deportations taught that survival is unexceptional, it is what people do. But as we know from accounts of 'survivors' guilt', surviving survival can throw up greater challenges than the ordeal itself. I think of this when I recall the dear old woman who lived in the shack in the woods, unable to communicate with the people around her, even her visiting grandchildren. Mum remembers her being extraordinarily preoccupied by death, by who had died and when and in what circumstances. In spite of this, she gave her grandchildren, and those of her great-grandchildren old enough to remember, some of their seminal experiences, reinforcing their hybrid identities by wrapping them in the warm blanket of childhood holidays. It seems almost fantastical that the journeys her daughters experienced at the same stage of their lives began with deportation from eastern Poland and ended with arrival, some seven years later, in Britain. Their traumatic journey provided us with our Eden. This paradox originated in the violent historical forces of the twentieth century; it's already proving to be a very twenty-first-century story.

2

Life in the Wild Lands

Rafał Ryżewski was born on 2 November 1899, the first son of a highly respectable Polish family in Bielsko-Biała, a town in Austrian Poland. His was a family of professors, teachers and artists, members of Poland's intellectual class or, as they were known in the census, intellectual workers.[1] A studio portrait, taken shortly after the 1914–18 war, shows Pan and Pani Ryżewscy, Rafał's parents, with their three daughters and three sons. Their eldest sons, Rafał and Stefan, stand like two sentries, impressively bookending the family group, haughty and proud in their Polish army uniforms. Rafał, the eldest, displays four service medals. The three daughters, modest in dress and deportment, are interspersed within the group. Elżbieta, the youngest, sits to the right of her mother, Renia stands next to Rafał between her seated mother and father, and Wiesia sits to her father's left. Józio, the youngest son, is on the brink of adolescence. He stands between Stefan and Renia, fresh-faced in his cadet's uniform. Graduating as a doctor in the mid-1930s, Józio, along with his father, would disappear without trace at the beginning of the war. It's quite likely they were among the first Poles to be taken to a Nazi concentration camp. All this was in the terrible future.

It is the parents, sitting face-on, who command attention. She has a lined face and seems slightly absent, her half-closed slightly Asiatic eyes suggesting indifference; it's not clear that she sees much value or purpose in the photograph. Józef sits confidently, squarely facing the camera. He wears a black suit, which firmly encloses his compact but tautly fat figure; from his shining bald round head, dark eyes challenge the camera, seemingly flitting between defiance and complacency. In photographs from the 1930s he looks bigger and flabbier, but here, in the prime of his life, Józef is the proud patriarch marking the moment of Polish independence with a visual record of his own achievement.

Pan and Pani Ryżewscy are remembered as forbidding and strict parents, so much so that interested young men had not much chance of getting close to their daughters, leaving them little prospect of marriage. Nothing in this photograph suggests otherwise. But as I've come to know Rafał, the eldest child of these formidable parents, I increasingly think of him in this photograph as acting out his role as dutiful son and Polish patriot. Released from the frame of this set-piece image, he seems to have been little confined by the restraints of bourgeois respectability the photograph so successfully evokes. From his later letters and the memories of his daughters emerges a man very different from this arrogant young soldier. Nonetheless, one way or another, Rafał would be in uniform until 1947. He was at ease in positions of authority and though he exercised this with a lightness of touch, earning the respect and affection of his men, this picture conveys the sense of entitlement that would carry him through life.

Rafał was educated at Gymnasium II in nearby Kraków, the region's cultural capital, where his schooling was interrupted by the outbreak of war in 1914. Following a successful military career, Rafał settled in the east of Poland. There he trained as a schoolteacher, married Hanna, another young teacher, and together they had two daughters, Wanda Irena and Maria Danuta. When war broke out in 1939, Rafał's and Hanna's young family was thriving: Rafał was head teacher of his school in nearby Postawy and Hanna, a full-time teacher in their home town, had temporarily held a headship; they were laying the foundations of the house they had long planned to build on their land; and their daughters, now aged twelve and eight, had become bright and pretty girls. A year later all four would be in the Soviet Union, having lost everything. Hanna,

Wanda and Danusia (as Danuta was known) would be living and working on a collective farm in Kazakhstan; Rafał would be a prisoner of war in a Soviet camp.

The move east and then the catastrophic change in the Ryżewski family fortunes was intimately bound up with the history of the reborn Polish state. In Poland, as elsewhere in Europe, the interwar years were experienced as a period of crisis and disorder. The Polish political classes struggled to reconcile democratic political practice with stability and order. Consequently, the state lurched between liberty and authoritarianism, drifting progressively towards the right. In their small way, the Ryżewscy were deeply implicated in this dynamic and to make sense of their particular fate one must situate their personal histories in the history of the territory that became Poland's eastern borderlands after World War One, one of the most contested strips of territory in modern Europe.

In the 1930s, the Ryżewscy rented a house in Hruzdowa in eastern Poland, a small town now in north-east Belarus near Postawy. It can be found on the latitudinal line between the Lithuanian capital Vilnius and the Belarus city Navapolack, and in road maps of the time it appeared more prominently than it does now. Nearby they had modest land holdings, always referred to as *Działka* (pronounced 'Jowka'), simply meaning land or allotment, looked after by a local family.

I'm talking about this house and the town with Rafał's two daughters, my grandmother, always to me Nana but often in this book Danusia, and her elder sister, my great-aunt Wanda. We're at Nana's house in Tavistock and Wanda is visiting from Canada. We drink tea and Nana ensures there is a steady supply of sweet snacks. Conversation turns first of all to their house. It was a typical *kresy* house, Nana says. *Kresy* simply means borderlands in Polish, but as will become clear the idea of the *kresy* is important to this history. The house had one floor and was built from timber logs, with an overhanging thatched roof. A stork nested on one corner. Later, in Karachi, Danusia saw a stork in the zoo and immediately thought of Poland. There was also a pond, which Wanda insists 'was not *that* big'. Water came from a well; the bucket was raised and lowered with a rope on a pulley. In front of the house to one side was a flower garden and to the other a vegetable garden. It would have looked something like this:

Aneska, an old woman, looked after the house and the garden until Ciocia Marysia (aunty Marysia), their mother's sister, came to live with them. She prided herself on her high standards and on arrival insisted the carpets be taken up and beaten. On laundry day the house would be abuzz with activity; local girls were brought in to help.

Hruzdowa was then a small market town, one of the commercial hubs of the region. It had fifty-two buildings, Wanda says decisively, which included the offices of the local administration, houses and businesses – often one and the same. There was a Polish general store and two Jewish grocery shops, one of which doubled up as a café, selling cakes, coffee and beer. After church, people gathered here and the shop was important to the social life of the town, providing a place where parents gossiped and did business, children played, and young adults could chat and flirt. Something of the importance of the café-shop is obliquely captured in *A World Apart* by the Polish writer Gustav Herling (1919–2000), the classic Polish account of life in a Stalinist labour camp. He describes visits to the camp shop, which as a productive worker – a Stakhanovite – was one of his privileges. Almost always void of goods for sale, the shop never-theless provided an easy atmosphere, a place where tobacco smoke mingled with conversation and inmates found solace in this parody of life back at home: it was a 'comedy', Herling writes, set 'in a small theatre without props'. We talked, 'as if we were meeting in a village wine-shop after Sunday-morning service, discussing the weather, the work, the news from other camp sections, our favourite dishes and the price of alcohol'.[2]

Hruzdowa also boasted a town hall and a police station. Wanda knew the mayor's son, a sure sign of both their social status in the town and the intimacy of small-town life, while Nana remembers the seductive, heady smells of the tannery.

The tanner, she says, was a Tartar. Whenever she talks of the ethnic background of the townspeople she takes pleasure in their exoticism, enjoying the sense that people had come to this place from far away, whether physically or in the imagination. It was the presence of such people that gives memories of life in the borderlands an other-worldly feel, and both Nana and Wanda tend to exoticise their past lives. But as one delves deeper, trying to fathom where these two girls stood in relation to their childhood haunts and trying not to schematise their memories, it nonetheless becomes clear that their experience was shaped by their privileged position in relation to the rest of the community.

Romanticising youth, whether through sepia-tinged accounts of the struggle against poverty or the evocation of a lost domain of a carefree innocence, is common enough, but also at work here is the peculiar form nostalgia takes when the places of the past remain out of reach. Revisited sites from childhood seem much smaller to adult eyes, everything built at two-thirds scale. Our adult selves 'correct' these memories and situate them in a chronological, developmental scheme, but for the place that must remain forever in the memory, they are difficult to rationalise or relativise and such places grow with us. Imaginatively recreated on the cusp of the present, past sensations can be recalled or re-experienced with a vividness often lost when continuously living in the same place. Nana sits on the sofa in her house in Devon. She is a seventy-five-year-old mother of two and grandmother of six. She says that Ciocia Mama, monitoring her table manners, forbade her from looking at the devils under the table during meals. This Danusia promptly did and Nana lifts her feet from the carpet, dangling legs unable to reach the floor, and then ducks her head under the imaginary table. She sits up suddenly wide-eyed; the cat was there, under the table, with devilishly green eyes. Nana, momentarily Danusia, laughs with mock horror, suddenly the playful, lively child who lived life in a theatrical spirit. It was one of those 'exceptional moments', described by Milan Kundera, where a gesture reveals the 'certain part of us that lives outside of time'.[3]

It's clear how differently Nana and Wanda remember. Wanda, four years older than Nana, remembers things Nana has no understanding of and Wanda can be relied upon for facts about people and places, about names and sometimes dates. Nana remembers things with a different eye. She's a painter and she *sees* her memories, which makes her recollections differently effective from Wanda's grasp of exact detail. She explains this carefully: to remember something I've read, she says, I must imagine the page of the book or the newspaper. In their letters from the 1940s their differences are strongly evident: Wanda relays facts, Danusia provides vivid description. Wanda just knows things, as the elder sibling must, whereas Nana seeks verification. 'Of course,' Wanda will say, commencing to answer a question or responding to a query from Nana. She'll then pause, before beginning a more detailed exegesis. Nana always wants to speak first, but she usually accepts her sister's clearer judgements with grace. Despite being separated by the Atlantic, they're a good team, who recognise each other's strengths and weaknesses, and are generous in their praise. Wanda, it seems, sees the creative, imaginative sunniness of Nana, forgiving her folly. She is one for the quiet word when her more ebullient sister is out of the room. She lets the talkative talk, waiting for the opportunity to steal a moment, making sure that something crucial has been understood. Nana will do the same, but late at night, pottering about the kitchen, as guests prepare for bed. At these moments she becomes meditative. 'I thought to myself,' she'll begin, her accent thickening, softening her English.

Nana's strong visual memory makes it possible to construct an impression of their home. It was a bungalow built to a rectangular floor plan, the logs stacked horizontally. The front door in the centre opened on to an entrance hall, which contained a large flower basket. The rest of the house horseshoed around this entrance, a door on the left opening into the kitchen, one on the right leading to the family room. Above the kitchen door hung a crucifix, a feature common to Polish Catholic homes. The family room, large and rectangular, was divided in half by screens. On entry, one was immediately confronted with the 'huge' fireplace and the smell of woodsmoke which pervaded the place. A large bookcase-dresser held her parents' many books and to the right of this was a big, squashy, plush green sofa. Above it hung a tapestry, which decorated and insulated the room. 'Some king or coronation,' says Nana, waving away the question.

The books were important to the girls. Danusia would hunt through them, looking for pictures. Nana has a vivid memory of a witch, with pointy hat, cloak and talons. Again she acts, imitating its malevolent pose, hunching in her chair, crooking her fingers into a crab-like shape before her face. She was known for telling stories – it's something her mother would later mention in letters from the camps – and guests she liked would be treated to pleasant tales, while those she didn't got 'awful, dreadful stories'. Wanda concurs – 'she was good at that' – as if Danusia had been carrying out a valuable service.

There was a radio, interjects Wanda, which Nana doesn't remember. It was under a window. When storms came they checked the radio was properly grounded so it wouldn't attract lightning and positioned their icon in the window facing the oncoming storm. Old superstitions alone wouldn't save them from the risks of new technologies. Wanda would play inquisitively with the dial, finding many different voices and languages – a typically *Mitteleuropa* experience. She remembers her father identifying them, making her aware for the first time of this Babel of tongues. Few others in Hruzdowa had this window on to the outside world.

As Nana's memory-eye pans around the room she fills it with objects. She comes upon a small picture, an embroidered image of poppies. She remembers the cane or raffia furniture, the set of table and chairs about which her parents entertained friends and neighbours, and the huge rubber plant that having reached the ceiling now arched downwards. Would they have to cut a hole in the ceiling to let it grow, she asked her father. Again, she delights in her naïve girlhood. There was an Ottoman too, one of those old-style, backless settees often present in late-nineteenth-century literary interiors. The floor was wooden and highly polished, inviting the girls to slide across it, wearing holes in their clothes. Ciocia Mama had things to say about that! They both insist there was an almost life-size photograph of their parents on their wedding day. This, almost more than anything else, suggests the women only remember this world through a child's eyes. To these two small girls the photograph seemed life-size and so, in a sense, it was.

Wedding photographs of Hanna and Rafał show a handsome couple. He is compact and spry, with fine features on a narrow face. He wears a white tie, his small moustache is cut and carefully maintained in the then-fashionable style. She is a little sturdier, with the broader, heart-shaped face of the Slav. Her wedding dress is finely made and delicately suggestive of the 1920s Flapper style and her notably elegant shoes complement the look. Though her face arches upwards towards her husband's as he looks directly out, her eyes are not directed towards him in the classic patriarchal arrangement but outwards towards us. There is something a little imperious about this couple, he confident of his position, she having arrived where she felt she belonged. Their different physiognomies seem to signify their different social backgrounds, he the scion of minor Polish gentry, she the clever daughter of small farmers who took advantage of new educational opportunities.

The Ryżewski household was a sociable one. Rafał's absence in Postawy during the week meant that his return home often had a festive feel, and the girls remember Hanna buoyed up in anticipation, the samovar on the table ready for tea. Particularly fun were the times Rafał would entertain his fellow officers. Ciocia Mama would cook and then 'glow with pleasure' as the officers flirtatiously congratulated her on her prowess in the kitchen. She would later marry Pan Aleksander Stanczak (Olek to the family), who owned the general store. At this point, Miecia, the girls' spirited older cousin – of whom more later – came to live with the family and help out. In contrast to the lives of their children, it's clear Hanna's and Rafał's social circle was closely determined by their class status. They kept up with the officers in the local police force, local politicians, and priests, both Catholic and Russian Orthodox. Also fun were parties at the Orthodox priest's house, who almost certainly was married with children. They didn't mix with local farmers; their friends were Polish and middle class.

Though in Nana's and Wanda's memories explicit ethnic or religious tensions barely register as a feature of their community, they both recognise the significance of certain incidents. Wanda remembers her classmates being Catholic and Orthodox, and the only Jewish boy in the school would go home during religious services or instruction. Jan Bednarz, a *kresy* Pole now living in retirement in Axminster in Devon, wrote in 2006 that he cannot remember any racial discrimination among his friends at school, 'although I can't speak for the grown-ups'. He occasionally went to the synagogue with a Jewish friend and was often invited to join his friend's family for their evening meal on Friday at the beginning of Sabbath. Given the injunction against work on the Sabbath, he says he happily lit the stove for this family and a number of their neighbours. 'Maybe this experience taught me to be tolerant to other religions and cultures.'[4]

Wanda, however, admits resentment of the Jews, particularly in the years immediately prior to the war, which she ascribes to their ability to set up businesses and succeed in commerce. It's because they were different, she says simply. Polish-Catholic memories of life in the town of Brańsk in the 1930s, gathered in the 1990s by the Polish-Jewish writer Eva Hoffman, often contain such confused thinking. Memories of affectionate relations between Polish Jews and Catholics are frequently tempered by remembered resentment of Jewish wealth.[5] As children, Wanda says, they 'played tricks' on the Jewish children and would pull their side locks.

Jewish traders, however, were welcomed to the door. Most memorable was the tailor, 'old Jankiel' (probably a generic name for a Jewish trader), who brought cloths and the especially prized 'English tweed', complete with a certificate of authenticity. Hanna was particularly conscious of the quality of collars and when the seamstress came to stay for several weeks, outfitting the whole family, she and Hanna would closely consult fashion magazines, ensuring the family were dressed in the latest style.

Historians have attempted to explain the paradoxical nature of Jewish life in Poland, working hard to find the right form of words that capture its contradictions. Daniel Stone summarises the situation at the end of the eighteenth century:

> Like other European countries, Poland isolated Jews geographically and socially and refused to admit them to the national body politic. Initial functional distinctions eventually turned into prejudice so that Jews were barred from state offices, even when they possessed sufficient training and talent to fulfil the duties, and were restricted by law in their residence and occupation. Nevertheless, compared to other countries Poland allowed Jews to live and work in relative freedom so that Poland became the largest centre of Jewish residence in Europe.[6]

No such formal restrictions existed in the interwar years and Ezra Mendelsohn, insisting that we must examine Poland comparatively, argues that Jewish/non-Jewish relations were generally better in Poland than elsewhere in Europe, suggesting that present-day Jewish ideas of Polish antisemitism are exaggerated for the 1920s and less but still so for the 1930s. For him, the paradox is that as a free but relatively antisemitic society Poland provided the environment which both stimulated and allowed the growth of a vibrant, often Zionist, Jewish politics, not least because Polish Catholics provided Polish Jews with a model of heroic nationalism. 'Interwar Poland', Mendelsohn concludes, 'was a relatively free country, a highly nationalistic country, and an anti-Jewish country.'[7]

Hoffman, an unfailingly fair-minded observer of Jewish and non-Jewish relations in Poland, observes that in the interwar period Polish politics became 'increasingly obsessed' with the 'Jewish Question'. Hoffman argues that only a small minority of extremists dabbled in the biological racism characteristic of German Nazism, suggesting instead that Polish Catholics in this period began to see Polish Jews as part of another nation, fundamentally different in character from themselves. 'Jews were becoming . . . not so much a part – no matter how loved or denigrated – of the symbolic and social entity that was Poland, but an entity unto themselves, which was experienced as somehow foreign, and which could be mentally detached or expelled from the symbolic universe of the self-contained Polish state.'[8] This should not obscure the concrete aspects of the political struggle which surrounded the so-called 'Jewish Question' and the emphasis the Right, chiefly representing the interests of an emergent urban bourgeoisie, placed on the need radically to reduce what it perceived to be the stranglehold Polish Jews had over the economy. The Left, and the Polish Socialist Party in particular, deserve notice for their consistent pluralism, inevitably attributed by the Right to the influence of 'international Jewry'. After Józef Piłsudski, whose conservative and authoritarian dominance was seen by many Jews to have held the line against political antisemitism, died in 1935, there was a surge of right-wing activism which often led to violence against Polish Jews. Though nominal Piłsudskiites remained in power, they maintained the line against the populist Right by adopting aspects of its agenda. A law of January 1937 restrained ritual slaughter, confining it to Jewish areas, thereby significantly disrupting the Jewish meat trade; with the backing of some church leaders – teaching hatred, to borrow a phrase, in the sublimity of their sacerdotal authority – there were boycotts of Jewish businesses;[9] the long-standing struggle over the number of Jewish students enrolled in the universities intensified, with some institutions introducing segregated seating in the lectures (the notorious 'ghetto benches'); and the long-touted idea that the Jewish Poles should migrate to Madagascar was widely discussed. Between the end of 1935 and March 1939 it is thought that 350 Polish Jews were killed and 500 injured in antisemitic incidents. One pattern that emerged in some parts of the country was the tendency for the non-Jewish community to punish the Jewish community collectively when a Jew was suspected of the murder of a non-Jew. How this evidence is read is open to debate. Norman Davies argues that persecution of Polish Jews was objectively mild by Hungarian, Romanian, Ukrainian or German standards, and though William W. Hagen implicitly agrees, he suggests that from these actions it is *possible* to 'conjure-up' a direction of travel towards the 'compulsory ghettoization, economic entrophy, cultural exclusion, and forced emigration' of Poland's Jews, thereby following the path already taken by Hungary, Romania, and Slovakia.[10] Fear and hatred of Germany saw rapprochement between the mainstream Right and Jewish Poles immediately before the war, but this was not enough to see the dissolution of the 'hateful notions' that had became commonplace in Poland in the late 1930s and would condition later actions during the war.[11]

The conflict between idyllic childhood memories and a more complex political context is equally evident in how Danusia and Wanda remember their land holdings outside of the town. Działka, the Ryżewski land near Postawy, was in the settlement of Korzyść. The land itself comprised fifty-eight hectares; a Belarus family looked after it and earned their living from the land and lived in a primitive cottage. Knowing the size of the plot allows us to situate the Ryżewscy a little more precisely on the social scale. In 1931 their holding was one of 2,536 in the Wilno area larger than fifty hectares; there were a further 1,516 holdings larger than a hundred hectares. They were among the 0.47 per cent of the entire Polish population classified as large landowners who owned approximately 30 per cent of the land in the Wilno region. (In Postawy County, the dominant landlord was Konstanty Przeździecki, whose giant Woropajewo estate comprised 31,000 hectares, most of which was forest and marshland.[12]) Some sense of the value of this property can be gleaned from records detailing their losses when it was confiscated by the Soviet authorities in 1939. The total value taken was put at 58,158 zloty. Working on the basis that one zloty in 1939 was worth about eight in 2004, the total value was something like £85,000. Given how cheap land in the east was and the absence of a house beyond a simple cottage, this indicates property of considerable value. The Ryżewski holding included a two-hectare orchard and 1.5 hectares of cultivated woodland, which suggests a rich supply of fruit. They grew a range of crops, including rye, wheat and potatoes, and kept cows, horses, pigs, chickens and geese. There were a brickworks, a pigsty, a barn and various sheds. Also listed as lost in the confiscation were a radio and a bicycle, and a much greater value in clothing and linen. Bricks worth something in the order of 2,400 zloty (around £3,500 by today's values) are listed, which gives some indication of how advanced plans were for building the house. Rafał would show off their achievements by riding through the rye to demonstrate how his abundant crops now reached the height of his horse's back. Nonetheless, as a commercial enterprise, Działka was in its infancy; the family's principal income came from teaching.

It is when recounting time spent at Działka that Nana and Wanda become most wistful. It is the fantastical domain they never quite laid claim to. On weekend trips, when it was just the girls and their father, they made the two-hour journey by bicycle, Nana perching precariously on the handle bars, Wanda clinging on to the back. It is easy to imagine this unstable threesome laughingly negotiating the poor roads, the girls bathing in the undivided attention of their father. On these trips they would sleep in a haystack, which never felt like a hardship. If Hanna came they took the pony and trap. On longer summer visits they rented a white house with a veranda. It seems other parents, also new to the region, brought their children out of the towns and into the country at the weekend or during the summer, reinforcing the cross-generational solidarities of the privileged and Polish. Rafał's brothers and cousins visited, wending their way by river and canal from Silesia, a journey that – apparently – took four or five days. Wanda's future husband Henio remembers selling boiled eggs to rich kids such as these heading east for their holidays. Days that were not spent supervising the development of the property – 'grooming it with loving care,' says Nana – might be spent kayaking, fishing, or picnicking, their dad putting them through their paces, keen to teach them something of the survival skills he'd learnt in the army. Canoeists would be invited to join them for tea or a meal; long lazy days would be spent at Lake Narocz.

Wanda says the Poles in the east were resented as 'occupiers' by the Belarussians. Like the antisemitism at the school, there were sometimes minor disputes between the children. Much of this was petty, the typical cruelties of schoolchildren encountering difference, but its significance lies in the extent to which it reflected attitudes picked up from the adults around them. Life in the east, for these pioneering young Poles, was a false paradise. Miłosz observed that the ongoing Polish–Lithuanian or Belarus conflict 'was in large part a class conflict between landowners and peasants; or, rather, between gentry traditions (regardless of how much property was owned) and peasant tradition'.[13] Perhaps so, as the friendship between Rafał, Hanna and the Orthodox priest suggests, but the advent of new nationalisms was adding an additional layer of ideological significance to class tensions.

Something of this malaise is caught in two casual observations made by Wanda. First, she says, much of the land in the area had been 'recovered' by Poland. The idea of recovery carries a dual meaning, indicating both bringing into cultivation non-agricultural land and the restoration to Poland after the First World War of its 'historic' lands. People were moved off the land to make way for new Polish settlers or, as the Belarusian family that tended Działka found, the departure of one set of landlords saw the arrival of another. Second, Wanda says, 'a lot of land didn't belong to anybody' and she insists that though granted land, Rafał was determined to pay for it, being willing neither to accept charity nor to face accusations of theft. This may be so, for there is documentary evidence of him having a mortgage and a great deal of work was needed to render some of the land granted to the settlers suitable for cultivation, which can only have enhanced the sense that this was virgin territory.

The kresy, however, was not an uninhabited land devoid of history. New settlers represented the imposition by a distant government of a new socio-economic elite, often alien in language, religion and culture. Many settlers saw themselves as pioneers, renewing an age-old Polish commitment to the east and though the state was obligated by international treaty to respect the cultural traditions of the 'national minorities', the extension of new state and government structures was experienced as 'Polonisation'. Many settlers sincerely believed Polonisation meant not cultural imperialism but progress, shining the light of a sophisticated European civilisation on a primitive and impoverished people of indeterminate identity. There is some truth in this. But part of this reality was Poland's overriding aim to consolidate its hold over land whose ownership, whether at a personal or a national level, was deeply contested.

How had this situation come about? The answers are to be found in Poland's long and complex history of intimate engagement with territories far to the east of its current borders.*

In the 1920s and 1930s Hruzdowa was in the northern part of the Polish *kresy*. This huge stretch of land straddled territory which now cuts deep into modern Poland, Lithuania, Belarus and Ukraine. Although Polish had been long established as the language of the elite and the educated, historical and ethnographic maps show a region comprising peoples that spoke many different languages.[14] By the twentieth century, numerous regional dialects had gradually evolved into the languages recognised today as Yiddish, Lithuanian, Belarusian and Ukrainian; in much of the region over 15 per cent of the population was Jewish and it was not unusual to find towns and cities where more than half of the population was Jewish. This linguistic plurality was echoed in religious practice. The peoples of the *kresy* worshipped in the Catholic, Russian Orthodox, Greek Uniate and Jewish traditions. Among the Christians, the religious rituals followed were not always clearly distinguishable from one another. Excepting the Polish-speaking elite – which might comprise Catholic, Jew or Orthodox but was dominated by Catholics – modern national identities could be very weak. To assume, as Poles and Soviets later did, that the peoples of the *kresy* could be divided into clear national or ethnic groups risks imposing on people of pre-modern, localist and religious identities the nationalist essentialism that would prove so destructive to life in the region in the twentieth century. Indeed, even to claim that this was a place of cultural hybridity is problematic. The peasant dialects of *kresy* villages may have been a mixture of words identifiable as Polish, Ukrainian, Yiddish (itself an amalgam of central European languages), but this teeming variety was a culture in and of itself, a pre-modern Babel rather than a degenerated admixture evolved from foreign influences.

From a western European perspective, Poland's history seems exceptionally unstable, and this is immediately accountable by its position between the imperial aggressors Germany and Russia. In many respects this made its experience typically central European. The Poland of the twentieth century was one of several nation-states built out of the rubble

---

* I should like to acknowledge the particular debt this discussion owes to Timothy Snyder, *The Reconstruction of Nations. Poland, Ukraine, Lithuania, Belarus, 1569–1999* (Yale, 2003).

of the Russian, Ottoman and Austro-Hungarian empires, proof that the Allied victory of 1918 was also a victory for the principle of the nation-state in Europe, if not in the overseas territories of the imperial victors, Britain and France.

Poland's perspective on these events, however, was exceptional. Among the new nation-states of interwar Europe, Poland was unique in having had a previous history of full independence and of being the ascendant partner of a powerful European state. Between 1569 and 1795, Poland dominated the Polish–Lithuanian Commonwealth, which at the time of its greatest reach comprised territory stretching from the Baltic in the north almost to the Black Sea in the south. Its northern extremity was a little south of Tallinn, the capital of modern Estonia, its southern extremity was a little north of the Crimea, and therefore included much of modern Ukraine; its most western point was considerably closer to Berlin than Warsaw, and in the east it penetrated land beyond the Dnieper. In short, its eastern borders approximated to the Russian Federation's western borders today.

The Commonwealth was established in the sixteenth century in response to the rise of Muscovy, the new power in the east. Under the dynamic and expansionist leadership of Ivan the Terrible (reigned 1530–84), Muscovy began to expand westwards, coveting the territories of Rus'. This land was held by the Polish and Lithuanian nobility, under their respective monarchies, and both realised that if they were to preserve their ascendancy in eastern Europe they had to cooperate. The resulting Union of Lublin, 1569, created the Polish–Lithuanian Commonwealth. Under the Commonwealth, the Polish and Lithuanian Crowns were unified and a single parliament was established, which was responsible for electing the monarch. The new arrangements preserved separate Polish and Lithuanian legal and administrative systems and instituted the principle of unanimity within the parliament (the *Sejm*). Intended to maintain the Commonwealth as a union of equals, unanimity made reform very diffi-cult and this requirement was a profound weakness when faced by author-itarian neighbours able to force their states to develop more effective military machines. Nonetheless, in the sixteenth and seventeenth centuries, the Commonwealth proved a considerable success. As Muscovy developed into Russia, the Commonwealth managed to protect its eastern borders and pacify the Cossacks, finally achieving their submission in 1658. The union failed, however, to secure the Ruthenian lands to its east and these were ceded to Muscovy in 1667.[15] As M. K. Dziewanowski observes, they

failed to transform the dualist Commonwealth into a tripartite federation.[16] In the Polish historical imagination this is forgotten in the light of
the union's famous 1683 victory against the Turks when the Polish King
Jan Sobieski led his troops to the rescue of Vienna. For later Polish patriots
excited by Commonwealth glories, successfully holding the line against
the 'barbarians' of the east was a source of deep inspiration.

The long history of the Commonwealth can only be described here
in general terms, but there are one or two crucial features worth emphasising. The first is that citizenship of the Commonwealth – and the
political rights that went with this – was limited to the nobility, known
in Polish as the *Szlachta*. Parts of the *Szlachta* were very impoverished
but this does not seem to have undermined its strong sense of corpor-
ate identity: the political rights and status that membership conferred
were not invalidated by poverty. In a sense, these privileges were caste-
based rather than class-based and their legacy was profoundly important.
For example, when describing his student life in Wilno in the 1920s and
1930s, Miłosz foregrounds the consciousness of difference which continued
to animate descendants of the *Szlachta*, among whom he included himself,
despite their embarrassed financial state and the bourgeois occupations
of their parents.[17] Rafał Ryżewski shared something of these attitudes.
One of the legacies of the *Szlachta* is the false perception in the east that
the Poles were all 'Lords', a notion later manipulated by the Soviet occupiers. As one of Miłosz's fictional characters asks, 'How can Surkont be
a Lithuanian when he's a gentleman?'[18]

In the Commonwealth period, the *Szlachta* was Christian, but its members
could be Catholic or Orthodox, though initially the Poles tended to be
Catholic and the Lithuanians Orthodox. When the debates shaping the
Reformation penetrated the Commonwealth in the mid-sixteenth century,
King Sigismond II (1548–73) promoted religious plurality, stating that he was
the 'King of the people, not of their consciences'.[19] This attitude, essential
to the survival of the Commonwealth, was reinforced by the Confederation
of Warsaw (1573) which established toleration for all within the Christian
nobility, with there being no distinction between Catholic, Orthodox or
Protestant.[20] There was no place for the Jews within the *Szlachta*, but on
the whole Jews were tolerated, though this should not obscure the occasional bouts of antisemitic violence that scarred the region's history long
before the 1930s. Catholicism became predominant among the *Szlachta*, not
least because it was closely associated with the Polish language, the vehicle
for Polish cultural and political ascendancy within the Union.

The ascendancy of the Polish language owed much to the fact that by the time of the Union it had replaced Latin as the language of Polish government. For the Poles, the languages of the public and the private spheres were the same. By contrast, before 1569, Chancery Slavonic was the language of Lithuanian government; Lithuanian or Ruthenian was the language of the domestic sphere and the medium through which the nobility communicated with its serfs. Often mistakenly referred to as Russian, Chancery Slavonic was a distinctive language which had a strong Polish element. Under these circumstances Polish was advantaged and the seeming inevitability of its ascendancy was indicated at the very outset of the Union when the acts of the Union creating the Commonwealth were recorded in Polish only.[21] Polish gradually became established as the language of politics and culture throughout the Commonwealth. Consequently, in describing the Lithuanian nobility as Polish, we are identifying an evolved cultural identity rather than describing an alien nobility planted on to Lithuanian soil by a movement of Polish aggression. Until the later nineteenth century, the only major challenge to Polish cultural predominance throughout the former Commonwealth territories was Russian.

Emblematic of Polish linguistic-cultural ascendancy is the epic poem *Pan Tadeusz* (1834) by Adam Mickiewicz, a native of Wilno. Written in Polish, it continues to be recognised as *the* Polish epic and is a fundamental of Polish schooling today – rather as Shakespeare is in the English-speaking world. Yet *Pan Tadeusz* recounts the lives of the Lithuanian gentry just prior to the Napoleonic invasion of Russia in 1812. It opens with the cry 'Lithuania! My fatherland!' To those schooled in the ideals and logic of the Commonwealth, Mickiewicz's celebration of Lithuanian Polishness carries no contradiction. And it is a tradition that lived on in the work of Miłosz, another Lithuanian Pole. Though acutely conscious of the hatreds animating life in the East, Miłosz saw the pluralism of the Commonwealth as a nostalgic counterpoint to the ethnic nationalism and Soviet communism that has since shaped the region. This earlier tolerance, Miłosz believed, brought into question the historical imperative that the nationalist challenge to Commonwealth ideals claimed to represent. As Milan Kundera said of the similar complexity of the Czech lands, for some Poles ethnic nationalism was 'un-obvious'.[22]

While Polishness may have thrived, the Commonwealth itself soon entered a period of dramatic political decline, culminating in its disappearance in the late eighteenth century. Popular historical memory

may hold the 'last king of Poland' personally responsible for this catastrophe, though more recent historical work demonstrates that the
Commonwealth failed as a state, proving unable to meet the challenge
posed by aggressive new Continental powers. In 1772, 1793 and 1795 it was
partitioned, bit by bit, by Austria, Prussia and Russia, the latter taking
the lion's share.[23] Warsaw, Wilno (in Russian Wil'na), Kijów (now Kiev),
and Minsk became part of the Russian Empire; Kraków and Lwów were
snatched by the Austrian Empire; and Gdańsk was taken by Prussia.
Nonetheless, as the nineteenth-century poetry of Mickiewicz and many
others suggests, Polish culture thrived in these new circumstances, and
Wil'na University, where tuition was in Polish, was the largest university
in the Russian Empire. Russian dominance saw an intensification of Polish
sentiments, and Polish nationalist politics, still bound in the east to the
aristocratic ideals of the Commonwealth, oscillated between an emphasis
on the nurturing of Polish culture within the Empire and the desperate
urge to shake off Russian dominance.[24]

A strongly romantic vein shaped much of this Polishness. Poland,
according to the Poles, was *the* martyr nation, and for some to suffer in
the name of noble ideals was regarded as an authentic expression of
Polishness. As in Ireland during the same period, some nationalists began
to see heroic failure in the name of the nation as preferable to the passive
acceptance of the status quo. This sacral nationalism, in which commitment to the nation becomes an obligation comparable to those demanded
by religious belief, was present in all nineteenth-century European nationalisms. But where the odds were especially high and a more constructive
politics stymied, sacral nationalism proved particularly seductive. Just as
Christ had died to redeem mankind, it went, so might dying for the
nation bring its redemption. In 1830 and, more significantly, in 1863
the Polish gentry rose against Russian rule. The revolutionaries of 1863
were caught between a serious attempt to overthrow imperial rule and
a reckless urge towards self-sacrifice. It was, perhaps, the last hurrah of
the old Polish nobility. It was also a total failure and the Russian response
was predictably harsh. Thousands were killed in the campaign of pacification that followed, thousands more were deported to Siberia – later
waves of Polish deportees would stumble upon the remnants of the '63
generation – and Moscow embarked on a concerted campaign of
Russification. They were determined to root out Polishness, which they
identified as the source of disloyalty and instability in their vulnerable
western borderlands.[25] Their Soviet successors would take a similar view.

Russia had good cause to act decisively. Throughout the Continental empires, restless peoples were embracing the dictums of nationalism, and demanding political rights and some measure of territorial independence. Many people in the nineteenth century believed nations were God-given timeless entities, bound to a particular language, territory and religion. For nationalists the Rights of Man could only be realised in confluence with the rights of nations and the individual could only achieve an authentic or fulfilled life when his or her historic national community was able to develop free of alien cultural and political influences. The 1848 revolutions, the 'springtime of the peoples', were an expression of these ideas and that year cast a long shadow. In France, 1848 might have been a bid to extend political rights further down the social scale, but elsewhere the fever of revolution was also driven by social and cultural elites within the Continental empires claiming political liberties as their right as members of distinct nations. In Hungary, Italy and elsewhere empire was under threat. Less than a decade later some claimed to see something similar happening in India.

The Russian reaction to 1863 was strongly conditioned by this context. Polish-language instruction was forbidden in schools and in some parts Catholics were forcibly converted to Russian Orthodoxy. This opened up space for other ethnic groups, busily inventing national identities, to assert themselves. Throughout the old Commonwealth territories people excluded from the privileges of the Polonised gentry began to demand of the Empire political rights on behalf of their community. Wider educational opportunities and improved access to communication technologies, such as newspapers and publishing, helped create new literate classes. Excluded from the Polishness of the elite, demands for new rights were predicated on the grounds of Ukrainian and Lithuanian nationality – Belarusian territories were less developed and similar movements would not emerge in that region until later. Intellectuals codified the Ukrainian and Lithuanian languages, turning dialects into languages of literature, history and philosophy. Often drawing on Polish writings, they began to write new histories demonstrating the existence of ancient national cultures destroyed by Polish cultural imperialism.[26] Modern print cultures ensured these ideas began to disseminate. Though much of the rural peasantry, in whom this nationalist authenticity was often supposed to reside, had no comprehension of these developments, by 1900 nationalist movements had emerged throughout the eastern part of the old Commonwealth lands. For each of these new nationalist movements,

Polishness was their most significant 'other', the standard against which they identified, and consequently their enemy.

In this context, Polish attitudes towards the *kresy* do not easily lend themselves to summary or generalisation. The very idea of borderlands suggests ambivalence, denoting a space of conflict peripheral to the indisputably Polish territories of the nation's geographical core. Nonetheless, for many early-twentieth-century Poles, the *kresy* was fundamentally Polish because its life had been shaped for centuries by Polish influence. Lwów (Lvov) and Wilno (Vilnius) were Polish cities, dominated by Polish-speaking people and culture. The surrounding lands were held by the Polish gentry, whether wealthy or impoverished, and the process of Polonisation continued after the partition of Poland between Austria, Russia and the German states in the late eighteenth century. Polonisation, with its strange echoes of colonisation and pollination, was not perceived by Poles to be a process of colonial or cultural subjugation but was the fulfilment of a role bequeathed to Poland by history. Poland's historic duty, these patriots told themselves, was to defend Europe's vulnerable eastern flanks, and therefore civilisation *tout court*, against Eastern barbarism, be it Russian, Tartar or Islamic. At its most extreme, exponents of this view regarded the Russians as Asian, racially distinct and inferior to the Slavs.[27] If Western civilisation's soft underbelly was the pre-modern peasant peoples of the *kresy*, Polonisation was the developmental project that aimed to protect it.

Something of Polish attitudes to the *kresy* can be found in the extraordinary run of historical novels written by Henryk Sienkiewicz in the late nineteenth century. The Ryżewscy were great fans, and Wanda and Danusia will later be found avidly reading them with friends in a Polish refugee camp in Karachi.

In a series of gripping narratives that combine blood-curdling description, romance and history, Sienkiewicz describes the Polish Commonwealth's decline in the sixteenth and seventeenth centuries during the wars against the Tartars, the Cossacks, the Russians and the Swedes. In the first of the sequence, *With Fire and Sword* (*Ogniem i mieczem*, 1884), the most eastern parts of the Commonwealth are described as the 'Wild Lands' and it was here, beyond the Dnieper, that Polish writ ran weakest. This lawless and undeveloped place, populated by simple, vulgar Cossacks, was permanently vulnerable to Tartar incursions – the brutality of which Sienkiewicz describes with graphic verve. Though theoretically loyal to the Polish Crown, the Cossack is shown by Sienkiewicz to be fickle and self-serving, available for hire to the highest bidder. For nineteenth-century readers, the Cossacks were identified as the forefathers of the Ukrainians and their seeming readiness to cooperate with the Russians in the post-1918 period can only have confirmed the assumptions held by Poles schooled in the Sienkiewicz tradition. In a classic act of re-appropriation, Ukrainian nationalists reclaimed historic Cossackness as evidence of their identity and rootedness in these lands, thereby re-imagining the Polish periphery as the Ukrainian centre. For Sienkiewicz, however, benevolent despotism was the only way to limit the damage caused by Cossack folly in the East and the Polish nobility stalk Sienkiewicz's Wild Lands, haughtily bringing chivalric and civilised values to this primitive people. As Sienkiewicz wrote, 'To hold these elements in bounds, to transform them into peaceful settlers and to enchain them in the fetters of civilised life, a lion was needed at whose roar all trembled.'[28] At first, Polish military might would inspire Cossack loyalty, but in time the very idea of the Cossack would become moot as Polonisation generated assimilation and the best of the Cossacks were integrated into the Polish nobility.

In a key passage, Skrzetuslei, the Polish hero, argues with his captor, the fierce Cossack rebel leader Khmelnytsky, condemning his decision to enter into an alliance with the Tartars. Khmelnytsky retorts that his loyalty to the Polish king is absolute but he cannot tolerate the despotism of petty kings and princes which comprise Polish government in the periphery. Skrzetuslei accepts that such grievances might have some validity, but is outraged that he might accept the Tartars, the 'heathen' enemy of Christianity, as his ally. For Khmelnytsky, the struggle is Pole against Cossack, for Skrzetuslei, Khmelnytsky has pitted 'younger brother against the elder brother' and made the Cossacks 'parracides'.[29] Sienkiewicz's sympathies clearly lie with the struggling Poles, trying to hold the line against Eastern barbarism.

Sienkiewicz, then, does not sanitise Poland's role in the East. He recognises that Polish ascendancy had to be achieved through a combination of force and persuasion; where the Cossack could not see beyond short-term interests, it was necessary to force him into submission in the name of historical imperatives evident to the more far-sighted Pole. Lithuanian, Belarusian and Ukrainian nationalists saw in history no such prescription, rejecting this as a nationalist fabrication intended to obscure Poland's selfish irredentist ambitions in the east.

As the popularity of his novels suggests, Sienkiewicz's views chimed strongly with popular Polish sentiment, but the political implications of this attitude towards the East were far from clear. At the turn of the twentieth century Polish nationalists were engaged in intense debates concerning what the future Poland should be. Broadly speaking, on one side were those promoting an ethnic nationalism which looked to build a new Poland rooted in the Polish-speaking Catholics living in the historic Polish Crownlands, territories corresponding to the Polish territories preceding the 1569 Union of Lublin. These ethnic nationalists anticipated the eventual collapse of the Russian Empire and believed it was crucial for Poland to become a compact and unified nation-state able to stand up to the growing power of Germany. A new Polish people, purged of polluting influences – and the Jews in particular – and apprised of the dangers of miscegenation, needed to be strengthened, ready for the inevitable struggles with rival neighbouring peoples. By the 1890s this strain of nationalism had generated a new political movement, National Democracy, known in Polish as *Endecja*, whose leading ideologue was Roman Dmowski. As the movement became more confident, so its territorial ambitions grew and it developed theories of national struggle and cultural expansionism that would justify expansion eastwards into the former territories of the Commonwealth. As Dmowski argued, 'A nation that does not want to acquire anything, does not want to create anything new in the future, that has no demands, but is satisfied with what it has, must shrivel and ultimately die.'[30] In the territories between Poland and Russia, Dmowski saw only 'a wide belt of land not belonging culturally to anyone, land on which two mutually hostile influences do battle, which is destined for whomever will be able to conquer it culturally.'[31] Russification could only be met with Polonisation. Dmowski's vile politics, so strongly rooted in antisemitism, has seen him placed among Europe's nascent fascists.

The contrary view was held by those inspired by the old Commonwealth ideals. These men and women, often of the déclassé nobility and living in the East, bathed more deeply in the romantic self-sacrificial waters of 1794, 1830 and 1863. For them, the enemy was and always would be Russia, and the only way to sustain not only Polish but European civilisation in the East was to recreate the Commonwealth, but on a newly inclusive basis with federal structures. This vision developed a significant purchase on the Lithuanian nobility in the generation before the First World War and, above all, would become indelibly associated with Józef Piłsudski. Piłsudski was the dominant personality of the first years of Polish independence, combining in his person military leader, head of state and cult figure. It was Piłsudski's policies and example which led people like Rafał Ryżewski to leave Poland's heartlands and settle in the East. Piłsudski's neo-Commonwealth idealism looked to nurture an association of nations that would allow the new nationalisms of the East to coexist, brought together by economic interests and, in Dziewanowski's words, 'the stern necessities deriving from the geo-political situation', that is, Russian imperialism.[32] Miłosz, in his melancholic meditation on his 'Native Realm', writes sympathetically but realistically of Piłsudski's vision. Piłsudski, he says, was more poet than politician and his ideas 'either an anachronism or too modern – depending on how it would have been realised in practice.'[33]

By this reading, Piłsudski was a deeply romantic figure, who fetishised the idea of Polish independence achieved through the nation-in-arms. In the decade or so before 1914 he embraced the idea of 'phys-ical force', nurturing terrorist cells alongside building up an open military organisation, which would evolve into the famous Polish Legions of the 1914–18 war. None of this was unique to Poland. Military voluntarism and citizen-armies excited nationalists throughout the Continent. At the same time, Piłsudski was a realist, recognising that Poland had very limited room for manoeuvre. He did not expect the Great War to bring Poland outright independence, but saw it as an opportunity to align Poland with Germany and Austria–Hungary against Russia so that the Poles could participate in the defeat of the great enemy in the East.[34]

The Polish Legion was a modest success, having some 12,000 recruits by 1916 organised into three brigades.[35] Riding the surge of Polish patri-otism energised by the war's nationalist potential, it became more impor-tant as a symbol of the Polish nation in arms, especially after the war, than it was for its concrete achievements. Rafał Ryżewski caught this wave of excitement. His army record shows he became a Legionnaire on 16 September 1914, some two months before his fifteenth birthday. From this moment on, Rafał actively participated in the major events leading to the achievement of Polish independence: his seminal experi-ences as an adolescent boy were not only the seminal experiences of the new state, but by joining the Legion, Rafał took the first step along a path that would render his fortunes utterly enmeshed in the future of the Polish state the Legions sought to create. It was one of those moments when a biography and a national history become so closely intertwined that in accounting for the fortunes of the ordinary individual the narrative of the state becomes the overriding frame of reference.

Everything suggests this boy would become a kindly man of great charm and a slightly frenetic energy. Nana and Wanda clothe their memories of their father in heroic garb; he was the charismatic centre of their childhoods, a man remembered as a devoted father who enlivened any social gathering. His simple, homespun truths and the aplomb with which he faced adversity left a deep impression. His first job in the army was banal enough. He was assistant to the field cook, the best place for a fifteen-year-old boy. Faced for the first time with a huge pile of potatoes to peel – and perhaps for the first time with domestic drudgery – he would later tell of how his disappointment drove him to tears and almost saw him abandon the military for the road home. For his girls there was a simple lesson to be learnt, and it is a leitmotif that runs through their telling of their story: 'You grit your teeth and you get on with the job.'

The way Nana and Wanda say 'my father', while usually referring to their mother as 'Mum', suggests pride in being his daughters. His granddaughters speak of him in similarly reverential tones and one sometimes feels an object of pity for not having known him, though to be thought in any way like 'my father' or 'my grandfather' is high praise indeed. In the stories told of him, it is difficult not to discern an adventurer with the aristocratic *joie de vivre* so beloved by film-makers and romantic novelists. In the movie of his life, he'd have been played by Alain Delon – and as romance demands, he *had* run away from his Kraków school to join the Polish Legion.

Though recognising that the Legion must cooperate with the Central Powers, Piłsudski was adamant that any alliance would be voluntary, with Polish forces retaining the independent command proper to an army of a nation-state, albeit one only virtually established. It was a tenet of almost all nationalist movements that a truly achieved nation had the capacity to defend itself and conduct an independent foreign policy. Consequently, volunteer citizen armies, throughout this period, played a key role in nationalist politics, whether it was the volunteer armies that threatened Ireland with civil war in 1914 or the various private fascist militias that undermined democratic European states after 1918.

The Legion's relationship with the Central Powers was tumultuous. The Central Powers, far from reconciled to the idea of Polish independence, hoped to channel Polish patriotic energies against their Russian enemy. Questions of loyalty dogged the relationship until the inevitable crisis finally came in July 1917 when the Central Powers demanded an oath of loyalty from the Polish Legion. Piłsudski refused, rightly seeing this as fundamentally compromising the Legion's ideological foundations. He was imprisoned, his army broken up, and many of his men were interned or dragooned into the forces of the Central Powers.[36] Rafał was carried along by these events. Initially recruited as rifleman, in September 1915 he was promoted to the rank of gunner and worked as a signalman. He picked up an injury and had his first experience of a military hospital between July and September 1916 at Cheb, a little town that found itself in Czechoslovakia after the war. Following another year's service as a Legionnaire, like many others, Rafał was forced into the Austrian army from 23 October 1917.

For eager young men like Rafał, Piłsudski was a simple figure, the principal symbol of Polish heroism and national integrity. In reality, in 1917 Piłsudski's position was decidedly precarious, facing political and military circumstances which called for careful calculation rather than reckless heroism. Faced with the hostility of the Central Powers to an independent Polish military capability, it was clear that to have waged a guerrilla war against those powers would have been at odds with a strategy which relied on the Central Powers defeating Russia. Piłsudski's imprisonment, there-fore, could not have been better timed and, as is often the case in the careers of revolutionary nationalists, timely imprisonment paid huge political divi-dends. While in prison Piłsudski's reputation grew, developing the cult that would sustain his political status in later years. Imprisonment also proved a seminal experience for many ex-Legionnaires. Many Poles drafted into the Austrian army were taken prisoner-of-war by the Germans in February 1918. Just as prison cemented Piłsudski's reputation, so too did it strengthen the solidarity of these young Polish patriots, allowing them to develop a more sophisticated understanding of their political struggle.

Rafał's experience was characteristic. According to the personal state-ment preserved in his army record, later validated by his senior officers, he fought on the Austrian–Italian front until being badly wounded during the December 1917 offensive. When he learnt of the 'Charge at Rarańcza' in February 1918, a famous event which saw Polish forces under Austrian and former Russian command link up, Rafał ran away from hospital carrying false papers. He was determined to join the renewed Polish struggle. Reaching Biała, in the Małopolska region, he was placed in command of a platoon of the POW (Polska Organizacja Wojskowa: Polish Military Organisation), a semi-clandestine Piłsudski-ite organisation. Following the defeat of Germany and the collapse of Austria–Hungary, the Polish prisoners-of-war and Piłsudski were simultaneously released, reinforcing the individual Legionnaire's sense of affinity for the great man. Piłsudski returned to Warsaw in triumph. The Regency Council, the body entrusted with overseeing the establishment of Polish independ-ence, named him Head of State. On 11 November 1918, the day of the European armistice, Piłsudski declared Polish independence. Around the same time, Rafał was posted to the 1st Bielsko-Biała infantry base, though he was not to remain in his home town for long.

On the first day of Polish independence Rafał was just nine days past his nineteenth birthday. He was among the nation's heroes and would carry this aura with him throughout his adult life. He had served in Poland's nascent national army from the beginning of the war. He'd been promoted from rifleman through to gunner, lance-corporal and finally corporal. He has suffered injury but had also enjoyed the camaraderie of the Polish Legions. He had grudgingly served in the Austrian army but had also seen some of the further reaches of the Empire. Since he had run away from hospital, Poland's prospects had been transformed. Russia and the Central Powers had entered negotiations and in March 1918 they signed the Treaty of Brest-Litovsk. Russia conceded massive territories in Eastern Europe, handing Poland and her neighbours over to the Central Powers. Russian withdrawal from the war and the transfer of this territory appeared to simplify the Polish position. Rather than being caught between the two warring sides, Polish nationalism faced a straight struggle for independence with the Central Powers, among whom Germany had achieved ascendancy. The eventual defeat of Germany and Austria invalidated the Russian treaty, leaving Poland surrounded on all sides by powers keen to dictate Poland's future but without the military capacity to determine it. For the first time in more than a century, there was the chance that Poland might have charge of her own fate.

Piłsudski's triumph was somewhat hollow for his personal prestige was not matched by party political support. Though he could count on the loyalty of the army, the support of the socialists, and the sympathy of minority political interests, the greatest political influence was wielded by the National Democrats, the leaders of which returned from exile in Paris to Warsaw at the moment of Polish independence. In the event, the question of Poland's borders, far and away the most pressing problem the new state faced, was determined first by military action and then by political negotiations with Moscow led by the National Democrats. The victorious Allies, meeting in Versailles to determine the shape of postwar Europe, had little 'hard' power in eastern Europe. Poland's eastern borders were not secured through a process of negotiation and compromise leading to the establishment of a federal state, but through the annexations and treaties which followed further war and a succession of small and highly localised military struggles. The year 1918 saw the end of one war in the East and the beginning of another.

The cities of Wilno and Lwów were particular flashpoints, bringing into focus the political and ethnic divisions that now shaped life in these territories. Both had significant Polish majorities, but for a new generation of Belarusian, Lithuanian and Ukrainian nationalists, schooled in the new medievalism, this Polishness was judged an imperial imposition. Wilno was claimed by both Lithuanian and Belarusian nationalists; Lwów was not only thought to be Ukraine's historic second city, but among Galician Ukrainian nationalists, intensely hostile to Russia, it was the capital of a putative West Ukraine. Given that the populations of these aspirant nations were predominantly rural, these urban centres became all the more significant to the futures of their imagined nation-states.

On 5 January 1919 the Red Army took Wilno, and it became Vilnius, the capital of the Soviet Socialist Republic of Lithuania (SSRL). Further Bolshevik success in the south saw them absorb Belarus territory which, when amalgamated with SSRL, was named the 'LitBel' Soviet Socialist Republic. Back in Warsaw, though all were aghast, political opinion was divided over the proper future of Vilnius. Should the city and its surrounding country be annexed to Poland? Should Vilnius become the capital of an independent Lithuania? Or was Piłsudski right to want it to become part of a new Polish–Lithuanian federation, a modernised Commonwealth? What was clear is that Polish opinion, intensified by the first exultant flush of national independence, could not stomach abandoning to the Bolsheviks a city considered quintessentially Polish. Political debate in the *Sejm* was increasingly dominated by the National Democrats and a succession of resolutions called for the incorporation of Vilnius and surrounds into a unitary Polish state, a rejection of Piłsudski-ite ideals. Nonetheless, Piłsudski marched the Polish army east, declaring that he was there to facilitate Lithuanian self-determination, and won a victory freighted with symbolic significance: independent Poland had inflicted a defeat on the historic enemy! But this outcome was far from decisive. Lithuania was now divided between Polish-occupied territories and the new Soviet Lithuanian republic with its capital at Kaunas.[37] For many of Piłsudski's young Legionnaires, Rafał among them, this event and those of the following two years would prove seminal, generating a tremendous loyalty towards the Marshal and a profound commitment to the Polishness of the eastern borderlands.

While the Bolsheviks licked their wounds, the Poles continued to debate the future of Wilno (as it was again) along lines heavily determined by their differing ideological perspectives. Complex manoeuvrings by the Bolsheviks saw the Lithuanian nationalist leadership in Kaunas grant the Red Army free passage in July 1920 on the understanding that once the Poles were driven from Vilnius, Lithuanian territorial integrity and independence would be achieved. This time the Poles were pushed back and the Bolsheviks kept advancing, seizing the advantage. In August 1920, with the Red Army on the outskirts of Warsaw and the new state facing defeat, the Poles somehow turned the tide.[38] This gave birth to the myth of the 'Miracle on the Vistula', the idea that the Virgin Mary had intervened on Poland's behalf. More prosaically, it was a crucial moment in the formation of modern Polish national identity and the history of twentieth-century Europe. Independence was the product not of Polish victory but of German-Russian defeat; now, though, the nation had been secured through arms, dignifying Polish independence (nationalists hoped) in the eyes of the world. Moreover, and this can be easily overlooked, the Polish victory played a significant part in the Bolshevik decision temporarily to abandon their revolutionary expansionism in the west.[39]

This time of terrible uncertainty and fervent patriotism is captured in letters written by Emil Ryżewski. Emil was the oldest brother of Józef, Rafał's father. Born in November 1868, he emigrated to the United States at the turn of the century, from where he anxiously observed developments in Poland. According to press coverage seen by Emil, the Ryżewskie family's extensive country estate in the Ukraine, known as Pawelca, had been overrun by the Bolsheviks. Desperate for news of the family, Emil fired off a series of frantic letters in August 1919 to all the addresses he could think of. Eventually learning that the family had been neither destroyed nor, as he had feared, sent to Siberia, in subsequent letters he breathlessly celebrated 'the rebirth of Poland' and the thrilling news of Rafał's and Stefan's record as Legionnaires. Might his son Romek, enviously following events from the safety of Massachusetts, cross the Atlantic and join the fight? Poland, he was proud to say, had survived experiences worse than those prospected in Dante's *Inferno*: the hordes had been pushed back and Poland's mountains now stood proud. Maddened that the Minister of War Kerensky had unnecessarily taken the war into the vicinity of Pawelca, he was ecstatic that Poland had fought for nearby Lwów ('Bravo! Bravo!!!'). All this triggered reminiscences of life in Poland, of mushroom picking and 'the awful faces' of now banished 'oppressors'. Interestingly, he says that during the war large numbers of Poles did not return to Poland from the States to join the struggle because they feared they would be forced to fight Poles enlisted in the Austrian and German armies. It's a striking observation that echoes the dilemmas of Piłsudski himself.[40] Emil's letters over the following decade or so, though preoccupied by disputes regarding the control of Pawelca, were infused by regret at his voluntary exile. The new Poland was a place in which he, as the eldest son of a propertied family, might by rights have been a man of position.

The backdrop to Emil's enthusiasm was continued manoeuvring,

negotiation and war. At Riga in September–October 1920 the Poles and
the Bolsheviks agreed an armistice line that left Vilnius part of Lithuania.
Various shenanigans led to Piłsudski marching his Legionnaires into
Vilnius in the hope that a federal settlement might still be possible given
the Bolshevik readiness to accept a Polish presence in Belarus and Ukraine.
Detecting a Bolshevik betrayal, Kaunas, Kiev and Minsk were furious,
while the west Ukrainians were becoming increasingly suspicious: they
realised the Poles were more likely to absorb Galicia than facilitate its
independence. Shortly after, the Bolsheviks offered Minsk and the eastern
territories of Belarus to Poland. This would prove to be a defining
moment. Would it see the triumph of Piłsudski's idea of a new
Commonwealth, creating a new order in Eastern Europe overlooked by
a benign but ascendant Poland? The Polish representatives, dominated
by the National Democrats, turned down the offer. The gulf separating
the head of state and the army leadership from the political leadership
had been decisively exposed. For the National Democrats, a federal state
in which the Poles were not numerically and culturally predominant was
unacceptable. In the words of Timothy Snyder, the coinciding interests
of Warsaw and Kaunas had generated 'a silent alliance of modern nationalists' intent on creating 'new nation states' and burying 'the early modern
traditions of the Polish–Lithuanian Commonwealth'.[41] As a result,
Poland's eastern borders were set some way east of the line running
north–south from Wilno to Lwów, the so-called Riga line. This left angry
Poles, Lithuanians, Ukrainians and Belarusians on both sides of the border.

Piłsudski's federalism was dead in the water. Nationalists, rooted in
the Polish Crownlands, with little understanding of the complexity of
the eastern territories but who regarded Wilno and Lwów as inalienable
centres of Polish nationality, had triumphed. Ukrainian, Lithuanian and
Belarusian nationalists recognised that the Bolsheviks were unwilling to
fight Poland on their behalf for territories they judged to be theirs and
settled for what they could get. In effect, Warsaw and Moscow had carved
up Eastern Europe and in doing so created a very unstable geo-political
situation. To the east of the Polish border were three states with irredentist claims on Polish territories; to the west of the border existed a
Poland with large national minorities, many of whom were uneasy about
their inclusion in the new state, some of whom would actively oppose
it and, in part stoked up by Moscow and Berlin, would conspire to undermine it. Poles schooled in similar brands of ethnic nationalism dominated public debate in the new state, questioning whether the national

minorities, including the large Jewish population, were Polish at all. For many Poles the answer was 'no' and attempting to Polonise the *kresy* was the natural, defensive response. However, for Poles steeped in the romantic traditions of the Commonwealth, Polonisation meant not cultural imperialism but the fulfilment of a civilising mission; Polonisation aimed not to convert one national group into another, but to bring a peasant culture into modernity. Above all, however, Polonisation meant the reversal of Tsarist Russification: for many Poles, implausible though this now seems, Polonising looked a lot like decolonising.[42] Such thinking was outmoded, naïve and insensible of new realities and identities in the *kresy*; crucially, it also established more common ground between the Dmowski-ites and the Piłsudski-ites than many would have been willing to admit. And as a consequence, in the interwar years, the Polish state lurched between conciliating, pacifying and oppressing its national minorities in the *kresy*, often all at once and sometimes with considerable brutality. Periodically, non-Polish schools were shut down, political organisations were banned and Orthodox religious practice restricted.[43] In equal measure, the political movements of the national minorities swung between coexistence and militancy: some urged accommodation with the new Polish state while a small minority met the forces of the state with terrorist tactics. Over time both sides became more ideologically absolutist in their thinking and more dependent on political violence. On the eve of the Second World War parts of the *kresy*, particularly in the south, were very unstable, with Ukrainian radicals in a state of near-insurgency and the Polish military and police periodically resorting to counter-insurgency tactics.

Many of Piłsudski's Legionnaires became deeply implicated in this dynamic, not least Rafał and Hanna, who both had successful careers as teachers in the *kresy*. Like many Legionnaires, Rafał acquired land in the *kresy*. It is not entirely clear whether he was one of the many former soldiers who were granted land as payment for his military service by a state little able to meet the costs of its soldiers. Either way, Rafał would have been associated with men known as 'military settlers' and they were required to remain in the Reserves, comprising a permanent military presence in the region. Some 9,000 Polish officers were granted land in the Belarus territories until the scheme was halted in 1924.[44] The purpose of this programme of colonisation was to strengthen Poland's position in the East and to develop these lands. Further Polish families, facing the harsh economic conditions of the 1920s, took advantage of the availability of government assistance and cheap land in the *kresy*, adding to the migration. Often armed by the government, they created in the *kresy* a permanently settled garrison and though many of the settlers would have been ineffective as soldiers, there were enough experienced military men among them to reinforce the state's authority in the region when necessary. Michael Kulik says eighty-five members of his grandfather's cavalry regiment settled on plots, which he describes as 'mostly barren and uncultivated countryside' that had previously been used by the Russian military;[45] other lands were redistributed following the state break-up of the landed estates of the old Russian regime. According to the official figures Kulik cites, 2,654,000 hectares were subdivided; of this total, on 1,431,800 hectares were planted 153,600 new farms. Some of this was socially progressive, granting Ukrainian tenant farmers land, but a very high proportion went to newly arrived Poles. One set of figures suggests that between 1926 and 1929, 560,000 hectares occupied by Ukrainians were forcibly granted to Polish settlers and military colonists; perhaps as many as 21,000 new families were settled in the Ukrainian province of Volhynia alone.[46] Tadeusz Piotrowski, an unapologetically patriotic Polish-American historian, describes the land-grant policies as 'disastrous'. 'For the most part,' Piotrowski argues, 'these colonists were regarded by the local population, who had expected to receive the land, as squatters, thieves and enemies of the people.'[47]

Uncomfortable though this is, Rafał's and Hanna's story is a part of this account of an insecure state in action, determined to consolidate its authority. Hanna's experiences in particular demonstrate how the *kresy* provided new opportunities for an ambitious young woman of humble background. Born in 1903 in Wara, a village in the south-west corner of Poland not far from Rzeszów, Hanna Szpiechówna was one of nine children, the daughter of Franciszek and Zofia (née Łuc). In marked contrast to the Ryżewscy, the Szpiechowie were simple hard-working country people, strongly rooted in their locality, whose land had been held by their family for generations. They adhered to the traditional dictums of the Catholic Church and are remembered for their strict morals. In their daughter Hanna they had an unusually bright child whose diligence at school paid off and whose teacher persuaded her father that she should continue studying. Again, as Nana tells the story of the teacher going to see the father, there is a cinematic quality. In the movie, the girl's father would resist, disown his daughter when she insists on following her dreams, and much pain would follow before their reconciliation in the closing sequence. In reality, it seems he agreed readily and paid part of the costs in kind, taking the produce in his

cart to the landlord of the pension where Hanna lodged.

If Hanna's and Rafał's wedding photograph suggests something of her

determination to live a different kind of life, further photographs suggest precocity, if not hauteur. In one, as a teenage girl, she is laughing amidst seriousness, just as her younger daughter would in photos taken twenty-five years later. In her elder sister's gloomy wedding photograph, which shows a simple country wedding, she looks ill at ease, not that anyone seems to be having much fun.

Photographs taken a short time later show her in her element, nicely dressed and hanging out with her friends.

But Hanna's success was not merely the story of an individual achieving against the odds. In the early years of independence, young Poles were exhorted to play a constructive role in the building of the new nation, particularly in the education sector in the east. It is no coincidence that in 1921, after working for a year in the accounts office of the electricity board in Kraków, Hanna was sent to train as a teacher in Nieśwież, a town deep in the *kresy*, a little to the west of Baranowice and not far from the then Soviet–Polish border. All this was to the far north and west of the Poland she knew and to leave Kraków, a beautiful university city, for the north *kresy*, one of the least developed parts of the new state, must have felt like a form of voluntary exile. She travelled alone by train and later told of being pawed by workers in her compartment. The story has an emblematic quality, describing her rude exposure to the risks young womanhood faced on the journey east.

Rafał also took a circuitous route to the *kresy*. After the war he was posted to Chełmno, a town north-west of Warsaw which had come under Prussian control in 1874. By now a second-lieutenant, he had seen experience as a company commander and had flourished as an infantryman, coming fourth in a class of 125 following four months' infantry training in 1920. A brief period of service in the tense border territory of Upper Silesia, where Poles and Germans fought an intermittent war, led to his second military injury. In September 1921 he was released from hospital in Dziedzice (now in Silesia Province near Katowice) and was transferred back to Chełmno where he commanded a company for fourteen months. In December 1922 he was transferred to the border guards at Nieśwież where he commanded his company for seven months, including a three-month stint in Warsaw for further training. In July 1923, after nine years in the army, Rafał was granted his release papers and entered the Reserves. He was a twenty-three-year-old man, with considerable experience as a military commander; he had picked up a nice collection of service medals and an injury or two, both of which he would add to over the coming years. His military career had not been focused on the *kresy*, but that last posting east and the availability of land to military settlers sealed his fate. He too trained as a teacher at Nieśwież.

Rafał, as an experienced soldier, was given the task of coordinating a team conducting part of a major census. Their aim was to gather the information needed for education planning. Part of their task was to

seek out isolated country dwellings (*chaty*) and persuade parents to
release their children for schooling. Parents could be very reluctant,
given the important economic role children played within the impov-

erished rural household. Hanna was part of Rafał's team and on one
occasion a defiant father set his dog on the young educational missionary
who'd come to his door. Hanna was scarred for life by a nasty bite.
Like the repeated anecdote of the incident on the train, it is another
story signifying how the *kresy* was experienced as 'other', a place where
children were kept from school to work and she, bringing enlightenment, was attacked.

Makeshift schools were established to plug the gap before a more permanent provision could be made and it seems likely it was in such a school in
Kleck near Nieśwież that Hanna worked until 1927. In the Wilno area alone
some 120 'Piłsudski schools' were soon established and teachers assigned to
them. A pioneering spirit animated these young people sent to educate
Poland's periphery, convinced they could bring the future to a backward
and unenlightened people. Capturing something of this utopianism – and
providing a literary counterpoint to Sienkiewicz's novels of the Wild Lands
– were the works of Stefan Żeromski (1864–1925). Pained by the poverty
and ignorance of the peasantry, and inspired by the romantic nationalism
of 1863, Żeromski believed that Poland could only develop into a civilised
nation if the intelligentsia, rendered inconsequential by Russian tyranny,

recovered its proper role working for the enlightenment of the people. As the nineteenth-century dictum had it, the intelligentsia must 'enter the folk and become the folk', thereby restoring the nation's organic unity.[48] It is hard to say whether Rafał and Hanna adhered to Żeromski's syndicalism any more than they did to any other set of precise political ideas, but fuelled by their youthful optimism and a little wine, strong bonds quickly developed between them. Nana tells of how her parents later talked of evenings around the campfire singing songs and talking of the future. And it was song that brought Rafał and Hanna together, he noticing the pretty girl with the fine soprano voice, she intrigued by the ebullient young officer. Tentatively at first but soon with more confidence they sang army songs together, their harmonising entertaining their friends. Many years later, Rafał wrote to Hanna recalling their first meeting. It was on 10 August 1922 'when you, darling woman, had burnt your face with some acid and it made you terribly self-conscious. It is 24 years ago and it still stands before my eyes as if yesterday.' In this intense atmosphere love quickly developed and they were married in Kleck in April 1924, alongside two other young couples.

As Eric Hobsbawm hints when writing of relationships between young communists, intense ideological affinities could generate a peculiar form of love, where partnership was built on comradely commitment and mission, salted with a sense of superiority and separateness.[49] Perhaps something of that quality characterised those three weddings that day in Kleck and there is little question that marriage had a more transactional quality at that time than the ideals of romantic love might allow: these young people were laying the foundations for a life in a relatively hostile environment. Nevertheless, as Hanna's and Rafał's later correspondence shows, this was a marriage of love cemented by powerful family bonds. On 26 April 1928 Wanda Irena, their first daughter, was born; Maria Danuta, their second, followed on 15 June 1932.

Though this picture of a seething *kresy*, rent with ethnic and ideological tension, should not be painted in too lurid colours, such divisions gradually evolved into the political forces that would determine the region's future and the fate of many families like the Ryżewscy. But this awareness of the broader process of historical change should not be allowed to obscure the complexity of the situation on the ground. For much of the 1920s and 1930s, socialist rather than nationalist parties were more likely to attract the support of the discontented national minorities, and this was particularly the case in the Wilno region. Moreover, in much of the *kresy*, and for much of the time, social or ethnic conflict scarcely went beyond the petty, largely pre-political resentments characteristic of small-town or rural life. In parts of the south, however, things could be very different, as Shimon Redlich's study of the town of Brzezany, now in Ukraine, demonstrates.[50] Here we can see how full of hatred the politics of the *kresy* could become and how these enmities were manifested within a small community.

Roughly equidistant from Lwów and Ternopil', in the 1930s Brzezany had a population of 13,000 which was 50 per cent Polish, 30 per cent Jewish and 20 per cent Ukrainian. As was typical of *kresy* towns in this region, the surrounding country was 60 per cent Ukrainian. Formerly a part of the Austro-Hungarian Empire, most educated people spoke German as a second language, but in the public life of the town Polish predominated, though in private people also spoke Ukrainian and Yiddish. Language, the strongest indicator of identity, tended to coincide with religious affiliation: most Poles worshipped in the Catholic tradition and Ukrainians in the Orthodox tradition.

Political life in Brzezany was strongly conditioned by conflict between

Polish and Ukrainian nationalisms. Polonisation, particularly through schooling, was the order of the day. This was reinforced by a strong Polish military presence and the town's garrison, including wives and children, brought a further 1,000 Poles to the region. Regular military parades reinforced the ascendancy of Polishness, decking the town with the symbols of the state, and brightening it with the red and white of the Polish national flag. Such displays were less a manifestation of Polish confidence than an action in an ongoing struggle with Ukrainian nationalists determined to resist Polonisation. Ukrainian activists established Ukrainian cultural institutions in the town and the surrounding regions. Among them were schools, libraries and reading rooms, all of which formed part of a wider network encouraged by the Ukrainian government and, ultimately, Moscow. Thousands of Ukrainian children joined the Plast, the leading Ukrainian Scout organisation, a typical adjunct to any nationalist movement in this period. Later on, as refugees, Wanda and Danusia became enthusiastic Scouts and it is clear that their patriotic feelings were strengthened by the organisation. Much Ukrainian cultural nationalist activity came under the direction of the Ukrainian National Democratic Alliance (UNDO), a moderate nationalist organisation that looked to promote the Ukrainian language and culture within the confines of the Polish state.

No easy equilibrium was ever reached. Memories of the military struggle of 1918–19 between Ukrainians and Poles were reinforced by the arrival of settlers intended to consolidate the Polish possession of the territory. Polonisation reinforced old and new enmities and rising Ukrainian militancy provoked a series of 'pacification' police actions by the government. What initially seemed the legitimate actions of a government determined to establish its authority developed into a vicious culture war. The local authorities received very mixed signals from Warsaw. The National Democrats disputed the legitimacy of Piłsudski's governments, which relied on a combination of minority and left-wing parties, arguing that a government could only be legitimate if backed by a majority of ethnic Poles. By implication, the Right believed that the Pole should have a superior status to other citizens, despite the constitutional guarantees of equality. More progressive observers became increasingly timid, tending to turn a blind eye to questions concerning the minorities. After Piłsudski took power in a military coup in 1926, Warsaw signalled the need for a new pluralism but Piłsudski, aware of his political vulnerability, held back from lending this his personal prestige and embattled Polish officials in the localities came under little pressure to hold to a moderate line. Politicians, often ignorant of the East, increasingly voiced their scepticism about the fundamental loyalties of the minorities and isolated crackdowns on anti-state activity in specific areas generated great publicity, further antagonising opposition groups. Spiralling conflict strengthened the Organisation of Ukrainian Nationalists (OUN), the radical alternative to the ONDO, which proved particularly popular with Ukrainian students.

In the autumn of 1930 the government upped the ante, instructing the police and the army to close down large parts of the Ukrainian voluntary sector. Searches led to the confiscation of weapons and seditious literature, buildings and other property were destroyed, and, inevitably, much of this was accompanied by physical violence. Activists were arrested, tried and imprisoned. Polish sources suggest that between July and November 1,739 Ukrainians were arrested and 211 were still in prison a year later.[51] In 1931 the pendulum swung again, and some institutions were permitted to reopen, but the confrontational dynamic quickly re-established itself, with the National Democrats continuously keeping up the pressure on the government to take a hard line. Arrests of further activists accused of anti-Polish activity in 1933 saw severe sentences handed out for relatively petty misdemeanours like distributing seditious leaflets. Further police actions followed in 1934 but failed to put a halt to periodic violence. For example, in May 1936 Ukrainian activists in the Brzezany area desecrated the graves of Polish policemen and soldiers, and embarked on a campaign of political assassination. The official Polish reaction was predictably severe; the unofficial reaction increasingly mirrored the actions of Ukrainian militants. In March 1936 a group of Poles, mainly high school students, marched through the town carrying a coffin marked 'Ukraine is dead'. A few days later the bodies of Poles thought to have been participants were found in a nearby river.

Polish–Ukrainian, Polish–Belarusian and Polish–Lithuanian conflict in the *kresy*, though varying in intensity and a long way off civil war, reflected in microcosm the politics of 1930s Europe. Race and nation had increasingly become the lens through which resentments were understood, gradually subordinating class-based motivations. Poland, fearful of Germany and the Soviet Union, drifted towards the right, seeking to form itself into a compact body of determined, purified Poles able to resist all comers. The voices of an older Piłsudski-ite ideal became less and less audible, experience demonstrating the Piłsudski-ite dream to be a naïve anachronism. And Piłsudski himself, Poland's authoritarian head of state after leading a *coup d'état* in May 1926, increasingly governed in a manner incompatible with his ideals. He relied, argues Snyder, 'upon

military force and personal charisma to keep majority views at bay'.[52]
The old lands of the Commonwealth were not populated by a simple
peasantry ready to be enlightened by benevolent Poles, but were thick
with new thinking and ideas. Maybe a pluralist Poland that did coincide
with the extent of the old Commonwealth would have been viable, where
federal structures would have allowed four cultures to coexist in a defensive pact against the Soviet Union, but the power politics of 1918–20 and
the ethnic essentialism of the National Democrats made this impossible.
By the 1930s the Soviet Union was ready to exploit the political and ethnic
tensions of the *kresy*, happily stoking up trouble where possible.

Following Piłsudski's death in 1935, German aggression in the west and
intensifying ethnic conflict in the east fuelled a savage reaction. Subsequent
governments made a significant lurch to the right. State policy became
identifiably antisemitic and the government, backed by army opinion,
fiercely anti-Ukrainian, with further police actions culminating in the closure
of all Ukrainian cultural institutions in early 1939. As a consequence, the
Ukrainian nationalist movement was forced ever more underground,
becoming increasingly radical and militant.

Caught between the Poles and the Ukrainians were the Jews. Both
sides accused the Jews of aiding and abetting the enemy, being either
agents of Polonisation or co-conspirators with the Ukrainians. And though
some Jews were attracted to communism, Ukrainian nationalism held
little appeal and could not be relied upon to be any less antisemitic than
the Polish version. Between 1923 and 1937 perhaps as many as 100,000
Jews emigrated from East Galicia to Palestine.

The Ryżewscy family's 'life in the wild lands' had a brutal coda that cannot
be passed over. It forces us to scroll forward to the latter stages of the
Second World War, when Polish–Ukrainian political tensions in parts of
the kresy bore the foul fruit of ethnic cleansing. A series of brutal murders
threw into sharp relief an unpleasant family dispute over who should control
Pawelca in the 1930s. These specific events, related to me in a letter by a
relative living in Poland today, can only be relayed in bald outline but they
fit with what we know of the kresy in the last years of the war. There
were five brothers, sons of Klemens (1839–1888) and Aniela (1846–1926)
Ryżewscy: Emil (b. 1868), Zygmunt (b. 1872), Rafał's father Józéf (b. 1875),
Władysław (b. 1878), and Marjan (b. 1880). Following the deaths of their
parents, Pawelca passed into their hands. Emil, as we know, had emigrated
to the United States, taking many of the estate documents with him; Józéf

moved to Bielsko; Władysław went to work as a head teacher in Silesia; and Marjan lived on the estate. Władysław died unexpectedly in 1924, leaving behind his wife Stefania, also a teacher, and their four children. Stefania and Marjan fell into a legal dispute over her right to a share of the estate and the courts eventually found in her favour. My relative explains that Marjan did not have a good reputation. He managed the estates badly, gambled away his money and enjoyed travel, selling off parts of his land to finance his debts. He met his first wife, apparently an actress or a singer, when travelling, though she soon grew bored of country life and ran off with another man, leaving Marjan and their two-year-old daughter. Marjan later married his Ukrainian maid, with whom he had another daughter. One day, in the winter of 1933-4, the house at Pawelca was subject to an arson attack and family hearsay unhesitatingly blames Marjan, saying it was an insurance job. Emil, still in the US, learnt of the fire from the Polish press and immediately wrote to Józéf demanding information and smarting at the house being described as belonging to Marjan. Emil was particularly angered because the house had been on his share of the land. Marjan successfully lodged a claim for insurance and then rebuilt the house on his land. In the months following the fire he bought Emil's portion of the land for 3,162 złoty, about $600.

This episode seems typical of the tensions that arise between present and absent landlords, when both are deriving income from land held jointly and where the boundaries marking ownership and individual rights are blurred. Safely distant in time and place, and made more so by the displacements that have occurred in the meantime, this fraternal rivalry and Marjan's apparent deviousness makes for an intriguing narrative. But can these obscure events bear a weightier analysis? Did Marjan's crime amount to an ethnic transgression? As patriots, the Ryżewscy considered themselves to hold Pawelca in trust for the Polish nation and Marjan's action meant Ukrainians might inherit land guaranteed to Poland through war – remember Emil's 'Bravo!' It seems plausible that to marry a Ukrainian family into the land in the period of Piłsudski-ite optimism might have been judged an act of assimilation, but to do so in the bleak days of the mid-1930s was a national betrayal. Marjan, Emil implied in his letters, had been disloyal to the Polish nation. That said, Emil's letters to Józéf about the affair – the only original documentation I have seen on the controversy – are hived with paranoia, supposition and self-pity. Consequently, this ethno-analysis, derived from such sketchy traces and though possessing its own logic, is speculative, an example, perhaps, of the historian's dark arts. When Marjan eventually learnt what was being said about him he wrote Emil passionate letters of protest, aghast that his brother could entertain such thoughts.

Marjan died of natural causes in 1941, leaving his enlarged share of the estate to his wife and children. Stefania continued to take care of her interests and occasionally this brought her to the estate, as in early spring 1944. On the day of her arrival, the rain was so hard that the journey from the railway station to the house, along wet and muddy roads, had to be abandoned and she stayed with her friends Pan and Pani Postołwscy. That night strangers came to the house requesting a warm drink. They forced Stefania and Pani Postołwska to accompany them to a nearby house, where they and nine other people were hacked to death using axes and knives. The murderers then set fire to the house and the corpses. Pan Postołwski, witnessing the crime, is said to have run down the railway tracks towards Stanisławow to get help. He lost his mind soon after. Inevitably, the tenant with whom Stefania was at dispute over rent was suspected of involvement in the crime. In a similar incident, one of Zygmunt Ryżewski's sons, a doctor, lost his wife and two children. He left the region soon after.

These murders were almost certainly the work of the Ukrainian Insurgency Army, or UPA, and were a part of their systematic campaign of 1943–4 to remove Poles from western Ukraine. Thousands were killed, often in extremely nasty ways. Polish reprisals, thought resulting in fewer deaths, could be just as savage. To this day Polish–Ukrainian relations are troubled by disagreements concerning what happened and why during these terrible years, with both sides offering responses ranging between confession, apologia and vehement self-justification. In the aftermath of the war the new Soviet-backed Polish authorities forcibly expelled Polish Ukrainians to Ukraine. At the same time, some of those Poles in western Ukraine that survived the UPA, including Marjan's family, were deported by the Soviets to Siberia. When these Ryżewscy were permitted to return seventeen years later they were granted a small parcel of land, which still provides some of their basic needs today. My relative notes that it is the family's poorest branch that today retains a little of the land that had once been the basis of its wealth and status.

Rafał and Hanna were heavily implicated in state-led attempts to integrate Poland's eastern periphery. In the cold language of the historian – or, indeed, the Lithuanian nationalist – Rafał and Hanna, teaching through the Polish language in an ethnically diverse area, might be identified as the agents of a colonising state and their daughters the beneficiaries of ethnic and class privilege. As a reservist, Rafał can be fingered as part of the near-military government pertaining in parts of the *kresy*. This young man, rapidly promoted, was comfortable not only as both educator and soldier but also as part of an ethnic elite. And yet, as historical understanding advances, it has become clear that old models of Polish colonialism and nationalist resistance – or models older still of civilisation and barbarism – are too crude to take altogether seriously.

In this world, as claimed by Danusia and Wanda, Piłsudski had an almost palpable presence in their childhood home and schools. And though the ideals of the Marshal were fundamentally compromised by Poland's permanent crisis of legitimacy, there was a meaningful difference between his patriotic pluralism and that of his far-right arch-rival Dmowski. It seems emblematic of these differences that Rafał's army record states that he could read and write German, Russian, Ukrainian and Belarusian, and could speak Czech and Lithuanian. The German and the Czech, of course, stem from his origins in Silesia, but it can be safely assumed that though Rafał taught in Polish, he acquired proficiency in Ukrainian and Belarusian through interaction with his pupils.

On one occasion at Działka, amid the hazy heat of summer, Rafał and the girls were out picking wild strawberries. They came to some mysterious earth mounds and Rafał quietly urged his daughters tread softly for the sleeping warriors were not to be disturbed. They must rest, conserving their energies for the moment they were needed. These mounds contained the graves of men who had fallen during the 1914–18 war and had been buried where they fell. The myth of sleeping warriors, awaiting their call, is common to many cultures living under the threat of an enemy. It resonates with the myth of the final judgement, a time when the accumulated actions of the people would be brought to account. Poland would indeed face an apocalypse, but its judges would not be of holy inspiration, but the product of ancient enmities funnelled through the ideological malignancies shaping twentieth-century European history. On 23 August 1939 Soviet Foreign Minister Molotov met his German counterpart Ribbentrop. In a secret pact the Soviet Union and Germany agreed to partition Poland, bringing to an end Poland's brief and chaotic period of independence. On 1 September 1939, as the German tanks rolled in, the warriors slept on. The Polish people, not without some justification, would think themselves martyred once again.

3

Deportation

Often it was the banging at the door with rifle butts, the shouted demands and the scuffle of heavy boots on snow that signalled the beginning.[1] It was almost always in the small hours of the morning, around 3 or 4 a.m. As the door was opened, standing on the threshold of the home would be Red Army soldiers or local militiamen, with an NKVD* officer, a policeman or a local official presiding. Poles from the Soviet-occupied Ukrainian territories bitterly remember the Ukrainian militiamen drafted in to enforce the will of Soviet officials. The arrest team were armed and their guns were trained on the family member standing in the doorway. Sometimes they simply barged in, snow- and mud-covered boots soiling washed floors. L. Cabut remembers it simply as 'a break-in',[2] a criminal violation of a family's private, domestic space. Screeched threats and foul abuse guaranteed the greatest impact, reducing the household to an immobilising spasm of fear. Wesley Adamczyk, at the time a boy, was transported on the night of 14–15 May. Their rifle-butt on the door came at 2 a.m. when soldiers entered and trashed the house. Shortly afterwards an officer came to inform them they were under arrest. '"You are Polish elite," he scornfully said. "You are Polish lords and masters. You are enemies of the people."'[3] When the Kulik family was deported the Russians were accompanied by a Ukrainian militiaman. They were told it was happening because 'locals object to you'.[4] By contrast, the official might calmly announce the arrest, giving instructions, telling the named persons they had anything between fifteen minutes and a few hours to prepare for departure. Although it was very frightening, Helena Szafrańska does not remember the soldiers behaving badly. They were just 'ordinary men', she says, who acted 'quietly and peacefully', and memories of soldiers acting sympathetically are common. Kindliness, even civility, with

* Soviet secret police.

perhaps a word or two of mumbled apology was not unusual. There are even reported instances of Red Army soldiers being in a state of near-despair. One deportee later recalled a tearful militiaman saying that his grandmother had taught him that 'there is a prophecy in the Scriptures that the Polish army will save us from Communism, and we are taking you to Siberia, how is this so?'[5]

Where present, fathers and older brothers were forced to face the wall or sit in a chair, guns pointed at them, while mothers and sisters rushed through the house gathering possessions together. Mothers were told to pack as much food and as many warm clothes as possible. Sometimes this came as an instruction, sometimes as whispered advice. Anna Bielińska, a February deportee, remembers milking the cow while her husband killed some chickens. The milk froze as it was poured into the bucket.[6] Sometimes the soldiers helped with the packing, telling the depor-tees they would be travelling a long way in the terrible cold. One soldier suggested the Szafrańscy bring their sewing machine but his officer over-ruled this. In other cases the officer insisted the sewing machine *was* brought. It's a telling detail. Sewing machines were crucially important to families of reasonable means and there is evidence of Polish women lugging them across extraordinary distances. Not only did these weighty machines help them keep children clothed but a sewing machine meant access to paid work, whether for money or barter.

Like all deportees, Nana remembers the night of her and her family's arrest vividly. She tells the story with drama, verve and, as ever, without self-pity. Like other deportees who were children at the time, she readily admits to finding the prospect of the long journey exciting. Whenever she writes or talks of any of the events described in this book, she emphasises that as the youngest child with the fewest responsibilities, she experienced much of her journey as adventure. Others, with the benefit of hindsight, say the moment of deportation marked the end of childhood and inno-cence, an innocence particular in the memory to the rural simplicities of *kresy* life. In the words of Danuta Gradosielska (neé Mączka), writing in the 1990s but slipping into the present tense, 'I am 14 and very deeply feel all that is happening; this is the end of my childhood.'[7]

On the night of 12–13 April 1940 Nana was staying at Ciocia Mama's. Nana tells of a quiet tap on the door at dawn awakening Ciocia. A shadowy figure whispered something and was immediately gone. Already there is an air of mystery and adventure suffusing the telling of the tale. 'Danusia, get dressed, you're going on a journey,' said her aunt. 'Any travel used to be a joy,' writes Nana. 'Some excitement rose in me.' Her aunt, however, understood immediately what was happening – everyone knew about the first transportation that February. Despite Danusia's protestations, Ciocia made her little niece dress in twice as many clothes as usual and then warmly wrapped her baby Jagusia. On the way out, she gathered supplies in the shop, pouring sweets from the jars. She was crying and though Danusia couldn't understand why she knew one had to be sympathetic at such times. The girl moistened her eyes with her own saliva.

Danusia stumbled after her aunt, hugging the brown paper bag full of sweets, feeling 'elated'. They crossed the square and hurried down cobbled streets – imagine not an orderly arrangement of pavement and road, but those of a simple country town, with grass growing between the cracks and mud everywhere. Nana remembers her family's house and its low thatch coming into view through the linden trees; it sat, she says, 'like a brooding hen'. The stork had long since migrated for the winter, the nest now standing empty, and 'the pond gleamed in the early light like an eye about to witness the event'. Outside the house stood a horse-drawn cart and some armed soldiers with fixed bayonets. Inside a search party was turning over the house contents, professing to be seeking arms, which they did not find. Wanda, Nana notes mischievously, was still in bed, refusing to budge: 'She loved her indulgences.' When she recalled these events two years later, Wanda claims to have answered the door herself. A further conflicting memory, quickly resolved through conversation, was the fate of their dog Karuś. Wanda says the dog was shot by the soldiers when they arrived, which Nana rejects, suggesting that a soldier may have temporarily stunned him with a whack from his rifle butt. This disagreement makes for a starkly contrasting impression of those brief moments. The crack of a rifle shot in a confined space, the dog instantly halted in its step, and the needless spilling of Karuś's blood in front of the two girls adds a whole additional brutality to the arrests. Wanda readily accepts Nana's version of the story, implicitly acknowledging that her memory was more a trope of Red Army brutality than the strict truth. Sometimes, as a means of conveying the reality of a situation, an emblematic fiction can seem to contain more truth than a mundane reality.

Faced by the magnitude of the situation, Hanna stood in the middle of the room 'stunned'. This was a common response and Jan Gross notes the time lost for packing by people momentarily stupefied by the suddenness with which their world was turning upside down.[8] 'Paralysed with fear we had no idea which way to move,' writes Henryk Grubczak. 'Laments and crying only further muddled our thinking.'9 'You have two hours,' the officer barked at Hanna, jolting her back to full consciousness. 'Siberia!' she screeched as he retreated from the room. The anger had exploded out from within her and she slammed her fists on to the table. Almost immediately those fists spread into helplessness, as she sagged under the weight of her awesome new burdens. She and her two young daughters, aged seven and eleven, were being transported to Siberia. It was the fate that haunted all Polish interactions with Russia. Hanna was quick to grasp the significance of the arrest, seeing how it fitted into a familiar narrative of Polish suffering at the hands of this mighty but crude neighbour. The young guard left behind to supervise this squalid operation whispered insistent advice: 'Warm clothing and food, lady.'

Ciocia Mama, who was not under arrest, offered to spirit Danusia away, letting her live quietly with her for as long as possible. No one would be any the wiser, she said, but Hanna refused, determined the family would stay together. Given the evidence of Soviet efficiency in compiling the lists of deportees and the routine of roll-calls that followed the arrests, it's unlikely Danusia's absence would have gone unnoticed. Miecia however, Hanna stated, must stay behind. She was a guest of the family and had not been placed under arrest. Miecia was outraged by the suggestion. To leave Hanna alone with the two girls would have been tantamount to desertion and to reinforce her insistence on this point she tore around the house like a 'tornado', gathering their things together. In these rapid-fire debates, where willpower rather than logic presided, decisions were taken that would shape the rest of their lives.

Danusia and Wanda were permitted what could be crammed into their school satchels. A tiny rag doll and the deflated football went into Danusia's, along with some school books. Wanda had her eye on a particular pair of her mother's shoes. They had high heels and cherry-coloured tassels. She liked to shuffle about in them. Hanna, in the heat of the moment, gave permission. Children obsessively attach themselves to inanimate objects, those small things they can possess, and it is hard to miss the poignancy of these two girls, at the moment they were ripped from all that they knew, wearing several layers of clothing and eccentrically clinging to a deflated football and a coveted pair of adult shoes.

The situation was similar in the Szafrański household. Helena remembers her mother packing into two large wicker baskets clothing, bedding and saucepans. Her grandmother emptied all the jam from the pantry into a large milk churn; jam made from the previous year's fruit harvest and a core part of their diet. Now the officer urged the family to take their icon of Our Lady of Częstochowa. Częstochowa, a city in south-west Poland, is the country's most important site of Catholic pilgrimage, attracting thousands of penitents and tourists each year, particularly during the summer months when it is traditional to walk to the monastery where the image hangs, approaching it prostrate. The Black Madonna binds together Polish patriotism and Polish Catholicity, and freighted with centuries of myth and legend it is one of the most potent symbols of Polishness. Its cult, like so much else in Catholic Poland, was renewed by Pope Jean Paul II, despite the communist government's avowedly secular vision for the state.

Helena's grandmother refused to take the painting, saying that she would not take it down with her own hands (*'własną ręką nie zdejmę'*). Helena is unsure as to the significance of her grandmother's words, but some clues might be found in the legend of the Black Madonna itself. St Władysław, determined to save the image from the repeated invasions of the Tartars, decided to take the icon to the more secure city of Opole, his birthplace. He broke his journey in Częstochowa where he left the icon overnight in the small wooden Church of the Assumption. Loaded up and ready to leave the following morning, his horses refused to budge. Władysław took this to be a heavenly portent and decided to leave the image in the church, around which a monastery subsequently developed. The icon is credited with having protected a small group of Polish defenders against a much greater Swedish army in 1655. Pious Poles sometimes attribute the 1920 'Miracle on the Vistula' to her intercession: the victory, quite literally, was a miracle. Consequently, for the wife of a Legionnaire, the icon might be thought to have brought them to the *kresy*. And to leave the Madonna in its place was to become a part of the legend that she was not to be moved. As they packed their things, refusing to take down the icon, they emulated Władysław. Hanna, however, decided to take their copy of the icon with them and this symbol of Polish good fortune and religious devotion accompanied her throughout the years to come in exile. My aunt now looks after it. The Szafrańscy later returned to Poland; the Ryżewscy never did.

Helena remembers that last moment in their home. Their time to prepare was up and Helena's aunt, holding her infant, had one last look round the room. Whether it was a moment of sadness or of rapid calcu-lation – a quick assessment of the possible use of things they had left behind – cannot be known, but her eyes alighted on a porcelain coffee set the family had brought from their Kraków home. It seems an apposite symbol of the cosmopolitan, sophisticated city of the family's origin, where to take coffee with friends was an ordinary daily occurrence. It is another small reminder of what the move east had meant. She took a single little cup, thinking it might be useful for feeding the child. Helena still has the cup.

Whether it is a small cup or the copy of a famous icon, historians sometimes talk about such possessions as 'memory objects'. From them a picture of a lost life can be reconstructed. The blue cup has a blue saucer, it was kept on a shelf, or a dresser, or in a cupboard, which in turn sat on a floor, tiled, wooden, carpeted, which was part of a room, which was part of a home, which was part of a street or a farm or a plot of land, which was part of a village or a town or a city or a country or a continent. Who drank from the cup? Was it for everyday use or special occasions? The small, insignificant object becomes a doorway into the past.

Food and water would become a luxury but for the time being the Ryżewscy were better placed than many. Dough had been routinely prepared the night before and it was hastily put in the oven, where it rapidly baked, producing a circular loaf of over a foot in diameter. At the last minute, Miecia had a moment of inspiration and, using a ladder, disappeared up the chimney. She emerged triumphant, carrying a whole leg of smoked pork which had been hanging in the preservation niche. Soon Danusia was sitting in the cart, wrapped in Rafał's best coat, with the ham tucked behind her and the warm loaf on her lap. The saddest moment, Nana admits, was when she and Wanda had to say goodbye to Karuś, who to them looked 'so lost and forlorn'. The dog left behind is another motif of the deportation, a typical adult memory of a child's preoccupations. As the cart pulled off, Ciocia Mama picked up the dog, promising to look after him. Danusia's and Wanda's last sight of home was Ciocia, her baby under one arm, the dog under the other.

The square, silent and empty an hour or so before, was now packed with carts en route to Postawy railway station. As they began to move off, Hanna refused to get in, declaring 'I will walk, no one is going to drive me out.' Smartly dressed, she strode on, a hand always on the cart, leading her girls out of the town. The roads were sloshy for the thaw had begun and Nana recalls that despite her galoshes, her mother's shoes became dirty. It was the first time she had ever seen this. And as the convoy slowly moved forward, the hooves of the horse and the wheels threw up mud and dirty snow, ensuring ugly wet patches grew on Hanna's coat. Battling dirt and struggling to maintain outward signs of respectability are important themes of the narratives of the deportation and it is striking how Nana recalls her younger self noticing the dirty shoes and wet coat. For Danusia, the familiar furs of her father's coat reassured the exhausted little girl: the 'coat around me felt like his arms, safe'. They passed 'the sleeping warriors', a symbol of Polish hope. What was this 'Siberia' that made Mamusia so angry? Danusia's thoughts became scattered as she drifted off to sleep.

Danusia drifting off to sleep is credible enough, but the almost blissful atmosphere she evokes less so. Though it might have been that her mother's determined dignity in the face of catastrophe reassured the child, protecting her from the surrounding chaos, research by Jan Gross into the night of the February deportations paints a very different picture. Depositions later written by deportees suggest an atmosphere of great distress. People were inconsolable with grief and fear, and the sounds of human distress accompanied every stage of this process. 'People were frightened,' Gross writes. 'It was very cold, they were not equipped for the journey, some of them were dying. From the moment they stepped out of their houses, deportees were surrounded by wailing, screaming, and crying.'[10]

When the Ryżewscy arrived at Postawy station that early April morning they met this chaos. Women herded their children and baggage, often followed by bewildered and fragile grandparents carrying their few things. NKVD men and soldiers stood guard while baggage and people were loaded on to the cattle wagons, the elderly and the exhausted helped as they clambered over the high lip of the wagon entrance on to the bare wooden floor. Their confusion can be imagined as they faced the empty wagon, with its hole in the floor and furnished with only two *prycze* (bunks) at either end for sitting and sleeping. According to Moscow regulations, each train had fifty-five wagons.[11]

Family and friends sought each other out, finding comfort and reassurance in familiars. Hanna spotted her friend of many years Pani Anna Blaszczakowa with her children Helena and Rysio. By keeping close together they managed to get into the same wagon. It soon held forty people. Once loaded, the openings were boarded up and the doors padlocked. When her eyes got used to the dark, Danusia noticed a well-dressed and well-mannered boy who had detached himself from the other people and was reluctant to join them on the *prycze*. His mysterious behaviour was soon explained. There was the wrenching sound of splitting wood and the boy was propelled backwards by the sudden release of effort, a piece of plank in hand. A beam of light shot into the wagon. They now had daylight and an observation post. There was spontaneous applause: it was a minor victory, a moment of jubilation.

These few intense hours in the dark of the night were the first stage in the process of deportation which would take thousands of Polish citizens to a new kind of life in the interior of the Soviet Union. Establishing exact figures for the numbers deported is impossible. Traditionally, Poles say that during the twenty-one months of Soviet occupation at least 1.5 million Polish citizens were swept from their homes in the dead of the night and on to cattle trucks bound for Siberia. Historians question these figures, one calculation suggesting that perhaps 1.25 million Poles ended up in the Soviet Union either as deportees (900,000), POWs, Red Army and labour battalion conscripts, or as voluntary migrants.[12] Natalia Lebedeva explains that the confusion arises from the fact that until the collapse of the Soviet Union historians were denied access to the Soviet archives.[13] The most recent revision suggests that during the period of the Soviet occupation between 309,000 and 327,000 Poles were deported to the Soviet interior in the manner described here.[14]

The deportations came in four main waves. The first and most deadly was that of 10 February 1940 when people were forced from their homes in temperatures of around minus forty degrees centigrade – it is this deportation that seems to have provoked the most distress. The second deportation began early in the morning of 13 April 1940, the third in the last week of June 1940, and the fourth in the second half of June 1941, just days before the outbreak of the Soviet–German war. These later deportations did not create quite the same level of anguish. Partly this is because the weather was less threatening. Something of the trauma suffered on the night of 10 February stemmed from the terrible cold. People who live in communities exposed to extremes of temperature develop effective ways of coping. They avoid going out at night when temperatures reach their lowest point and they certainly don't expose their children or the elderly to such appalling conditions. By making the arrests in the earliest hours of the morning, apparently to minimise the fuss that might be caused by local townspeople, the Soviets accentuated the dangers the process posed. A second difference between the February and the April and June

deportations was that those in the second and third waves had a chance
to prepare and there are plenty of stories of people hoarding food or
stitching money and other valuables into their clothes. A third, and perhaps
the most crucial, difference was the various destinations of the deportees.
Those in the first wave were indeed sent to Siberia, to the remote northern
and central regions of the Soviet Union, those in the second, third and
fourth to Kazakhstan and the Altai region. Finally, the June deportations
comprised some of the hundred of thousands of refugees from Nazi-
occupied Poland, mostly Jewish Poles.

Hanna's furious assumption that she was being sent to 'Siberia' is telling.
In part, this simply reflected what she knew of the first deportation, but
the very idea of 'Siberia' was important. For Poles, and for many
Westerners brought up during the Cold War, Siberia is a place of mythic,
terrible significance, a synecdoche for all that is dreadful about Russia. It
was to Siberia the Tsars banished their political enemies. This form of
exile did not necessarily involve formal incarceration but instead a relatively free life in primitive conditions far from home and with severe restrictions on the right to free movement, particularly back to European Russia.
In the Stalinist era Siberia became synonymous with the Gulags, the prison
labour camps, which embodied the regime in the popular imagination,
Western or Eastern. Named after the state institution that ran the camps,
a series of extraordinary accounts of sentences served in the Gulag – most
famously Aleksandr Solzhenitsyn's *Gulag Archipelago* (1973) – made the term
a byword for Stalinist barbarity and the systematic abuse of human rights.
Anne Applebaum, a leading authority, suggests that between 1929 and 1953
(the Stalin era), 18 million Soviet citizens passed through the camps.[15]
Gulags, however, were not death camps in the way that the Nazi concentration camps were. People were sent to the camps to work, not to be
killed. The camps served a dual purpose, providing a place where enemies
of the regime, real or imagined, might be imprisoned and a means by
which the vast natural resources of the Russian wilderness might be
tapped. As with most modern penitentiary regimes, the Gulag professed
a moral purpose, seeking to reform prisoners: through the humbling experience of hard work they might develop an understanding of their rightful
place as a part of the 'dictatorship of the proletariat'.

Nonetheless, in the camps an extraordinary disregard was shown for
the value of human life. Food, clothing and accommodation were utterly
inadequate; the labour was physically very hard and often carried out in
savage conditions (forestry work in the Siberian winter or the Kolyma

gold mines meant probable death); there were harsh punishment regimes, which brought many inmates close to death; and the hierarchies that existed between the prisoners and helped sustain discipline led to further abuses, particularly against women. Above all, prisoners lived in a state of perpetual uncertainty, learning through experience that any hope of release – and many were released, sometimes in mass amnesties – might be dashed at the last moment for seemingly inexplicable reasons. According to one Polish inmate, people died through neglect and despair, whereas people lived because they were constitutionally strong and came to terms with the fact that the Gulag was their life.[16]

Siberia, however, is not just a symbol. It is also a distinct place to be found on any map of the Soviet Union or contemporary Russia. It is a place of clear geographical borders and administrative units. Large industrial cities were developed in its milder southern reaches along the route of the trans-Siberian railway, one of the great achievements of Russian engineering. Siberia was a place of terror and misery, but it was also – and, more than ever, is – a place of ordinary, everyday life.

The indifference towards human life shown in the Gulag also characterised life in the trains. Boarding the train was the beginning of one of the most miserable parts of the experience of deportation; descriptions of the railway journey feature heavily in all the memoirs. The deportees travelled usually for three weeks crammed into cattle trucks which held thirty to forty people, though accounts suggest some took double this number. Most had a stove in the centre, set in the floor, though this did not provide adequate heat and fuel quickly ran out. During the first week of travel the trucks were often not opened. The fetid atmosphere can be imagined. Food was in very short supply. According to NKVD instructions, 'the deportees shall receive free hot food and 600 grams of bread per person once every twenty-four hours', though few, if any, were so treated.[17] The deportees were heavily reliant on what they carried and this was shared, though the Soviets occasionally supplied bread, water and a very thin soup. All remember the trains coming to a halt and the doors being unbolted to reveal bleak, snow-covered landscapes, the light piercingly bright after days in the gloom. A volunteer would be sent to collect a vat of soup. Those in the February transport faced especially low temperatures, which ensured the experience was particularly miserable. Overnight, the frost would stick clothes and hair to the carriage walls, freezing people in place. The old and the very young were particularly vulnerable to the cold, and there were deaths from hypothermia.

One account recalls the anguish caused by the death of a baby. The mother refused to give up the child, clinging to it for several days. The stench of the decaying corpse made already awful conditions very much worse. Her fellow occupants took a collective decision to wrench the baby from her arms and to push it through the carriage window when she fell asleep.[18] It was just one of many bodies – sometimes stripped of clothes too precious to waste – discarded at the side of the track.

All the transported remember the toilet provision on the trains. It was a hole in the floor by one wall and waste fell directly on to the tracks. In most cases a curtain was made from cloth to create privacy. Nana remembers how things were a little more comfortable in her wagon because someone had brought a chamber pot. In Wesley Adamczyk's account the insanitariness of toilet provision constantly recurs, with the author convinced that it formed part of the psychological warfare inflicted on the Poles. Forced to abandon standards of privacy and hygiene, the transported became less themselves. He describes the anxiety and shame associated with going to the toilet on the trains. 'My stomach tightened up like a drum and for three days Mother had to massage my abdomen before I was able to return nature's due.'[19] It is difficult to establish whether the primitive toilet facilities actually were a deliberate psychological tactic, as Adamczyk insists, but as people became weakened with illness and hunger they began to smell, their breath became foul, they broke wind, they got lice. When describing the experience of cramped and insanitary Soviet prisons, Gross refers to how the body became a 'shameful burden to everyone'.[20] It's an insight which equally applied to the experience of the trains.

Franciszek Herzog remembers that when the train reached the last stop before the border many hands stretched out of the barred windows, pleading for people outside to give them a handful of Polish soil. When he buried his mother in Siberia, a little of that soil was sprinkled on her coffin. As they crossed the actual frontier, people began to sing 'We will not abandon Polish Land'. The song carried from wagon to wagon, until all were singing.[21]

The conditions on the trains led Jan Gross to comment: 'The half-million people, most of them women and children, who were deported from the Western Ukraine and Western Belorussia in 1939–1941 were not singled out for resettlement. They were meant to be destroyed.' This is hyperbole, unless Gross's claim is somehow metaphoric. As Applebaum points out, when the Soviets killed en masse, their preferred method was the bullet in the back of the head. Deportation was not execution by stealth, though there can be no question that the way the transportations were organised directly caused the deaths of many people. To unpick Soviet motivations, it is necessary to look at how the deportations fitted into the wider history of the Soviet Union and the conquest of Poland.

What purpose lies behind the military conquest of another country or territory? An obvious question but not one which invites obvious answers. States invade other states for many reasons and the desire to conquer is not always one of them. The Soviet takeover of eastern Poland needs to be understood in terms of state ideology, the perceived long-term strategic interests of the state, and the short-term pressures brought about by the war itself. Just as analyses of the Nazi 'Final Solution' increasingly emphasise how the particular form the Holocaust took was shaped by the immediate circumstances of the war, so too must deportations be seen as less the result of a careful plan and more a response to immediate pressures, fuelled by deeply embedded attitudes. There is no doubt that the balance of power in Europe, particularly in the context of Nazi imperial aggression, was at the forefront of Soviet thinking, but the ways in which the Soviets established their authority in former Polish territories were consistent with the broad thrust of Soviet policy in the 1920s and 1930s.

Eastern Poland was to experience a planned revolution, imposed from outside, which would proceed through logical steps and of which the deportations became an integral part. The deported Poles of the *kresy* were deported because they were of Polish nationality. This becomes clear if the June 1940 deportation of Jewish refugees from Nazi-occupied Poland is examined more closely. Auxiliary agents of the NKVD were ordered to institute a census in which the refugees were asked two questions. Did they wish to adopt Soviet citizenship or did they wish to return to their country of origin? It was not clear what the most advantageous answer was. Those who declared themselves Polish were arrested and deported.[22] This action was consistent with the fact that from the moment of the invasion the Poles were not merely a military opponent. The order issued to the Red Army on the Belorusian front on 16 September 1939 stated: 'We come not as conquerors but as liberators of our brother Belorusians and Ukrainians and the workers of Poland.' Their aim was a 'lightning, crushing blow' which would 'rout the lordly-bourgeois Polish troops and liberate the workers, peasants, and labourers

of Western Belorussia'.[23] This order is striking for the way that it im-
agines that the class enemies of communism in eastern Poland could
only be Polish, falsely suggesting that there were no Ukrainian or
Belorussian owners of capital. Following the invasion, 240,000 Polish
soldiers were captured and the NKVD were ordered to open files on all
prisoners of war with any history of political activity. They searched out
anyone known to have been 'conducting anti-Soviet work, suspected of
espionage activity, and those belonging to the PPS [Polish Socialist Party],
"Piłsudski-ites", National Democrats, Social Democrats, anarchists, and
other c[ounter]-r[evolutionary] parties and organisations, as well as the
entire officer contingent'.[24] Later orders from Laventiy Beria, the head of
the NKVD, demanded that POWs among the rank and file who were
members of 'fascist military and nationalistic organisations' be flushed
out.[25] In effect, any involvement in the civil or political life of pre-war
Poland made one vulnerable to the charge of fascism, communism's
greatest enemy (notwithstanding the Nazi-Soviet Pact), making one
not merely a POW but an enemy of the state.

Anti-Polishness – and hostility for the military settlers – does not alone
explain the deportations. They were also consistent with the broader
Soviet approach to the 'nationalities question' in the Soviet Union as a
whole. Since the 1917 revolution, the Soviet authorities had been aware
that nationalism posed a serious centrifugal threat to the Soviet Union.
According to communist thinking, nationalism was a reactionary creed,
which worked in the interests of the bourgeoisie by blunting the class-
consciousness of the proletariat and the peasantry. In short, the seductive, cross-class, vertical allegiances of nationality prevented the working
class from developing internationalist class solidarities. Nationalism was
a 'masking ideology', which obscured the capitalist system and kept the
proletariat subject to the ascendant bourgeois minority. Faced with the
emergence of internal nationalist challenges to Soviet authority, Stalin
argued, 'The national flag is sewn on only to deceive the masses, as a
popular flag, a convenience for covering up the counter-revolutionary
plans of the national bourgeoisie.'[26] Nevertheless, according to Lenin
and Stalin, the predominance of national over class identity was a historical phase that all communities must go through. The proletariat would
learn through their experience of the nationalist state its bourgeois
realities and, as Stalin said in relation to this debate, 'It is impossible to
go against history.'[27]

Given these unavoidable historical imperatives, the radical solution to the grave threat national sentiment posed their sprawling multi-ethnic state was to come to terms with it. Lenin and Stalin both argued that over the long term national sentiment would be neutralised not merely by allowing it to thrive but by actively promoting it, making it the stuff of state policy. Between 1923 and 1932 vast resources were dedicated to building up numerous indigenous elites throughout the state, creating cultural and educational institutions dedicated to nurturing ethno-linguistic cultures. The thinking was simple: national groups would not develop separatist tendencies if the state fully recognised their right to exist. This policy was applied throughout the Soviet Union. Resources were lavished on the so-called historically advanced nationalities of Belarus, Ukraine and Lithuania (including their Russian, Polish, German and Jewish enclaves) as well as the 'culturally backward' nationalities of the East and Soviet Asia – in 1932, ninety-seven such communities were identified.[28] One of the most striking aspects of the nationalities policy was that it demanded the suppression of Russian culture outside the core Russian heartlands, recognising that Russia was a minority culture too. Soviet nationalities policy, albeit briefly, created among communist Russians anxiety that the creation of the Soviet Union was an exercise in Russification.

Crucially, the policy did not lead to federal political structures. National groups were not granted regional autonomy within the state. The Soviet Union remained profoundly centralised. Instead, the idea emerged of creating thousands of pseudo-democratic micro administrative units on the basis of ethnicity. These, of course, were known as Soviets. As Terry Martin has argued, this policy was applied with notable vigour in the USSR's porous borderlands, particularly in the Ukraine where special efforts were made to placate a restless and vulnerable Polish population.[29] In 1929 the number of Polish National Village Soviets in Soviet Ukraine was put at 150; in Soviet Belorussia the figure for 1933 was forty.[30]

It is difficult to exaggerate the significance of this approach to the Soviet nationalities in the development of the new state. It is also diffi-cult to exaggerate the difficulty the state faced in sustaining these prin-ciples against resistance to collectivisation, the state's overriding priority from the late 1920s. Collectivisation was a colossal undertaking, which aimed to end private property in agriculture, creating a vast infrastruc-ture of state farms managed through the local Soviets but driven by targets dictated by the centre. Collectivisation was accompanied by tremendous violence and had a catastrophic effect on the productivity of agriculture throughout much of the Soviet Union. Popular uprisings and famine became commonplace in the early 1930s, not least in Soviet Ukraine, which became profoundly disturbed, with one set of figures suggesting that in February and March 1930 the region saw 3,145 disturbances involving 937,210 people.[31]

An important component in the motor driving collectivisation was dekulakisation. The kulaks were not the great landlords – they had already been deprived of their properties – but the small and medium farmers who produced surplus goods for the market, employed farm workers, let smallholdings and had thrived under the relatively liberal conditions of the 1920s. Collectivisation demanded, above all, that land held by the kulaks be expropriated and the Soviet authorities stoked up a great deal of anti-kulak sentiment, fomenting a class war throughout the Soviet Union. Collectivisation aimed to liquidate the kulaks as a *class*, but not to kill them as individuals. In practice, the passions released and the cycle of resistance and counter-resistance that followed ensured many thousands were murdered (often with the tacit approval of the local authorities), many thousands were executed as counter-revolutionary enemies of the state, many thousands were deported to new settlements, and many thousands ended up in the Gulag. More still – kulak and non-kulak – died in famine caused by the disruption to agricultural production.

All this was profoundly significant for Poles in the Soviet Union. From the Polish–Bolshevik war onwards, the Poles were suspected of counter-revolutionary tendencies. One report written about the Ukraine in 1925 argued that 'The German, Polish and, to a degree, the Czech colonies are a foothold for spreading the influence of their governments, nests of spies in support of these governments.'[32] These suspicions were compounded when there was a surge of illegal emigration by ethnic Poles to Poland in the late 1920s and early 1930s. In 1930, Poles demonstrated their anger at being prevented from emigrating by staging mass marches to the border, sometimes comprising up to 2,000 people. Though resistance was not exclusive to Poles, in 1930 the Politburo decided that in the border regions of the Ukraine and Belorussia, the collectivisation of kulak households of Polish nationality must be the first priority.[33] With Moscow having set this tone, over the course of the collectivisation campaign it became common to associate Poles and other 'western national minorities' with the kulaks. This could lead to some crude thinking: 'You are being dekulakized not because you are a kulak, but because you are a Pole.'[34] Here the precise sociological terminology of the Soviet revolution was corrupted, allowing all opposition to be design-ated kulak, providing a carapace for a more ancient Russian fear of the Poles. Hostility towards the Poles became more and more evident: in Belorussia it was claimed the legitimate development of Polish culture under the nationalities policy was being exploited by 'Polish fascism', which aimed to Polonise Soviet Belorussia itself.[35] By closely associ-ating Poles with counter-revolution, Polishness itself became crimi-nalised and Soviet officials blamed the failures of collectivisation in the region on counter-revolutionary Poles.

With much of the Soviet Union in turmoil and the peripheral border territories in a state of profound unrest, it became clear to the Soviet authorities that a class-based policy was not enough. Dekulakisation was augmented with ethnic cleansing. According to Terry Martin, the first time this occurred was in December 1932 when the entire Cossack town of Poltava in the Ukraine was moved to the far north. Within months, a further eight Cossack towns in the area were emptied, moving perhaps 100,000 people. Though a small number when contrasted with the 1.8 million individuals deported as kulaks in 1930–1, the Cossack deportations represented a very significant change in policy.[36]

As paranoia about the border territories in the west increased, Moscow decided to establish a 7.5-kilometre-deep 'forbidden border zone', acces-sible only with special NKVD permission.[37] From 1933 NKVD agents began to worry that the Polish Military Organisation (POV), which dated back to the Polish–Bolshevik war, was again active in its territories. In her important book on the Soviet borderlands, Kate Brown argues that the POV had long been defunct and that it was 'conjured' back to life by the NKVD.[38] The aim of the POV, according to the NKVD, was to provoke a mass exodus to Poland, which would have been a propaganda disaster and might have triggered a Polish invasion.[39] In effect, the NKVD invented the POV in order to account for the resistance to collectivisa-tion and in the arrests and 'confessions' that followed, the NKVD engaged in the work so characteristic of Soviet terror, creating its own reality. Brown thinks Soviet persecution of the Poles stemmed less from a crude anti-Polishness than the observation that rates of collectivisation were significantly lower in areas of Polish (or German) than Ukrainian settlement. According to Soviet thinking, areas of Polish settlement in Soviet Ukraine, though considered 'advanced' under the Old Regime on account of being bourgeois, were now thought 'backward' for the same reason. 'Backwardness' itself became a signifier of 'sabotage' and the

Poles, collectivisation statistics taught, counter-revolutionary.[40] More
contentiously, Brown argues that Polishness in the Ukraine itself was a
problematic concept. The Soviet apparatchik, clipboard in hand,
conducting nationality surveys, often found *kresy* peasants baffled by his
questions. Nationality meant little to them. They were from 'here'. They
identified with their church. They spoke a dialect that was only broadly
speaking Ukrainian or Polish or Yiddish. Still, the system demanded that
each individual was classified: they had to be of one nationality or another.
The apparatchik had to tick a box and the box he ticked could have
untold consequences for that individual.[41]

In 1935–6, the problem of under-collectivisation was addressed. Half
the households classified as Polish or German in the Ukrainian border
area were deported. In the three waves of 1936 some 15,000 families were
forcibly moved.[42] Over the course of that year, the Ukrainian authorities
and the NKVD sought permission to deport additional Polish families,
identifying them as 'counter-revolutionary nationalist and anti-Soviet
elements'.[43] At the same time a significant proportion of Polish and
German national institutions in Ukraine and Belorussia were closed down.
They were described as 'artificially created',[44] the suggestion being that
at the point of creation they were surplus to need, the state having been
hoodwinked into creating them by crafty Polonising Poles. Due recognition of national identity was one thing, creating the means by which that
nationality might be proselytised to a credulous peasantry was quite
another. The logic was clear: if the revolution was to progress, Polishness
in the Ukraine must be uprooted.

The 15,000 families were sent to Kazakhstan. They were granted the
status of 'special settler' (*spetspereselentsy*), a status shared with deported
kulaks. This meant they came under the supervision of the NKVD and
could be used as forced labour. In practice, many were put to work on
pre-existing *kolkhoz* (collective farms) or were required to establish *kolkhoz*
farms on the Kazakh steppe. It is enough for now to note that the same
fate awaited the Polish deportees of April 1940.

In August 2007 I met Albert Lewkowski in Warsaw. He told me his
story of deportation from the Ukraine in 1936. Born in 1927 in the village
of Czerniawa in the Woloczyski region of the Ukraine, Albert was the
son of the blacksmith and the second of three brothers. He describes his
family as having always lived there and the village as half-Polish and half-
Ukrainian. No Jews lived in the village but two kilometres away was a
Jewish shtetl. Relations within the community were good, he insists,

though when quarrelling people resorted to ethnic slurs: 'Polish pig' was common. There was a consciousness of difference, he says, but ethnicity did not determine social status.

On the night of 21 May 1936 the knock came. The family was one of nine in the village to be placed under arrest and instructed to prepare to leave. Albert cannot say for sure why his family was singled out, but he wryly notes that local officials had to meet a quota and he thinks the 'Polish spirit' was strong in the families selected. He firmly rejects the idea that Polishness was the product of the classifying impulses of the Soviet census takers and says that his family were strongly conscious of their Polishness and always spoke Polish together. Few restrictions were imposed on the baggage the 1936 deportees were permitted to bring. They were allowed to fill two carts and could even take a cow or two. Given that these regions had been collectivised, and that consequently individual families owned very little livestock and farm equipment, the deportees could bring the bulk of their movable possessions. The Lewkowscy killed a piglet, which sustained them during their journey, and they took their painting of Christ, which Albert's brother in Moscow now has. During the eighteen-kilometre journey to the station, on this grey drizzly day, they stopped in a primarily Jewish village where there was a Catholic church. Women, he says, cried quietly, the men stood in silence. Their destination, they soon learnt, was Kazakhstan. After two miserable weeks in the cattle trucks, they arrived. It was a grim place, undeveloped and desolate, with little evidence of human settlement. Under the supervision of the local Soviet authorities they were to establish a *kolkhoz* out of nothing. Difficult times lay ahead.

It is perhaps now clear how profoundly the absorption of the *kresy* into the Soviet Union changed the status of the Poles. They were transformed, almost overnight, from being a part of the national majority to a minority within a vast hostile state. Previously, they had enjoyed a very special status. Every Pole in the *kresy* was, in some respects, an envoy for the Polish state. Whether they thrived or not was of interest to the state in a way quite distinct from that of Poles in territorially non-contested parts of the country. At a stroke, the defeat and partition of Poland removed that protection and that special status, isolating the Poles of the *kresy* from territories where their fellow Poles were a strong majority.

The effect of this was felt immediately. The Polish defeat of September

1939 was inflicted by the *Wehrmacht* – the German army – who then with-
drew from eastern Poland to make way for the entry of the Red Army.
In the meantime the Polish government fled to Romania, along with
many officials from all over the country – thousands abandoned their
posts, leaving behind a power vacuum. Though many skirmishes followed
between the Red Army and the chaotic remnants of the Polish army and
its border defence force, the Soviets essentially faced a clean-up operation. They occupied eastern Poland and took 240,000 POWs at a cost of
3,000 casualties, which was cheap for 200,000 square kilometres of territory and 13.5 million new subjects.[45]

For the Polish Christians and the Polish Jews of the *kresy* the brief
period between the collapse of the Polish government and the arrival
of the Soviet army was a time of extreme anxiety. In parts of the *kresy*,
a peasant *jacquerie* sprang to life, converging on the towns and villages,
and Poles, fearful for their lives and property, responded by forming a
Citizens' Guard. Though these forces were uncoordinated and largely
spontaneous, here were the makings of the civil war that the politics
of the *kresy* had long threatened. Poles, Christian and Jewish, suffered
violent attacks and looting, with these early days bringing the first wave
of murder and pillage, which would scar the region throughout the
war. For both groups the lesson was clear: their safety depended on
strong central government and it is this which explains why some
welcomed the Red Army. Among the older generation there was fear,
and scattered accounts survive of men abandoning their wives and
children and even committing suicide.[46] Among the military settlers
fear of reprisal for the Polish–Bolshevik war was great and in the waves
of arrests that characterised the occupation, evidence of participation
in that past war was taken as proof of counter-revolutionary thought
in the present.[47]

These sinister times are remembered for the disappearances. Accounts
by deportees, remembering those days through their childhood eyes,
write of fathers and other male relatives going missing. Some testimonies
begin simply by saying on such a date 'My father disappeared, never to
be seen again.' Rafał, Nana says euphemistically, stopped coming home.
Olek disappeared. A police officer, the father of Danusia's friend Wercia,
vanished, as did the fathers of many of their friends. Some may have
been kidnapped and murdered by the *jacquerie*, though it was more likely
they were reservists, mobilised, and then almost immediately taken prisoner by the Red Army. This was Rafał's fate. Their mothers kept to their

homes, in public they huddled together, talking in whispers. Wesley Adamczyk remembers the pervasive atmosphere of secrecy and gloom.[48] Similarly, Nana remembers the tension in the public spaces, the disputes and fistfights that began to disfigure the social life of the town. People, she says, were being forced to take sides. In Hruzdowa a strange beggar was talked of. He carried a large cross close to his chest and blessed anyone who showed him kindness. Perhaps this was just another destitute old man muttering religious incantations, but in the feverish atmosphere of those early weeks of defeat he attracted attention, seeming a portent of the difficult times to come.

Nana recalls the moment the Russians arrived as one of trepidation and curiosity. Though small advance parties of troops and political workers had signalled their imminence, for many people the first sign of the impending arrival was the distant rumble of tanks. The impact of this awesome noise, gradually approaching, is one of the more brilliant sequences in Steven Spielberg's World War Two film *Saving Private Ryan* (1998). Though people confined themselves to their homes that day, Nana says she sneaked into the garden and hid behind the picket fence and shrubs to watch the army march past. In fact, the conquering army did not march but 'trudged, looking very tired and unkempt'. Their greatcoats were unhemmed and frayed. It's common for Poles to remember the poor state of the Red Army, contrasting it with the well-equipped, well-dressed Germans, who in many cases were seen leaving the same neighbourhoods just days earlier. One of the more peculiar features of the Soviet occupation was the spending spree many Soviet soldiers quickly embarked on. The new authorities declared the rouble the legal currency and the troops appear to have been supplied with money in advance. They bought everything they could get their hands on. Soldiers gorged themselves on sweets and pastries, often wolfing them down as they stood in the shop or on the street. Particularly prized were watches, which they bought up by the dozen. Goods were purchased rather than looted and it seems that many soldiers felt intimidated and humbled by the relatively high quality of life they found in the *kresy*, the poorest part of Poland.[49] This difference in expectation between the Poles and the Russians would be a leitmotif of Polish–Soviet interaction throughout the war. It would later get Miecia into very big trouble.

As the rhetoric of dekulakisation had legitimatised mass violence during collectivisation in the Soviet interior, so did anti-Polish sloganising

in the *kresy*. From the moment of the Soviet arrival, propaganda fingered
the Poles as imperial oppressors from whom the people should be liberated. Languages of class and ethnicity again overlapped, until all Poles,
rich or poor, civilian or military, became identified as the people's enemy.
Though in some communities anti-Polish violence was minimal and the
local population proved reluctant to take the law into their own hands
as the pronouncements of local officials seemed to allow, it is hard to
exaggerate the appalling barbarity many Poles suffered. Through the
patina of ideological justification protruded an atavistic fury. In areas
where ethnic enmity was most intense, large groups of peasants attacked
isolated Poles – in some parts public humiliation became common, while
the unlucky were stoned, mutilated, tortured or beaten to death with
farm implements. Poles took to hiding in the woods, sometimes for weeks
at a time, while the Soviet troops routinely ignored pleas to restrain the
peasantry. Violence by the Red Army itself was less overt and more
focused. Their purpose was to root out the Polish 'counter-revolutionary'
elite, so they directed their efforts mainly against Polish officers, policemen
and landowners. There were well-attested massacres of Polish officers,
but much of this violence against Poles went on behind closed doors, in
prisons and makeshift interrogation units.[50]

Though uncoordinated, this violence was neither spontaneous nor
meaningless. In a few short months a revolution was brought about. The
Polish elite were replaced by a newly created Soviet elite drawn from the
'reliable' parts of the population and organised through new local Soviets.
Often hopelessly ignorant of the conduct of government, the new elite
was foisted upon the people and then confirmed in its position through
staged elections in October 1939 and March 1940. These elections were a
triumph of Soviet organisation, producing exactly the mandate Moscow
sought. Most notoriously, convicted criminals were elevated to positions
of power within the community. This was consistent with a conveniently
crude interpretation of Soviet ideology: their criminality should be recognised as a form of rebellion against the bourgeois state. Bourgeois
society, Soviet ideology taught, criminalised its class enemies, allowing
the true criminals to hold on to power. A criminal conviction, now judged
symptomatic of a subordinate class status within bourgeois society, signified
the potential to become model Soviet citizens. Under the new conditions,
any achievements or status, professional, political or plutocratic, were a
liability, an indication of counter-revolutionary tendency.[51] Society was being
turned upside down.

Much energy was invested in de-Polonising and secularising the new territory. According to Soviet orthodoxy, the aim was to reduce the influence of Poles to a level that reflected the Polish proportion of the population. Of central importance to this project was schooling and the reduction of education in the Polish language. It is hard to know if this met with approval from non-Poles, for Polish had long been associated with advancement. Like many deportees, Nana remembers the changes brought about in her school. Prayer was forbidden at morning assembly, religious symbols were removed, and portraits of Piłsudski were replaced with Lenin. These changes were enforced throughout the *kresy* and many non-Polish parents were deeply troubled by secularisation. Wanda described the process as a Polish school being turned into a Belorussian school. In every classroom a large chalk sign appeared declaring 'Let Live Belarus'. With the help of three classmates – a daughter of the church organist, the son of the Orthodox priest and the son of the mayor – she changed it to 'Let Die Belarus'. It caused a scandal. Each class member was summoned to the principal's office and questioned, but the culprits were never identified. 'If they had found out,' she says, 'it could have been very bad for my parents.' Her act of rebellion was part of a wider informal movement of non-cooperation among schoolchildren and students, which included Poles refusing to attend school, so exposing their parents to the terrible risk of prosecution for counter-revolution. In June 1940 at Czortkow in Tarnopol, Ukraine, a student rebellion led to 600 students being rounded up. An unknown number were taken away and shot, and thirteen of the twenty-eight who were brought to trial were executed. The thirteen-year-old boy who had his death sentence commuted was the exception proving the rule.[52]

Teachers had a very uncertain status under the new regime. School principals, as the leading agents of Polonisation, seem to have been rounded up early on and it is easy to see why Rafał – as a school principal, reservist, civilian settler and ex-Legionnaire – was targeted for arrest. Hanna, on the other hand, continued to work, and there is evidence that the Soviets prized teachers for their valuable skills. For example, they were put to work collecting census information in the run-up to the elections. Conditions at work, however, changed radically. With Poles constantly mocked in Soviet propaganda, pupils became less respectful and discipline harder to maintain. Pupils were encouraged to inform on their teachers and some, empowered by the new certainties brought by the excitement of revolution, zealously rose to the task. On the night of the deportation, Nana remembers Hanna's new boss mockingly waving them goodbye. Hanna shook her fist, impotent yet furious.

Property, naturally enough, was requisitioned, expropriated and redistributed throughout the *kresy*. The long-term aim was to establish collective farms, but in the short term feeding and clothing the Soviet army was the priority. Ciocia Mamusia's house was requisitioned and she and her baby moved into the back of her store. When Danusia stayed, as on the night of the arrests, she would sleep in the linen basket, 'like Moses'. Thanks to the demands made on the dwindling supply of foodstuffs by the army, it became impossible for Ciocia to meet orders. Feeling the pinch, Hanna sent a man to Działka to collect provisions. When he returned empty-handed she demanded an explanation. The reply was army requisitioning. Fuming, she drove the *bryczka*, their small passenger cart, to Działka herself, bringing Danusia and Wanda along with her. It was, perhaps, the first time she made the journey to Działka without her husband. Why was I not told of the requisitions? she demanded, futilely remonstrating with the Belarusian caretakers that the security of the holding was in the interest of them all. When the whole property was requisitioned, Hanna's handwritten comment on the document detailing the transfer of their property says simply, 'We lost everything.'

While Hanna tried to put her affairs in order, the girls went to find their friends, the two Belarusian boys. There followed an exchange, which became seared onto Danusia's memory. Danusia and the older of the boys watched their siblings play jacks, at which Wanda excelled. Where's Reks? asked Danusia, noticing the absence of the dog who was normally their constant companion. The older boy made a slitting motion across his throat. Horrified, Danusia said, 'Wait until Tatuś [daddy] gets back!' With a menacing hiss, the boy again made the slitting motion, to indicate the fate of their father. Wanda stood up, looked at the boys, said sternly, 'We will see,' and walked away. Nana remembers tearfully stumbling after her 'brave and fearless' sister.

Back in Hruzdowa the strange beggar with the cross was found dead in the bottom of the well.

There is a final dimension to the deportation that brings this complex of factors into brutal focus. Documents which have become available since the collapse of the Soviet Union demonstrate the connection between the decision to deport the families of 'western Belorussia' and 'western Ukraine' and one of the regime's most notorious crimes, the massacre of 14,500 Polish army officers, police, gendarmes and civilians at Katyń, Mednoye and Kharkov, locations in the Soviet Union. These men had been held at POW camps at Starobelsk, Kozelsk and Ostashkov where they were inadequately fed, restricted in their religious practice and constantly subjected to interrogation. Stalinism had little time for the Geneva Convention. The decision to execute them is generally thought to have been made by or on 5 March 1940. Beria's memorandum recording the Politburo's approval of the step is signed by Stalin and other senior figures alongside the simple word 'za' meaning 'for'. Describing the prisoners as 'all hardened, irremediable enemies of Soviet power', the NKVD recommended that their cases be examined and, where appropriate, 'using the special procedure, apply to them the supreme punishment, shooting'. The men would not be presented with charges, a document of indictment, or be questioned.

Less well known is that the order was also to be carried out against 11,000 further Polish POWs of lower status but still thought to pose a counter-revolutionary threat to the new state. The fate of these men is unknown, though documentary evidence points to 7,305 being shot in prison, with surviving lists accounting for some 3,435 of the total.[53] One source suggests that in all 21,857 prisoners were summarily executed.[54] For Poles, these murders are signified by the word 'Katyń' after the forest where many were shot and buried in mass graves. It was not until the final years of the Soviet Union that the crime was finally admitted and it became possible for surviving family members to discover the fate of their missing relatives.

Almost to the day the order was given to commence the POW investigations and executions came another order to deport to Kazakhstan the families of the prisoners held in the camps. On 7 March 1940 Beria instructed that lists be compiled of the Polish POWs and their families.[55] On 20 March Beria directed that the People's Commissar of Internal Affairs Kazakh SSR prepare for the reception of 75–100,000 people, the 'twenty-five thousand families of repressed former officers of the Polish Army, police, prison guards, gendarmes, intelligence agents, former landowners, manufacturers, and prominent officials of the former Polish state apparatus being held in prisoner-of-war camps'.[56] There is no documentary evidence directly linking the execution order to the deportation and specialist historians are reluctant to assert that the execution order triggered the deportation order.[57] Natalia Lebedeva, a leading Russian expert, suggests a slightly different way of explaining the chain of events. In order to strengthen the Ukrainian border, Nikita Khrushchev, then First Secretary of the Ukraine, proposed creating an 800-metre-deep frontier strip from which would be removed the families of those who had been executed or imprisoned. They were then deported to Kazakhstan. Beria supported the suggestion and gained Politburo approval on 2 March 1940.

Can it be that this decision inspired Stalin to have shot the heads of the families subject to deportation?[58] It's a compelling argument, not least when one considers that the first deportation of February 1940, comprised mainly of Poles from around Vilnius, had included fathers. It is the presence of men that meant Siberia was a feasible destination. It was out of the question that the former Polish elite, those 20,000 men judged by the regime the most dangerous group in the Soviet Union, would have been released to accompany their families east. But rather than this determining the deportation of the women and children to Kazakhstan, choosing Kazakhstan – the development of which was something of an *idée fixe* for Khrushchev – led to the decision to execute the soldiers. The Katyń murders loom so large in the Polish memory of the Second World War that where the link has been made to the deportations it has been implicitly assumed that the deportations must be of secondary significance. Lebedeva's analysis suggests it was actually the other way around, the decision to deport triggering the decision to execute.

All this leaves an unanswered question. What of Rafał? He, surely, was of the class who were executed that blood-coloured spring? He was not among the 14,500 officers held at the special camps but it is hard to imagine he was not among the 10,000 junior officers held as counter-revolutionaries. Family legend says Rafał escaped Katyń and it is just possible this is true. Piecing together a detailed account of Rafał's experience is impossible, but if the little evidence that survives can be seen to bear out family lore, then it is a most extraordinary story. He and Hanna kept in touch by letter during this time, but only one letter survives. Dated 2 February 1940, it is addressed from Simno, a town seventy miles west-south-west of Vilnius. 'My Darlings!' it begins, characteristically upbeat. Rafał explained that he was doing some kind of concreting work, noted that everything was run by and for the state, and observed how he was 'a well-known artisan and highly valued', an ironic comment on his new status as a Soviet worker. As in many of his later letters, he had a special message for his elder daughter. 'Wanda, please take care of

yourself and understand that every lesson is a good one and can benefit
you. What you see and hear now is all knowledge which can benefit you
in life. To become acquainted with such interesting sources as you have
there is a priceless treasure house of knowledge, which money simply
can't buy. You must make use of it while it's there.' It's exactly the kind
of attitude Nana associates with her father. Of his 'darling' Danusia he
simply asks after what she is 'doing', an affectionate question, reflecting
his consistent view, even as she got older, that her scampish innocence
protected her. Finally, he turns his attention to his wife. 'You, Hanna, I
kiss your ears especially so they are turned up and stand proudly.' It's a
sweetly uplifting image from the family's chief cheerleader. 'Everything
you do is all right,' he continues, 'as I believe it is wise.'

Rafał's positive outlook masked some serious dilemmas. He refers to
earlier (now missing) letters which had considered the offer of Soviet citizenship to the kresy Poles. 'In connection with this you will understand
that I thought and meditated about what to do with this chance. Your
position inclined me to a favourable relationship to the whole story.
Thanks, however, to your loving letters and your negative point of view,
my peace and courage returned.' It's a striking closing statement. Rafał,
seemingly agonised by indecision, was tempted to trade his Polish for
Russian citizenship, thinking it would be to the advantage of himself and
his family at this time of appalling vulnerability. Hanna's repudiation –
and it is easy to imagine her scorning any such idea – renewed his
certainty, liberating him from the possibility of compromising his nationalist principles. Moments such as this, achieved through an exchange of
letters, also served to renew their marriage, confirming the meeting of
minds when they first met in the kresy.

Why was Rafał working as a concreter? The most logical explanation
is that like the great majority of the Polish POWs he had been released
and was among those drafted into the work brigades. There is an alternative explanation, long established as family lore. Following the invasion,
Rafał was placed under arrest along with many officers and put on a
train 'destined for Katyń'. As she tells the story, Nana's language here
is clearly a little loose but it is conceivable that he was en route to the
officers' camp at Smolensk. Similarly – and this fits the myth a little
better – he may have been among those junior officers transferred to
Ostashkov Camp at the time of mass POW releases in October 1939.[59]
Perhaps it was during this journey that a high-ranking Russian officer
was taken ill and an urgent search was made for a doctor among the

Polish prisoners. Perhaps it was then that Rafał stepped forward and declared his fictitious medical credentials. Did he approach the officer in character, adopting the appropriate mannerisms and making the appropriate noises, murmuring and grunting his way through an examination and diagnosis? (The many subsequent performances in the parlour at Haye Down Farm can be imagined.) It was serious, the 'doctor' pronounced, the officer needed hospital attention at once and must be accompanied to the hospital for the possibility of relapse was high. Sometimes it is said he took his chance to bolt through the window of the toilet of the slow-moving train and landed in a potato field, crawling to cover, other times that he took his chance once they had arrived at the hospital . . .

One day, while on the run, says Nana, he overheard Polish-sounding

voices and came upon a group of people burying someone. They were free travellers or gypsies and they agreed to shelter him. He lived, or so the story goes, for several months as a gypsy. They gave him the papers of the dead man and thereafter he lived as Franciszek Zawadzki, growing a rather peculiar beard as a way of disguising his identity. Hanna is supposed to have heard while in Kazakhstan that Franciszek Zawadzki was safe and well, though only Wanda, the 'sensible daughter', could be trusted to keep the secret. He sent a photo.

This fantastical story might just be true. His army record briefly states that he saw action in the September 1939 campaign with the 86th Infantry Regiment before being interned by the Lithuanian authorities on 25 September 1939. It then states that he lived under an assumed name from 27 October 1939 until 14 June 1941, at which point he joined the new Polish forces established in the Soviet Union. In a decidedly oblique letter to Hanna dated 28 August 1940, Rafał lurches from subject to subject. He begins by surveying his work over the past six months or so, and explains how having been freed he is now paid for his work. What he means by being freed is unclear and it might simply be that he was released from the POW camp, as many officers had been. But it might also be a euphemism for his escape.

He says he worked at a mill for seven months, mainly unpaid, until in August 1940 he picked up some work as a land surveyor. Now, though, it was farm work, simple labouring, 'fetching and mowing'. He was particularly concerned with Hanna's housekeeping needs and was frustrated that she did not specify her exact wants so he could prepare a package of essential goods. He then dropped in a curious parenthesis: 'The psychological evolution I have been undergoing took a very calm course.' It's hard to know what to make of this. It chimes with his earlier relief that Hanna had made the decision not to accept Soviet citizenship; it might simply refer to his new situation, but it is tempting to see it as a reference to living under an assumed identity. Either way, Rafał clearly recognised that Hanna had it very much worse than him, shouldering much greater responsibilities. Living in the Ukraine, Rafał was in familiar territory, with some family members close by, and he ends the letter hoping that he might yet be permitted to work in a Ukrainian factory.

A year later, from a new location in Ukraine, he wrote of his current circumstances in a similarly intriguing way: 'Staying in the town is becoming impossible for a multitude of reasons. Unaccustomed to the new conditions, and particularly being in a group, a person begins to fidget – not dangerously, but unnecessarily. This is why I mainly spend my time in the hut of a bricklayer I work with.' Again, thinking about the possibility of Rafał living incognito, this fidgeting might be read to mean he had allowed little bits of information to slip out.

'Through the slits in the carriages we peered to see our beloved Polish land. When the train departed and we crossed the border we bade farewell to the fatherland through the narrow windows and slits of the truck; in tears and in great sadness we sang "God, who loves Poland" and the national anthem.' So wrote Wanda two years later.

As the train pulled its human cargo east, deep into Russia, the Poles looked out at a land that grew ever more empty, grey and shabby. People could be seen at their work, bent double in desolate fields: Russian primitiveness and the human cost of collectivisation were seemingly confirmed by many fleeting but monotonous impressions. Aware of the hundreds of eyes hungrily peering out from those dark wagons, workers in the fields would straighten up and 'cross themselves as though the Devil himself carried those wretched souls to the abyss'. Most ironic of all, however, were those that flocked to the railway wagons, keen to receive the *kasza* (a kind of porridge) supplied by the Soviets and discarded as inedible by Poles still surviving on the scanty provisions brought from home.

How different it is to be carried today along that same stretch of track by PKP, the Polish railway, in the relative comfort of a second-class coupé. The journey from Warsaw to Moscow, which passes through Belarus, takes a little over a day. It's early evening on the day I left Warsaw and I'm sitting in the restaurant car sipping green tea. The train somnolently rattles on through the dusk. We're an hour or so from the Belarus border. The waitress is pretty and friendly, and we exchange a few words as I try to come up with the right change. Frustrated at being unable to instantly see the combination of coins needed, I resort to a five-zloty piece and accumulate yet more change. My paper cup warns me in Polish, German and English – but not Russian – that the contents are hot. *'Uwaga! Gorący napój!' 'Achtung! Heiß Getränk!'* 'Warning! Hot drink.' I'm sure this reflects commercial calculations rather than politics, yet still it chimes with the continuing Polish wariness of the Russians.

I've come to the restaurant car to escape the large group of Russian boys in my carriage. They're on their way back from a sports trip to Poland. I share a compartment with the two who, I guess, pulled the short straw. They have murmured conversations and fiddle with their mobile phones and hand-held Playstations. Their friends stick their heads round the door and the hierarchies that exist between the boys are evident. Becoming more confident, their behaviour grows a little more intrusive. Soon they're playing music through their mobiles. 'Rock Around the Clock', 'Smoke on the Water', 'The Show Must Go On' and other 'soft metal favourites'. I smile indulgently, recognising the opening bars of yet another dadrock classic. These kids are very uncool indeed and, as if to prove it, each time they leave and enter the carriage they deferentially say 'sorry' as I move my feet.

In the restaurant car, two guys sit at a table on high stools fixed to the floor. They talk quietly in Polish over a beer. The chef is a table or two behind me, taking a break from having very little to do. The waitress has reappeared and I wonder about her. Will her life be spent working on this train? Is she a student and this her summer job? Perhaps she'll graduate in a year or two and get a job in the new Poland or maybe she'll follow the thousands of young Poles who have migrated to the UK? There she might serve Londoners caffè lattes and brownies in a chain café, before returning home with hard-won savings. Or perhaps she'll have a successful professional career and settle in England, starting a family. Her mobile phone goes off. It's a familiar ringtone, a powerful advertisement for a huge international brand.

Villages and small towns roll into and then out of focus. Soviet housing developments flit past, seeming incongruous in this semi-rural environment. Grids of low wooden houses, each fenced in its own cottage garden, line the track. Though they look scruffy, containing bits of gardening equipment and rusting old junk, these are clearly gardens in which things are grown to eat. I think of the old ladies selling good fresh vegetables on the street. It's a trade threatened by EU membership and its attendant 'food standards'. People walk along paths, evidently on their way home from work. It's that time of day, but seemingly at all times tiny round old ladies in long skirts and headscarves trudge along, swinging a little from side to side, long-handled cloth bags hanging from limp arms. They make good but monotonous progress. It's hard sometimes to discern where they've come from and where they could be going. Everywhere is tall yellow grass; it sprouts at the edge of cultivated fields or parks, it borders dusty paths and stony roads, it provides a wispy border just outside every garden fence.

It's begun to rain and the windows have become cross-hatched with water. Fat liquid blobs run down vertically while the forward motion of the train creates a fine tracery of crossing lines, running parallel to the horizontal of the window frame. We're now very near the border at Terespol and freshly painted red and yellow railings line the track. I'm shooed back to my compartment to be ready for the border guards. They treat me with absolute courtesy and there is none of the intimidation described in lurid warnings in the Lonely Planet guidebook.

Just beyond the Polish–Belarus border the train is backed into a huge, gloomily lit shed. Burly men in fluorescent jackets get to work with hoists, and for the next two or three hours metal cranks and clanks, the carriage jolts and judders. It takes a moment or two to realise what is happening. The train is being converted from the standard gauge that is near-universal in Europe to the broad gauge used by the Russian railways. As the passengers wait in their compartments, each carriage is decoupled from the train and then lifted so that the bogies can be run out along the track from under the train. The new wider bogie is then wheeled into place and the carriage lowered and re-coupled. It is now possible to continue the journey into Russia.

Standard gauge is 1435mm, broad gauge is 1520mm. Much can be read into these eighty-five millimetres. In 1866 the first broad-gauge railway was opened in Poland running from Warsaw to Brest, the first stage of the journey to Moscow. Around the same time, the Russian general staff declared that only broad gauge should be used in Russian territories, thus simplifying the transfer of troops and supplies around the vast empire. During the First World War the Germans and Austrians standardised the network in the territory under their control. In the interwar years, to travel by train from Warsaw to Moscow meant changing trains at Niegoreloje on the Soviet–Belarus border. Standardising the railway network in the *kresy* was, of course, a practical matter. But as with all such practical matters, assimilating the infrastructure of borderlands with the rest of the country was another Polonising act, of removing difference.

The *kresy*, as a place of ethnic and cultural pluralism, no longer exists. In the 1920s and 1930s, Polish nationalism failed to destroy the *kresy* through Polonisation; in the 1940s the Soviet methods – de-Polonisation, annexation and deportation – succeeded. And though the deportations did not remove all Poles from the region – the process was brought to a halt by the Soviet–German war – Polishness became an ever more marginal presence as the area ceased to be ethnically and culturally diverse. As part of the same process, Poland itself also became mono-cultural, not least owing to the systematic murder of three million Polish Jews by the Nazis. As the journey east today demonstrates, the annexation by the Soviet Union of this territory brought the *kresy* a different future. Lithuania, Belarus and the Ukraine were fully integrated into the Soviet Union in a way that Poland, Hungary, Romania, Bulgaria, East Germany, Czechoslovakia and Albania never were, and the change in railway gauge continues to reflect this.

Lodged in a particular kind of Polish consciousness the *kresy* continues to exist. Miłosz once lamented the neglect of Vilnius's Catholic churches, seeing a Polish cultural inheritance going to rack and ruin thanks to Soviet ideological disregard.[60] Today such buildings are being restored and Lithuanianised. But it is not just the older generation who think of Vilnius and Lwów as Polish places beneath a carapace of something new. A friend of mine, who has no particular connection to the city, says that though Poles harbour no irredentist claim to Lwów it has a 'legendary' hold over the Polish imagination. Even young Poles feel wistful when visiting the city, finding an elegance that seems quintes-sentially Polish. I'm astonished when she says that, though dirty and run-down, Lwów is more beautiful than Kraków. This seems an extraor-dinary concession. Lwów is a piece of our colonial history, she explains, it's good to visit and say we were here. Ukrainians find such attitudes extremely irritating, evidence once again of that ineffaceable Polish sense of superiority.

The Soviet ethnic cleansing of the *kresy* is shadowed by a heavy irony. After 1940 the deportees were always behind the front line. They were not in eastern Poland during the Nazi occupation (1939–45) and did not experience its attendant brutalities; they were not exposed to the ethnic conflict of the *kresy*, which raged throughout the war; they were in a place of relative safety at the time of the battle of Stalingrad (the death toll from fighting, illness and hunger: 2 million) and the '900 days' of the siege of Leningrad (aka St Petersburg; death toll from fighting, illness and hunger: 1.5 million). For those in the *kolkhoz*, as the next chapter will explore, their lives were comparable to those of ordinary Soviet civilians at a time of great shortage and hardship. Though the deportations led to thousands of premature deaths, Stalin's attempt to liquidate the Polish 'kulaks' from the *kresy* ensured, indirectly, that many survived.

4

In 'Siberia': Life in Kazakhstan

The April deportees – among them Hanna, Wanda and Danusia – were not sent to Siberia but to Kazakhstan, the vast Soviet republic which lay to the south of Siberia. Nor were they sent to the 'Gulag', the notorious Stalinist labour camps, but were instead employed as labourers in the *kolkhoz*, the collective farms created in the 1930s, and on other projects, notably building the Kartaly–Akmolinsk railway, which cuts across northern Kazakhstan. The precise status of the deportees is significant. Some were *spetspereslentsy* or special settlers and came under the control of the NKVD, the Soviet secret police, and so were a part of the Gulag administrative structure, others were *wolni sylni* or free deportees, who had greater freedom of movement and were not forced to work, but necessity ensured they generally did.[1] On paper, at least, their status was the same as that of many former kulaks, the class of peasant farmers who had done well out of the New Economic Policy of the 1920s and which the Soviet state had sought to 'liquidate' through internal exile and re-education when it embarked on agricultural collectivisation in the early 1930s. But, as we shall see, the history of the *spetspereselentsy* – and hence the context into which the Poles were deported – was more complex than this.

The system of special settlements was a form of internal colonisation intended to unlock Russia's colossal natural resources. Establishing forestry and logging operations in Siberia was the first priority, but setting up mines and other projects in the Urals, the Northern Territory, the Far East, and Kazakhstan came a close second. The scale of the operation was huge. The beginnings of collectivisation in 1930 saw the first great disruption, when some 60,000 'counter-revolutionary kulak activists' were sent into internal exile and placed under the direct control of the OGPU, the forerunner of the NKVD. A further 150,000 'kulak activist' families also faced internal exile, but they were thought less of

a threat and so came under the authority of the host regional governments. In 1931 the second phase of dekulakisation saw a further 265,795
families exiled, marking the end of this first wave of forced mass migration.[2] Much government ink was spilt planning the process. Blueprints
were drawn up, targets set and orders issued. Each new settlement was
to be self-sufficient and conditions standardised, with every family or
individual living according to a clear system of rights and obligations.
In theory this would be Soviet social justice at work, each kulak granted
the possibility of achieving redemption through hard work in the cause
of the revolution.

This 'penal utopia', to use Lynne Viola's phrase, bore little resemblance to reality.[3] Local authorities, with neither the resources nor the
time to prepare for the exiles, faced huge demands from Moscow. At all
levels in the food chain tensions emerged as one set of officials, faced
with the demands of their superiors, insisted on greater efforts from their
subordinates. As a consequence, existing communities were forced to
bear the costs of absorbing the new arrivals, plunging them into great
difficulty. Local families were sometimes required to take in special settlers,
but exiles were just as likely to be dumped in exceptionally hostile environments with little or no existing infrastructure. As one official admitted,
'The plan of resettlement . . . has been put together in a hypothetical way
with no pretension to reality.'[4] Local officials were ordered to establish
new communities on marshland and other inappropriate environments
and, when suddenly confronted with new arrivals, rapidly improvised.
With often only a day or two to build shelters before work 'norms'
(targets) were issued, living conditions were very harsh. Extreme weather,
inhospitable environments and food shortages ensured thousands became
ill or died in the critical first few weeks. The construction of self-sufficient communities was a fantasy because work norms were prioritised
over building of settlements or establishing new agriculture. Food rations
were assigned according to the degree to which a worker met the work
norms. Rules were frequently violated to enhance productivity: children,
women and the elderly were made to work, and the right of children to
an education, as established in law, was frequently disregarded.[5] In short,
life in the special settlements was dictated by the norm – fulfilling it was
the only way people could expect to have their most basic needs met.
The inhumanity of the process derived from a combination of the weakness of the state and an ideological disregard for certain categories of
people. Not all officials were cruel and some felt an affinity or sympathy

for the settlers, but the possibility of kindness was minimised by deep structural inadequacies.

Older historical writing on the Soviet Union, particularly when filtered through the lens of the Cold War, tends to emphasise the strength of the state and its capacity to organise all aspects of the people's lives. Viola's study of the 1930s suggests the oppressiveness of the system was equally a symptom of weakness. Paranoia about subversive and counter-revolutionary elements was part of a wider struggle by the state to achieve control over its vast and unruly territories. Plans and blueprints created an illusion of order, a fantastical veneer to the disorder of Soviet life. And when attempts to reform the system failed, the state fell back on the only foolproof method at its disposal: coercion. Faced with chaos, localised rebellions and fractious officials, the Politburo brought the special settlements under the control of OGPU, the secret police. Having overseen the transfer of the populations, the OGPU became responsible for all the settlements and hundreds of thousands of lives, transforming the special settlements scattered through various jurisdictions into one centrally-controlled system, 'the other Gulag'.[6]

Kazakhstan proved particularly resistant to Soviet order. Reports on the arrival of the first settlers in 1930–1 judged the situation 'disastrous', with the local authorities 'unable to guarantee even minimal living conditions'. Some 15 per cent of the settler population died almost immediately.[7] By the mid-1930s reports were more optimistic, emphasising stabilisation and self-sufficiency. A series of high-profile trials saw forestry officials convicted of illegalities and abuses, seemingly demonstrating to the settlers that the state would not tolerate abuses of power by local officials. Moreover, with dekulakisation thought complete, the state moved towards a policy of normalisation, granting settlers certain civil rights and permitting them to live less constrained lives. Their right to free movement was still severely restricted, but granting permission to families to build individual homes and keep small numbers of animals seems to have helped stabilise the settlements. This suggests that when restrictions on individual initiative were relaxed, people's productivity and standard of living improved. From the Soviet perspective stabilisation vindicated the upheavals of the previous years, demonstrating that sound thinking had underpinned the earlier period of accelerated change.

Stability, however, was short-lived. The second great disruption, the 'Great Terror', came in 1937–8. Most infamous were the Moscow show trials of leading communists, but as significant was the less noticed second

wave of dekulakisation. By 1937 the term 'kulak' had ceased to refer to
individuals belonging to a clear socio-economic category and had come
to signify any enemy of the regime. These included 'socially dangerous
elements' from the cities, suspect ethnic groups, citizens of wartime
enemy nations and people judged to be 'socially alien'.[8] Dekulakisation
in 1937–8, the outcome of the notorious order 00447, resulted in 1,575,259
arrests, 1,344,923 trials and 681,692 executions (for which quotas were
issued to the camps in July 1937). A significant proportion of these figures
is accounted for by fathers being lifted from the Special Settlements and
transferred to new labour camps, which were judged to be more efficient, including some in Kazakhstan.[9]

The April 1940 Polish deportees – 'kulaks' according to this revised
definition – were absorbed by this system. Not only did they become a
part of the workforce available to the Gulag system and under the control
of the secret police, but, where separated from their fathers and older
brothers, they fitted the family profile of many special settlements. In
effect, the Soviet Union had created family units incapable of reproduction. They had also transformed the status of these Polish women, making
mothers the sole breadwinners, challenging the gender stereotypes long
nurtured by patriarchal ideals of Polish family life. Our understanding of
Polish women's experiences in the Soviet Union during World War Two
has been greatly enhanced by pioneering research done by the historian
Katherine Jolluck on the many accounts such women wrote shortly after
the war. According to Jolluck, Polish women deported to the Soviet Union
made sense of their experience through these challenges to Polish ideals
of womanhood. To some extent they survived the ordeal – when they
did – by maintaining a mental adherence to these ideals despite the practicalities of survival rendering them impossible to sustain in practice. In
many accounts of the deportation, and particularly those written by men
long after the event, mothers are pictured as heroic figures, battling
against the odds to keep their children warm and fed. Some mothers,
particularly those with young families, saw child after child die of disease,
their children's chances of survival diminished by shortages of food and
clean water, the intense cold, and the lack of medical care. Others, often
ill themselves and despairing of their inability to feed their children, chose
to give them up to Soviet orphanages, broken-hearted by loss and the
sure knowledge that they would be Sovietised. 'I preferred parting with
them for ever,' wrote one woman, 'so as not to see their eyes when they
asked me for a piece of bread that I didn't have.'[10]

Polish mothers battled hard to sustain the Polish identity of their children, seeing it as their duty to maintain traditional practices, the Polish language, a sense of Polish history, and, of course, the distinctiveness of Polish Catholic practice. Mothers, at all stages in this experience of exile, were the principal carriers and defenders of national tradition. For many, deportation to 'Siberia' enhanced their sense of national identity, making them a part of that long historical succession of Poles forcibly exiled to Russia. 'Somewhere in the recesses of my brain arises the thought,' one Polish woman later wrote, 'just like our ancestors.' Another wrote, 'We were tracing the steps of our forefathers, who also were heroes exiled to Siberia for the cause of Poland.' Exile could be experienced as the ultimate fulfilment of Polishness: 'I was proud that I experienced, that I came into contact with, Polish reality, that I was a part of an unyielding whole.'[11]

For Hanna, Wanda and Danusia this Polish reality began in Pavlodar, a small town on the river Irtysh in the north-east of Kazakhstan. Pavlodar today is an attractive town displaying all the signs of post-Soviet development. The new mosque is a commanding presence in the centre of the city. It looks a little inter-Galactic to the untrained eye. On the river and slightly north of the city centre is the new Orthodox cathedral, a typical sight in the former territories of the Soviet Union.[12] Thanks to waves of settlement like those described here, Kazakhstan today has a large Russian minority and the ecumenism reflected in the two new churches is one of the forces holding society together, preventing somewhat resentful Russians and generally optimistic Kazakhs from coming into social conflict. Indeed, though the majority of the population adheres to the Muslim faith, which the state recognises, the impression the visitor gets is that Kazakhstan remains broadly secular – women are visible on the streets in the cities and Islamic dress is rare. Similarly the emphasis is laid on a moderate Kazakhising rather than Islamising the state. This secularism, salted with strong commercial links to the US, is perhaps one of the more beneficial legacies of the Soviet era.

Another legacy of the Soviet era is urban living. Soviet modernisation in Kazakhstan forced a nomadic people to settle. In the post-war period great energies were expended on irrigating the steppe in an effort to make it a second Soviet bread basket to rival the Ukraine. Soviet art of the time shows enthusiastic Kazakh apparatchiks, smart in their uniforms, bringing the good news to their merry-eyed elders seated outside their yurts, cattle grazing peacefully in the background. As a part of this process, in the

1950s and 1960s thousands of Russians were induced to settle in the country under the 'virgin lands' scheme, a favourite policy of Nikita Khrushchev. Though more coercive, aspects of the policy resembled Polish attitudes towards the *kresy* in the 1920s and 1930s. All this came at a huge environmental cost. Massive irrigation projects drained much of the Aral Sea, once the world's largest inland body of water; the land will take decades to recover from the unrestrained use of fertiliser and pesticides; and the nuclear testing in Semipalatinsk has left large parts of eastern Kazakhstan uninhabitable. All this is invisible to me as I survey the Irtysh from its east bank and Pavlodar's impressive new esplanade, the city's social focus. Looking across the river to the unbanked west side, it is possible to imagine something of what must have greeted Hanna and the girls when they arrived here at the beginning of this long period of modernisation and urbanisation. They were earmarked to play a role in the process.

Nana remembers being unloaded from the train and onto lorries, which took the Poles to a number of local destinations. She remembers four lorries at a time being loaded onto a raft to cross the Irtysch. Conditions were treacherous. The thaw saw high water levels and gushing spring tides: great lumps of ice swept past 'angrily and threateningly'. Safely across, their group was taken to Gresnovka, a small settlement east of the river. Initially they were placed with a Russian family, who gave them a friendly welcome, made space for them in their front room and gave them hot food. It's likely these were special settlers from 1930–1. Their two teenage children, a boy and a girl, neatly dressed and wearing their red Komsomol (Scout) neckerchiefs, were engaged in the good Soviet activities by which the whole family might be rehabilitated.

Wanda remembered her first experience of Kazakhstan as follows:

Mummy arranged the bedlinen and we lay to sleep. I, so weary and tired after the fortnight-long journey, fell asleep instantly, and slept marvellously, and it felt as if it was all a dream and I would awake in my own bed. But no, I awoke on the floor on the same bed that I fell asleep on – it was no dream, it was reality. I quickly dressed to go outside and look around the new horizon. When I came out of the house I saw a broad flatland on which far far away one could see little black dots, these were sheep, and even further a large city Pavlodar, which seemed as small as children's toys. This city was sixty kilometres from where we were.

I was overcome by fear, and my heart beat fast that we find ourselves in the middle of such a vast and flat land, so vast as to be impossible to penetrate.

With no hope and no return to Poland I re-entered the house with a huge
weight on my heart and broke into huge tears like a child. And so started
the sad and monotonous life on the steppe, with no change.[13]

Written about eighteen months later, under greatly changed circumstances, this passage shows how Wanda was shaping her experiences
into a narrative. The menacing alien landscape and the sense of despair
and hopelessness, expressed through metaphor and image, formed part
of a wider schema established to give expression to her later miraculous deliverance from the Soviet nightmare. Doubtless the basic facts of
this narrative were true – the sleep, the fear, the tears – but the meaning
imposed on these experiences was retrospective. Of particular significance was Wanda's reference to her childlike tears. Deportation and exile
forced the girl not only to reclassify certain behaviours but also herself,
denying herself the right, as a child, to childish responses. Her later
letters and writings show how she veered between embracing and
resenting her new responsibilities, distinguishing herself from her
younger sister, and allying and aligning herself with her mother and
her mother's concerns. Adult Wanda, however, was a brittle carapace
and time and again, particularly in her later letters to her father, she
cautiously sought permission to resume the old position of dependant.

The new arrivals had much to learn. When Miecia began unpacking
their things, the Russian girl took a keen interest in everything, closely exam-
ining their few clothes and possessions. Excited by a nightdress Miecia laid
out, she exclaimed how lovely it would be for dancing. Miecia, 'being Miecia',
was forthrightly dismissive, boasting of the wonderful dresses women wore
back home to balls and the like. This, she said, was only a nightie.

There is no reason to disbelieve this story but it is striking how strongly
it echoes stories of Russian women in Poland, deprived of nice things,
wearing nighties or slips out to parties or the theatre in the evening.[14]
Two days later the NKVD came to search their possessions and ask questions. Miecia, then seventeen, was arrested, charged with spreading propaganda and taken to a labour camp. After this shocking experience of
NKVD power, the girls learnt to keep quiet and closely guard their few
possessions, making sure not to draw attention to them. Chief among
them, of course, was the icon and a photograph album, as well as some
jewellery Hanna kept stitched into her clothing.

Nana describes Gresnovka as an outpost village situated in a vast
desolate land, cold and hungry. When I went to see it in 2007, it was a

little under an hour from Pavlodar by taxi, located just north of the main road stretching east out of the city towards the Russian border and had a population of about 2,000 people. On the way, we passed an industrial town, with what looks like a power station standing four-square on the flat landscape, the dark silhouette reminiscent of Durham Cathedral. Gresnovka itself is a little further on, just over a small river. The village is spread over three sites and is part-constructed on a grid system, the low single-storey, ramshackle wooden houses lining wide earthen roads. It is apparently populated only by beaten-up cars and a few animals, but as soon as we stop our little party gathers quite a crowd. Kazakh men and boys, with one or two women, appear from where I'm not sure. They're small but look strong, with square faces and smiling black eyes. Not for the last time I feel the Kazakh charm and they also remind me of men and women from Soviet-era propaganda paintings. Amid raucous laughter and jokes, which I'm assured reflected only amazement at my presence, they directed us towards the village centre. On a warm summer's day like this Gresnovka is pleasant enough – though the enormous dragonflies are alarming – and it is enjoyable being an object of curiosity and, consequently, generosity, but at the same time it's easy to imagine the biting winds of winter whipping across the steppe.

We'd hoped to find an elderly Bulgarian woman who was said to have been deported in the 1930s, but according to the young woman who opened the door to the house she was out. Presumably this was her granddaughter – her Kazakh features but very pale skin suggested she was the product of a mixed marriage. She directed us to the school headmistress. This was the person visitors were directed to. She was Russian and had been in Gresnovka for four or five years. She had that bosomy confidence female teachers of a certain age often exude and, accompanied by her little daughter who hid behind her leg most of the time, she showed me the school museum. The school was the largest building in the village and the most modern. The poverty of the school's interior spoke volumes, as did the rickety museum display, but equally eloquent was the size of the building, its central position in the village, and the very existence of the display itself. It is also significant that the teacher was Russian in what seemed an overwhelmingly Kazakh village. When I haltingly told my story and reason for being there, its telling was immediately grasped, with the word Stalin provoking vigorous nods. These people knew of the significance the region had played in the history of the Soviet Union, with the 1940 Polish arrivals one of several waves of population movement to the area.

As I wander around Gresnovka in the heat of high summer I think of how there is nowhere in Britain like this. Nowhere of permanent settlement so generally underdeveloped, so decaying, so primitive, so corrugated. Even places of rural isolation have concreted roads, pavements, reliable electricity, easily available clean water, a good postal service and transport links. All this is here in Gresnovka but only to a degree. In Britain our foundations are, literally, sunk deep into the soil; here people live on its surface: a giant hand could easily sweep it all away. So many of our metaphors of stability and security concern getting closer or becoming one with the soil. We dig in, we become rooted, grounded, we lay strong foundations. Those that rest on the surface are vulnerable, easy to lever off or be scraped from the rock if caught by surprise. Less than a century ago, most here were nomadic, living in yurts on the steppe. Hanna, Wanda, and Danusia had come to a place where the settled community's grip on the land was even weaker than it is today. Many of the deportees later talked of how the transportation came after seventeen years' work spent taming the hostile *kresy* environment, and now they were, in the different context of Soviet collectivisation, being told to go through the whole process again. Rafał's few surviving letters from 1940–1 show he was acutely aware of this predicament: they concern neither the regime nor politics nor the war, but the elements, the environment and the climate.

Admitting he is 'writing only in theory', Rafał informs his wife that she lives 'in a particularly dry continental climate':

> Summers are scorching, but winters, though sharp and cold, are not stormy. As strong as the frosts are it is more tolerable than with us. It is only necessary to warn you that in the first moments outside you must cover your mouth, as the frost cracks the lips and pneumonia is almost guaranteed. Acclimatisation must be gradual, especially for the children. Have a couple of little chats beforehand and especially explain all this to Wanda.

Having fulfilled his husbandly and fatherly duty insofar as he is able, he signs off with characteristic warmth and encouragement. 'All my thoughts are with you all. And I count on us being together soon . . . Cheer up and be of good heart and, if you can, send photographs of the children. Stay where you are. I'm as strong as a horse. I don't lack energy. Hug the children.'

Like most of the population of Gresnovka, the Poles were put to work on the *kolkhoz*, the collective farm, under the supervision of the Stakhanovites, the exceptional workers named after Aleksei

Grigorievich Stakhanov (1906–1977), the Soviet miner whose zeal saw
him made the symbol of the ideal Soviet worker. Following Miecia's
arrest Hanna and the girls were moved from the Russian home to live
alongside some Kazakhs in dugouts on the edge of the village. Nana
describes it as like an underground terrace, damp and windowless; you
had to stoop to get in. It's not clear whether the move was a punishment or a routine reassignment. A little Kazakh boy, their neighbour,
took a liking to Danusia and called her Danak, his version of Danka.
This, apparently, was the local term for the shell of a kernel, 'a nothing
thing'.

That life in Gresnovka was difficult and often traumatic is not in doubt. The mortality rate was high, people were often seriously ill and food was in short supply. Harsh work regimes defined the lives of the Polish mothers and Nana remembers them being 'reduced to workhorses', their time entirely taken up with struggling to keep their children alive. This created new anxieties for mothers who worried about their children running free all day, confirming their hostility towards a system that seemed not to respect the proper needs of society. Fathers, the providers, had been separated from the mothers, the carers, meaning that mothers became the providers, leaving no one in the role of carer. For many of the deportees, employment had always been a normal part of everyday life, but as Jolluck has demonstrated, 'Poles found it outrageous that the physical difference between male and female bodies – understood as integral to their respective natures and proper roles in society – was not the organizing factor of the labour force in the USSR. This situation undermined Poles' sense of order and signalled the Soviet system's perverse nature.'[15]

There is also evidence that middle-class women were given particularly difficult jobs as punishment for their formerly privileged lives. A report addressed to Beria, the head of the NKVD, recorded that local Communist Party officials instructed that the Poles might be issued 'norms' fixed at double the standard rate for which they could expect half the normal rate of pay. This disadvantage was compounded by the restrictions placed on their participation in the local economy. Moreover, vulnerable to exploitation by the local population, Poles often faced demands for extortionate rents in exchange for unacceptably poor accommodation. Regretting 'that the living conditions of the exiles do not meet the minimum requirements to secure a normal life', the senior officials who authored the report were moved by the plight of some mothers and children. Anna Motyl and her 'thirteen little children' lived on the street dependent on begging because no family would take them in. Varvara Paniuk had tried to leave her six children to the care of the NKVD. 'Take my children', she reportedly said, 'They are starving and I cannot feed them. If you refuse to take them I will have to drown myself.' Their fate was unknown.[16]

Hanna's experiences as a collective farmer saw her work weeding the grain fields (a hectare a day being 'the impossible norm', says Wanda) and distributing water among the workers (which involved mastering a cart pulled by two wilful bullocks). Nana recalls an occasion when her mother nearly drowned. She had taken the cart to the river to fill the barrel and had lost control of the bullocks. Disaster was averted by a fisherman, who plunged into the river, swam over and managed to take control of the animals, turning them round and leading them on to the bank. This rapid intervention had prevented her drowning and from losing

a valuable possession of the *kolkhoz*. Her drowning would have seen the girls sent to a state orphanage, while the loss of the barrel would have had a severe impact on their rations.

Perhaps it was this near disaster which saw Hanna transferred to the night watch; a scarcely less treacherous occupation. Winter was approaching and nights out on the steppe were freezing, with temperatures often reaching minus forty. The girls would help their mother dress for the night. Two cushions were put under her coat, one at the back and another at the front. A piece of rope was then used to tie them in place. They wound her legs with rags, straw, newspapers and anything else that came to hand. Thus semi-mobile she set off into the night. When Hanna fed the cattle, filling the racks with straw and the troughs with dense animal 'cake' they surged forward, puffing heavily, butting her with their horny heads. Her padding, that makeshift defence against the cold, also protected her from serious bruising. The cake, the girls discovered, was edible. By scraping away at the hard surface with their teeth a nutty flavour was released.

The children's response to the frequent absences of their mother varied. In her 1941 testimony, Wanda wrote of how she and Danusia were 'left alone', she having to fetch firewood and water for the bath. She crossly noted, 'I was for her as if a maid. I had to obey her every whim.' By contrast, Nana remembers them developing a new sense of responsibility. They quickly came to terms with the fact that their normal expectations would not be met and that crying was no use. She and Wanda learnt to value the *kiziak*, the animal dung used for burning and the only fuel available for free. All the children competed to collect the most from the

steppe. Someone came up with the idea of mixing fresh dung with dry grass, which when dried burnt even more effectively. Nana pictures a scene of each child selecting a cow and following it with a bucket. She is sometimes apologetic that her memories have this irrepressible touch of comedy, given the universal hardship, the premature deaths, and the separation from fathers and other family members. Other child deportees have similarly vivid, almost euphoric memories. One Pole, who has spent her adult life in South Africa, described to me the beauty of the Kazakh spring and summer, remembering the extraordinary moment when the steppe became ablaze with colour. 'There was nothing like those flowers,' she says. 'I've never seen anything like it before or since.' Danusia was one of the younger children able to adapt fairly readily to new circumstances and she lived relatively carefree, while Wanda, as the elder sibling, felt greater responsibility.

In late 1940 Hanna contracted pleurisy and the two girls faced the responsibility of keeping the family fed while their mother lay ill. Wanda wrote (again, in the 1941 testimony) of how 'for the first time in my life I have to look after a sick person and be like a "Sister of Mercy" to her'. The girls probably benefited from the generosity of their neighbours, for there was often a strong sense of solidarity among the Poles, particularly when children found themselves in a vulnerable position. Workers' kitchens, selling soup and other foods, were sometimes a godsend. Nana remembers on one occasion during her mother's illness hearing that the kitchen was selling a *lapska* soup, a kind of pasta soup. Off through the snow the eight-year-old scurried, clutching a jug, only to be met at the kitchen by what seemed a solid wall of *valonki* and *fufajki*, the padded winter clothes worn throughout the Soviet Union. As she wriggled her way through the crowd, ducking in and under legs, someone grabbed her, pulling her up, exclaiming, *Eta rebionek*, a child. She babbled something about Mamusia being ill and her jug was taken from her hand, voices demanding the *rebionek* be given some food. Exhilarated by her success she hurried back, slipping and sliding over the hard icy surface of the snow. She didn't take enough care and at one point she sank suddenly, half the jug's hot contents spilling and rapidly seeping away. Resisting the tears of frustration that threatened, she hastily collected the scattered strips of pasta and topped up the jug with a handful of snow.

The next of Rafał's surviving letters comes from around this time, dated 16 October 1940. Hearing that Hanna had been ill he was so worried by the news that a note of reproach enters his comments: 'Why do you not look after yourself, darling? I don't know your living conditions, but I do know that you have our treasures by your side, whom you must lead to some peaceful ending. You must think about this and remember it.' It is perhaps a good thing that we don't know Hanna's response to this extraordinarily unfair articulation of his own sense of helplessness. Fatherly duty again makes an ineffectual appearance, as well as a hint of impatience: 'I have written once about the fact that in those places people fall ill from scurvy and I wrote to Marysia to send you some dried onions. I will try, if it's possible, to send you some cranberries and wild strawberries to put in tea.' Again, though, he was to be frustrated in his role as provider. 'I am always with you in my thoughts and do shopping for you, only rather ironically I can't send anything because I don't have the postage and don't know when I will. I hope, however, that I will conquer these difficulties.' It's clear that Rafał's mood had begun to deteriorate under the emotional pressures caused by the long period of separation. He ends the letter with his most heartfelt and unguarded words to date:

I dream often of you and the children and I am so overwhelmed that I walk around in a daze. Darling, please keep going and time will work for us. There are rumours among us that it will be possible to move freely, maybe some possibilites will open up then . . . I miss you terribly and the smallest glimmer of hope keeps me on my feet. I am immeasurably grateful to Wanda and Danusia for the cards . . . For now I hug you all very very much.

He signs off simply 'Your Rafał'.

This letter also contains the striking suggestion that as Hanna was born in territory which was then German she might appeal to the German consulate in Moscow to intercede on her behalf with the Russian authorities, seeking permission for her return west. I don't think this bears too much scrutiny. That this patriot Pole should be reduced to proposing an appeal to the former imperial power and present occupier of Poland suggests a man clutching at straws rather than anything more sinister. To Hanna, stuck somewhere in the Kazakh steppe, it can't have seemed very helpful.

Rafał wrote two months later, upset that he had not heard from Hanna and the girls for four months. He begins extravagantly – 'My Most Beloved Darlings!' – striking a note at odds with the increasingly desperate words that follow: 'I have had no direct word from you all for four months now, though I send letters weekly. I have been, in truth, in despair as I had no word about you from Stefka and Maryśka. Any messages are incomplete but if they don't come my nerves may not hold up. Write at least a few stereotypical greetings, darlings, so I can be certain you are there.' He goes on:

> When I have had no word from you at all for months the worst assumptions go through my mind – that you have perhaps started back. I had a very upsetting dream that I received a letter from you on a bit of brown paper with the words 'I end your earthly correspondence' and a few dots and a collection of half-formed words with the signature Hanka. It was the night of the sixteenth last month. It put me in a foul mood.

It seems Rafał hoped that as the new regime established itself and a more ordered life returned to the *kresy* – or the new Soviet republics – travel might become possible. At that moment he was expecting new identity papers, a sign that the bureaucatic necessities of the modern state were returning to the occupied territories. And though the idea that Hanna and the girls might abscond reveals how little Rafał knew of their situation, his emphasis strongly suggests he expected to obtain permission to come and join them, if not to bring them home. It seems he and family members had been lobbying the local authorities. Though off work with lumbago and spending time warming his hurting shoulders against the stove – enforced idleness always led to Rafał brooding over the present and the future – Rafał assured Hanna that he was physically well and earning reasonably good money, now as a supervisor on a building site. He signs off exhorting Hanna to look after herself so she can look after the girls, finishing, 'Darlings, I am with you in my thoughts and truly believe that it will not be just thoughts for ever. For now, my dearest little Siberians, I hug you.'

The strain had begun to show that winter in Gresnovka, too. For Nana evidence of frayed nerves was captured in one particular incident. Her friend Ala was helping her increasingly tetchy mother. Instructed to fetch a little of their small supply of flour, Ala spilt some on the floor and her mother lost her temper. 'Lick it up,' she yelled, furious that the child could be so careless. She grabbed the girl by the back of the neck and forced her face to the ground. Hanna, still ill in bed, was horrified. 'It's your only daughter,' she cried, 'you, you . . .', but the insult didn't come.

Instead she yelled, 'Run, Ala, run.' Enraged, Ala's mother launched herself at Hanna. Grabbing her by the throat, she tried to throttle her. The commotion brought their neighbours running and the 'fiendish' woman was dragged away. Danusia found Ala, her face streaked with flour and tears, and the two little girls wept together.

Ala's mother, Pani Kowalska, may have been at her wits' end for reasons the girls could only half understand.[17] By the time of this incident the Kowalscy, the Ryżewscy and a number of other Polish families were living in 'Kantora', an old disused municipal office in Gresnovka. With winter approaching the Poles had urgently wanted to move out of the dugouts and had their eye on the building. One day in late 1940 news reached Gresnovka that Ali Bek, the head of the regional authority, a formidable and splendid Kazakh pasha, was to visit the settlement. He was known as a hard taskmaster who rarely dismounted from his horse owing to his lame leg. As he was respectfully addressed by the people, nervously taking the opportunity to express their concerns, he would flick his polished boot, 'as though punishing his gammy leg'.

On this occasion Pani Kowalska stepped forward out of the crowd. She was a young and attractive woman 'dressed to impress'. A fine black coat with a sumptuous fur collar encircled her fair head. She approached the horseman and looked up, her blue eyes pleading. Ali Bek, betraying no more than a flicker of a smile, acceded to her request, saying they might take Kantora for the winter and that he would return to see them settled in. Pani Kowalska, who had taken a liking to the Ryżewscy, saying that Hanna looked after her children well, invited them to share the best room in the building with her. For the first time since leaving Poland they had a degree of comfort. The room was divided by a chimney breast which lent the two families some privacy, though there was little furniture and no curtains. Hanna, Wanda and Danusia shared a bed, Wanda sleeping by the wall, Danusia in the middle and Hanna on the outside. In the morning Wanda would awake to find her hair frozen to the wall, a grim reminder of the nights in the cattle wagons. Ali Bek took an interest in the comfort of the Poles, occasionally bringing tea, once commonplace, now a luxurious reminder of home. One moonlit night Danusia woke up and saw a pair of shiny boots by the door.

There is no question that Polish women suffered sexual exploitation and abuse when in the Soviet Union. Rape was widespread in the labour camps and a form of economy existed among the men regarding who had the right to rape whom. Women gained certain material advantages by attaching themselves to a man with either formal or informal authority, but this rarely protected them over the longer time for such men often became bored and soon took an interest in someone new. In the camps it was felt a matter of pride that Polish women were not susceptible to these arrangements, though this is impossible to verify.[18] Outside the labour camps Polish women were vulnerable in different ways. Fear of sexual attack was a constant for many, while men in authority are known to have pressurised their female subordinates into sex, sometimes in exchange for goods, sometimes not.[19] Prostitution seems to have been common and was for many a necessary survival strategy, but accounts of prostitution are very oblique and almost always indirect: people wrote either of rumour and the actions of others rather than their own or used veiled language to describe sexual demands or sexual assault. Little noticed by historians is the fact that 3,000 prostitutes – or rather women classi-fied as prostitutes by the NKVD – were among the April deportees.[20] Relationships of other sorts are likely to have occurred and it is possible that Polish women freely chose to become involved with local men and that real affection could grow out of this. Indeed many of these women were widows or had good reason to think that they were. In the partic-ular case of Pani Kowalska, it is impossible to be certain of the nature of the relationship with Ali Bek or her motivations. The only evidence we have is an adult's realisation of the meaning of her childhood obser-vations and though it chimes with what we know of other women's expe-riences it is still only based on supposition. Moreover, if there was a sexual relationship between Pani Kowalska and Ali Bek, it seems likely her actions had an enormously beneficial effect on all those Polish families permitted to live in the building during that bitterly cold winter.

Faced with indifferent officialdom, petty cruelties, shortages and an unknowable future, mental resilience was one of the keys to survival. Work was important in this regard, providing both income and divers-ion. As one woman, a forty-one-year-old former obstetrician who worked as a logger, put it: 'I went to work for reasons of the "pay" of 400 grams of bread, and so as not to go mad from despair and the gigantic longing for my country that I can't even describe.'[21] Despair, it seems, could kill, and the following story is perhaps best told in Nana's own words:

Just a couple of doors from us in Kantora were two sisters from Poland like us taken to Siberia. The younger one was engaged to be married at

Easter. I can't recall their names, but it was known to all residents in Kantora that she, the bride-to-be, [had] completely lost the will to live. She would not even get up from the bed, or eat, just wasting away in some melancholic dream.

One day she behaved most oddly. Being children we followed the commotion and through the open door observed a most bizarre scene.

The 'bride' almost naked sat on the bed amid her trousseau performing some kind of dancelike movements. The black gossamer fabric [was] enveloping her body and flowing through her fingers like a caress.

Open-mouthed we watched this weird but beautiful phenomenon until someone closed the door on us. The next day we learned that the lady was dead.

The shroud of death was her bridal trousseau.

What to make of this remarkable story? The woman, possessed and beautiful, seems to be performing a private ritual. She acts out not merely her final anguish but also her status as a young woman betrothed to be married. She displays her trousseau, gathered in preparation for her wedding and carried across Russia, against her body, the symbols and actuality of what she was ready to give over to matrimony. Her agonies and ecstasies may well mark the onset of madness, the final stages of illness or malnutrition, but interpreting her condition in medical terms sits uneasily with the seeming acceptance of the people around her that she died because she 'lost the will to live'. Perhaps there is something of historical significance taking place here? Might it be that what marks this woman out from the steely determination of those like Hanna, with her children to live for, is that she was deported just as she was to become a wife, and in all probability, soon a mother? Deportation denied her the opportunity, according to Polish expectations, to realise herself as a woman. There was more at stake here than a broken heart.

Practical needs were met through barter. Things brought from Poland took on a new exchange value in Kazakhstan and this precious currency had to be very frugally spent. In the already cited report to Beria, mention is made of local people taking advantage of Polish women's desperation, offering very low prices for the relatively luxurious goods they had to sell. This might be borne in mind when reading the following account of a transaction Hanna made, as recalled by her youngest daughter.[22] Chief among Hanna's possessions suitable for trade was Rafał's fur coat.

Hanna had held on to it since April, knowing that when the 'black hour' came it might make the difference between life and death. It was a magnificent item, lined with tiny pelts stitched together into an intricate pattern, the little tails hanging. Danusia had fallen asleep wrapped in the coat as the cart led her away from home on the first night of the deportation.

One night, as Nana tells it, Hanna secretly slipped away from the settlement in search of a good place to sell the coat. As she crossed the frozen river she nearly fell through the ice, then again as she clambered up the far bank, once more narrowly avoiding drowning. Tired, wet and cold, she knocked at the door of the first seemingly suitable house she came to and was invited in by sympathetic Kazakhs who sat her by the fire, fed her and gave her a stiff drink. She managed to communicate the purpose of the visit and soon a great deal of interest was sparked in the luxury item. Nana insists that once the people understood that her purpose was to raise money to feed her *rebionki* the Kazakhs, with their strong family and tribal loyalties, became supportive of her efforts, setting in train a traditional Kazakh auction. She got a good price and returned to Kantora quietly triumphant.

Indeed, things were generally looking a little more positive. Being at Kantora gave the Poles an address allowing them to send and receive letters and parcels. One of the most remarkable features of the experience of deportation was that the post got through. Hanna wrote to Ciocia Mama and received a reply full of various items of gossip about the situation at home. Ciocia Mama no longer ran the shop, for there was nothing to sell, and her property had been absorbed into the new collective farms established by the Soviets. The strange beggar with the cross turned out to be a German spy and hidden in his cross were maps and information about the region and the people. Pan Dawid, the schoolmaster Hanna had so disliked, had been exposed as a German collaborator. Karuś, the Ryżewski dog, had died pining for the children. He had refused to eat and repeatedly returned to the deserted house waiting for the family to come back. More hopeful was Ciocia Mama's promise to send some flour if Hanna thought it would get there safely. The parcel arrived in time for Christmas, though, as Nana coolly points out, the timing was propitious because they had run out of things to barter. Exchanging the coat had been the last resort, though one assumes Hanna's small items of jewellery were still somewhere about her person. Most important was Ciocia

Mama's news that Pan Franciszek Zawadzki, Hanna's 'acquaintance from Latvia', was alive and safe. 'That pleased Mamusia no end . . .'

The two girls were now going to school and becoming increasingly proficient in Russian. Some of the mothers regarded the danger of Soviet indoctrination as comparable to the perils of running wild. One child in a Soviet school remembers the 'militant atheism' and anti-Polish content of the teaching. 'In school they taught us that Poland no longer exists, that there is no God.'[23] In her testimony, Wanda said they 'paid no attention' to this. Nana too remembers the propaganda content of the teaching but also her readiness to toe the line when it suited her. This was most evident in an incident that occurred during their first Christmas away from home. Towards the end of term, news arrived that 'Baciuszka Stalin' had promised every school a Christmas tree. Danusia's class were thrilled and Dmitriy, a Russian boy, a skilled dancer, leapt to his feet to cries of 'Padrygas, Dmitry, Padrygas!', ('Dance Dmitry, dance!'). And so he did, gyrating Cossack-fashion and kicking vigorously until his already worn-out valonki, the compressed felt boots everyone wore, spat bits of felt around the room to the delighted laughter of his classmates.

The Sovietised Christmas tree arrived to great ceremony. It was positioned between the school's portraits of Lenin and Stalin, the most prominent place in the building, and topped off with a red Soviet star. The children gathered to mark the occasion with songs of the Soviet youth movement. Nana remembers the older Polish children from Kantora deciding to boycott the celebrations, claiming they couldn't sing owing to sore throats and similar complaints. They were told that any child who volunteered to step forward and recite a poem might choose an item from the tree. Danusia became fixated by a blue bauble hanging next to the red star: 'I wanted it with all my being, as it twinkled at me.' Wanda and the other Polish kids reprimanded her, condemning her covetousness as a betrayal of Poland, but still Danusia stepped forward and recited a poem, her eyes fixed on the shining blue ball. 'Asked what I wanted, I just pointed my finger at the desired object. Offers of other things did not tempt me. My finger still pointing at the blue bauble, I stood unmoved.' Relenting, the teacher stood on a chair and reached for the bauble.

Christmas came to have great symbolic importance among the deportees, a time when the rituals and traditions of home could be followed and reaffirmed. Recreating a proper Polish Christmas was an act of Catholic piety and of Polish patriotism. For Danusia, her strong visual memory developing, the blue glass bauble evoked memories and longings. When talking of this incident, her reminiscences turn to Christmas in Poland, to the vigil she and Wanda kept by the window on Christmas Eve, waiting for the first star to appear and signal the beginning of the celebrations. The girls were then called to the table. A thin layer of hay was placed under the tablecloth, a reminder that Christ was born in a manger. The table was laid for all those present plus an extra place should a stranger arrive seeking hospitality. At the heart of the celebration was the sharing of bread and salt, a traditional ritual of welcome, and the breaking of the *opłatek*, the consecrated wafer. Today Poles send pieces of the wafer to relatives abroad, allowing each family member, however distant, to eat from the same unleavened bread. In the Ryżewski household, pieces of the *opłatek* were shared with the household animals, Rafał taking the girls to the stables to thank them for their 'service', suggesting that perhaps this year they might hear them speak with human voices on this holy night. Traditionally, twelve dishes were served and Christmas was the only time Rafał was to be found in the kitchen, where it was his job to prepare the carp in what Nana describes as the Jewish style (in a sweet sauce with raisins) and to see to his cellar 'duties'. Lastly, the family attended Midnight Mass, that great communal get-together, before coming home to the sound of carols and ringing bells. Covetous though Danusia's desire for the blue bauble may have been, it was anything but a betrayal of nation.

Danusia's imagination should not obscure realities. By the new year the Poles in Gresnovka – 'our lot', as Nana describes them – 'did not look so good'. Malnutrition, the harsh weather conditions and illness were taking their toll. Sanitation had become a major problem; for with the earth frozen solid by temperatures of minus forty it was difficult to dispose of human waste. People had grown weak and some were dying. The death rate of Polish deportees between 1940 and 1942 was very high, but exact figures don't exist. Some idea of scale is suggested in Zofia Bukowica-Lipska's estimate that in her settlement of 450 families, 180 people died, with the death rate of children at 50–60 per cent. Certain family histories tell of nothing but horror. The Ognowski family lost five children; the Ropelewski family lost the father, six sons and two daughters from a combination of disease, exhaustion and hunger.[24] So far the girls were faring pretty well, but Hanna was still in a bad way, paying the price of the long nights out on the steppe tending the cattle. Necessity, however, soon forced her back to work, and she took a job as a cleaner and fire stoker in the school. Whether the Gresnovka settlement was particularly badly afflicted remains unclear, though my mother remembers how, old and widowed, Hanna constantly talked herself through a litany of specific deaths, describing them in detail.

Rafał wrote again in the New Year and though he wished more letters had reached him from Hanna and the girls, it is clear that he had received the keenly needed assurance that they were alive and reasonably well. He seems to have been about to be on the move again and his old optimism and irony had returned. 'Journeying into the unknown is good,' he declared, although admitting that the continual vigilance needed to stay out of trouble rid travel of 'delight'. According to the letter, he had acquired an American visa, perhaps with the help of distant relatives, and a Japanese transit visa, but had not been successful in getting a Russian exit visa. This, he surmised, was because he had refused to accept Russian citizenship – he must have meant Soviet. These scattered references to visas are all the evidence there is of the possibility that he might have left the Soviet Union, though it seems inconceivable that his plan did not include taking Hanna and the girls.

The letter is also peppered with references to the health of family members in Poland, where the news was mixed, and Rafał promised that he would keep Hanna informed of what he knew. All this was set against a summary of his working life, which gave very little time for a break or a rest. He was unable to afford sufficient clothes, but could live reasonably well, if very simply, provided he kept working. Away from his dependants, Rafał saw his material position as relatively privileged, although the circumstances in which he now lived were, of course, dramatically reduced. Once again, the advice was for Wanda: 'I kiss Wandziunia and Danusia very very much and ask them to obey Mummy and learn everything there is to learn. Did you know, Wandzia, that your Daddy went into the world at about your age and with a similar level of education, and, however, thanks to the fact that he kept his eyes and ears open and a keenness for learning that the years haven't quenched, he went to people and others helped him?' Jumbled though these thoughts are, it's clear that Rafał's experiences as a teenage Legionnaire were etched deep into his psyche. And though those exciting memories did not always quite sustain his optimism, they did at least offer him a clear standard by which to face his immediate difficulties. 'Hanek, darling! Tell her about this often and gently, for she can understand now, and keep a close eye on Danusia.' Little Danusia needed not advice but a short leash.

A letter from Rafał suffused with hope generated by the new spring survives from April 1941. He was enjoying the 'bountiful and healthy' country and was living in reasonable comfort – he had bedlinen – and was only spending between a third and half of his earnings, which meant he had saved 120 roubles for Hanna and the girls. It was not obvious how he could get the money to his family. All this meant he had been able to repair his boots, pay off the debts built up over the winter, and buy some much needed replacement underwear – he now had more than one pair. Though there was snow and the rivers were still frozen, the classic signs of the end of winter, one of the great subjects of Russian painting, could be seen. Despite the minus-ten-degree frost on the day of writing, there had been several warm spring-like days. The larks and starlings had been back for two weeks and Rafał had seen lapwings on the mudbanks. 'The easterly winds bring us warmth,' he sonorously observed. 'They also bring us a new energy in the veins, as well as the hope of a better tomorrow.' When the ice started to melt and the rivers to flow, then winter would truly be over and the hope of travel real.

Though still harping on the visa situation, he turned his attention to Hanna's concerns in the letter's closing passage:

> From the last letter I understood, darling, that you are working hard like Adamczykowa and have such worries on the subject of your appearance, so believe me darling that it's all silliness which you shouldn't pay any attention to. And my view on this is as it was, and even stated that it's more conservative than ever before. Don't worry about it, just as I don't, save your humour and time working for us and our lot. Keep your chin up as in the best of times though some things press upon us. Not everything can be described, but believe me that there is everywhere a rise in spirit, and it grows stronger as a change comes nearer.

This rather mysterious ending, combined with the heavy emphasis on the dawning of spring, carried a distinct political charge, though whether Rafał anticipated the impending German invasion of the Soviet Union is impossible to say. The comfort he provided his wife concerned about the deterioration of her looks might not have been quite the reassurance she needed. For the proud woman of Postawy, always careful of her appearance, a well-groomed exterior was a signal of the very respectability to which she aspired as a dutiful parent and Pole and to which Rafał, the 'conservative', surely referred.

'Kiss Wanda and Danusia very very much for me,' the enraptured father closed, 'and remember my embraces till your last breath.' Not the most sensitive close to a letter under the circumstances, it was loving nonetheless.

For the Poles of Gresnovka, the thaw did not bring an improvement in their working conditions. Orders came that they were to be assigned to new work. Packing their few things, they were loaded on to steam-driven lorries. As the driver steered the panting vehicle onwards, its passengers fed the boiler *churka*, the nuggets of wood that fuelled the beast. Nana remembers spending a few days chugging slowly across the seemingly endless steppe until they reached a railway station. There they were loaded on to wagons similar to those that had taken them from Poland, though these had small stoves, and they slowly progressed into the heart of Kazakhstan. Hours were spent waiting in sidings, but this time they had greater freedoms and at stations they could scavenge for food and for fuel to feed the small stove. It was a chaotic, ill-organised operation; trains departed suddenly and without warning and according to a number of accounts people were often left behind. Terror-stricken children would find themselves in the darkness of the wagon, the doors locked, and the train setting off, their parents having not returned in time from a foraging expedition. This happened to Wanda and Danusia. Wanda did the only thing she could think of. She instructed Danusia to pray to her guardian angel and the two girls knelt in the middle of the rocking wagon resolutely keeping up their pleas.

What had happened to Hanna can only be sketched. Along with the other mothers she had learnt that the station had a soup kitchen and there she ordered five portions. To her surprise the soup came with five glasses of wine. It seems she took a moment to enjoy the wine, drinking from two glasses and passing the remainder to a local man sitting opposite, who seemed curious that this woman should be emptying five portions of soup into her canister. Nana says they established a kind of rapport over the drink. For Hanna and the other mothers, this must have been a brief moment of respite, the alcohol relaxing them a little.

The train, however, had gone.

In the panic that ensued, the man came to their rescue, identifying a goods train going in the same direction. Hanna travelled in the hot engine room, grateful for the hospitality of the engine driver, who declared himself a family man. She later joked that he stoked the fire more than was needed in the hope that she might unbutton her coat. Mother and daughters were reunited and they devoured the soup and the tin of frozen peas the engine driver had given Hanna at the moment of departure. To this day, Nana says, she cannot resist crunching on a pea or two when she takes the bag from the freezer.

The train came to halt. They had reached the end of the line. All they could see in every direction was barren steppe. The great central part of Kazakhstan is just this, a vast grassland, hot and dry in the summer, and freezing cold in the winter. Savage winds wreak havoc, spreading fire or tearing up shrubs that form *katuns*, the Kazakh equivalent of tumble-weed. Rolling into balls, these careen across the steppe, pirouetting and prancing. Though colliding with a *katun* could be potentially lethal, they were a valued fuel, free to all, and during a *katun* storm everyone would be mobilised to run as many to ground as possible. Farmers would be similarly mobilised when fires were spotted inching across the steppe. This occurred on one occasion while the Poles were at Gresnovka and when the news arrived, the tractors were immediately put to work, digging trenches to protect cattle and crops.

The Poles had been moved so they could form a core part of the work-force building the Akmolinsk–Kartaly railway. Kartaly is a small Russian town to the south of Chelybinsk, just beyond the western border of Kazakhstan. Akmolinsk is the old Russian name for Astana, the present capital of Kazakhstan. In the 1990s President Nazarbayev decided to transfer the Kazakh capital from Almaty, the pleasant leafy city in the foothills of the Tien Shan mountains in the south-east of the country, to Astana. His motive seems to have been a perceived need to assert the Kazakh character of the northern territories where the Russian presence was strong, to situate the capital more centrally and to distance it from any possible threats from China. In the past decade or so an extraordin-ary new capital has been built almost from nothing on the site of Akmolinsk. In the middle of the steppe can now be found a mall, lined with government buildings, a huge new mosque, swanky shopping outlets and apartment buildings, and, at one end, the massive presidential palace, and at the other, a giant yurt, a large-scale performance space. Though clearly inspired by Washington DC, the architecture has Islamic detailing and the dominant colour is the warm, watery Kazakh blue. The construc-tion has clearly been hurried and the quality of finish is not far from Washington's exceptionally high standards, but there can be little doubt that a very significant proportion of Kazakhstan's new oil and mineral wealth has been invested in ensuring the Kazakh capital is the showpiece of the new central Asia. How long it will take the civil servants, the embassy staff and the political classes to become reconciled to the move from cosmopolitan Almaty remains to be seen, but there can be no question that all have bent to the president's will. None of this can have been foreseen when Hanna and the girls joined the workers building the railway, but as with the great stretches of Russia covered by the trans-Siberian railway, the positioning of this track, eventually dissecting the whole of northern Kazakhstan from east to west, would have a profound impact on the development of this huge area.

The journey from Poland in the cattle trucks was perhaps the only part of the experience of deportation to rival the unpleasantness of life as a railway navvy. Nana remembers the workforce comprising political dissidents, old men, a few Russian workers, and large numbers of women and children. Some were there as punishment, others by choice but in circumstances where there was no viable alternative employment, and some, like the Poles, were effectively forced labour. They lived in dugouts, sleeping side by side, with two rows of people lying feet to feet: each person had just enough space to lie down. In the middle were small cylindrical heaters, which provided minimum heat and an inefficient way of warming food or drying the sodden rags used to swaddle feet. There was no privacy and no water with which to wash: people soon stank. Conditions were not merely 'primitive and vile', but the physical isolation of the workers left them utterly dependent on the regime. They had no choice but to do exactly as they were told, knowing that their rations depended on their full cooperation. This was in stark contrast to life in Gresnovka where barter and a little ducking and diving got many Poles out of very difficult situations. As railway workers, isolated from the complex functioning of even simple rural societies, the Poles now lacked all autonomy and were entirely at the mercy of the authorities. This was the closest Hanna and the girls came to experiencing life in a labour camp.

The work was arduous and the working day filled the hours of daylight. They handled a constant supply of bedrock, gravel, rails of 'enormous lengths', and heavy wooden sleepers. All tasks were carried out by hand with shovels and pickaxes. They built the embankments on which the tracks sat, spreading the gravel and hauling the rails into place. Accidents were an inevitable part of this process and Nana remembers an incident in which a woman shovelling great heaps of gravel off the supply train was carried along by a minor avalanche and thrown off the wagon on to a recently unloaded rail. She was badly hurt.

As the railway advanced and their parents edged further away from the makeshift camp, the children spent longer periods of time unsupervised. They realised that the tar-soaked railway sleepers would burn well and one day, like ants struggling with a large object, they managed to drag a sleeper away and out of sight where they set to work trying to break it up, using sharp stone wedges to lever it apart along the grain into large splinters. Overall, though, they were becoming bored and reckless, and took to playing chicken on the railway. Nana thinks they were saved from a nasty accident by the arrival of a supply of the coarse cloth used to make coal sacks. For a few kopecks – the smallest unit of Russian currency – they were offered work stitching them together and most took it.

Soon the Poles were on the move again. New orders came announcing the end of their work on the railway. At some point in the summer of 1941, lorries arrived to take them on a long journey south through the vast and desolate Golodnaya steppe – the 'hungry steppe' – towards the Tien Shan mountains and the cotton fields of Kyrgyzstan. The relentless monotony of the journey left few memories. Nana remembers only their water running low and the hopes raised by the distant silvery glint of a lake, dashed when they came upon a salt plain where it once had been.

Their destination was Andizhan, a town in Uzbekistan close to the Kyrgyz border. It was a journey of some 800 miles. At the southern Kazakh border the landscape changed radically. They left behind the steppe and entered the great Tien Shan mountain range of central Asia. At Andizhan, some of the deported Poles of Kazakhstan were reunited for the first time since they had been split into work groups at Akmolinsk. Danusia saw Ala for the last time. Her friend was deeply distressed. Ala's mother now had a Russian boyfriend and a baby. Ala begged Hanna to take her with them. It wasn't possible.

At Andizhan the Poles were split up, often into single families. Hanna and the girls were assigned to a Kyrgyz man with a rickety cart whose ancient mule had to be coaxed forward every step of the way. Night was falling as they headed deeper into the mountains, going steadily uphill towards an unknown destination. The girls clung to their mother, fearful of the dark shapes that hung above them silhouetted against the night sky. The tension was increased by the agitation of the Kyrgyz man, who rummaged continuously among his things. Hanna asked tentatively what he had lost. Money, the money he had raised that day selling his sheep. They needed light to search properly, Hanna said, and she kept the man distracted until they came upon a tea house.

The mushroom-like *chajchana*, tucked in close to the rock face, seemed too good to be true. And so, in some respects, it turned out to be. It was a tea house without tea. But inside this low circular building of stone and mud, with smoke pouring out of the hole in the roof, was warmth and good company. On a raised platform in the centre of the room the fire burned, heating a black pot of *kipiatok*, as water kept on the boil is known. All around the room was wooden decking where the guests sat over their *chai* and gossiped. Hanna and the Kyrgyz man thoroughly searched his cart and the money was found. Elated, he insisted they spend the night in the *chajchana* and he would pick up the bill. Nana remembers the chatter of Kyrgyz and other voices going on late into the night . . .

It was another day's travel to their new home, a small Kyrgyz hamlet, and they didn't arrive until nightfall. They were to share the home, 'a shed', with a grandfather and his two grandsons. They were Jews from Bessarabia, the strip of territory arching up from the Black Sea occupied by the Russians in 1940 and later split between Moldavia and Romania. The old man had tuberculosis or something similar and their shed was cold – when the wind blew, it gusted through the room, when the rain fell, the roof leaked like a sieve. It was not a satisfactory arrangement and Hanna did her best to patch up the roof and bring some order to the lives of these three rather helpless men. When an old Kyrgyz man died in the *kibitka* opposite, Hanna acted decisively, moving the girls in as soon as the body had been removed. Danusia was ordered into the bed. Be sick, her mother told her, be the evidence they needed to lay claim to the house. It worked, though there was a nasty price to be paid. In the morning they awoke to discover the hut was infested with lice. There were thousands of them everywhere. They traced them back to the matted piece of sheepskin the old man had used as a bed cover and under which the girls had slept that first night. It was, Nana says, 'a living platform'.

Lice are a fact of life for people living in unhygienic, primitive and crowded circumstances, and for Poles held by the Soviets in overcrowded and unsanitary lodgings large parts of the days were spent fighting the losing battle against infestation, competing to see who could crack the highest number between their fingernails. When the temperature dropped, the lice headed for the warmest parts of the body. Polish women recalling life in Kazakhstan carried visceral memories of the Kazakh's chief Sunday activity being sitting around 'killing lice with their teeth'.[25] Fighting lice turned the body into a battleground, adding to the physical and emotional energy expended on maintaining certain standards of dress, hygiene, attitude and deportment that were alien to the local population. Resisting local norms was a way of maintaining a sense of self and there can be little doubt that a sense of superiority empowered women like Hanna, generating in them an air of defiance unimaginable in their former lives. And here, of course, attitudes were shaped by both the former class status of the deportees and their age. Hanna's state of mind can be made sense of in these terms. On the one hand, her class status was a little shaky. Her marriage had been facilitated by her own upward class mobility, brought about by education and fresh opportunities provided by the new Polish state. On the other hand, she and Rafał, a young married couple, were still in the process of securing their status as members of Poland's comfortably off, propertied middle class. Deportation meant huge material losses and through this a great deal more was jeopardised.

Still, they adapted. The girls and their mother learnt how to mill the tough grain that was given to workers instead of bread. A Kyrgyz neighbour allowed them to use his grinder, while the nearby miller, some two miles away, would take pity on the two girls standing in his queue with their small supply of grain and would add it to his bigger jobs, giving them their share of the flour. Fuel, as ever, was a precious resource and the girls learnt to hack the stubby dry bracken from the mountainside with the axe-like tools used by the locals. They were taught to bake bread. First, they built the oven, a small beehive-shaped construction made of mud and stone, and hollow inside. They burnt whatever small pieces of wood or bracken were available, heating up the inner walls. When the flames died down to cinders, a piece of dough was flattened between the palms and quickly slapped on to the wall of the oven. When baked, it was easy to peel off.

They became friendly with the local children and had their hair plaited Kyrgyz-style, each pigtail representing a year of their lives. There was no schooling and the two girls quickly adapted to a way of life where customary skills were passed on from generation to generation; they complemented their Polish and basic Russian with a rudimentary knowledge of the Kyrgyz tongue. So comfortable did Danusia feel that she took to hanging around the old patriarchs, watching them chew betel nuts and *uruk* (apricots) while putting the world to rights. Danusia's quest was always the same, to get *uruk* stones. Hanna was horrified when her daughter demonstrated an essential skill learnt from the old men. To express contempt or astonishment, the little girl explained, you must spit through clenched teeth 'like a camel'. She continued the demonstration, explaining the subtleties of the ritual. The further you can spit the greater the emphasis. From later letters we know that Hanna took some delight in the cheeky high spirits of her younger daughter, but spitting was not to be indulged.

Being the only Poles in the community and living in their own hut afforded Hanna and the girls some privacy. A door that could shut out the world was a luxury not experienced since they were forced from their home in Poland. Ritualistically, they would unroll their ragged bundles and examine those things grabbed that night in April 1940 which had not yet been sold or bartered. The coat had gone and the shoes, but still they carried the icon, the photos, the football, the rag doll, and the ham bone. They told each other that the bone, though by now put in the pot many many times, still yielded a little flavour as evidenced by the eyelet or two that occasionally floated to the surface of the simmering broth. It – the bone – reminded them of that moment of triumph when Miecia remembered the ham stored in the chimney. Now the girls reverentially laid the bone on the windowsill 'as if it was some precious talisman'. This small and slightly ludicrous gesture, the solemnity doubtless a little mocking, is a powerful indication of their changed domestic situation. In a sense, for the first time since leaving Poland, they *had* a domestic situation. And the laying of the bone is exactly the kind of ritual middle-class parents enjoy, seeing in such private cultishness evidence of their offsprings' imagination, free spirits and urge to affirm the family itself. Of greater value, of course, was their icon and the photo album, and the unwrapping of these items must surely have seen prayers for their father, family members and friends. The ceremonies complete, Danusia become re-acquainted with her long-forgotten deflated football and little rag doll.

The bone, the ball and the rag doll would soon be gone too. When Danusia was home alone a big black dog, which hung around the village, would trap her in the hut and lie outside the door growling. One day, in desperation, she took the bone and gingerly pushed it out of the door. At once the growling ceased and the dog became their 'best friend and guardian', accompanying the girls to play and sleeping outside the door at night. Perhaps there had been a little goodness left in that bone. It was not to be the last time the girls would adopt or be adopted by a dog. The loss of the ball did not result in such a good trade-off. Again, Danusia was alone at the hut, this time kicking her ball around. A group of boys came upon her and demanded the ball – *'dawaj miacz, dawaj miacz'* – but she ran inside and shut the door. The boys laid siege to the hut, swarming around it, their faces pressed up against the window. Frightened and fearing the fragile pane of glass would give way, she chucked the precious leather ball out of the hut at the boys, 'and like magic the siege was over'. The laughter and joy of the boys was scant reward for the football she would never see again.

Danusia gave up the doll in very different circumstances. She became horribly ill with what she thinks was Asian flu. As her temperature soared, her sight became impaired and she lost her hearing. Fearing her daughter was going to die, Hanna took drastic action. She swaddled her in a home-made poultice. Howling in agony at the increasing heat, Danusia imagined she was burning as if 'on a spit'. She begged her weeping mother to remove the bandages, praying to her as 'if she were a god'. But through her tears Hanna held fast, resisting her daughter's pleas, and soon, little by little, Danusia's temperature began to fall, her hearing return, and her sight become focused. She had survived. During time spent recuperating Danusia was kept company by a little Kyrgyz girl. The focus of their games was the doll, to which her companion took such a liking that it was increasingly difficult to persuade her to give it up. On one occasion the Kyrgyz girl, as Nana remembers it, became so hysterical in the inevitable tug-of-war over the doll, that she let her take it for fear of being accused of hurting the child.

The bone, the ball and the doll had gone. Minor incidents, perhaps, but evidence nonetheless of the vulnerability of Hanna and the girls in this strange environment. Danusia seemed to have recognised that the theft by the group of boys and the neediness of the girl reflected their poverty, and it was strange to be in such reduced circumstances and yet still possess objects of desire. As the nightdress incident in Gresnovka demonstrated, the Polish exiles in the Soviet Union carried with them a powerful sense of the superiority of their previous lives to those lived by their new neighbours, and this was reinforced by episodes like those of the doll and the ball. When talking of the incidents that saw her lose the last of her personal possessions, Nana is forgiving of the Kyrgyz kids, arguing that they wanted her things more than she did. Perhaps this was the case or maybe her sympathy is no more than a retrospective rational-isation, but I think it also stems from the fact that Hanna and the girls never lost the certainty that eventually they would return home to their former way of life. This was a temporary aberration, soon to be reversed, and the Poles, when not revolted, felt pity for those for whom scratching a living was normality. Soviet sneers that the 'Polish Lords' had better get used to the new conditions, for the only alternative was death from hunger or illness, were not necessarily echoed by locals who often looked at them pityingly, saying they were made for better things. Indeed, Pan Lewkowski, the Ukrainian Pole deported to Kazakhstan in 1936, remembers the *kresy* Poles arriving in 1940. Their situation was easier, he said, for the founda-tions of the *kolkhoz* were already laid. And they were different, too. We from the Ukraine were agricultural workers, he says, but those from the *kresy* were the best Poles. They were well educated and well clothed; some were wealthy. They were highly cultured people who spoke perfect Polish. They were beautiful people. We taught them how to survive, but they brought us something too, we looked up to them.

One day Hanna and the girls were invited by an affluent Kyrgyz neigh-bour to join him and his family for *chai*. They lived in a big *kibitka* surrounded by a walled courtyard. On first entering, the girls were aston-ished; it was, says Nana, a revelation. To their young eyes the family lived in a state of extraordinary luxury. Their wealth was displayed in the quilts, sheepskins and blankets that lined the interior from floor to ceiling. In the centre of the room was a large, low table covered with a thick over-hanging cloth. Beneath the table was a *sandal*, a deep hole filled with cinders, creating a radiator effect. All present sat on the floor, their feet directed towards the hearth, and each was given a blanket to cover his or her lap. Tea and tasty foods were passed round as Hanna and the girls waited expectantly, mystified by the great 'privilege' of Kyrgyz hospitality.

Satisfied that his guests were comfortable, the head of the household addressed Hanna. 'I want to buy your daughter Danak as wife for my son Sieroza.' The discussion, it seems, went something like this:

– I will give you four sheep and two sacks of *uruk* (dried apricots).
– I'm grateful to you for your very generous offer but Danak is too young to be married.
– Oh, but they won't be married just now. First, she needs to be groomed in all the skills expected of a Kyrgyz bride. You can be sure that she will

be well looked after. Also, this will make you quite well off, allowing you to pick a new husband.

Danusia and Sieroza sat watching each other. The boy was sixteen; his black eyes stared out from under an unbroken eyebrow; he seemed like a young eagle, watchful and alert. Danusia glowed with importance, delighted to be talked about. 'I actually was worth something. I, that scruffy urchin scratching in the dust looking for *uruk* stones to crack and eat the kernel, the stones that someone had spat out.' Wanda, I'm sure, can't have been too impressed. Hanna, seeking a diplomatic way of refusing what must have seemed an offer that could not be refused, met like with like.

– My husband may still be alive and, like you, we too have traditions to observe. And tradition says that it must be the father who gives his daughter away. I cannot make this decision. I'm afraid such a decision will have to wait for the time being.

What Hanna thought of the proposal we cannot know, but evidence suggests propositions like this were not uncommon. They were, after all, a normal part of Central Asian life and there is no reason to think that the father had at heart anything but what he regarded as the best interests of all concerned. What should be made of his readiness to bring these Polish exiles into his family cannot be said with any certainty, but it does suggest the absence of a religious or ethnic essentialism or any fear of miscegenation. Indeed, it is possible that a European bride for his son might have been a source of status. Other evidence, however, suggests that Polish mothers tended to be horrified by such offers, whether targeted at them personally, their daughters or girls that had come into their care. Accounts of Kazakh life written or recounted by Polish women near the time almost without exception portray the Kazakhs as a dirty, violent, ignorant and primitive people, sexually threatening and repulsive in their everyday habits. Marriage, as the product of some kind of pecuniary transaction, tended to be pointed to as the ultimate evidence of the primitive barbarity of the people of Soviet Asia. It is only in accounts written in the 1980s and 1990s that the Central Asians are portrayed more sensitively. Adult memories of childhood experiences are more differentiated, less shaped by racial stereotyping, more sentimental about Kazakhs that treated them well, and readier to see the Kazakhs also as victims of Stalinism.

The paradox, perhaps, is that in being more historically nuanced memories can serve to obscure how people felt at the time. Nana might present the offer of marriage as a rather genteel proposal that gave the 'nothing thing' sudden importance but there is no reason to suppose that Hanna, for all her diplomacy, regarded the offer with anything but disgust.

5

Leaving the Soviet Union

Everything changed on 22 June 1941. The largest single military operation in world history began when the German military attacked the Soviet Union. Operation Barbarossa saw untold horrors; it also overturned at a stroke the system of alliances that had driven the war thus far. The Soviet Union and Germany ceased to be allies in the most decisive way possible. The British Prime Minister Winston Churchill immediately pledged British support to all those fighting Nazism, effectively announcing a new alliance with the Soviet Union. When the Japanese attacked the American airbase at Pearl Harbor in the Pacific in December, the course of the war was set. Germany, Italy, Japan and their allies faced Britain, the United States, the Soviet Union and their allies in a war that would eventually lead to the surrender of Italy and the defeat of Germany and Japan, with the Red Army overrunning Berlin in April 1945 and the Americans dropping atom bombs on Hiroshima and Nagasaki in August 1945. Total War led to Total Defeat.

For the Poles June 1941 was momentous. The Polish government had been exiled to London early in the war and was recognised by Britain and her allies as Poland's legitimate government. Poland's Prime Minister General Władysław Sikorski presided over a Cabinet in London. If the Soviet Union and Britain were now allies, Britain's allies were now Soviet allies and Poland was among them. The question immediately arose regarding the basis on which Poland and the Soviet Union would re-establish diplomatic relations. Sikorski seized the initiative. On 23 June he broadcast to the Polish nation. Though taking a conciliatory line towards Moscow, he assumed that the new circumstances meant the Soviet Union would consider the 1939 Nazi–Soviet Pact redundant. Consequently, Polish–Soviet relations would automatically return to those established in 1921 at Riga. Moreover, Sikorski insisted, given that Poland and the

Soviet Union were now allies any Poles held captive by the Soviet Union should be liberated.[1]

Complex diplomatic manoeuvrings followed in which it was immediately clear that the Poles did not have a strong hand. They were under great pressure from the British government to reach an accommodation with the Soviets in order to strengthen the alliance and they understood only too well that the sooner an agreement was reached the sooner their people in Soviet captivity might be helped. Moscow announced that it would create National Committees in the Soviet Union to represent the interests of the Poles, as well as the Czechoslovakians and Yugoslavians on their territory. Sikorski was rightly suspicious. The Poles already had a National Committee in the form of the Polish government-in-exile and they feared a 'Red' National Committee would challenge their ultimate responsibility and authority over Polish citizens in the Soviet Union. Moreover, Sikorski saw in the new committees a Pan-Slavism, in which Russia would be the dominant partner. A rival representative body might come to undermine the Polish government's claim to manage the reconstitution of the Polish state after the war. Indeed, the 'Red' National Committees, though a response to transformed diplomatic conditions, were consistent with Soviet nationality policy and it was not unreasonable to see the National Committees as a precursor to the integration of the Poles into the Soviet Union. Hence, there began the long and ultimately fruitless struggle by the Polish government-in-exile to achieve international recognition for Poland's pre-war borders – no wartime government, however pressing its immediate war needs, could afford to neglect the ongoing diplomatic manoeuvrings intended to shape post-war Europe. Poland's position was hugely dependent on the goodwill and moral and diplomatic support of the British and the Poles had to play their hand very carefully, recognising that their national interests would be disregarded, however delicately, where they were at odds with the Allies' overall war aims.

Maisky, the Soviet ambassador to London, assured Foreign Secretary Eden that the Soviet Union was committed to establishing a Polish state, but he added the important caveat that this would be along ethnographic lines. As Keith Sword observes, Maisky's commitment to establish rather than re-establish a Polish state signalled that the Soviets did not intend to see a return to status quo ante.[2] Once again, Poland's right to self-determination was recognised but its territorial extent was subject to Great Power politics. A return to the uncertainties and conflict of 1918–21 looked likely.

A rickety agreement was reached on 30 July 1941. It left unresolved the question of Poland's future borders, but provided the basis for the re-establishment of Polish–Soviet diplomatic relations. In theory, the agreement saw the Polish government-in-exile recognised by the Soviet Union as an ally, on which basis it could expect to participate in future negotiations regarding Poland's territory. Two further crucial agreements were reached. First, Stalin agreed that Polish POWs would be released and that a Polish army might be formed on Soviet territory under a commander appointed by the Polish government. For Rafał – and many like him – this was a highly significant decision. Second, all Poles 'who are at present deprived of their freedom on the territory of the USSR either as prisoners of war or on other adequate grounds' would be amnestied.

The general amnesty of Poles was an extraordinary and unprecedented event in the history of the Soviet Union. A decree of the Presidium of the Supreme Soviet freed 50,295 from prisons and camps, 26,297 from POW camps, and 265,248 from special settlements and exile.[3] Evidence suggests that incredulity swept the camps, with Poles looked on with a mixture of awe and hostility by other inmates. Though there had been amnesties since the beginning of the war intended to fuel the voracious appetite for men of the Red Army, this sweeping treatment was entirely outside their experience of the system and it generated a kind of stupefied incomprehension. As the news slowly reached the furthest outposts of the Soviet Empire, many Poles felt jubilant, vindicated in their intense feeling of difference from the people around them.[4] The fact of their nationhood had proven as powerful as they had always believed it to be: Polishness had once again determined their fate, the general amnesty cocking a snook at the Polonophobic Soviet propaganda machine.

Close readers of the protocol were angered by its implications. What were the 'adequate grounds' it referred to? Nowhere did the Soviet government accept that imprisonment or deportation may have been wrong or illegitimate. From the Soviet perspective, their actions were diplomatically and politically logical. The Poles had occupied territory (the *kresy*) that rightfully belonged to Soviet allies (Lithuania, Belarus, Ukraine). This position had been reversed and with the German invasion the Poles were now allies, meaning those previously considered a threat to the Soviet Union could no longer be so. And as long as the government-in-exile was recognised, any Polish resistance to the Soviet Union could not be considered representative of the legally constituted, if somewhat virtual, Polish state.

Poland's president Raczkiewicz refused to sign the protocols and three members of the Cabinet resigned over the failure to persuade the Soviets to agree the Riga borders. Prime Minister Władysław Sikorski shouldered the burden, signing on behalf of the Polish government and people. He addressed the Polish nation and immediately achieved a heroic status among the Poles in the Soviet Union. His address was an exercise in spin laced with patriotic truisms. Correctly arguing that nothing in the agreement contradicted the Treaty of Riga, Sikorski implied that the re-establishment of Polish–Soviet diplomatic contact returned the relations between the two countries to the basis established in 1921. He might just as truthfully have said that nothing in the new agreement *affirmed* Riga. Either way, Sikorski observed that since the original late-eighteenth-century partitions, many such agreements had attempted to destroy the Polish nation, not least the Nazi–Soviet Pact. 'Such documents are only scraps of paper in the face of the dynamism and vitality of our nation.'[5] This came perilously close to saying that the agreement, despite its very concrete achievements, was no more than a diplomatic nicety. A somewhat reckless claim for if the Poles later disregarded the agreement, as Sikorski implied, so might Poland's neighbours. More revealing still was how readily Sikorski reverted to an older rhetoric, which prioritised the strength of national sentiment over the political functioning of the Polish state. Throughout the war the government-in-exile struggled hard to maintain the outlook and attitudes of a legally constituted national government, awaiting only the defeat of the Germans. Once again at the mercy of the Great Powers, it was hard not to take refuge in the old rhetoric of the martyred nation, especially when faced with the need to boost the morale of the Polish people. Crucial to this effort to retain legitimacy was the establishment of a Polish army under Polish command. Just as in the early decades of the twentieth century Piłsudski had believed that a national army manifested the nation by giving it will or agency, Sikorski also believed that when the peace came, the military contribution by the Poles would show as a credit on their balance sheet when the diplomacy began.

The Polish–Soviet Military Agreement was signed on 14 August 1941. A Polish land force would be formed in the Soviet Union, while the Polish air force and navy would be sent to Britain. Though the Poles would be under immediate Polish command, it was expected that they would fight on the Soviet–German front in accord with the operational plans of the Soviet High Command. The financial responsibility would rest primarily with the Soviets, though it was expected that equipment would come from Britain, largely financed by the Polish government. Over the coming years, a measure of the Polish government's legitimacy would increasingly come to rest on its willingness, rarely in doubt, to borrow money from the British and Americans in order to finance its activities. Soviet and Polish liaison officers were appointed in Moscow and London to ensure the smooth functioning of new arrangements and General Władysław Anders was appointed commander.[6] Anders' Army, as the new force quickly become known, is the stuff of Polish legend.

Though the amnesty and Polish army announcements were simultaneous, the army announcement had a more immediate impact. This was because the Polish POWs tended to be more geographically concentrated, with many still in the Ukraine and western Russia. Some of the high-ranking officers, including Anders, were held at the NKVD headquarters at the Lubyanka in Moscow. Consequently, it was no more than a month or so before POWs began to make the journey to the Volga region. The command post was established at Buzułuk, with infantry divisions formed at Totskoye and Tatischevo. Between October 1941 and January 1942, the Polish army was stationed at Buzułuk, south-east of Moscow and well behind the lines of the German advance.

The formation of the army would prove to be the necessary precursor to any serious change in the condition of the civilian deportees. Seen as the Polish infrastructure in the Soviet Union, when word of the army and the amnesty went out, it was to the army bases that the Polish began to move. News of the amnesty, however, spread slowly. Information was not widely available and its distribution tended to be controlled by the local NKVD. In small towns newspapers made only an occasional appearance and many people depended on the single radio held by the local Palace of Culture, often a very modest institution despite the grandiosity of the name. The NKVD was responsible for informing Poles of the amnesty and issuing them the 'freedom papers' testifying to their right to free movement within the Soviet Union and to leave the country. Permission for individual journeys still needed to be sought from the NKVD and many Poles became mired in its bureaucracy. When refused his freedom Gustav Herling, a prisoner of the Gulag, went on hunger strike. He was eventually freed.[7] Rightly distrusting the readiness of the

NKVD to convey news of the amnesty, the Polish army eventually sent out 136 plenipotentiaries to spread the news to the 2,600 or so places where deported Poles were living. This, however, was in the future. For the time being, little changed for the deported Poles and it was the army that was of most importance.

All accounts agree that the POWs emerging from the camps were in very bad condition. They were malnourished, emaciated and poorly clothed. A fairly intimate account of his experience in the new army is traced in the remarkable diary kept by Rafał in these months. He was in the 2nd Machine Guns Company, 17th Infantry Regiment, of the 6th Infantry Division. This Company of seventy or so men was part of an army that numbered 37,000 by December 1941 and would grow to 64,000 by mid-March 1942.[8] There is little reason to doubt that the experience of Rafał's Company was typical and the diary gives very strong evidence of how makeshift and under-resourced the whole operation was.

The diary begins with a little bit of doggerel, which immediately sets the patriotic tone:

> We walk through the mountains, and forests, and ridges
> For You, Poland and for Your glory

In Polish this rhymes.

Rafał goes on to provide a remarkably cogent precis of the Polish situation, which gives a fascinating insight into the state of the Poles in Russia in the early autumn of 1941. It is worth quoting at length:

July 1941 found huge numbers of Poles scattered over the endless territories of the USSR. They were prisoners of war of the Wojsko Polskie [Polish Army] from 1939, arrested in 1940 and 1941, displaced in 1940 and 1941, and a lot of youth contracted to work deep in the USSR lured by the hope of finding a living and pay in industry. Their numbers are not entirely known but are most likely to be between 1.5 and 2.5 million people (not distinguishing between sex or age). In the general mass there are also representatives of ethnic minorities. Especially the Jewish minority is strongly represented as it probably reaches 25 per cent to 35 per cent. They are not among the arrested or displaced, however, but were evacuated after the commencement of Soviet–German war activities in 1941. The evacuated 'echelons' are made up of mostly those from this minority. Among Polish

citizens there is a sizeable percentage of people who in difficult to determine circumstances found their way into the lands of the USSR before
1939 and some of whom even started families here. The moment the military activity of the USSR against Poland began, they were all arrested, and
currently a lot of them are being released and are part of the general mass.

The Polish–Soviet treaty found everyone in groups: in prisons, in camps,
or in forced resettlement. The prisoners can be divided into two groups.
The first is made up of those who received a sentence of four to sixteen
years, and those are mostly: settlers, officers, non-commissioned officers,
forest rangers, gamekeepers/foresters, detective servicemen and those
employed in public administration. The second group is those sentenced
to under four years for administrative infringements of the law, such as
crossing of the border, fights, fencing, receiving of stolen goods, stealing,
moonshine/home-made vodka, tax evasion, work evasion. The first group
do not leave the prisons and are kept alone, the second work under convoy.
In the camps there were officers, non-commissioned officers and soldiers
of Wojsko Polskie – either in closed fixed camps or mobile working camps.
The third group – of the displaced – made up mostly of the elderly, women
and children, were left in relative freedom and were employed only as
czarnoroboczy [black-labourers in Russian] with the right to move within a
three-kilometre radius. The last group had to find a place to stay and earn
money for food. Because the standard wages were v. low and prices v. high,
everyone was starving, of which the common vitamin deficiency illnesses
serve as proof. The state of clothing was even worse. If one wore out their
clothes during work, he/she wore rags as there was no way they could
buy a new set.

All of these groupings, it has to be added, were located north of the
line of Oret–Orenburg–Zmiejnagorsk–Mongolian border.

The news of the agreement and organisation of the Armia Polska
brought about general enthusiasm, among everyone regardless of sex,
nationality, and even political views. In the clusters of Poles, companies
began to form, and even regiments of volunteers of fifteen-plus years of
age – awaiting the possibility of leaving to join the Armia.

But not everyone left.

The reference to the Jewish recruits is a subject I return to below.

In September men began to arrive from Starobielsko in the Ukraine
and other POW camps. They were mostly dressed in tattered Polish army
uniforms and though their physical well-being was poor, at this stage

morale was high, sustained by a pervasive sense of deliverance. Anders recalled the first military parade at Totskoye, 14 September 1942:

> I shall not forget the sight as long as I live, nor the mingled pity and pride with which I received them. Most of them had no boots or shirts, and all were in rags, often the tattered relics of old Polish uniforms. There was not a man who was not an emaciated skeleton and most of them were covered in ulcers, resulting from semi-starvation, but to the great astonishment of the Russians, including General Zhukov, who accompanied me, they were all well shaved and showed a fine soldierly bearing. I asked myself whether I could ever make an army of them, and whether they could ever stand the strain of a campaign. But I found an immediate answer: it was sufficient to note their shining eyes, to see the strong will and faith there.[9]

Morale would ebb and flow over the following months, lurching between gloom and optimism as events dictated. The need to maintain the men's trust in the process, combating suspicions that they were being hoodwinked by the Soviets, was a pressing concern for the leadership throughout the army's history. For the first few weeks Rafał's Company camped in the open air, though there was room for a small number to sleep in sheds or stables. During this time formal military ranking of officers and men was established along Soviet lines. Owing to the Katyń murders there was a terrible shortage of experienced officers and for many recruits this meant rapid promotion, always a feature of an army suffering losses at war. On 18 September the Company took delivery of ten tents. Spirits were high and Rafał even describes their condition as 'v. good' and their new accommodation as 'warm'. The Company now comprised sixty-seven Polish Catholics, two Russian Orthodox Ukrainians, a Lithuanian Catholic and a Jew of unspecified nationality. On 26 September a Mass was held, which quickly became a regular part of the Company's routine, with a system of morning and evening prayer established. The 'Our Father' and 'Hail Mary' were said and 'When Dawn Breaks', 'All of Our Daily Affairs' and 'God, Who Protects Poland' were sung. Here again, religious and national faith become indistinguishable despite the presence of the national minorities within the Company. On 11 October a confession was 'ordered' and on the 12th they attended Holy Communion, a priest on his rounds having reached the Company. All, though, was not God and country. On Tuesday, Thursday and Saturday nights 'campfires' were scheduled, times when the company gathered together for songs and stories and other entertainments. Surely vodka was distributed then, though Rafał makes no mention of an alcohol ration.

By mid-October a programme of activities tending to the mind and the body had been issued by the central Command. Drill, gymnastics and military exercises, still conducted without arms, were to be supplemented with a programme of talks and seminars on military matters, moral and religious questions, and wider ethical or educational subjects. As we shall see, such programmes were typical of the Poles once given control over their own affairs. Attendance was low owing to more urgent work within the Company and sustaining an ambitious programme of cultural uplift was very difficult given their limited resources. At the same time a Divisional Field Court was established, sure evidence of the tightening of military discipline. And this, it seems, was needed. For although the camp infrastructure was slowly improving – the men had even been paid for September and inoculated against typhoid – the food supply was steadily deteriorating and, owing to the absence of anything for sale locally, they were wholly dependent on official supplies. Increasing hunger and dropping temperatures saw an increase in theft among the soldiers.

A major problem was that local agricultural produce was being wasted. The nearby collective farms were in a 'lamentable state', with potatoes and wheat going unharvested. The military call-up had left many such communities undermanned, with the routine of harvest and distribution severely undermined. When land wasn't worked properly subsequent yields dropped off dramatically, compounding the problem. Consequently, with the aim of improving the Company's provisions, thirteen men volunteered to work on the farms as paid labourers. Six returned on 10 November, bringing stories of fields so frozen that it was impossible to dig the potatoes. Most striking, however, was their reception by the local people. It was 'simply incredible', Rafał records, how warmly they were received. Their good manners and religiosity made a great impression, apparently even on the party apparatchiks, such as the teacher and other functionaries, who listened respectfully to their prayers and songs.

Uplifting experiences like this could only paper over growing discontent, brought on by the tardiness with which elementary needs were met. Rafał notes that though their uniforms were passable, in the middle of October many were still going without boots, their feet wrapped in rags.

On the 22nd the Company received twenty-two *fufajki*, those highly-valued padded jackets, eighteen pairs of padded trousers and fifteen pairs of shoes, the latter most eagerly accepted. Nonetheless, ten days later, Rafał complains again about the state of their footwear, adding that because it must be reserved for drilling, the men were reluctant to come out of their tents owing to the cold. Attention was also drawn to shortages in underwear, which compounded the inadequacy of their uniforms as autumn set in. With no firewood and everyone infested with lice, the mood was grim. On 26 October the Company faced disinfection and delousing, an unpleasant prospect given the cold, but one which ultimately cheered them up.

A month later new clothes arrived. This time they received nine *fufajki*, eleven pairs of padded trousers, 106 shirts, 108 pairs of long johns, and two sheets. A day later they were supplied with Soviet-style high boots. A definite improvement and they looked good, giving the men a more military bearing, but they were made of a thick impermeable rubber. They kept feet dry but not warm and came in a standard size. Having smaller feet was an advantage – boots could be stuffed with insulating rags – but for the large-footed the situation was not so good. In early November they took delivery of seventy-eight fur hats. Morale improved, though grumbles about the lack of cigarettes and firewood remained, not least because they were forbidden to cut down trees. By 20 November, following the delivery of further supplies, the status of the military uniforms was finally reported as 'very good'. Every soldier had an overcoat, a fur hat, a *fufajka*, padded trousers and high boots, as well as one blanket and sheet. Things were less rosy where undergarments were concerned, with hardly anyone owning a second set. Despite the delousing, all were again infested and the cold meant it was impossible to wash clothes – how could they be dried? – or oneself, a situation hardly helped by the absence of soap.

Particularly difficult was caring for the Company's twenty-eight horses, originally supplied in mid-October. There was no proper stabling but only a simple structure comprising a roof and fencing without walls. A lot of energy was spent trying to improve this situation for, standing unprotected in the cold, the horses were becoming ill. No help came from the quartermaster and the shed they pulled down for the planking made little difference. By the end of November the weaker horses were receiving larger food rations, while at the same time the Company was awarded five 200-gram portions of bread and hot soup for the most hard-working among them. The Soviet nature of this response cannot have been lost on the men.

Polish Independence Day is on 11 November and there were celebrations on the square: Masses were held, the soldiers paraded and in the evening they all gathered for a meeting. It was an opportune moment to announce some promotions. Corporals Sanko and Frontczak were nominated Lance-Sergeants and Lance-Sergeant Cadet Officer Rymkiewicz II, adjutant of the battalion, was nominated Sergeant Cadet Officer. Captain Józef Cader, Company Commander, addressed his men:

> Soldiers! Twenty-three years ago our Motherland rid itself of the 150-year shackles of enslavement. The great Polish nation began work in the Free State of Poland and employed it to further the happiness of its citizens to the envy of those abroad. By a decree of Providence, two years ago Poland was attacked by a stronger enemy. We fell, but the Nation did not cease its military fight. It did not forgive the enemy for the harm done, and is preparing for the final encounter, in all its strength. All over the world, Polish soldiers are gathering to take part in the last battle for the freedom of the Nation and a good future for the civilised world. And we will be honoured to participate in this battle. On Independence Day, I appeal to you to use all the power of your abilities and strengths so that this battle is crowned by our victory.

It was stirring stuff, which left 'the spirit among soldiers . . . elevated'. The reference to Providence again taps into the old idea of the martyred nation, whose determination against the odds should be an example to all, while intimations of the final apocalyptic battle are suggested by the reference to the 'final encounter' and 'final battle', the necessary preface to the achievement of paradise on earth. Once again, the Poles must gather their strength, preparing themselves for the opportunity that must arise. The 'stronger enemy' could be easily identified as Germany, though for these men, their direct experience of the enemy was defeat at the hands of the Soviet army. Who were the envious abroad? The Lithuanians, Belorussians, or Ukrainians? The Germans? Or, perhaps, it was the Russians themselves, still smarting from their defeat in 1921? Indeed, the Polish experience of the Soviet Union only reinforced the Polish sense that the Soviets had much to be envious of. And allusions to Poles mobilising throughout the world allowed these few men, freezing on a roughly made parade ground, to feel themselves a part of something much greater, taking in both the Polish Diaspora and the Poles serving in Britain and elsewhere. After the misfortunes of the previous years, Cader implied, Polish forces were regrouping, preparing to play a role that was not confined to the German–Soviet front. And though it is unclear who comprised the 'civilised world', it is hard to imagine it included their hosts, raising any number of questions regarding the kind of world these Poles hoped would emerge out of the war. These patriot commonplaces, expressed in a Polish army camp in the heart of Soviet Russia, are highly paradoxical and can only be decoded when the ironic subtext is fully recognised.

Two days later, on 13 November, Lieutenant Ryżewski was made Commander of the Company.

In December a buzz of excitement was felt through the force that General Sikorski, travelling from London, was to make an inspection visit. Not coincidentally, supplies began to arrive from the Western allies. British coats and socks provoked a mixed response. 'These are very beautiful and exceptional but they are not liked by the soldiers because of their too civilian look, which our soldiers are not accustomed to. Despite everything, we finally look like an army.' Much effort was made in advance of Sikorski's visit, including preparing a parade ground, which needed continual maintenance against incessant snowfall. Anders' statement, issued at the moment of Sikorski's arrival at central command in Buzułuk, was read out to shouts of joy from the men. Following a string of cancellations, Sikorski finally arrived in the Totskoye region on 12 December.

Ceremony and patriotic encomiom dominated that day. Inspections, first at Company level, when Sikorski chatted with the men, then at Division level, reportedly impressed the Allied representatives. Mass, a Divisional parade, and a large luncheon followed, at which Sikorski and other generals made stirring speeches. 'The day left an indelible impression on everyone.' It gave a concrete reality to the fact that Sikorski was not only the acknowledged head of the Polish nation but the Prime Minister of an internationally recognised government who had been accompanied by representatives of Poland's allies. His visit symbolised an extraordinary change in Poland's fortunes. Poland may have lacked a state or a territory, but standing on the freezing parade ground and before the international community was the strongest evidence of the nation's continuing agency, an army eager to join the war effort.

Sikorski's inspection had followed a momentous meeting with Anders and Stalin in Moscow on 3 December. Acutely conscious of the problems of supply and the harsh weather conditions – the Company diary recorded the astonishing temperature of minus sixty-three in January 1942 – Sikorski and Anders requested that the Polish army be re-stationed somewhere in the south with a milder climate. As Anders later recorded in his memoirs, 'Many of our men froze to death in their tents.'[10] In the meantime, following lobbying from the Poles, Churchill had indicated to Stalin that the British would find it easier to equip the army if it were temporarily removed from the Soviet Union, possibly to Persia, where the men could recuperate properly and be trained before returning to the German–Soviet theatre. Stalin agreed on the move south, but then dragged his feet about a date until March. Nonetheless, the positive signals triggered British–Polish preparations and later events showed Stalin was more or less right when he suggested at these meetings that the British would dragoon the Polish forces into the British army. This is exactly what Sikorski had been planning.[11]

In fact, evacuation had been on Sikorski's mind since the implications of the German invasion of the Soviet Union had become clear. He and Anders were determined that the Poles should fight on a number of fronts, not least because if war on the German–Soviet front led to a German victory, Poland would effectively be defeated for a second time, the political gains represented by the formation and recognition of the army lost. They also foresaw the danger of the Poles being dispersed along the front among the Soviet army, meaning they might be picked off gradually and effectively defeated irrespective of the overall outcome.[12] How much of the meeting with Stalin was reported to the men that December is hard to know but Rafał's diary suggests that the Company was laying plans for the development of their quarters in anticipation of the harsh winter. A detailed list of the materials required and the planned layout is recorded – collecting building materials demanded a three-kilometre walk to the forest. Consequently, when the order came to pack up and prepare for departure it must have gone against their expectations. On 19 January 1942 the temperature hit minus forty and Rafał reports the men having frostbite on their legs, hands and cheeks, only leaving their tents to gather firewood. On the 26th the temperature hit a low of minus sixty-three. As Sikorski and Anders recognised, inadequate equipment meant the army existed more on paper than in reality.

Preparations for departure began on 20 January. The Company had only a single railway wagon for equipment and men. When they began moving the equipment to the train on the 21st the temperature was minus forty-five. Loading itself commenced on the 25th in temperatures of minus fifty. On the 27th they received a wake-up call at 4 a.m. The temperature was again minus sixty-three. They hastily took down the tents and loaded them on to sleighs, which were dragged by the ailing horses to their sixty-ton wagon. It was a tight fit but the men were cheered at the thought of milder climes. As they progressed south they held the usual meetings, and practised emergency drill – they could get the essentials off the wagon in six minutes. Much of the process was hastily improvised, as Rafał's banal comment that sometimes they ate directly from the pot suggests. On their third day they encountered the first of the civilian transports heading south from Archangel: 'A picture of misery'. The people had no help from the government: left to fend for themselves, there was little cash in circulation and little to buy, especially at affordable prices: 'Children die like flies.' In one wagon thirteen children had died on their journey. The army transport helped where it could, 'but it is a drop in the ocean'.

On 3 February they stopped at Ursatiewskaja station for a day. They were bathed and disinfected. Two days later at seven in the evening they arrived at their destination, Jakkobad in Uzbekistan. It was raining. They ate and slept out under the sky. In the morning they marched to the camp, mud up to their ankles, and set up the tents. By the 8th the weather had cheered up. The wind dried the mud and order began to come to the new camp. Food was more plentiful and cheaper in the south. Dried fruit was readily available, but its purchase was forbidden for the authorities didn't want the soldiers disrupting the local economy. What's more, they'd travelled into a typhoid epidemic and Poles scattered throughout Russia were heading in the same direction.

Thirteen dead children in one railway wagon.

Rafał does not specify if the civilians travelling south were Poles but it is very likely, given their point of departure, that they were part of the February deportation and had been in one of the Siberian logging camps. Either way, news of the amnesty and the formation of the army in Buzułuk meant that beginning in the autumn of 1941 Poles in the north, determined to escape a second bitterly cold Siberian winter, began to move south. The Polish migration coincided with a much larger internal migration of civilians fleeing east in the face of the German invasion. Heading west into the paths of fleeing civilians were troop reinforcements, often in trains filled to bursting. Congestion saw trains stuck for days on end. It was mayhem. At the same time, the state prioritised the transplantation east of as much as possible of the industrial infrastructure of European Russia. It was a colossal operation and the rapid rebuilding of the Soviet military-industrial base in Soviet Asia was one of the most remarkable endeavours of the entire war. Apocalyptic descriptions of these new factories tell of the terrible working conditions and the determination of the Russian workers. As a result, the German war machine was met with simple but strong Soviet tanks, artillery and planes, which rarely broke down and could be easily maintained. That, and the effectiveness of Soviet supply lines, the skill of her generals and bravery of the soldiers, eventually repulsed the German army, turning virtual defeat into victory. Approximately 10.7 million Russian soldiers lost their lives – including 3 million in German POW camps – and maybe 14 million civilians were killed or died from disease and malnutrition. As Richard Overy argues, none of this is explicable as the product merely of Soviet coercion. 'The Soviet people', he writes, 'were the instrument of their own redemption from the depths of war.'[13]

Accounts of the Polish migration south tell of extraordinary good fortune and derring-do – building rafts and travelling south by river reoccurs in the accounts – as well as appalling hardship and loss. The journeys were frequently worse than the initial transportation to Russia and the death rate appears to have been higher. Irena Okulicz-Kozaryn (née Szunejko) was relatively lucky in picking up a train at Vologda, which took her directly to Tashkent. The journey took fourteen weeks, with delays in sidings sometimes lasting a week: 'My mother exchanged her wedding ring for a small bag of carrots to be shared among our group. What a feast!' Other journeys were frequently broken, with long periods spent in crowded stations waiting for the next train.

The experience of the Milewscy family was not untypical. They left their logging camp in northern Siberia on 6 January 1942 and reached the military camp at Lugovoy, where their father was the commander of an artillery regiment, at the end of March.[14] It took twelve days to reach Archangel, variously travelling on foot, by sled, horse-drawn wagon, truck and train; they slept in stations, stayed with 'Eskimos', and even managed a few nights in a hotel, sleeping in the corridor. At Yaroslav they 'had to spend two days and nights among the worst multitude of people imaginable: mostly released prisoners on their way to join the Red Army, some of whom were half dead, starved and even blind'. Night blindness, brought on by malnutrition, was common in the labour camps and the *kolkhoz*.[15] 'They were all dressed in dirty rags and were full of lice.

Thousands, crowding together like sardines, awaited the train for days at a time.' The journey – 'long and tedious' – continued in this fashion, repeatedly broken for days at a stretch. Army reinforcements took priority, though the presence of soldiers was an advantage, for they frequently shared their rations. On arriving at Kuybyshev, 'the town we had been dreaming of, the town with the Polish embassy . . . I ran to the embassy thinking that I would be welcome as a hero.' Instead, the Milewskis added to the growing problem. 'But they welcomed us like dogs. We were put in a school: a nest of dirt, disease and starvation. We had to sleep on the floor. I heard that forty-seven children had already died there in the last two months.' Eventually, with help from a military attaché, they got on to a military train and made the long journey into Kazakhstan, finally arriving at Lugovoy, completing a journey of over 5,000 miles.

It is impossible to calculate the total number of Poles who died on these journeys following the amnesty, but those forty-seven might be multiplied many times. During one week in November 1941, seventy corpses were found among Poles arriving by train at Tashkent. At Guzar, where one of the recruiting stations for the Polish army was established, several thousand Poles died of typhus between January and March 1942.[16] Other accounts give an impression of how deaths accumulated one by one.[17] Asleep on a train, Vala Lewicki (née Miron) woke to find the woman asleep next to her had died. Stefania Buczak-Zarzycka's friend Stasia lost her younger brother on the journey. Stasia's mother and another brother had died in Siberia, and her father and older sister had been left behind when the train left unexpectedly. They wanted to give the boy a Christian funeral but after three days of non-stop travel they decided the body had to be dropped on to the platform as they crawled through yet another station. Judging by people's memories, parents and older siblings being left behind at stations was remarkably common. Trains departed without warning and those who had gone to forage for food were frequently left behind – too many stories tell of small children left in trucks or carriages suddenly without a parent and the distress and panic can only be imagined. Sometimes mothers and other siblings could catch up with the train, running after it; others followed the track for several days, eventually finding the train had been brought to a halt by the inevitable delays; some families were not reunited for weeks, with small children dependent on the decency of the people around them; and some families could be separated forever, never to see each other again. Stefania's story carries that double charge. Did Stasia's father and sister eventually find her, only to discover that yet another member of the family had perished? Maria Borkowska-Witkowska's four-year-old brother died of measles. Sabina Kukla (née Lukasiewicz) recalls her brother Jureczek dying of typhus. She tells of a family of five in which only two daughters survived the epidemic and a Jewish family of seven, all but two of whom perished. Of her group of forty-eight, who having arrived in the south were sent to a *kolkhoz*, only twelve survived.

Mass movement of civilians had not been planned for and, locally at least, Soviet officials were ready to dismiss Polish demands for rations, saying they had their own government now. The Polish authorities agreed with the Soviet government that it was better for Poles living in tolerable conditions on the *kolkhoz* to stay put for the time being, but there was nothing they could do to prevent the migration in Uzbekistan. Military rations were shared with the civilians, and the military camps, rudimentary at best, became refugee camps, undermining their whole purpose. Necessity saw thousands who had made the journey – sometimes only too briefly reunited with husbands and fathers – transferred, often forcibly, to the local *kolkhoz*. A great deal of anxiety accompanied these moves and many resisted moving too far from the camps or railway stations fearful that their connection with the Polish authorities would be broken.

Polish actions, however, pulled in contradictory directions. As mentioned, plenipotentiaries were sent out to areas where deportees were known to be and their unexpected appearance in familiar uniforms provoked disbelief, then joy. Fathers, too, set off in search of their families. It was just such a search that led, one day and without warning, to Rafał appearing at Hanna's door.

According to the Company log, Rafał was granted leave on 15 February. As we might expect, the story of his search carries more than a hint of adventure.

Travelling by train towards the Kazakh capital Almaty, Rafał overheard people talking of Poles in the area attempting to register for the evacuation. Without hesitation, he threw his boots from the moving train and quickly followed after. From some point in southern Kazakhstan, through the heat of high summer, he began to walk along the track, enquiring at every stop after his wife and children. Along the way, casualties of wartime shortages and disruption were everywhere, often stranded at railway stations and badly in need of medical help. Thanks to his interventions, so the story goes, he secured medical attention for three people on the brink of death. It seems his officer's uniform helped him along the way, opening doors and allowing him better access to information.

It was at this point the Ryżewscy had their 'miracle'. On entering one of the Polish registry offices, Rafał was looked up and down by the official, who then pushed a photograph towards the Polish Lieutenant and said, 'Mr Ryżewski, you just missed your wife by a couple of days. She left this photograph with me.' Rafał was given directions and sent to the marketplace to hitch a ride. Luck was on his side for a second time that day. In the market, the Uzbek chief, the father of eagle-eyed Sieroza, was doing his business. It was he who would triumphantly and unexpectedly deliver Rafał to Hanna's door. Nana recalls: 'There are no words that can express our joy . . . I'd waited for almost three years for such a moment, seeing my beloved Tatuś. I was almost afraid it was an illusion. Whenever I had a chance to speak to Mamusia I would just whisper to her "Tatuś is here", as though I was afraid to shatter this wonderful dream by speaking aloud.'

The dream quickly became a nightmare. Rafał awoke the following day to find himself covered in the all too familiar red spots. He had contracted typhus. They rushed him to Almaty hospital, where the only vacant place was a mattress on a corridor. He fell into a delirium and, as he was highly infectious, it was some days before Hanna could visit. She found him very weak and emaciated – hardly able to stand – and his hair had fallen out. Despite this, he was determined to leave, anxious that they return to the camp. So pervasive was the sense of uncertainty that being away from the army generated a panicky paranoia, not helped by the illness. Hanna left the hospital that day with his exhortations ringing in her ears. They must leave, they must get back to the army, they couldn't risk being left behind. He insisted she bring his uniform the following day.

Amid the chaos of the massively overstretched hospital, Rafał struggled into his uniform and, supported by his wife, staggered out. Waiting outside with the girls was Danusia's would-be Kyrgyz father-in-law and his cart. Sieroza was very agitated. He pleaded with Rafał to take him with them, insisting he would make a fine soldier. Whether he could understand that as a non-Pole this was impossible cannot be said, but it is another small example of how ethnicity determined people's future.

They got to the station safely and the journey began, which for Rafał was terribly arduous. Ticket after ticket had to be bought, one for each stage, meaning he faced long queues, often nearly fainting and needing to be propped up by others. At these stops the girls and their mother would be tucked away out of sight, fearful that they might attract unwelcome attention from local officialdom. Along the way, they picked up other refugees and were soon quite a party; Nana says that Rafał's pass for four was doctored, becoming a pass for fourteen. Maybe so, though the official scrutiny of papers had become pretty lax in the chaos of early 1942.

Arrival in Jakkobad, the little Poland in central Asia, with its hustle and bustle of military and civilian organisation, Polish uniforms at every turn, Polish voices instructing and organising, brought a moment of euphoria. For the Poles, Nana says, Jakkobad meant 'freedom', a place of the imagination suddenly taken corporeal form, a Polish oasis in the Soviet desert. Looking back, Nana says she experienced freedom as 'feeling like a child again', of living 'carefree', of seeing her mother wearing a pretty floral dress and sandals, somehow preserved from her wardrobe back home. It's more likely Rafał had bought the dress and sandals in the intervening period, but still the image is striking, the feminine flash of colour and the relative unconcern it represented, a freely moving body no longer needing protection. Most delightful was discovering Miecia, released from prison and unbowed by her experiences. She too had made it to Jakkobad.

Rafał was immediately taken to hospital and the Company diary tells us that he was in for a rough time. Typhoid was rapidly followed by pneumonia and his recovery was not noted until 2 April, around which time he contracted malaria and was sent on leave. By the end of April he was thought fit enough to return to his duties. Nana recollects everyone being afflicted with some kind of physical complaint or other, with many recovering from serious illnesses. For her it was malaria and she remembers vividly the cold chills, the fever, the sweats, and the uncontrollable shaking. Jasio, Rafał's batman, and a great favourite of the two girls, was often on hand at these moments and he would hold her down until the spasm was over. Time, though, passed slowly, and Danusia took to picking poppies, which grow in great profusion in parts of Kazakhstan. Her self-appointed duty was to decorate the sick bay and the garrison offices. 'They grew in ditches; they grew on the flat roofs of the mud *kibitkas*. One day I walked into the offices and there was General Anders. He picked me up, saying, "For me, my little Kazakh," and gave me a big hug.'

The Company diary shows that routine military training and activities remained the order of the day. Route marches of fifteen kilometres or so and night exercises were now a part of their training. Numbering 124, the Company periodically lost men to Officer Cadet School and other training schemes, and in March and April eight men were dismissed for unspecified reasons to be replaced by new recruits. Disinfection became a regular part of the Company's routines and in early March they undertook the ten-kilometre march to the inoculation point where they received injections intended to protect them against smallpox and typhoid. An unlucky rifleman called Milewski contracted typhoid the following day. Easter celebrations loomed, as did occasional lectures, seminars and ceremonies, such as raising and lowering of the Polish flag. Obligatory literacy lessons were laid on for those unable to read. The death in March of the regiment chaplain, Captain Chorobański, stands out from the general run of activity.

Most notable, however, were two patriotic celebrations, which must have touched the civilians as deeply as the men and women in uniform. The anniversary of the signing of the 3 May Constitution in 1791 was

marked in some style. In guaranteeing the rights of the Polish citizenry
against arbitrary government, it lays claim to being the world's second
– after the American – and Europe's first liberal constitution. Like the
American original constitution, it is imperfect by modern standards, limiting
its award of full citizenship to certain social groups, but it was nonetheless
religiously pluralist (though privileging the Catholic Church) and progressive by contemporary standards. To this day, it is marshalled as evidence of
Poland's historic modernity, its liberalism proof that Poland was ahead of
the curve until diverted from its true path by the partitions.

Following a 5 a.m. wake-up call, the whole regiment assembled at
7.30. In battalion order they marched to the assembly area of the garrison
to join the whole Division. The Polish flag was raised and weapons
were presented. Shortly after, Major-General Tokarzewski, Commander
of the Division, accompanied by Soviet representatives, arrived to receive
the garrison commander's progress report. Following Mass, Tokarzewski
gave 'a most beautiful speech' about the Constitution of 3 May as a
prelude to the inevitable march past. At 11.30 the ravenous men returned
to their lodgings and tucked into 'a plentiful three-course meal, during
which one could notice the smiling faces of the soldiers'. There was a
'wonderful atmosphere'.

For the men the evening brought the festivities and comradeship of
the campfire, while the non-commissioned officers of the regiment were
assembled for dinner. A select few were invited to join the commander
and his staff in the 'casino'. During the dinner, a non-commissioned
officer gave a short speech to the commander of the regiment; subsequently the non-coms bellowed out a few military songs. Recitations
followed and the gathering came to an end with the rousing rendition
of the sombrely uplifting anthem 'Rota' ('Oath'). 'Rota', in 1927 a candi-
date for the national anthem, was written by the Kraków poet Maria
Konopnicka in 1908 and set to music by Feliks Nowowiejski in 1910. It
is said to have been first sung in public on 15 July that year, the 500th
anniversary of the Polish–Lithuanian defeat of the Teutonic Knights at
the Battle of Grunwald. As the lyrics suggest, it was a provocative – if
largely ignored – thing to do in Austrian-ruled Kraków in 1910 and newly
appropriate to 1942:[18]

> We'll not abandon the land of our folk.
> We'll not let our language be buried.
> We're the Polish nation, the Polish people,

Royal line of the Piasts.
We'll not let the foe hold us down.
   So help us God!
   So help us God!

To the last drop of blood in our veins,
We'll defend our spirit
Until into dust
Falls the Teutonic storm.
Every doorway will be our fortress.
   So help us God!
   So help us God!

The German will not spit in our face
Nor Germanise our children,
Our host will rise up in arms,
Our spirit will lead the way.
We'll go forth when sounds the golden horn.
   So help us God!
   So help us God!

We won't let Poland's name be crushed
We won't go, living, to the grave.
In our country's name and its honour
We lift our heads proudly,
The grandson will regain his forefather's land.
   So help us God!
   So help us God!

The most famous lines are those referring to the Germans and in the poem the contemporary struggle against Germanness, be it of Austrian or German origin, is made continuous with the Teutonic threat of the late Middle Ages. To sing this on 3 May reinforced that sense of Poland's self-appointed historic role as a beacon of progress and liberty, often only faintly glimmering under the maw of their barbaric, primitive neighbours. The Nazi and Soviet conquests renewed that sense of historic mission, liberating Poles from the problems they faced in actually living and governing by these principles in the 1920s and 1930s, allowing them to seek refuge once again in the 3 May ideals.

The strong emphasis placed on protecting the Polish language is linked to the home as fortress, signifying that Polishness is something to be nurtured in the family. If the language survives, the nation survives, irrespective of whether the nation possesses a state. Above all, to sing the 'Rota', voicing its assertions, is to realise Polishness itself – 'We're the Polish nation, the Polish people.' Once again, on that chilly parade ground the nation comes into being. The nation is reified – transfigured perhaps – through such ritualised performance.

Nine days later nationalist sentiments were stirred once again with the anniversary of the death of Piłsudski. A funeral Mass in the morning was accompanied by a short speech by the commander of the regiment. At 5 p.m. Lieutenant Leśkiewicz, commander of the 5th Company, lectured the whole battalion on Piłsudski's career and work in attaining Polish independence. At the campfire there was another lecture, this time by the education officer, before common prayer for the whole regiment at 8.45 p.m.

The quick succession of 3 May and the Piłsudski anniversary linked history to lived experience, reinforcing the sense of a continuous national struggle. Men like Rafał embodied those earlier triumphs and for young men, reared on the stories of their fathers' and grandfathers' heroics, the urge to etch their names onto the tablets of the Polish national tradition can only have been strengthened by the stories told by (relatively) old boys like Lieutenants Leśkiewicz and Ryżewski.

Perhaps the greatest ceremony in the life of the Company while in Russia was the Corpus Christi celebrations of 4 June. These processions are very important to Polish Catholic tradition, as they are throughout much of the Catholic world. Little girls walk in front wearing their first Communion dresses and scattering flower petals, the Church hierarchy follows in all its liturgical splendour, followed by representatives of civic groups, trade unions and so on. Religious paraphernalia are displayed in windows and people line the streets to greet the procession en route. Remarkable footage survives of the Corpus Christi celebrations in Warsaw in 1945, held in the immediate aftermath of the German defeat. The little girls in pretty white dresses stand in stark contrast to Warsaw in ruins. An altogether more raucous portrayal of a Corpus Christi procession can be found in Rossellini's *Voyage to Italy* (1953), one of the many cinema portrayals of this central ritual in Catholic life.

This holiday, in Polish Boże Ciało, on a scorching hot day, brought the whole Polish community together. Attending the 8 a.m. Mass on the regiment square were the army, the civilian population, and the children from the orphanage – 'the flower of our youth and our comfort and the pride of our Nation' says the Company Log. The Holy Communion wine and wafers, presented for adoration, provoked in the 'brotherhood' of soldiers a 'happiness in their eyes that they have lived to be free and take part in the religious celebration'. The description of this day provoked the purplest patches in our diarist's prose. Each of the four battalions had its altar and the torchlit procession that evening saw the Holiest Sacrament moved from makeshift chapel to makeshift chapel. Our diarist sees:

> a wonderful sight. The children from the orphanage scatter flowers in front of the Holiest Sacrament dressed as the committee could afford (generally beautifully). The altars in each of the battalions look most beautiful, the effort put in and artistic decoration is evident. The Soviet population and children take part in the procession. One can see in the soldiers' eyes happiness and tears for there is a reason to cry from happiness and being touched by what the human eye can see and it is difficult to believe everything but still it is so and God wanted for us to be people and love him with all our soldiers' hearts.

The routine of celebration and training, both of which became more extravagant and advanced as the months progressed, began to leave the soldiers restless and feeling frustrated. The partial arming of the Company on 13 May gave them a boost, leading to an intensified training regime, with some of the riflemen finally able to learn properly the skills of their trade. Likewise, many Company members were sent off on courses, which along with an improved diet, better clothing and better weather, meant the Company began to feel itself a genuine fighting force readied for battle. By late May a new intensity characterised the men's questions and conversations among themselves. How long would they stay in Asia, when would they be properly armed, when would they go to the front line, and 'when will they finally be able to pay the Germans back for the harm done'?

Their frustration was not simply that of a military force stationed far behind the front line during a war. It reflected the profound uncertainty about their eventual fate and the vulnerability of their position as a force wholly dependent on support outside their government's control. The Sikorski–Stalin talks, for all their uncertainties, had promised an evacuation to Persia. From the moment the Polish military headquarters was re-established at Yangi Yul in the south, plans were laid, but the Soviets finally agreed on 18 March to the evacuation of only 30,000 soldiers and 10,000 dependants. They were to be moved to the Turkmenistan port of Krasnovodsk and from there ferried to the Persian port of Pahlevi. Agreement became urgent when Japan's entry into the war cut anticipated United States wheat supplies to the Soviet Union and Stalin informed Anders that from 1 April the rations for the Polish army would be drastically reduced. When we remember that these rations heavily subsidised the civilian population attached to the military camps, we can see that a humanitarian catastrophe was imminent.[19] It is clear that the unplanned movement of Polish civilians into central Asia and the formation of the Polish army had created a serious political problem for the Soviet government. First, the army and the civilians placed grave pressure on Soviet supplies. Many of the Poles had gone from being productive members of society to dependants. Civilians sharing military rations was not a long-term solution to the problem. Second, the support the Poles were receiving from the British created tension in the region, with the impression growing that these foreigners, so often characterised as enemies of the Soviet Union, were receiving favourable treatment. When the British began to figure out how to deal with the impending refugee problem, they too were concerned to avoid provoking resentment among the Iranian population.

Britain only slowly began to perceive the scale of the refugee crisis it might face. Although the Poles exploited the British need for troops in order to get as many civilians as possible out of the Soviet Union, the British had nonetheless already cast at least half a sympathetic eye on the plight of the Polish deportees. Poles and their supporters in Britain brought the matter to the government's attention, these lobbyists getting a hearing in part thanks to the extraordinary prestige still attached to the Polish airmen, who had acquired a legendary status fighting within the RAF in the Battle of Britain.

Throughout the war and in the years that followed, all the major departments of state and many of the colonial governments of the British Empire became involved in the Polish refugee question. Notes between departments passed up and down Whitehall, all written with the formal grace characteristic of the British Civil Service: nothing was demanded, all was politely requested, and subtle nuances of language conveyed degrees of pressure, though expressions of urgency were acceptable. What blazing rows there must have been are kept from the record, where only hints of simmering tensions can be found.

The same was true of Whitehall's interactions with the colonial governments. Telegrams between London and Tehran, Delhi and Nairobi all passed through the communications hub at Cairo, where colonial administrators, perhaps better placed than any Whitehall civil servant to understand political pressures at work throughout the empire, provided comment on the information they forwarded. If good communications were the key to governing this vast worldwide empire, it was Cairo rather than London that gave the pink parts of the map its centre. Again, though, all was request and supplication, with the relative autonomy of the individual governor, such as a viceroy of India, fully respected. His assessment of the situation on the ground was taken as Gospel and the degree to which London did not tell Delhi what to do now seems remarkable. The empire was not governed through centralised diktats, but worked on the assumption that the governing caste, inculcated with the right sort of values, dutifully worked in its interests. If duty was done, the most appropriate solution to any given problem could not but emerge through exchanges of information and fair-minded assessment. Consequently, this could be a slow-moving and somewhat lethargic machine, institutionally complacent, a sudden crisis often necessary to trigger decisive action. Such would be the case with the Poles.

The possibility that the Polish deportees might be evacuated from the Soviet Union to India began to be discussed in the autumn of 1941. Barbara Vere Hodge, of the Women's Voluntary Service for Civil Defence, one of a series of remarkable civilian organisations established in response to Total War, became an early champion. She appears to have been alerted to the problem by Polish friends and through contacts with Professor Koskowski of the Polish Red Cross. Writing on 19 September 1941 from the WVS office at 28 Ann Street, Edinburgh, she reported to Paul Patrick at the Allied Information Bureau that discussions had taken place between Lord Tweeddale and the Polish Ambassador to London. Both agreed that a scheme to take Polish children from 'Russia' to India would be a good thing. Indeed, Captain Shanker Hayat Khan, the son of the Prime Minister of Punjab, reportedly felt that 'India' was 'rather hurt' because refugee children had been sent to other parts of the empire 'but not to her'. Any Indian scheme for the benefit of refugees, Khan insisted, would meet with 'a very warm response', particularly from Muslims.[20] People living in India, reported Hodge, were anxious to help with the war effort 'and to show their sympathy with those who have suffered in the cause of freedom'.[21] British government in India operated through the indigenous elite and was therefore dependent on their goodwill. It was a delicate balancing act and they had every reason to take such sensitivities seriously.

With her letter, Hodge included a typed memo outlining her scheme for assisting 30,000 women and children trapped in central Asia. She proposed that a small organising committee be sent from Britain to India. It should comprise a Polish officer who could lecture in English and introduce propaganda films like *This is Poland* and *With Polish Forces in Britain*; a retired Indian army officer 'conversant with all aspects of social life in India'; a Polish or English-speaking woman, possibly the anonymous author of *My Name is Million*, written by a British woman married to a Pole and who was in Poland during the invasions;[22] and an English woman with administrative ability who knew India. It was clear that Hodge thought such philanthropic work was best suited to women and, as plans developed, it was hoped the Viceroy's wife would take a personal interest in promoting the scheme. And in keeping with this, though she believed the scheme should be financed initially by the Polish government-in-exile and the Polish Relief Fund, she hoped an Indian branch of the fund would eventually be able to cover costs. A month or so later, Patrick counselled patience, reminding Hodge that organising relief through charity took time.[23]

More time would have to pass before the scale of the problem would become clear and the notion that it could be financed through charity abandoned. Somewhat comically, for this propaganda effort Hodge proposed as 'an example of the type of family who would benefit' Countess Sophie Czarkowska Golejewska and her two daughters, Rose aged eight and Nina aged six. The Countess, Barbara explained, was the daughter of Prince John Sapieha and was British by birth. It seems likely that relatives or friends of the Countess were among Polish friends of Hodge, though the notion that the Countess and her daughters were representative of the deported Poles is obviously dubious. That said, given her wish to appeal to the British and Indian elites, she might well have been right to suppose that the plight of Poland's gentry would touch the right philanthropic nerves.

Most striking, however, was how Hodge framed her proposals. Informally, she noted that the conditions under which the Poles were living were 'quite deplorable', but in the memo itself she emphasised a motive that went far beyond a mere humanitarian concern for the suffering. 'In view of the accounts recently received of the systematic efforts of the German Government to annihilate the Polish race,' she wrote, 'it is considered vital that everything is done to preserve these Polish families who are now living in exile.' She continued, saying it must be 'stressed that the aim of this proposal is the preservation of the Polish race, and therefore priority should be given to mothers with children, and to young people'. Though extreme in her fears, it's an idea that crops up in various forms in the documentary traces of the period, not least in Rafał's and Hanna's letters when they emphasise how their overriding duty, their reason for living, is to ensure their daughters' survival. They do not, however, express this in racial terms. Note also the euphemistic description of the Polish families living in exile. British documents on the plight of the Poles in the Soviet Union were often sanitising, obscuring the fact of the deportation and mass internments.

At this stage, the question of numbers was very vague. Though Leo Amery, Secretary of State for India, wrote in October to Lord Linlithgow, the Viceroy, mentioning 30,000 possible refugees,[24] at this point serious discussions were focused on relatively small numbers, perhaps as few as 500 children under the age of fourteen. Consequently, Amery readily took up the charge. Writing to Linlithgow, he expressed great sympathy for the Poles, but advocated assistance be provided not by the state but charity. In doing so, however, he indicated his awareness of the particular difficulties in accommodating non-Asiatic refugees in India.[25] Concerns regarding the climate and European vulnerability to tropical disease became a recurrent theme in British planning, though it was often noted it couldn't be any worse than it had been in the Soviet Union.[26] The Viceroy responded positively, saying he hoped they could rely on private hospitality but was less sure about how they could ensure adequate educational provision. Places in European schools were in short supply and, as he reminded the Secretary of State, European children, and girls in particular, could not be left unsupervised. It was possible that Catholic schools might have places and be willing to look after the children during the holidays, but perhaps the simplest solution would be to allow the mothers to accompany their children.[27] A month later the picture was becoming a little clearer and the Viceroy wrote on 23 December that it would not be possible to house the children privately: the provincial governments insisted that separate camps would be needed. Moreover, given that 'there were over a million Polish refugees in Russia and that they are comparatively well-to-do middle class families', the convent or mission schools,

having been built for Anglo-Indians of 'humble origin', would not be
suitable. They would have either to build or requisition buildings and
establish separate schools.[28]

By the end of January the British had communicated to the Soviets
that they could handle a modest 2,000 evacuees per week if given ten
weeks' notice. At this point the Polish army was receiving not far
short of this number of new recruits every day. At the end of March,
neither the British nor the Polish government had yet agreed that civilians would accompany that March evacuation (Anders was clearly
instructed that they must not),[29] though the British realised that the
morale of the Polish forces relied on them knowing their relatives
were safe.[30] In the event, 43,858 Poles arrived at Pahlevi over eleven
days, commencing 25 March, with the peak occuring on April Fools'
Day, when 12,241 bedraggled Poles poured onto the wharfs.[31] Evidence
suggests the Soviet authorities pressurised the Polish military leadership into squeezing as many Polish civilians as possible on to the ships,
irrespective of their papers.[32] The transfer of the Poles to the port
showed how efficient the NKVD could be. March and April conclu-
sively demonstrated how little control the British had over the numbers
of Poles that might come into their care. Careful plans, formulated
at a stately pace and predicated on an illusory orderliness, would be
swept from the table when sudden changes in circumstances demanded
ad hoc responses.

At first Tehran was unhappy with this state of affairs and the British
sought to assure the Persians that the Poles would soon be moved, though
London, expecting the Poles to be in Persia for some time, instructed their
local representatives to be very vague.[33] Soon after, however, the attitudes
of the Tehran authorities changed. Most immediately, they recognised the
danger of an epidemic if they did not assist in the provision of sanitary
accommodation, but more persuasive was the propaganda value of a
constructive response. A British representative in Tehran outlined the
delicate situation to London:

> Not only will Persia appear more generous and hospitable than the Soviets,
> but Russians can no longer upset Persian citizens by singing the glories of
> the Soviet Union, while Tehran is full of Poles who were starving in Russia
> and who admitted that Russians in the same circumstances were starving
> too. This may be awkward for the Russians but if it compels them to
> moderate their propaganda, that will be to our advantage and theirs.

If the Persian Government try to make capital overtly out of the refugees, I shall discourage them but so long as refugees stay in Persia anti-Russian propaganda by implication is unavoidable.[34]

By contrast, the Foreign Office was keen that the good treatment of the Poles in Persia was not trumpeted too loudly for fear it would encourage further evacuation, though as one official observed, now that 'the cat was out of the bag' regarding the state of the Poles in the Soviet Union, the Soviets had nothing to lose and everything to gain from more leaving.[35] The FO can hardly have welcomed this observation though at this stage there was no certainty that more Poles would be evacuated, not least because Sikorski continued to believe that Poles fighting on the Eastern Front would strengthen his government's diplomatic position. Continuing tension over the border question meant it was important for Polish troops to be directly involved in the liberation of Poland. Equally, Sikorski was concerned that if the Soviets were internationally embarrassed by the exposure of their incapacity to maintain the Poles in the Soviet Union, this might adversely affect Polish–Soviet relations in the future. Already, reports of civilian suffering, propagated to mobilise the relief effort, were undermining Polish–Soviet relations. Anders, by contrast, wanted to get as many Poles out of the Soviet Union as soon as possible. He was unconvinced that the Red Army would hold out against the *Wehrmacht* or that good Soviet–Polish relations would last much longer and can only have been too conscious of the growing desire among his men to be posted to Persia. Sikorski, aware of the froideur that had entered his contacts with Moscow, was gradually worn down by Anders' lobbying and eventually gave way.

Careful diplomatic manoeuvring gave the Soviets the opportunity to approve a further evacuation on the grounds that the strategic situation in the Middle East urgently needed an injection of additional troops. With the British eager for the troops and the Soviets glad to get shot of the problem, the Poles chose this moment to play their strongest card. The entire army would be placed at the disposal of the Western Allies if the families, auxiliaries and the Boy Scouts were permitted to accompany the troops, and if preparations were laid for the evacuation of some further 50,000 Polish children along with their 5,000 mothers or guardians. These conditions reflected a new nervousness among the Poles, triggered on the ground by the Soviets forcing civilians attached to the camps back into the *kolkhoz* and the evident cooling of relations at the political level.

The basic fear was that the men might become separated from their families for good. Moreover, there was the simple fact that 16,000 Polish civilians were dependent on the military camps. Take away that infrastructure and they would surely die.[36]

In June, Foreign Secretary Anthony Eden wrote to Amery, outlining the potential scale of the problem. Lobbied hard by the Polish government, Eden admitted that their own information concurred with Polish claims that the deportees remaining in the Soviet Union were 'living in harrowing conditions, diseased and threatened with death from starvation'. The Polish Ambassador in Kuibyshev, Eden reported, had begged his government to appeal to the British and the United States to help remove 50,000 Polish children. Clearly sympathetic, Eden emphasised that though it had been made clear to the Poles that the problem of their civilians in Russia was for them to settle with the Russian government, Britain's 'humanitarian interests' were re-inforced by political considerations. On the one hand, Eden reported the Polish claim 'that between the German extermination policy and the fate of their people in the Union of Soviet Socialist Republics the basis of their national life is being destroyed', while on the other, he was equally moved by Sikorski's warning that the condition of the Poles in Russia was 'an important obstacle to a full Polish–Russian understanding'. Despite the limitations which 'transport, supply and overriding military considerations impose on us' – which had been made clear to the Poles – Eden wanted 'to be in a position to say to the Polish Government that the possibilities of help were being urgently reviewed'. And, 'for the most immediate help, I can think of nowhere to turn but India'.[37] The response from India cannot have been very reassuring. They agreed to take a further 500 children but it would take them three months to prepare.[38]

Despite this lukewarm response, and the insistence that the Polish government was both diplomatically and financially responsible for the refugees, geographical and political logic dictated that the problem ultimately rested with the British. These realities were stated forcefully two days later when Cairo laid out some home truths before the Foreign Office. So large-scale might the problem become that it could no longer be treated as a purely humanitarian issue. It would have to be dealt with on a military scale and with the wider military strategy at the forefront of planners' minds. Refugees, Cairo reminded London, had had a disastrous effect on the battle of France and Cairo feared the presence of refugees clogging lines of communication in the Middle East. Now it was a war issue, Cairo implied, pressure needed to be put on the colonial and dominion governments: South Africa should take 50,000 Poles, mainly women and children; the East African colonies and Northern and Southern Rhodesia 30,000; Madagascar 10,000; Allied governments should be equally supportive, the Belgian Congo and Portuguese East Africa each taking 5,000. The US government should also be approached.[39]

At this point, the British in Tehran began to talk about preparing for the reception of 50,000 Poles and a shift in perception can be sensed in the FO's reference to 'Allied civilian refugees'.[40] Cairo, however, still kept its eye on the bigger strategic picture, giving harsh expression to what it perceived to be strategic realities. They must prevent any further evacuation before the authorities in Persia were ready:

> To put matters brutally if these Poles die in Russia the war effort will not be affected. If they [are allowed] to pass into Persia, we, unlike the Russians, will not be able to allow them to die and our war effort will be gravely impaired. Action must be taken to stop these people from leaving the U.S.S.R. before we are ready to receive them (and then only at the rate we are able to receive and ship them away from the head of the Persian Gulf) however many die in consequence.[41]

Shocking though this is, it is equally striking as a forceful articulation of British perceptions of their difference from the Soviets. The FO assured Cairo that the Polish government accepted the general strategic position and that no Allied government – in other words, the Polish government – would take independent action. Can they really have believed that a 'further exodus from the Soviet Union was improbable'?[42]

In the meantime, another blunt telegram arrived at the FO from Cairo:

> I have personally instructed that 10,000 refugees largely in Persia should be medically examined in due course as to their fitness to travel through the Persian Gulf during the hot season. Those not fit must await a more favourable season unless further exodus from Russia into Persia necessitates their immediate evacuation in which case the risk of death en voyage from heatstroke must be accepted as inescapable.[43]

Notwithstanding the assurances granted Cairo, after a little procrastination the British effectively acceded to the Soviet *fait accompli* that had come in the form of the decision to end the rationing of the Polish army.

Churchill made the necessary diplomatic gestures and on 31 July 1942 a Polish–Soviet protocol allowing a further large-scale evacuation was signed at Tashkent. At first glance it looks a great success for Polish diplomacy. The Polish army would find itself able to play a full role as part of the Allied forces and the 'military families' would be brought to safety. A second glance, however, reveals the weakness of the Polish position. The Soviets insisted a significant caveat was added to the protocols: of the former citizens of the Polish kresy who were in Anders' Army, only ethnic Poles would be permitted to leave.[44] The logic of this condition was that there was a fundamental difference of citizenship between the Poles and the national minorities of the kresy, and to accept it was implicitly to recognise the territorial conception of Poland established by the Nazi–Soviet Pact. To express it a different way, a proportion of the Polish citizens, whether men, women or children, who were originally imprisoned as POWs or deported from the kresy and who were now attached to the Polish army, would be debarred from leaving on account of their ethnicity. As such, the Soviet decision to permit the evacuation was continuous with the main thrust of the original deportations.

Did the Polish signatories recognise the significance of this caveat? Alexander Kot, the perceptive Polish Ambassador to Moscow, certainly did, and though Anders later argued they could not accept this condition he silently acknowledged that they had no choice but to do so.[45] A further implication of the agreement was that by removing the Polish army from the Soviet Union, it was almost certain to play no direct role in the liberation of eastern Poland and possibly the country as a whole – those Poles that eventually did were fighting as part of the Red Army.

Was a darker process at work in the establishment and then promulgation of the protocols? Throughout the history of Anders' Army, and particularly in its earliest stages, it was dogged by reports that its recruitment patterns and attitudes in the ranks were antisemitic. Jewish groups and their British sympathisers – often left-wing and sometimes distinctly pro-Soviet – publicised this information, putting the Polish Government-in-Exile under pressure to prove otherwise.

Surviving documentary evidence suggests that Anders did not hold to a strongly inclusive line – which he later vigorously denied in his memoirs[46] – and there is evidence to suggest that the Polish government recognised anti-Jewish sentiment in the ranks as a serious problem. Under pressure from the political leadership, Anders issued an order on 14 November 1941 stating that the victimisation of Jews was unacceptable, though in an accompanying note to his senior officers he stated that he shared the anti-Jewish views of many of the rank-and-file. There can be little doubt that the order was motivated in part by the Government-in-Exile's acute consciousness that accusations of antisemitism were very damaging to their cause.[47] It is clear that many Poles did not extend their 'universe of obligation' to include Polish Jews and the institutionalised Catholicity of the ritual of Polish army life was a manifestation of this.[48] Some indication has already been given of the nature of the Polish Catholic–Jewish relations on the eve of the war, but the anti-Jewish sentiment at work in the army and among the deportees does need further contextualisation.[49]

When trying to make sense of Polish Catholic perceptions, it is important to remember that it was the Germans who initially conquered much of eastern Poland. They introduced antisemitic laws and began to transport Polish Jews west, but at this stage in the war they were murdering large numbers from among the Polish elite. Consequently, the well-documented welcome *some* Jewish Poles gave the Red Army, in the carefully modulated words of Eva Hoffman, was 'to the Poles, a distressing and an alienating spectacle'.[50] In the early stages of the war, Polish Jews found Soviet occupation more acceptable than Nazi occupation, whereas for Polish Catholics such a preference generally did not exist. Despite the treatment meted out by the Nazis, the arrival of the Soviets was not generally considered an improvement. Be that as it may, all serious historical analysis indicates that generalisations about 'the Jewish welcome', still sometimes made in Poland today, must be rejected.[51] But the absorption of some Jewish Poles into the new Soviet infrastructure – be it refugees from Nazi-occupied Poland with few other options, Jewish Poles profoundly alienated from the old regime or Jewish communists – was an aspect of the Soviet conquest.[52] Polish POWs in the Soviet Union, however, did not directly witness the Jewish experience of Soviet rule in occupied Poland, which very quickly dashed any hopes that Stalin would deliver 'the Messiah's times', as at least one old Shtetl Jew hoped.[53]

Such partial memories were enhanced by widespread perceptions among ethnic Polish women that their families had suffered deportation owing to their ethnicity, whereas Polish Jews had been deported as punishment for speculation and theft, and Ukrainians because they were common criminals.[54] Jolluck's nuanced reading of Polish sentiment suggests that depositions by Polish women emphasised that some of 'our' Jews and national minorities had behaved disloyally since the invasions and had

actively persecuted Polish women in the prisons and in the *kolkhoz*.[55]
Such women articulated their anger at Polish Jewry in terms of their
actions rather than a priori assumptions, though such actions confirmed
more generalised perceptions about these groups, which dated back at
least to the 1920s and 1930s. Similarly, it is striking that in the Company
diary, Rafał distinguished the experience of the Polish Jews from that
of the Polish Catholics: the Jews were evacuees, saved by the Soviets
from the Nazis, rather than deportees and POWs, victimised on account
of their Polishness. Though some Polish Jews fled east with the retreating
Red Army at the time of Barbarossa and others had voluntarily migrated
to the Soviet Union, others still were imprisoned by the Soviets, and, as
discussed earlier, Polish Jews were principal among the deportees of June
1940 on account of their declared nationality.[56] Consequently, a significant proportion of Jewish Poles in the Soviet Union in 1941 had experienced Soviet occupation just as Catholic Poles had. Nonetheless, the
strong perception that Jewish Poles had played fast and loose with their
nationality, whereas Catholic Poles remained consistently loyal, meant
that as the prospect of evacuation came nearer there was a tendency in
the army to maximise the presence on the evacuation lists of Poles they
thought properly members of the national community.

It is quite plausible that when the Company diary mentions the
dismissal of eight men in March and April 1942 this refers to Jews, fallen
foul of the rigorous interpretation of Soviet-imposed ethnic regulations.
David Engel argues that the Polish army leadership used these regulations as a cover and that Anders' anti-Jewish sentiment, typical of his
rank-and-file, was easily exploited by the Soviets, leading many Jews to
'see his anti-Jewish feelings as the primary motivation for his stringency'
in applying the rule.[57] By contrast, when later accused of drawing up
antisemitic evacuation lists, senior Polish officers responded that the Soviet
claim that they would have not have impeded the evacuation of Jewish
Poles was false. Instead, these officers argued, they had to take seriously
the threat that the evacuation would have been halted should the Soviet
ruling on Polish ethnicity be contravened.[58]

A further factor at work was the pressure the British government put
on its Polish counterpart to minimise the number of Polish Jews allowed
to leave the Soviet Union. Knowing Anders' Army would pass through
Palestine, the British feared that mass Jewish desertions would add to
their difficulties in the Middle East.[59] These were not irrational fears: the
Zionist movement was strong among Jewish Poles and of the relatively

small number who were a part of the evacuation – some 3 or 4 per cent of the total – a significant number did desert. One set of figures puts the total Jewish desertions while Polish forces were in the Middle East at 2,972, though we might remember that some 850 Polish Jews fought in Anders' Army at the great battle for Monte Cassino (May 1944), the most famous victory of Polish arms during the whole war.[60] It is not unreasonable to suppose that the number of desertions would have been higher had there been more Jewish Poles among the evacuees.

Just as all Jewish Poles did not scatter flowers in the path of advancing Soviet tanks, so all Catholic Poles did not at that moment become polit-ically anti-Jewish, but it is clear that the experience of invasion, occupa-tion, imprisonment and deportation enhanced the ethnic divisions that had shaped Polish politics in the 1920s and 1930s. In 1942 the Polish lead-ership in Russia, dominated by Catholics, had at their disposal a very scarce resource – exit papers from the Soviet Union. The leadership was manipulated by, acquiesced in or openly embraced the Soviet view that Polish Catholics had rights as Polish citizens that did not extend to their Jewish fellow citizens. Consequently, though this book ultimately deals with the fate primarily of a group of Catholic Poles, it does not make the Jewish dimension of this history tangential to its concerns. The minority of Catholic Poles in the Soviet Union fortunate enough to be evacuated were marginally advantaged by an exclusivist idea of Polishness shared to a significant degree by Catholic Poles and Soviets alike, and convenient to the British.

On 1 August the Polish army issued the evacuation order. Between 9 August and 1 September the movement from Jakkobad and other camps to Krasnovodsk took place. Despite the insistence on strictly adhering to the rules, the NKVD efficiency of March–April was not much in evidence and the second evacuation soon became a headlong rush for the port. Poles from outside the camps did everything they could to get to the army or the port, desperately hoping to make it onto both the Polish and NKVD lists, which had to match if the evacuation was to be guar-anteed. Hanna was among those appointed to process the new arrivals and faced what Nana describes as the heartbreaking task of applying the selection rules. Where possible the rules were bent, with impersonation not uncommon, but it was essential that at least a plausible case could be presented when the lists were rapidly checked. Irena Okulicz-Kozaryn recalls her mother's horror at discovering from 'some bureaucrat' that having not seen her husband since his arrest in 1939 her family were not eligible to leave. Their 'Russian miracle' took the form of a soldier seeking his family, also sent to an Archangel labour camp and also from Nowogródek in Poland. Irena's mother explained their situation. 'Come with me,' he said, 'you are my sister and you can live.' 'We never saw the man again, but we remembered him in our prayers for a long time.'[61]

Luggage was restricted to twenty kilogrammes per person and much was left behind, dumped in ditches at the roadside. Amid the fevered preparations for departure, Rafał suddenly noticed that his elder daughter was missing. In a state of panic, he sent his men out to find her. She was found in the market, sitting cross-legged amid the traders, the pile of discarded Ryżewski rags neatly laid out, her round native hat cocked to one side. Seemingly every bit the hardened trader, she held aloft a pair of heavily patched pink flannel pantaloons, the winter wear of the Uzbeks, and attracted some brisk bidding.[62]

This latest train journey passed in a blur and Nana remembers little more than the atmosphere of urgency and, at one stop, the strident voice of a woman in charge of a group of evacuees from Tashkent. 'Tashkent, Tashkent, come here, come here, stay together, keep close, keep close', the demands of a 'mother hen keeping her brood together and safe'. At Krasnovodsk, the refugees faced a six-kilometre walk to the port and, as at all stages in this odyssey, there were fatalities, people breathing their last, ravaged bodies succumbing to the final stages of illness. And though the Poles never lost a sense of their collectivity, the fear that at the last moment they might be denied an exit led to an intense focus on the immediate family before all else. Bewildered children were instructed by frantic parents to keep moving and it is easy to imagine small hands tightly held as parents pressed on, their children stumbling along, looking back at the latest tragedy that had occurred. Recalling an earlier stage in their journey, Wesley Adamczyk has himself ask his mother, 'How much longer do I have to close my eyes or not look at the world around me?' God, the boy suggested to her, must be blind to allow this suffering. '"Wiesiu, it is a sacrilege to talk like this," she admonished me. And I remained silent.'[63] Many years later when Adamczyk sat down to write his memoirs that exchange inspired his title, *When God Looked the Other Way*.

Like Adamczyk, Nana too remembers the panicky atmosphere at the dock, the pushing and shoving, the hustle and the urgency, as people crowded forward, desperate to get on board. The cargo ship looked 'dismal': there was no passenger ramp and she recalls the few planks hastily improvised as a gangway having no rails. Soldiers at each end of this rickety arrangement passed the children across, leaving them momentarily suspended above the dark waters washing between the ship and the dock wall. People's possessions, sometimes carried from Poland three years before, were thrown on to the deck from the harbour walls and no attempt was made to retrieve those humble items that fell short and into the water below. Everything about the operation suggested time was short, though much of this sense of urgency came from the people behind, struggling to get their place on board.

Rafał stationed the girls against a 'mushroom-like iron post' and instructed them to stay on deck. The conditions on board were grim and could only get worse. All the ships used to ferry the Poles across the Caspian Sea were dangerously overcrowded and crammed aboard were many passengers suffering from diarrhoea and dysentery. The deck was covered with people, closely guarding their small space. Facilities were non-existent: a thick rope was set up to allow people something to hang on to while defecating or urinating overboard, but so weakened were some that they fell overboard and drowned. There was no possibility of a rescue attempt, especially at night, and the overloaded ship just kept going, completing its two-day voyage. By the journey's end drinking water had run out, the deck was streaked with urine, excrement and blood, and the sick lay covered with flies.[64] The position below deck can only have been worse. 'The crossing', Nana says, 'was horrendous, the choppy sea, the sickness, the stench, tested human dignity to the core.' 'But', she concludes, 'we reached Pahlevi somehow in one piece.' Between 10 August and 1 September 1942 twenty-six ships brought 69,247 Poles across the Caspian Sea. Of this total, 25,501 were civilians.[65] Rafał, Hanna, Wanda and Danusia had left the Soviet Union; they were now the responsibility of the British government. Any sense that the evacuation was a 'miracle' must be tempered by a consciousness of the misery, psychological and material, faced by the hundreds of thousands left behind. Finally, it might be supposed that in imprisoning or deporting the people intended to sustain the internal security of Poland's eastern borderlands, the Soviets removed a possible obstruction to the Red Army's later advance. This would be to forget the systematic decapitating of Polish society pursued by the Nazis, largely through murder, and the fate of the *kresy* elites would surely have been the same, depriving the Western allies of an important component of the forces that liberated Western Europe.

6

'We live in a state of tension':
A Year in Persia[1]

Disembarking on Pahlevi beach, 'somehow in one piece', civilians and uniformed men were immediately segregated and, for the brief time soldiers were nearby, Danusia occasionally caught sight of her father, working with his fellow officers in the distance. Assisted by British representatives, they were preparing to march the men out to their quarters. Though this start to their time with the British was dictated by unsentimental military routine, the overwhelming feelings shared by the Poles on arrival at Pahlevi were of euphoria and relief. Adamczyk remembered the moment 'the Polish escapees from the Soviet Union entered the protection of His Majesty, the King of England. I saw a British uniform for the first time, and my heart was filled with awe and gratitude.'[2] Stefania Buczak-Zarzycka recalls: 'Instinctively everyone, even the children, upon reaching land would make the sign of the cross in thanksgiving, while most of the adults knelt down on the yellow sand in prayer.' British observers, little understanding the overwhelming wave of physical and emotional relief flooding these wrecked bodies, were 'shocked', thinking the Poles 'religious fanatics'.[3] Ryszard Tyrk remembers his foot first touching 'free Persian soil a few minutes past eleven o'clock' on 15 August, the significance of the event evident in his memory of the exact details. Helena Szafrańska felt she'd entered 'another world'. She remembers Krasnovodsk as a bleak desert port, whereas the picture she paints of Pahlevi is of a seaside resort, with palm trees and a shop where chocolate and fizzy drinks could be bought. There might be a hint of poetic licence here, but the feeling of deliverance was almost universal. Jan Bednarz, a young Polish soldier arrested aged nineteen in 1940 on a trumped-up political charge, had been brutally treated by the NKVD, sent to the Gulag and then amnestied. Writing in retirement some sixty years later in Axminster in Devon, he remembered being met by 'smart British Indian soldiers' and he too felt he had arrived 'in another world'. 'For the first time after nearly two years in Soviet Paradise I saw eggs, milk and oranges.'[4]

Adamczyk, always conscious of the bodily and rarely one to allow rose-tinted memories to obscure realities, remembers the Poles who arrived in Pahlevi as diseased, suffering from dysentery, typhus and typhoid fever, many afflicted with nasty skin complaints. Everyone spent at least two weeks in quarantine and he reports some 650 Poles dying of illness, making a mockery of the dreadful journey across the Caspian. They were buried in mass graves in the Polish cemetery.[5] To know relatives were buried in 'free soil', says Anita Paschwa (née Kizicka), provided 'some comfort, but the loss was almost unbearable'.[6]

Nana remembers waiting on the beach while a team of medical inspectors made their rounds and, though many bad cases were immediately sent to the hospital, her memories ring with the same joy as Helena's. While the inspectors progressed, the kids stripped off their clothes and splashed into the sea. General Anders, who took a march past on the beach, wrote: 'It was heartening to see those emaciated men, women, and children express their joy at being free again, dash down to bathe in the sea and splash gleefully in the water.'[7] Adamczyk, observing, says they washed away Russia. It was symbolic cleansing at best; they emerged, to their 'mothers' lament', black with oil. All the better – in Nana's words – was 'the ablution, army style' that followed. Their lice-ridden clothing was incinerated; heads, armpits and genitalia were shaved to rid them of lice;[8] and these 'living, walking skeletons', enjoyed 'the delight' of going 'through a corridor of hot water sprinklers shooting from all directions.' 'It was bliss,' says Nana. Some children, not yet inhibited by adolescence, may well have wriggled and giggled their way through the jets but for others, subdued, withdrawn and sick, it was yet another ordeal. Bednarz says they were sprinkled with DDT before receiving new battledress and boots, transferring treasured photographs from old to new pockets. 'I saw our old uniforms were set alight and so were our companions – the lice. From that day I never saw lice again.'[9] Sabina Kukla remembers returning to the beach after the shower, naked and wrapped only in a blanket, to find their possessions being burnt, including items carried from home. As she watched, 'burning feathers from pillows were carried along the beach by the wind. An extraordinary sight – the flames were taking our last memorabilia from us.'

For the first time since the deportation, the Poles had decent accommodation and access to plenty of food. A warehouse depot near Pahlevi station had been furnished like a barracks and Nana says they were fed well and felt looked after. On arrival, writes Henryka Kłopecka (née Leonowicz), 'We were entranced watching a Persian man selling pancakes, hard-boiled eggs, cigarettes and oriental delicacies.'[10] Their diet, however, had to be carefully regulated. Fruit and vegetables were easily available, but few Poles could yet stomach the mulberries, figs, dates and pomegranates that flourished in the Persian climate.[11] Water, too, was treated carefully, Bednarz describing an Indian soldier stationed at the taps who would drop a small pinch of chlorine into the vessel being filled. As with the use of DDT, hygiene was crude but effective if not too good for long-term health. Digestive problems were more immediately threatening – and many deaths were caused partly by overzealous officials keen to feed the refugees after such a long period of shortage. Vala Lewicki (née Miron) remembers the heavy diet of rice and mutton causing Poles, 'especially young girls of my age', to die by the hundreds of dysentery.[12] Ryszard Tyrk confirms this: 'Many people, however, gulped everything down that was near at hand. The result: typhus, twisting of the bowels, a short stay in hospital, and eternal rest.'[13] When carefully controlled however, the new diet could bring a transformation. 'What a life,' remembers Tadeusz Pieczko, who was among a group of malnourished children sent to a 'special fattening-up camp', 'just eating, sleeping and swimming in the Caspian Sea'.[14] Likewise, little clouds Nana's memory of this place. What was oppressive in central Asia was celebrated in Persia: 'The sun was shining and the nights were hot and starry.'

The Poles had arrived into a complicated political situation. Military supplies for the Soviet Union passed through the country and in late 1942 the Allies still feared that the Germans might break through the Caucasus, transforming Persia into the front line. Persia had become 'one of the most important highways in the world' and, potentially, one of the most vulnerable.[15] Allied cooperation in Persia was textured by long-standing Anglo–Russian rivalry in the region. Since the nineteenth century the British had endeavoured to contain Russian influence owing to the threat it posed to the security of Britain's Indian Empire. Consequently, diplomatic engagement with Persia had long played a role in British foreign policy, though by the early twentieth century tensions had eased, with Britain and Russia accepting each had spheres of influence in Persia, respectively in the south and north. Early in the war the Shah effectively declared Persia a neutral power, refusing either to denounce Germany or to allow the Allies to use the railway system for the transportation of supplies to Russia. In response, in August 1941, Russia and Britain invaded Persia, occupying the country in line with their traditional spheres of influence: the Russians in the north, the British in the south. The following January the three countries signed a famous Tripartite Agreement. This established that the occupation was temporary, intended to last until six months after the end of the war, and in the meantime the occupying powers pledged to safeguard the Persian people and economy. A further declaration in December 1943 made the US government party to the same agreement. Having been under occupation, Persia became an ally and, inevitably, the site of a mini Cold War with the British and Americans on one side and the Soviets on the other.[16]

For the British, the 73,000 Polish military personnel who arrived in Pahlevi during the two major evacuations were relatively easily dealt with. They were sent to training camps in Iraq before an eventual transfer to Palestine, from where they were transported to Egypt to link up with the Allied Eighth Army. Anders' Army landed in Italy between December 1943 and March 1944, where it would play a prominent role in the campaign to liberate Western Europe from Nazism. By contrast, the 11,000 children who arrived in Pahlevi in April 1942 and the 25,000 civilians who arrived in August–September created a severe logistical problem. As strategic considerations meant the Poles could not stay in Persia, it was not immediately clear where they should go. Many of their difficulties were simply logistical. Where were the Poles to be housed, how would they be fed and clothed, and – importantly – who would pay for them? Initially, ad hoc arrangements, dependent on the grudging cooperation of the Persian government, had to suffice. But, as already mentioned, the Persian government became more cooperative when they began to see that not only was the provision of hygienic accommodation necessary if a dangerous epidemic was to be avoided but that the material and physical condition of the Poles acted to counter pro-Soviet propaganda. Five semi-permanent camps, four in and around Tehran and one at Isfahan, were quickly established. Two of the 'camps' were effectively orphanages.

The logistical problems created by the April arrivals were the subject of a series of letters written by Reader Bullard, British Ambassador to Persia 1939–45.[17] Many civilians, he wrote, divested of their lice-infested clothes, were transported to Tehran wrapped in nothing but the army blankets they were issued on arrival at Pahlevi. A group of English women,

led by Mrs Holman, the wife of the new Counsellor, with help from the
Red Cross, got to work with their sewing machines: 'In three days they
produced an incredible number of garments and sheets and pillow cases.'
Impressed by the physical condition and morale of the Poles, Bullard
wrote, 'They are a grand people in adversity, the Poles.' He thought the
troops 'hardy, like the Russians' and the children, though 'grey-faced and
neglected', had 'retained more energy and a greater interest in life than,
I feel, English children would do after living on next to nothing for two
years'. These admiring if patronising generalisations are intriguing for
how they contrast with Herling's observation that the Poles were less
likely to survive the Gulag than the people of the poorer Soviet republics.[18]
From the Soviet perspective the Poles were among the weak, but to the
Western European they appeared tough. That seems obvious enough,
but tough and weak are not straightforward categories. A person accustomed to hardship and demanding physical labour might be better placed
to stand the Gulag regime, but at the same time a life of privilege might
create healthier and stronger individuals more capable of withstanding
difficult times. A recurrent theme in Herling's *A World Apart* is the idea
that the physical basis of survival had a psychological dimension. To
survive meant the individual had to come to terms with the psychological strain of incarceration as well as develop a capacity to secure a steady
if meagre food supply. To reiterate a theme running through this book,
the consciousness among the deportees of the Polish people's history of
exile and oppression at the hands of the Russians was sustaining. This
martyr complex left them peculiarly well-equipped to make sense of exile
and great hardship.

Bullard confirmed Polish memories, reporting that many children died
soon after arriving, and he admitted that the medical facilities provided
by the British were poor. Under pressure from all sides, he hoped Russia
would not allow further civilians to leave, although he regretted 'that
few of those who do stay in Russia can expect to survive the hard conditions'. Earlier in his career Bullard had served in Leningrad and was
familiar with the basic functioning of the Soviet system, recognising that
the fate of the Poles would be determined by wartime priorities. The
needs of the individual, he believed, would be subordinated to the needs
of the state: 'The Soviet Army is well fed and well equipped, but the
necessities of life have to be distributed according to the importance of
the individual to the state in the present crisis.'

Two weeks later, Bullard struck a more optimistic note. The Poles were still living in overcrowded barracks and the supply of clothing was a problem, but the mortality rate was now falling significantly. 'Where the malady is malnutrition,' he wrote, 'it is astonishing how quickly an apparently dying child will recover if given a little orange juice and cod liver oil.'

The April arrivals, those first 11,000 Poles to disembark in Pahlevi, had left Persia before the second evacuation arrived. They were despatched by the British to camps in British East Africa and Palestine. Despite the best of intentions, conditions in those camps could be very primitive. In a remarkable 1944 survey outlining the enormous humanitarian problem 'displaced persons' would pose the Allies as Europe was liberated, Bertha Bracey described the conditions in which 4,000 Polish children had lived in Palestine. She wrote of 'hundreds of little boys . . . encamped under canvas under sand dunes' initially clothed in what the British army could supply: 'Youngsters of five or six were almost buried under army topees, while army shorts flapped around their thin legs.' In one hospital small boys spent the winter of 1942–3 'almost naked'; elsewhere, 400 boys lived a 'Spartan' life in a monastery. Months after arrival the absence of tables and chairs meant they still ate their food – half an army ration – standing up; 150 particularly unfortunate children had faced three months' isolation when they came down with a highly infectious eye disease.[19]

The second wave of Poles, two-thirds of whom were adults, proved less pliable. True, Pahlevi itself was decisively cleared of Poles by 16 October 1942 but that was the most decisive the process got. Most were transferred to camps near Tehran, where a continual but halting cycle of arrival and departure could be observed. As options for their removal were explored, a seemingly interminable process of enquiry and negotiation commenced. Among the possible destinations for the Poles were British East Africa, including Northern and Southern Rhodesia, India, the United States and Mexico. In most cases the Poles were a burden and to accept them was an act of charity, though the Mexican government was actively interested in recruiting people with agricultural expertise who could help develop the Mexican economy. Time and again, agreement seemed at hand, only for departures to be delayed by Polish objections or the impossibility of providing safe transit.

Diplomatic relations became a little fraught on occasion. When, in the autumn, agreement was almost reached concerning the transfer of some 500 refugees to Mexico via San Francisco, the US authorities began to question how the British proposed to finance the US stage of this journey. If the refugees departed from Persia, which was not British territory, the US government would cover the costs, but if the departure point was India – in this case Karachi – which was British territory, the US insisted Britain meet the costs. The Foreign Office, cabling Washington, insisted the Poles in British territory were in transit and not residents. Further complications arose when the US communicated the very stringent medical requirements it expected to be met prior to boarding. Eventually the US Congress agreed to use the President's emergency funds to finance the transfer to Mexico of up to 10,000 Poles, though in the event the Polish government approved the transfer of only 4,000. Things did not go smoothly. Minor diplomatic controversy followed when 'twenty rich Poles, wearing furs and jewels' arrived in San Francisco. Probably thanks to a bribe, they had got on board the ship sailing from Bombay. Rather than accepting their designated places in the Guanijuato agricultural settlement reserved for the Poles in Mexico, they had their US-Polish friends lobby for them either to be permitted to live and work in Mexico City or be granted domicile in the US. The US feared that its immigration officials might be susceptible to corruption (which provoked acid British comment) and though the British attributed the problem to those who allowed them on board the US ship in the first place, they recognised that procedures at the Indian end had put the whole scheme in jeopardy.[20]

Diplomatic embarrassment and transportation obstacles aside, further difficulties lay with the Poles themselves, whose government representatives retained considerable agency in the process. Though the British were infuriated by the difficulties caused by the spread of what they judged to be disinformation, including negative reports about the camps in India, they recognised that the Poles had certain rights as allies. The Polish government, credited by the British Treasury, was financially responsible for the refugees and, in theory at least, determined to spend the money as they saw fit. Ensuring the decent treatment of the refugees was an exercise in Polish national sovereignty. The British recognised this and so were reluctant to move Poles against their will: without approval from the Polish government such movements would be tantamount to coercion, and might even be seen as equivalent to the original deportations. Moreover, though supervised by the British, who retained ultimate control, the camps themselves were organised by Polish officials, who were constituted as agents and employees of the Polish government.

Whatever autonomy the camps had and however adept the refugees became at dealing with their local officials, ultimately inmates had little control over their individual destinies. Superior class standing or having an army officer as a relative was widely perceived to be an advantage, conferring a higher status on some inmates. Despite this, the extent to which the camps replicated the social divisions of pre-war Polish society was not as absolute as might be supposed. Habits of deference, already weakened by the experience of Soviet occupation, had been further weakened by life on the *kolkhoz*. Deportation was a levelling experience and while some families might initially have had superior possessions, once in the *kolkhoz* wealth or education secured few advantages and could prove disadvantageous – such as when Polish 'Lords' were given particularly difficult work details. When persons of high social status were subjected to hard work, suffering physical and, possibly, mental deterioration, this undermined their capacity to maintain their original social standing. With the status of middle-class Poles undermined in the Soviet Union, lower-class Poles were less willing to accept a subordinate position, particularly if it meant disadvantage in the camp.

Hanna was among the many who resented this. She and other officers' wives had a strong sense of their rightful place in Polish society and felt they were not accorded sufficient respect by the other women. Once the natural leaders of Polish society, they risked becoming marginalised if they were not willing to speak up. Rightly or wrongly, some felt their good manners and civility left them little able to assert themselves against noisier, pushier women who were once their social inferiors. These other women, Nana suggests, having survived Russia, were empowered by their experiences and began to take charge. Tension increased when among these women a 'Red' contingent emerged.

Throughout the war the army was the most powerful 'national' Polish institution and these insecure and anxious refugee families were determined to stay in Persia while the military was stationed in neighbouring Iraq and in Palestine. So determined were some Polish women to get to the Polish army bases that they illegally crossed the Iraqi and Palestinian frontiers, sometimes disguised as soldiers. Having made long journeys across the Soviet Union, often without official papers or money, and surviving the most hostile conditions, these women were often unperturbed by the obstacles placed in their way. Nor did they necessarily treat the British authorities more respectfully than they did the Russian. According to a British report these obsessive attempts to join the army were driven by 'a kind of mania' and it is not difficult to feel some sympathy for the British soldiers who had to deal with these determined women.[21]

A more effective way to ensure a longer stay in Persia was to become indispensable to the camps. As these became sophisticated social organisms, with complex bureaucratic, medical and educational infrastructures, skilled middle-class women were employed by the camp authorities and were thus less likely to be transferred than their compatriots. Much jockeying for position within the camps ensued and in time the camps became institutionally dependent on educated and articulate women who made themselves indispensable to their functioning. The British anticipated this, fearing the camps would take on an institutional life of their own, ceasing to be the temporary arrangements originally intended. And it is possible to observe a tendency for talent to gather in particular places: new arrivals could be moved on quite quickly, while more established residents clung to their positions. Later, when most of the Poles had been moved out of Persia, British reports suggest that those who remained behind were proportionately overprovided for; this threatened political embarrassment. Somewhat in vain, the British issued a directive insisting that a) all refugees receive equal treatment and b) the material circumstances of camp employees should not be too obviously superior to that of the local population.[22]

Despite the ways in which class generated differential treatment among Poles, their overall status as European allies placed them in a privileged position. Perceived to be of broadly middle-class background and the victims of Soviet ideology, socio-ethnic assumptions were invoked when considering the appropriateness of the facilities provided. Colonial administrators noted the importance of providing facilities that were appropriate for white Europeans, particularly where protection from disease and exposure to the elements were concerned. There were certain conditions that white Europeans simply couldn't be expected to tolerate and such assumptions worked to the advantage of the Poles.

An important breakthrough came in October 1942 when the government of India agreed that the Maharajas of Jamnagar and Patiala might, respectively, accept 2,000 and 3,000 children.[23] Jamnagar is located in Gujarat, not far from the modern Pakistan border, Patiala is in Punjab, north of Delhi. Reports suggested it would take three months to construct the camps and railway congestion meant only 500 children could be accepted at a time. An undated report by Major Clarke describes the preparation of the Jamnagar camp.[24] It was quite a task. The site at

Balachadi, adjacent to the Maharaja's own seaside resort, was seven-teen miles from Jamnagar and the nearest railway station, meaning all supplies, materials and labour had to be transported by road. The ground itself had to be cleared, the telephone system extended to the locality, machinery to ensure an adequate water supply installed, and contracts drawn up between local merchants and the camp authorities – these children had to be fed. All this was to be carried out by the state, which would also provide a doctor.

The first batch of 260 boys and girls, accompanied by twenty adults, duly arrived and were settled in under the supervision of Madame Banasińska, the wife of the Polish Consul-General in India. A second batch of children, numbering some 450, was held up at Quetta owing to the heavy floods immobilising the railway, but they soon made it through. The camp had a thirty-bed hospital and a dispensary. All who needed it received medical attention, including dental treatment and operations to remove the appendix and tonsils, and, by the time Clarke wrote the report, they were enjoying a wholesome diet and most were thriving. For the seriously ill, a separate medical block for their exclusive use was built adjacent to Irwin Hospital in Jamnagar. The children were well provided for. The Maharaja granted access to his gardens, tennis courts and swimming pool. He made a further building available for their schooling and a chapel was built. The commandant of the camp was a Polish army chaplain; following the evacuation from the Soviet Union no sizeable group of Polish refugees was ever without a chaplain. Everything suggests His Highness the Maharaja Jamsaheb Digvijaysinhiji did everything he could to make his guests comfortable. 'Do not consider yourselves orphans,' he said as he welcomed them to the camp. 'You are now Nawanagaris and I am Bapu, father of all Nawanagaris, including you.'[25] When Warsaw was rebuilt at the end of the war, Clarke was told by a representative of the Polish government-in-exile that a street would be named after the Maharaja.

For all the optimism of this report, with its powerful sense of a job well done, Balachadi remained under capacity. This would be a constant problem throughout the system of camps. Facilities were established and then would stand empty or half-empty for months as obstacles delayed departures of the Poles from the transit camps. A particular problem in the case of India was an agreement made with the Soviets to take the 5,000 Polish orphans in a separate evacuation arrangement. Following the negative propaganda prompted by the Caspian evacuations, the Soviets reneged on this and the 5,000 stayed put, facing a bleak future. In January 1943, the Indian government agreed to fill their quota by taking 5,000 women and children in their place. While preparations were made, they would be accommodated in barracks in Karachi, before being transferred to a specially built camp near Kolhapur in the southern Maharashtra in April.[26] Over the following year or so, thousands of Poles sailed from the Persian port of Ahvaz – where some lived in stables – to the transit camps at Karachi.[27]

Further bulletins arriving from Delhi at the Foreign Office in February 1943 testified to the complexity of the operation in hand.[28] Delhi reported that it had enhanced capacity at Karachi from 3,000 to 8,000 and advised that shipping facilities from Ahvaz in March would be good, so Tehran should prepare by moving to the Persian port as many Poles as possible. They planned on the refugees being shipped to Karachi, then on to Bombay, before travelling by train south to Kolhapur. An advance party was required to make preparations in the camp and, as the following list reveals, little had been left to chance. This was to be a properly run self-sufficient community:

1 camp superintendent

1 amenities officer

1 quartermaster

1 account officer

1 police officer

1 assistant police officer

23 (half of a total of 46) civilian police

2 clerks

1 chief physician

2 other medical officers (experience in malaria desirable)

2 dentists

2 security officers to organise a security service

1 matron

9 (half of a total of 18) qualified nurses

15 (half of a total of 30) probationer nurses

7 (half of a total of 14) hygienists for sanitary duties

4 (half of a total 8) compounders

India would brook no argument. They were looking to create a semi-permanent solution to the refugee problem, which would hold at least until the end of the war, and this had to be done properly. In an equally revealing report India instructed that children 'be sent in organised units with their own staff of doctors, hospital nurses, teachers and adult guardians, on a scale of two doctors, six nurses, forty teachers and fifty adult guardians per 1,000 children'.[29] It was clear that putting together such a team of experts, primarily drawn from the Polish community itself, would place great strain on the infrastructures of the transit camps, but India left Whitehall in no doubt as to the nature of their commitment. They could provide space, accommodation and access to local markets, but otherwise they were not in a position to organise or manage the day-to-day activity of the communities they stood to create. Most indicative of this overbearing attitude was the stipulation imposed by the Indian government that all the 8,000 Poles expected imminently at Karachi were to come with visas for Africa. The Indian government evidently intended to cream off the 5,000 that were to their liking and send the rest on.

A Foreign Office communication with Polish Ambassador Raczyński summarised the situation as of May 1943: 11,500 Poles had arrived in Uganda, Tanganyika and Northern Rhodesia; 1,000 had arrived in Southern Rhodesia; a further 3,500 could arrive immediately and 6,000 more places would be created by August once arrangements had been made to ensure good food supplies, bringing the planned total in Africa to 22,000. Despite newly cleared diplomatic ground, the departure of the 4,000 Poles allocated to Mexico was delayed by difficulties in arranging their transportation.[30] In June, Cairo reported that 15,000 Poles were still in Persia and 4,000 were awaiting transfer at Karachi.[31] Progress had been made by September: 3,000 Poles were now in Kolhapur in India, living in good facilities built to house families, and many of the newly available African places had been filled. Cairo, reporting that numbers in Karachi were now down to 750, were keen they were replenished.[32] Their strategic priorities had not changed. The more Poles there were in Karachi the fewer there were in Persia.

Hanna, Wanda and Danusia spent a year in Tehran, arriving in September 1942 before being shipped first to Ahvaz and then to Karachi in late 1943. The attempt to reconstruct their story is made significantly easier at this point owing to the survival of long sequences of their letters beginning in September 1942. Nana's impressionistic memories, the accounts of others and official documentation remain essential sources of information but their hand-written words enormously enrich our capacity to make sense of the Ryżewski's family experience. Distanced by time and place, the meaning of every detail and nuance of these letters cannot be fully understood. This is exacerbated by the fact that many of Rafał's letters are missing, making a one-sided epistolary conversation, which creates gaps in my understanding of his perceptions and feelings. This is the case, for instance, when attempting to contextualise Hanna's apparent hope that through family connections they might secure a right to emigrate to the United States. Similarly, without Rafał's replies it is difficult to guess to what extent he was able to determine the family's prospects from afar, though Hanna certainly believed he could. The letters instead give us a powerful sense of who these people were, of their characters and their hopes, fears and preoccupations. Despite the vast difference in life experience between the deported girls and the elderly women I know today, the timbre, tone and personality of their written words are uncannily familiar. It is a rare privilege to read the teenage letters of one's grandmother and great-aunt; it seems more remarkable still for a thirty-something to find two familiar spirits in the translated typescripts of a bundle of dusty letters written sixty years ago.

Hanna's epistolary voice is first heard when she writes to Rafał on 12 and 22 September 1942. Together with the girls she had just arrived from Pahlevi in Camp 3, Tehran. Their journey was fine – 'we have arrived without incident' – though when the possibility later arose that Rafał might visit them on leave, Hanna wrote of the treacherous roads and the dangerous driving. Flash images of hairpin bends, precipitous drops and crazy Persian driving pepper all accounts of these trips south, with temperament determining the degree to which they were experienced as frightening or exhilarating. As common, however, are memories of the beauty of the journey through the 'majestic' Elburz mountain range. General Anders later wrote of the journey from Pahlevi to Tehran along the 'most beautiful road I have ever seen':

> At first it ran not far from the shore of the Caspian Sea, with wide tilled fields on either side, but then it gradually climbed, passing through mountain gorges and dense forests, from which it emerged high in the mountains, to wind at a great height along the edge of a precipice, diving, at one place, into a tunnel driven through the rock. The road was open to traffic for only five months of the year: snow-drifts, avalanches and flooded mountain streams made it impassable the rest.[33]

Other journeys were not quite so meditative, as this description from the Milewski family memoir demonstrates:

> The serpentine road was very narrow and in some places the trucks had to make several attempts in order to negotiate the road's sharp bends. As we gazed into the chasm below we prayed that the truck would not fall off the mountain. The view, however, was magnificent and we could see picturesque Persian villages surrounded by date and olive trees in the valleys below us.[34]

'I will never forget that trip,' wrote Janina Żebrowski-Bulmahn.

> The narrow road that led through the Elburz canyon seemed so huge that it made me dizzy looking down. Our drivers, however, did not slow down but negotiated the turns and twists in the road at great speed. Many times we held our breath, thinking that any moment we would either be hit by the truck behind us or, with the driver unable to control the vehicle, plunge to the bottom. We did a lot of praying that the trucks would not veer off the road.[35]

According to one testimony, two trucks 'heavily laden with people' rolled off the road into the valley, though it is unclear whether there were serious casualties.[36]

As Hanna's voice becomes more familiar through her letters, it is easy to imagine her among the prayerful; her younger daughter, however, remembers the thrill of that journey.

Hanna's initial impressions of the four Polish camps just outside Tehran – their 'tent city' in Nana's words – were upbeat. Soon settled into tent 66, they found it was 'pretty enough' and the food, though monotonous, was a little better than what they had grown used to at Pahlevi. 'Communal' living she found fine and the tents themselves were an improvement, with no leakage from rainfall. 'We are living in American tents which are big enough for 60 people; only the fleas make it hard to sleep but, because there is a little time, we are hunting them.' Unpleasant though this occupation was, fleas were a distinct improvement on the lice they cohabited with in the Soviet Union. Characteristically, Nana remembers the tents as pitched 'among orchards of eastern fruit and shimmering brooks'. They were kitted out with standard military-issue facilities: the bathrooms had showers and there were well-equipped laundries with irons and washbasins. 'It's alright if you're healthy,' Hanna commented, a little grudgingly; evidently, they were comfortable enough.

A pass system allowed new pleasures like going into the city where most things could be bought at reasonable if increasing prices. After Russia, Tehran seemed a place of sensual delights, of colour, taste and scent, where lavish wealth shockingly coexisted with extreme poverty. In this city of gardens and groves, of rich men with their pretty women in Western dress, of bazaars selling rugs and engraved silver boxes, of magnificent mosques decorated with beautiful ceramic mosaics, few streets were without their beggars, the disabled, the unemployed and the destitute. Exotic though it was, for Poles, hailing from a land which becomes a giant fruit bowl in the summer and autumn, Persia felt familiar. Fresh fruit was supplied daily and soon returned the glow to sallow skin. [37]

For the Ryżewscy the only real material shortage, frequently alluded to in their letters, was of appropriate school books for the girls. The expectation that they might have something to read was another indicator of their changed circumstances. Quite how successfully Rafał made good their wants is unclear, but Polish books were now being printed in Palestine and the steady progress the girls began to make at school suggested he was successful enough. Among Hanna's requests were copies of patriotic songs for the girls.

Health matters, illness and concerns about the sick feature prominently in almost all of Hanna's letters. With life and limb secure, her greatest worry – and she was prone to anxiety – concerned when and where the family would be reunited and how, in the meantime, they might recover and retain their good health. Illness had become routine and the whole family could now be matter-of-fact about quite serious maladies. Both girls, for example, had malaria in May 1943 and Wanda spent time in the sanatorium. In June, Hanna reported Wanda's recovery, saying the X-rays had shown her lungs to be healthy. On arrival in Tehran both Hanna and Wanda were taken ill, Wanda suffering some kind of 'jaundice', Hanna losing her appetite and becoming 'very thin and shaky'. It could be a three-day wait for an appointment with the camp doctor, but they quickly recovered once more: Hanna now had an appetite for 'treats' and was 'even eating bread', while Wanda boasted 'she could eat a whole kilo of grapes', a boast again indicative of changed expectations. More generally, their appetites were good. 'We love the goulash, especially when it's with cabbage – then we eat it all.' The Poles were Polonising their food.

Not for the last time, Hanna reminded her husband of his physical vulnerabilities. On this occasion, he was told to be careful of his liver (a reference to drinking?), 'because it can be a pesky thing in its consequences', another time he was instructed to 'wrap up well'. In other letters she voiced her fear he would aggravate his asthma or risk the return of his malaria: 'You men sometimes trivialise everything and lose your health' (24 March 1943). Rafał can't have been too displeased at Hanna's suggestion (21 August 1943) that 'beer is very good for malaria, so you can use it as medicine'. In a repeated refrain she reminded him of the significance of his good health: 'Your health, Darling, is *the health of our children* and my own'; 'your health is our health'. On occasion, Rafał would remind her of the same.

Living in the camps meant the Poles were now much less isolated from each other. Friendships renewed or begun in the Polish camps in Soviet Asia were sustained, and Hanna's letters were peppered with news of the whereabouts and well-being of their acquaintances. If not quite a social whirl, their sense of living in a community was very strong. 'Of our friends,' she wrote, 'Wickowska is here, Kizikowa in Camp 3, Hasowa in Camp 2, Szczerbicka in Camp 2, though I haven't seen her.' Linked to these reports were enquiries about certain of Rafał's fellow soldiers and Hanna wrote on behalf of friends and acquaintances convinced that as an officer he had access to information denied to others. Requests that Rafał investigate the whereabouts and health of this or that soldier who had lost contact with his family became a feature of her letters and the belief that she had access to such information accorded her some status among her fellow camp inmates.[38]

Hanna was conscious that her community, dominated by women in the prime of life, had certain charms, particularly for the soldier on leave or curious local men. In these first letters she reported that Pan Tarkowski, a member of Rafał's Company visiting the camp while on leave, was enjoying 'flirting with the girls', exclaiming, 'I tell you, Raf, it's like a harem here with so many women and children.' Slightly suggestively, she observed that 'the Persians often give the nicer ladies lifts from town in their limousines'.

Such gossipy moments were rare and Hanna's letters naturally reveal that her primary concern was for her daughters. With assistance from the British, the Red Cross and other agencies, the Poles ran schools and chapels in the camps – at one point the priest, speaking from the pulpit, denounced dances organised by some of the inmates. Hanna reported assiduously on the girls' progress, proudly reporting that Danusia, now twelve, was preparing for her First Communion, to be taken on 18 October, a 'sacred day'.

The children were filmed, shared a Communion breakfast, and had photographs taken. Danusia can be seen grinning right in the centre of one of the back rows. It is evident many of the children had been returned to sturdy good health and there is something at once understated and dramatic in Hanna's observation, 'I am pleased that it was here and not in "Paradise".' So many children had died in the Soviet Union, and continued to succumb to illness, that her younger daughter's first step towards adulthood carried more than the usual significance. The overriding importance of her children's health is further revealed in another letter (24 October). Hanna observes, 'I presently feel entirely healthy, and the children too (only there are isolated cases here of scarlatina and diphtheria). Iza, the Pietoniowie's daughter, died of scarlatina – a shame, for she was her parents' only child.' It's a grim summary, particularly in its contrast between their good health and her relativist appraisal of the loss. If not quite heartless, Hanna's reserves of empathy had been depleted by her struggle to keep herself and her daughters alive and well. If they were OK, all was OK.

Iza's fate reminds us that the colour which returned to their cheeks might at any moment begin to drain away. They continued to live in a context of high mortality, with the risk of contracting a potentially fatal illness ever present. They also lived among people who had suffered many such losses, of mothers stricken by the grief of child after child dying or those who did not know the fate or whereabouts of their offspring. Some searched the orphanages again and again, firing off desperate letters, clinging to the possibility attached to the last known address; they lodged missing person pleas with the massively overburdened Red Cross; they hoped a child given up in Russia to an institution might appear among the latest arrivals. Maddened by their pain they seized on children in the orphanages, claiming them as their own, becoming enraged when met with the child's denials. Troubled transactions were sometimes proposed. One woman remembers a rich woman who had lost a daughter offering to take her off her mother's hands, promising the child a fine life, in the hope the adoption might comfort her husband. The exhausted mother seemed ready to let her go but the girl refused. 'Stop crying,' her mother eventually sighed, 'no one is sending you if you don't want to go.'[39]

As the girls grew older, Hanna noted how they developed as they passed the '"idyllic" times' of childhood. Adolescence had yet to leave a clear mark on Danusia, but at fifteen years of age Wanda was suddenly showing all the outward signs of coming adulthood. She was 'quite the young woman' (8 January 1943) and had 'grown so you probably wouldn't recognise her; she is almost a young lady and in three years will be the same age I was when I married' (24 March 1943); at the end of the year she had grown still more 'and is a pretty girl' (24 November 1943). Photographs attest to this. Wanda had become a prettily blonde teenage girl, with fine features, strong cheekbones, and a slightly stern look. Through malnutrition and repeated illness, she and Danusia proved resilient. Hanna's more general impressions of her daughters' developing characters implied strong contrasts between them. Wanda, as will be evident in her letters, was thriving in the camps. In particular, she was an enthusiastic Scout and enjoyed the order of organised activities. She also took on many of her mother's concerns, echoing her mother's words in her own letters to her father. Hanna's letters, however, do not provide a very strong sense of Wanda's personality and focus mainly on her achievements at school and blooming womanhood.

It was quite the opposite with Danusia. In scattered remarks she comes across as charismatic and charming, the carefree and self-centred younger sibling free of the watchfulness of her older sister, who was always a little confined by her exaggerated sense of maturity and proximity to the adult world. In describing their New Year's Eve celebrations Hanna pictures Danusia as charting 'a course amongst us, telling . . . stories' (3 January 1943); at school Danusia 'constantly falls behind and then (abruptly) jumps ahead and is always promising she won't skip'; she 'is probably just like you for she is constantly busy' (24 March 1943); she remained 'the same rascal as in Jakkobad, she attends third grade and is a good student though she is such a chatterbox' (2 April 1943); she was 'as chatty as she ever was' (15 May 1943); and 'apart from her school life her time is filled with cavorting' (14 June 1943): in sum, 'Danusia is always a little whirlwind and is well; she goes to Scout meetings, takes part in their parties, and never has any time' (30 June 1943).

As had been the case in Russia, customs were closely observed, rituals helping to sustain their affinities for home, family and Polishness. On Rafał's saint's day he received rapturous letters from his adoring wife and daughters, while just after Christmas long letters described their celebrations under canvas. As in Kazakhstan, they laid the table in the traditional way, with straw cushioning the tablecloth and *opłatek* broken and shared. A substantial meal was prepared, including borscht and potatoes, fried pierogi, fish and compote, all washed down with wine. 'In general the mood was cheerful enough,' Hanna reported, 'our only lack was you among us.'

This lament, repeated throughout Hanna's letters and particularly emphasised when describing moments of celebration, reflected a deeper malaise that she struggled hard to keep in check. In September, at the beginning of their time in Tehran, she described how they lived 'in a state of tension'. In January, though insisting her health was fine, she admitted that 'from time to time something ails me in my heart', and though she felt 'sure this silliness will come to nothing' her concern surfaces periodically in later letters. In particular, she had learnt enough through her experiences to know that physical ailments could be symptomatic of a fragile psychological state. On one occasion she felt 'cursed, that is, engulfed by a typical funk'; on another she explained that 'it is not good to miss you too much, because it has an effect on the health and may cause undesired illness' (20 February 1943). Most revealing was her *cri de coeur* in June: 'I would very much like to see you, for I really do miss you and feel strange psychologically – everything upsets and enrages me, I don't know why, but it is nothing serious.'

Mood swings and irrational anger suggest Hanna was suffering from depression and when stressed she admitted finding it difficult to order her thoughts on the page. Part of the problem was that Rafał did not write often enough, a serial complaint in her letters, though because his letters from this period have not survived it is impossible to know whether her grievance was legitimate or, indeed, to adjudicate on what was enough. Nonetheless, Hanna was evidently distressed by what she perceived to be long silences – 'the lack of word from you unsettles us very much' – and she resented feeling that other wives received more frequent letters. Moreover, she confessed, going to the post room was humiliating when there was nothing to collect and she asked that he always write to tell her in advance when he was sending a parcel so she could avoid speculative visits. When her resentment occasionally crept into letters it was evident that a lot of it stemmed from her basic dependency on parcels and money from him. Having always worked in the past, she hated having to rely on handouts and was conscious of all the time wasted to inactivity. When a long letter from Rafał did arrive, such as that received in March 1943, it had an immediately soothing effect, announcing a period of 'calm' and eliciting from Hanna a more reflective and less breathless response.

Nonetheless, Hanna's considerable psychological resources kept her on track and Nana remembers her mother as formidably determined. Like her husband, her mood was lifted by spring and she wrote in May how, 'With us, the brooks flow and there is so much greenery and so many scents of spring that we sit with pleasure by the bushes in the camp recalling our old acquaintances' (14 May 1943).

Hanna's agitated frame of mind and her occasional vehemence were

not without good cause. Her deep anxiety stemmed from the profound
uncertainty under which she was living and the lack of control she had
over any part of her future. Feelings of stability and calm could only ever
be fleeting, as was the sense of reprieve which followed any postponement
of their inevitable onward journey. Their existential state was one of fundamental uncertainty, so while that 'state of tension' varied in its intensity,
they always lived 'full of nerves' (20 February 1943). Rumour and counter-
rumour preyed on all and in the evenings when the women gathered
together their hushed discussions inevitably turned to a consideration of
their possible options, assessing the veracity of hearsay, repeatedly going
over the pros and cons of one destination or another. At the outset they
lived 'under the shadow of Africa', which for unknown reasons Hanna
immediately took against. An early crisis was triggered when they thought
they would be forced on to an African transport leaving on 5 November.
Hanna was convinced that if she could prove Rafał was due to visit on
leave they would be allowed to stay and she implored him to send a telegram
announcing his pending arrival. Wanda picked up on this panicky mood
– and Hanna's panacea – and pleaded with her father:

> Therefore, Daddy, if you want to find us please hurry to get here by the
> fifth because many people come here and find no one left. If Daddy gets
> here soon then maybe he can keep us here but any later and definitely
> not. Because everyone will be forced to leave. Those for whom husbands
> are coming are kept here. They do not look at letters where someone
> writes that he will come shortly because everyone is doing that and the
> whole camp would stay here that way. And now they've decided they won't
> pay any attention and will force us and there's an end to it! Please, Daddy,
> we ask you to get here as quickly as possible because otherwise we shall
> perhaps not see each other before we are in Poland again.

Wanda was always – and touchingly – her mother's ally and this letter
was more frankly revealing of their anxiety and the atmosphere in the
camp than those written by Hanna. In the event, the transport was delayed,
the crisis passed, the women went back to waiting and speculating. 'Every
day brings changes,' Hanna wrote, 'first a journey, then a postponement . . .
Will we hang on? I don't know.' During the fifteen months spent in the
camp it seemed possible they would be sent to Africa, India, the United
States, Canada, Mexico and Argentina, but as long as the men were still
stationed in the Middle East, Hanna was determined they would not leave.

Hard lobbying, she was convinced, could prevent their being sent away and in various letters she describes her approaches to officialdom, sometimes a little reproachfully – a reminder to her husband that she was doing her bit. These encounters saw her face the genial goodwill of senior figures and the hard-faced attitudes of lower officialdom. One period saw her approach the Chief of Staff, the Base Commander, the Office for Military Families, the Polish Consul, the Central Registrar for the Delegation, a camp assistant, 'and so on'. Of these 'bigger and smaller fishes', she wrote, 'the bigger the fish the more pleasant' and 'the local fish . . . the toughest'. At times like this she felt Rafał's absence acutely, convinced that as 'a woman on her own' she was 'just a face in the crowd', unable to get a fair hearing. Other women, however, had learnt to be forceful operators: 'Those who have "snout" and backing are alright but the rest are just a crowd.' As Hanna became more reconciled to the fact that they might find themselves in a situation with no choice regarding their destination, she began to settle on the idea of Mexico, though her letters give no indication why. It's probable the Poles were enthused by the personal interest Sikorski took in the Mexican option, which included his visit to the country in December 1942. Africa, certainly, she did not like the sound of and we have already noted that the Poles' initial impressions of the Indian options were negative.

Solace was found in God and Hanna professed a strong belief in the power of prayer. Her religious faith was integral to her conviction that the family would one day be reunited and return to Poland. She described how her daughters 'ask God to guide you to Poland and allow us to be happy again once more'. The notion that God might 'allow' their return signifies more than her adherence to commonplace beliefs about the existence and power of God's will. Their trials and tribulations, combined with their lack of agency, had given conventional expressions of piety about godly intervention new meaning.

Hanna's dreams sometimes had a visionary quality and the most remarkable from her time in Tehran is described in her New Year letter to Rafał. It is an astonishing amalgam of religious, cultural and national symbolism, a paradigmatic expression of a particular kind of Polishness; it was also touchingly particular, evidence of how deeply she had internalised the idea that her family's fate and the fate of the Polish nation had become one. It should be quoted in full, just as she wrote it herself:

Now I'm going to describe to you a remarkable dream I had on the night of the 3rd/4th January – I dreamt that we girls gathered together, the clouds ringing with the sound of falling rain and storms from all sides, and from inside opened an oval star and we – that is, the children and I and others – watched and began to count the arms of the star. When there were 17 an altar was made from this with stained-glass pictures of the saints and angels and suddenly around us appeared some male figure in a dark suit and hat with beautiful, noble features. We watched, asking secretly 'Who is that?' and the figure took up an enormous brown cross on the altar, saying to us: this is the symbol of faith, and then the figure took the form of Christ and took up his place on the cross again, saying this is the sign of suffering, and he covered the altar with a shroud. The figure moved to the older children, asking: you surely know me? And he kissed them on the head and the children stood and with awe and wonder said it is Adam Mickiewicz and when he returned to Danusia she took him by the hand on which there was a large rectangular ring with some pictures I could not see on and he said it is the sign of the Polish Scouting move-ment. To me this figure said, madam, you feel bad here; you must live for these children's tomorrow, and tomorrow will come, it must come. And at this I awoke and it was the break of day.

The apocalyptic weather and the oval star that opens to reveal an altar immediately evoke Catholic devotional painting, echoing any number of altar pictures of Christ bathed in celestial light. Does their guide, a beau-tiful man and an awe-inspiring patriarchal figure, dressed in a dark hat and suit, carry a sexual charge? Crude Freudian analyses notwithstanding, is this the dream of a woman long starved of her husband's company? He carries the Cross (Simon from Cyrene?) and then becomes Christ Himself, and in 'again' taking up his place on the Cross are we to think that Hanna had dreamt of Him initially descending from the Cross, the resurrection occurring before her eyes? For Christ to be transformed into Mickiewicz, the great poet of the Commonwealth ideal and symbol of the Polish nation, was extraordinarily audacious – even by the standards of the subconscious. Christ is Mickiewicz, Poland the martyr nation, and Christ-Mickiewicz blesses the children in turn, kissing their heads. It seems significant that it is the children, in their innocence, who are able to recognise him and as Danusia guilelessly takes Mickiewicz by the hand, is she claiming what is rightfully hers or does she merely wish to look at the ring, always transfixed by shiny things? Though the blessing bestowed on the Scouting movement seems a parochial touch, much devotional art connected the transcendent with the local and particular. Finally, Hanna received her instruction, which, as we have seen, echoed like a mantra through her letters. 'You see, Tatuś,' she wrote, 'I describe for you many beautiful dreams.'

Wanda's letters – and she wrote regularly – shared many of her mother's concerns. They often began formulaically and formally, aping adult concerns and language, asking after her father's health, hoping that 'malaria and other diseases are not bothering you', and reporting on her well-being. But the formulaic language could collapse, allowing less inhibited concerns to break through. On one occasion she mentioned that 'Mummy is constantly worried about you and thinks you are ill or that the malaria has returned'. No doubt this was true, but it was also an expression of her own anxiety for she went on say, 'I ask you one thing, Daddy, which is to please not drink anything cold as it brings on the malaria.' Her father may well have smiled at this request. Sometimes she sent greetings to his fellow soldiers, name-checking Major Cader and others, all further gauche indicators of her understanding of the concerns and niceties of adult life. Thereafter, she would turn to her educational achievements, charting her progress and prospects. Throughout the year the main question concerned at what point she would take the examinations necessary to progress to the Gymnasium.

Her mother worried that Wanda had missed so much school that she would never properly catch up. Wanda was more optimistic, keen to emphasise that though she was working steadily towards this important goal it would be unwise to attempt the examination too soon. She was unsympathetic towards those who got ahead of themselves and then struggled to make the grade: 'Some girls are taking the exam . . . but it isn't going very well and everyone laughs at them.' She had made progress with her English lessons, seemed to get through maths without too much difficulty, despite the amount of fuss everyone made about the subject, and particularly enjoyed Polish and history, which was taught by a very impressive teacher. In April 1943 she boasted that she had 'executed' the best sketch of a map of America of her class, though, as she explained to Rafał, she had 'wanted to do it as you used to sketch, but it didn't quite work out'. At the same time they had been learning about Marshal Piłsudski and she had been tested by Inspector Pialuch on her knowledge of the partition of Poland: 'As I know this the best, it went well.'

Most touching, however, were her often fulsome expressions of love for her father. Sometimes she might simply sign off 'bye for now' (*pozatem pa*) but she was more likely to send innumerable kisses, writing, 'I kiss you very, very much' (or 'very, very, very much'). In signing off 'your daughter Wanda', she expressed more than merely love and attachment, but signalled her need to feel she was under his protection. She could also write movingly of how much she missed her father, occasionally letting her guard down. 'After having written in my last letter about our trips and gatherings with the Scouts I have often thought about how we used to go with you to Korzyść and see various things. I often have various whims, such as, for example, if you could be here with us or if we could go to you and we could go on some trips.' Her yearning that the family unit might be whole again is felt in every phrase of this tentative confession. If today Wanda remembers those weekends at Działka before the deluge as the best of times, this is continuous with her teenage self. Significant too was the slightly apologetic tone, that reference to 'whims' suggesting such sentiment had to be kept under wraps. Pining for the past, as Hanna understood, would not help them survive the present. Further poignancy is to be found in this teenage girl's growing awareness that those earlier times must always be in the past for a girl fast becoming a young woman.

The way to keep that past at bay was to be busy in the present and Wanda was devoted to the Scouts. 'I joined the Scouts, which is very good for me and I'm happy because I have many friends with whom I never quarrel because in the Scouts no one argues or quarrels.' Her troop was called 'Spring' and her division 'Future', and she loved the drill, the organised activities, the outings and Scouting's provision of clear goals, like developing the skills needed to win badges. Wanda now remembers herself as a solitary child who was not as socially at ease as her more carefree younger sister and it seems that the organised fun of Scouting gave her the social structures she needed to integrate. As a consequence, her descriptions of Scouting activities are a little zealous, driven by the enthusiasm of a child for a new best friend. As she put it herself, 'I like Scouting from the point of view of the discipline and obedience.' She expressed similar sentiments in her New Year letter, reporting that it was 'the Christmas holidays until the 7th so we are making the most of the time and horse around so we don't waste time during the term'. This rather self-righteous justification of having fun leaves open to question quite how much horsing around she really did. Was she, secretly, looking forward to the return of order the new school term brought or simply writing what she thought her father would want to hear?

Most striking was Wanda's struggle to express herself through writing and her developing sensitivity for the effects of language. Though little evident in her prose, constrained by its mimetic maturity, the effort and the effect was a little clearer in her poetry. Seven poems survive the year or so spent in Tehran. They are patriotic, Catholic and deeply sentimental. Inevitably, perhaps, they are highly derivative and tell us much about the patriotic schooling the Polish children received in the camps and through the Scouts. They are also very personal, revealing something of the concerns and attitudes of the teenage girl that wrote them. The first, a poem to her father on his saint's day, falls into this category:

> We wish Daddy happiness and endurance
> That God can lead you happily to freedom
> Today on your saint's day your children wish
> That you hurry back to your family home.
> Not wandering the world in these Eastern deserts
> But sitting in the Polish land and feeding the hungry
>
> So wishes on your saint's day your older daughter

This is straightforward enough with the penultimate line the most revealing, suggesting how the girl idealised her father's former role in Poland, a view consistent with wider Polish attitudes regarding the *kresy*. A later longer poem described how Polish soldiers fought for Poland far from Poland:

> Polish soldier, you go to the fight
> The bloody fight so far away
> Over sea, mountains and forest
> To build strong walls for Poland
> Strong walls of your own breast

In the poem Wanda refers to Poles on the Siberian steppe, on the need to 'defeat the German before the Polish gate', and her hope that soon it will be over:

Far from the Polish border
Far from Polish towns, villages and huts
You gave your life
You spilled your blood
You will not fight many more years
O, my soldier from these Polish huts.

And the comments that immediately follow these literary flights? 'Apart from this,' she prosaically signed off, 'I kiss you very much and ask for a letter.' In a later sequence, if that is not too grand a word, she achieved a more sophisticated melding of patriotic and religious ideas. The first, 'O, Mother', ran as follows:

I
O, Mother the fatherland has
Something to accuse you of
That you did not save me
From these terrible wanderings
II
Though I know for you yourself
Covered us with rivers of tears
When we left
And with tears bid your farewell
III
Please do not cry, Mother
I will return to you
And then I shall not leave
And die in the soil of the fatherland

After the striking opening couplet the meaning of this poem becomes a little confused. The metaphor of mother and fatherland contains its own logic, suggesting that through a return to one a return to the other might be effected: as the last stanza suggests, to go back to Poland was to be reunited with the bosom of the Catholic Church. There is little reason to suppose that this poem suggests Wanda's 'terrible wanderings' had brought on religious doubt – Mary had cried tears for the Poles – but only through return could spiritual wholeness be achieved.

The theme of return dominates the remaining poems in the sequence. 'The Underground Voice' laments that Poles are dying 'on the frozen

Siberian steppe', 'in dark prisons', 'from great hardship and work /
Pleading in great pain'. Much of this stemmed from first-hand experience – the exceptional cold, the heavy labour – all reinforced by what
she heard of the adult talk around her, particularly stories and anecdotes
of imprisonment. She pleads that the Virgin, '*niepojęta* Lady',[40]

> deliver our country from slavery
> Quickly not slowly
> For we die like flies

returning them to their 'pleasant fatherland', to 'sacred Poland'.

Ten-year-old Danusia's letters throw up few problems of interpretation.
They are rare, hastily scribbled and short, each reporting in a few brief
sentences a couple of basic news items. She wished her father wrote more
often; she missed him; at school year 3 is going better than year 2 had; the
days are hot, the nights cold; the tent is leaky but only in the middle, which
is not where they sleep; she has started to study geography and natural
history; they now have desks and no longer work on stones; she sends the
regards of various friends in the camp to Rafał and his various colleagues;
she is sorry that her writing is so untidy but she simply doesn't have time
to be tidy; but 'Daddy's daughter Danusia kisses his hands and embraces
him truly and kisses him very, very, very much'; indeed, 'Danusia your
youngest little daughter', 'sends hugs, very big, very, very big 100,000 times.
And for the whole battalion and the whole company.' So that's all right then.

Here is her Christmas letter of 1942. Short and sweet, it is the only
one which hints at her developing talent for observation, foretelling what
makes her later letters a charming, if – her father might have added –
occasional delight:

Darling Daddy,

We spent Christmas a little sadly because you were not here. We had
a communal Christmas tree with the whole tent. On the tree were angels,
winter flames, candles, nuts, sweets, fish in gold wrappers with angels on,
Italian apples and stars which I made. From the angel I received a diary
and stockings. Mummy bought me a doll which was Jesus in a nativity
scene, Wanda was a Cracovian in the nativity play.
Danuta for Daddy
2.1.1943

The angel was probably a little optimistic in giving her a diary,[41] but the list of decorations, the reference to the tree, the gold wrappers, the candle flames, the model nativity scene, and the nativity play, with girls like Wanda dressed in traditional costumes, comprise the detail, dutifully reeled off by a little girl needing something to write, which make these letters so precious. We know this occurred in a large army-issue tent in a Polish refugee camp outside Tehran in December 1942. We might be familiar with traditional Polish dress and the sound of Polish Christmas carols; we've probably seen or at some point, long ago, been in an old-fashioned nativity play, with its innkeeper, shepherds, kings and baby Jesus, the stage gradually filling as the final tableau is created. We know the special festive warmth generated by bodies crammed inside on a cold winter's night – and nights in Persia were cold, as the letters testify. To this scene, Danusia's list adds the play of light, bringing the glimmer of gold and the flicker of candle flame, the red shine and sweet smell of apple, an echo of glowing faces, with their heart-shaped Slavic cheekbones. But we can also sense – and how acutely this was felt – that the warmth of this gathering was only partial, that it was limited by the absence of fathers and husbands. And if on that winter's night a traveller did chance upon the scene, she or he would have found only women, children and a few old men, and might have wondered whether these people had suffered a ghastly catastrophe.

In early August 1943 Wanda and Danusia were at a Scout jamboree a short distance from the main camp. Word came that the Ryżewski girls had a visitor. Danusia knew all about this. She'd been expecting it, long expecting it. She scampered off, abandoning her post, breaking her Scout pledges. Her Tatuś had been granted leave. None of the shyness of his miraculous Uzbekistan appearance was felt this time. Together for just three glorious days, the highlight was a trip to Tehran and an enchanting visit to the extraordinary Golestan Palace complex, the Shah's official residence. The splendid Peacock Throne, now on display alongside the Iranian Crown jewels in the Central Bank of Tehran, etched itself on to Danusia's memory. With expectations running high, it was perhaps inevitable the day would end in tears. Rafał had booked a room for him and his wife in a Tehran hotel and arranged for the girls to be taken back to the camp. Surely, Danusia insisted, she could stay too. She was only small. She could curl up at the bottom of their bed. They'd never notice her. She'd be as quiet as a mouse. Her mother gently explained that there really wasn't room and she must go back with Wanda. The elder daughter, a little embarrassed, half comprehending, helped usher her tearful little sister out of the room. When applying for leave, Rafał said something to his senior officers about wanting another child. It wasn't to be. Hanna and the girls would not see Rafał again until 1947, over three years later. Those few magical days are memorialised in their most perfect family portrait.

Following the joy of the visit was the inevitable plunge in mood, not helped by another period of epistolary silence from Rafał: 'Rafku!' Hanna exclaimed, 'why did you not write from the road? I was so worried after your departure that I became a little ill.' When in Tehran, Rafał and Hanna had discussed the possibility of the family joining the army camp. Hanna clung to this hope, arguing that if Rafał were to send paperwork to this effect she might continue 'defending' their position with the authorities, though it is clear she was coming to accept that before long they would be put on a list for removal. In this same letter (30 August 1943) she suggests that the authorities were becoming irritated by her continual attempts to safeguard her family's position. A Tehran report for the Foreign Office around this time noted that, excepting 500 volunteers who had chosen Mexico, the 12,000 Poles remaining in Persia were all earmarked for East Africa.[42] In the meantime

the 'Brimfield' train (named after the code word for the second evacuation from the Soviet Union) began to make regular runs from Tehran
to the transit camp at Ahvaz, some ninety miles from the Persian Gulf
port of Khorramshahr, each time carrying 800 passengers.[43] Hanna could
not close her eyes to the fact that the Tehran camps were now being
liquidated. On 2 September she continued her letter, now more reconciled
to the inevitable move. 'You will always be in our thoughts wherever fate
sends us,' she wrote, 'and we ask God to allow us to meet again in our
free land . . . We kiss you a hundred times, always the same'. Ten days later
the next stage of their journey began:

> Most Darling Raf!
>
> Today we move on and I assume that they will not turn us back from
> the station. We feel completely well and healthy. We don't know how long
> we will be in Ahvaz. There is presently the possibility of Mexico, but we
> think we will choose Africa for the moment. I don't know for how long
> the correspondence between us will be broken . . .
>
> We kiss you a hundred times. See you in Poland.
>
> Your Hanka.
>
> PS I would prefer to be together with you and I would certainly enjoy the
> army, but I see that fate has left me among the civilians.

Nana's memory of the journey south, which she says for them was by
truck rather than train, suggests it was as exciting and as invigorating as
that which had taken them from Pahlevi. 'The convoy of military trucks
and fearless drivers took us on this mountainous adventure all the way
from Tehran to the Persian Gulf. It was a hairy but wonderful experience.
Winding serpentine roads, sheer cliffs on one side and bottomless ravines
on the other. Spectacular scenery, fantastic flowers and mountain springs
so cool and refreshing.'

Hanna was happy with their new location and on 12 October wrote
Rafał a more upbeat letter. Though it contained the usual uncertainties,
requests for letters and information about their health (poor Wanda was
sick again with malaria), Hanna had decided to accept whatever was
coming her way. With the Polish army moving on and following Rafał's
reassurances regarding Africa she was a lot less fearful: 'Recently I have
not crossed even my toes in my shoes.' Sustained by memories of Rafał's
recent visit, she closed on a happy note, a testament to one of her most
important camp friendships: 'Urszulka reminded me that it was good

when we were here together and I think so too and often recall the pomegranates hanging overhead. I kiss you, always.' A month later she reported that Wanda had finished her third malaria cure and was finally well and, with the scorching heat of summer easing, they were enjoying the warmth, happy to be going out in summer dresses.

Hanna's bright mood had other sources, too. Bertha Bracey, writing in 1944, recognised that one of the major problems in the refugee camps was the 'lack of occupation for these thousands of mainly peasant women'. 'Food, shelter and clothing do not provide the whole needs of human beings,' Bracey wrote, 'particularly when they are not constantly engaged in the winning and preparing of them.'[44] Hanna would have concurred, having experienced the demoralising effects of dependency and inactivity, her depression stemming in part from lethargy. Now, in Ahvaz, she had taken up teaching again and though not yet in a permanent job the work was doing her the world of good, renewing her sense of purpose. She liked earning her keep and being less dependent on handouts or money arriving from Rafał. It also allowed her less time to brood on their fate or bother the authorities.

Instead, she wrote of a new talent in the family: while in hospital Wanda had learnt to tell fortunes. Was it true, her daughter wanted to know, that near Daddy there were two men, one dark-haired and the other fair, writing letters? Finally, Hanna reported, Wanda had lost their copy of Sienkiewicz's *Fire and Sword*, part of the great Polish trilogy. Were these the same copies Rafał had read in 1940? Hanna was unsentimental about the books themselves and simply asked that Rafał send replacements.

On 29 November 1943 Hanna wrote that there was nothing further to be done. They were about to leave and for now they must remain apart: 'We miss you very much, Darling, but we keep our spirits up so that if our paths should not cross, the one thing we cannot renounce is that humour and loving devotion that is most Polish.'

The following day Danusia, getting under her mother's feet as they prepared to depart, was sent to write a letter. Her mother's voice almost can be imagined in the background, dictating details:

Dearest Daddy!!!

Mummy cannot write a letter because we have received notice of departure for Karachi, without any exceptions, whether someone works or not. All the teachers from our classroom are going. Wanda is also helping

Mummy pack so she also has no time. Therefore I am writing for Mummy
and Danusia. We depart on the first of the 12th, 1943. So if you want to
have contact with us please write to Karachi. Apart from this I send sincere
best wishes from Mummy, Wanda and Danusia. We all kiss you very very
much.

By the end of 1943, 23,788 men, women and children had been evacuated by ship from Ahvaz to Karachi. Among them were the Ryżewscy.
A British report from Tehran dated April 1944 recorded that only 8,200
Poles remained in Persia: 1,000 were at Ahvaz awaiting shipment, 2,300
were staff and residents at the children's colony in Isfahan, and the
remainder were either the sick and their relatives or camp employees.[45]

Almost all the Poles who passed through Persia left with an indelible
impression of the beauty of the country and the riches of its food and
culture. Few experienced anything quite like it ever again. And though
India would mark their memories more strongly, Persia was their place
of deliverance. Nana remembers a particularly joyful moment in the
camp at Tehran. One day a new supply of clothes arrived. Hanna and
the girls did pretty badly out of what was left but with a little imagination much could be made of little. That evening a young actress stepped
on to their makeshift stage. She was transformed by her new outfit into
an elegant cabaret artiste off the Warsaw boulevards. Her high-heeled
shoes were set off by a pair of long johns (a size too big), a sumptuous
boa and wide-brimmed straw hat. As she made her slinky way across the
stage she brought tears of laughter and joy to the gathered women and
children. 'Suddenly we didn't feel like we were in a displaced persons
camp, but felt as guests of the Shah of Persia entertained in his beautiful
garden.'

7

Karachi

Today, Karachi is a huge sprawling city, the Islamic Republic of Pakistan's largest and, after India's Mumbai, second-largest in the world. It has grown rapidly since India's partition in 1947, when its population was boosted by Muslims fleeing India for the Sind, and it now hosts in excess of 15 million people. A simmering mix of the rich and poor, cavernous social divisions are manifest in gated communities, slums and everything in between. According to Western governments, Karachi is now one of the world's most dangerous cities, a place where liberals and Islamists are locked in a political struggle to shape the ethos of the city, internation-alist ideologies overlapping with ethnic turf wars. It brims with life. Everything can be bought at the bazaar, at traffic lights the city's legendary transvestites collect money from tolerant motorists, beggars throng the Muslim shrines, motorbikes carry entire families (often with only the father wearing a helmet) and the famous buses, each a shining kitschy work of art dripping in silvery decoration, are packed to the gills, people spilling out, hanging on as they can, seemingly unconcerned that it is for dear life. As throughout the subcontinent, the cheapest resource is people. The affluent hire armed guards, keep servants and have drivers. Generators shield them from the frequent electricity cuts; air conditioning protects them from the sweltering heat. Arriving fresh and staying fresh takes substantial resource and effort: to live or not to live an air-conditioned life is one of the key markers of social status. There is no tourist trade to speak of and securing a visa can be tricky. At the embassy in London's Kensington, charming women in Islamic dress sell samosas and teasingly warn of how hot it's going to be. Steely officials are less charming: their business is scrutinising paperwork, demanding to know the detail of your exact itinerary and accommodation: and when they say it's dangerous, the threat feels real. At Karachi International Airport a similar atmosphere prevails, despite incongruities – a Muslim prayer area next to the Costa coffee stand – and the chaos of repeated security checks. In pristine English and with unimpeachable courtesy uniformed men make precise demands for information before permission is granted to pass through.

In 1943 this was a very different city. Then a part of Britain's Indian Empire and the subcontinent's third-largest port after Bombay and Calcutta, steady growth over the previous century saw Karachi become a major commercial centre with a population in 1941 of some 435,000 people. During the war, Karachi's strategic importance meant it became a major military base for British and American troops.

The Polish passenger liner M/S *Batory* made the runs between Ahvaz in Persia and Karachi. Dubbed the 'Lucky Ship', it already had a legendary status. Named after the Polish King Stefan Batory (1533–86, elected 1576) and built at Trieste in 1936 for Polish Oceanic Lines, it weighed 14,000 tonnes. Like its unfortunate sister ship, M/S *Piłsudski*, sunk off the Yorkshire coast in 1940, the struggling Polish state acquired it in exchange for coal. Designed to carry some 760 passengers in varying degrees of luxury,[1] it saw continuous military use between 1939 and 1945, serving under the Polish flag and participating in some of the most momentous events of the war. The *Batory* took part in the 1940 Norwegian campaign, evacuating Allied troops (including Poles) from Narvik; it was on hand again to help evacuate Allied troops from Dunkirk, picking up stranded soldiers at St-Nazaire and St-Jean-de-Luz; and it acted as a troop carrier for landings in North Africa (1942), Italy (1943) and Normandy (1944). Most famous, perhaps, were its two civilian missions later in the extraordinary summer of 1940. In July, under heavy military escort, it carried to safe-keeping in Canada some of Poland's greatest art treasures, rescued from Wawel Castle, Kraków, and millions of pounds in Bank of England gold bars. On its return it was entrusted with evacuating 480 schoolchildren to Australia. This journey on the 'Singing Ship' is affectionately remembered in a touching memoir which glows with affection for *Batory*'s Polish crew.[2] In 1946 it returned to civilian use, working transatlantic and Poland–India routes, carrying many Polish émigrés to North America. Decommissioned in 1968, attempts to make it pay as a restaurant-hotel in Gdynia failed, and the ship was sold as scrap to a Hong Kong ship-yard two years later. *Batory* made its final voyage in 1971.

For Poles, boarding the *Batory* at the height of the war felt special. 'We arrived very happily and pleased,' Danusia wrote to her father, 'because we travelled on a Polish ship. It was very pleasant for us to travel on a Polish ship with Polish seamen.' Throughout the journey Polish voices were heard giving orders, making decisions, exercising agency; it was like a little piece of autonomous Polish territory. The atmosphere was further enhanced by the commanding presence of Jan Matejko's magnificent canvas *Batory at Psków*. Matejko (1838–93), possibly the greatest visual articulator of Polish nationalism, portrays a scene from the Livonian wars of the sixteenth century in which Russia and its western neighbours fought for control of territories now part of Estonia, Latvia and Lithuania. The twists and turns of events – not so dissimilar to those of 1918–21 – saw Batory turn the tide against a powerful Russian advance and lay siege to the city of Psków in August 1581. Richly coloured, the painting shows Poland's resplendent king receiving the homage of the Tsar. Batory sits on a chair in his field tent, wearing armour, a gold cloak and blue velvet trousers. His stance exudes a Sarmatian machismo: he holds a sword across his legs, which are set wide apart, and his golden boots with golden spurs are firmly planted on a black bearskin. Pennants fly, his look is imperious, his moustache as black as his hat. Before him, accompanied by despondent knights and imploring priests, kneels the Tsar, holding, in supplication, a tray of bread. His red, gold and blue cloak, matching hat, and long hair and beard mark a frivolous contrast with the martial bearing of the Polish warrior-king.

In reality, the siege was lifted following negotiations and though no such homage was made, the Polish–Lithuanian Commonwealth did emerge triumphant, its territories extended at Russian expense.

On arrival at Karachi the Poles were given waterproof caps and, in true Raj style, pith helmets, which they were instructed to wear at all times. They were then taken to the Country Club Refugee Camp. It was, says Nana, located on the edge of desert terrain, a place of hot sands and dry winds. Long since swallowed up by the dusty, rubble-strewn city and now known as the Aero Club, the site is just off the University Road in the Gulshan area. When I visited, wedding preparations were under way, days of celebration anticipated in the carpets and chairs being laid out and the fancily decorated dais prepared for the bride. Though a size-able gathering was expected, the wedding would take up a relatively small area of a site the size of several football pitches. Surrounded by a white-washed concrete wall, much of it looked derelict, with only a small office and a few corrugated-iron shelters and some washing hung out to dry indicating the place was inhabited. Mountains of carpet were to be found in sheds and though they looked unusable, a dense rotting mass of damp material, the wedding preparations hinted at how rough-and-ready decorations might bring life to the place. Most impressive was the old whitewashed clubhouse. Badly run-down and seemingly little used, it was easy to imagine the former Raj elite assembling on the grand terrace in evening dress, a glass in one hand, a cigarette in the other.

After halting negotiations, I was allowed a quick look inside. In a small office stacks of yellowing documentation crept up the walls, though it was impossible to tell how far back those records reached. The most impressive space, long and rectangular, with French windows opening out on to a terrace, was just the place for a dance; I wondered if those doors had been opened of late. A neighbouring room contained a bed and some basic cooking facilities; still another boasted a table, chair and some less ancient files: an office in regular use. Now I thought of it, the key had turned smoothly in the lock. Until one learns to see things properly, in Karachi it is easy to take a dilapidated building for an unusable one.

Run by the British military authorities, with assistance from two hundred or so Polish staff, a camp was established here over sixty years ago, under stretched canvas (another military-issue job) with the 'rather dapper' and fondly remembered Captain Allan serving as its commandant.

Though revolving around a core group of Polish organisers, the camp was integrated into the local military and imperial infrastructure – British and American – and the choice of this site strengthened these links. Official records, memoirs and the Ryżewski letters convey strongly how the camp functioned. Nonetheless, it should be emphasised that little in these records speaks of the worry that must have permeated camp life, particularly in the first half of 1944 when the Polish II Corps saw almost continuous military action as part of the Eighth Army, the great Allied coalition force that fought its way northwards through Italy, driving back the Nazi occupiers. In the camp Polish families awaited word of their relatives just as they did in Britain, the United States, New Zealand, Australia, Canada, India, Greece, Rhodesia, South Africa and France. When Hanna wrote to Rafał worried that she had not heard from him, circumstances once again meant her conventional expressions of concern, exhortation, or love came freighted with greater, more literal, meaning. Also on their minds were friends and family stuck in the Soviet Union and Poland. In an undated letter Wanda wrote plaintively to her father: 'I received a letter from Stasia, from which I discovered Stasia's mummy died and that Zosia has been left alone in Russia. So something must be thought up to try somehow to deliver Zosia from there.' Another orphaned child. Another futile plea.

Everything the refugees needed was provided, from showers and toilets to a sickbay, a hospital and a laundry. Most impressive were the dining areas, large tents with open sides, cement floors, and row upon row of tables and chairs: 1,000 adults were fed in one, 500 children in the other. When Wanda celebrated her sixteenth birthday she graduated to the adult dining tent, joining the mothers; Danusia continued to eat in the melee that must have been the children's dining area. Indian kitchen staff prepared the food, summoning everyone with a gong at mealtimes six days a week; on their day off, a military field pack was

issued. The Catholicism of the great majority of the inmates was amply
catered for. Nana remembers the 'lovely though simple' altar erected in
the open: regular attendance at Mass, of course, was a routine part of
camp life.

Father Gasper of the Goan community, which comprises the core of
Karachi Catholics, remembers the Poles clearly. Born in 1925, he trained
at the seminary near the camp between 1942 and 1951, before being transferred to Quetta. Tall, thin, bespectacled and softly spoken, he muses on
evening visits to the camp, repeatedly emphasising the Catholic piety of
the Poles, their extreme sociability and their tolerance. Wanda's and
Danusia's letters describe how they participated in religious processions
wearing national dress and Father Gasper adds that these would have
taken them to Karachi's St Patrick's Cathedral where ceremonies took
place before the huge monument to Christ the King. Both the cathedral
(consecrated in 1878) and monument (erected in 1931) testify to the past
wealth and power of the Catholic Church and the success of the Jesuit
mission in the city. Unlikely though it may at first seem, the Poles were
peculiarly well suited to life in Karachi.

Church was only one aspect of camp life. Plays and sketches were performed on a makeshift stage; the songs of the Scouts, in which virtually all children were enrolled, were to be constantly heard. American soldiers, 'like children . . . only bigger' says Nana, were a great hit, not least because they set up a cinema screen, bringing the glamour of Hollywood to the desert, and introduced the children to chewing gum, much to the irritation of their mothers. Thanks to their boisterous presence, a handful of engagements and weddings ensued, as well as one or two unaccounted for births. Dignitaries – political, military and religious – put in regular appearances, entertained by Polish children called on to sing patriotic songs and dress up in national costume (Krakówian and Carpathian mostly), sometimes brought from Poland, sometimes made on site.

On occasion, special privileges might come their way, such as the time the British Governor-General opened his doors to them, allowing a walk in his gardens and a splash in the pool. Day to day, schooling and Scouting dominated the life of the camp and the lives of the Ryżewski girls in particular. Hanna, keen to work, got a regular teaching job and soon succeeded Pani Żurowska as headmistress. She was assigned an office and library space (an extra tent) and when not in the classroom her time was spent juggling rotas to ensure that despite the constant arrival and departure of teachers, the 500 students were properly taught. It was these responsibilities that kept them in Karachi so long. As Hanna had observed in Tehran, this environment was strongly feminine and, despite the exoticism of the location, strongly domestic, centred on the care of children.

Camp life was not without its hazards. Though mild and pleasant in the first months of the year, Karachi is then exposed to extremes in temperature and the fierce rains of the monsoon season. Generally, it is hot and dry, the sun beating down from high in the sky, exposing the Poles to the risk of sunstroke and other related ailments. High winds were a problem too, whipping up the sand, hot and sharp, which stung skin, left eyes raw, watering and sometimes infected, and got everywhere, including food, leaving every mouthful gritty.[3] At the other extreme the monsoon season brought heavy rains, perhaps ten inches a month in July and August. The moment the weather broke was always joyful – as when the arrival of the first birds signals the coming of spring at the end of the Russian winter – but this joy did not prevent tents from collapsing under the weight of the water or pegs coming loose in the sodden sand. 'We are swimming in the tents,' wrote Wanda in July 1944. Nothing could be properly waterproofed against the onslaught and to leave anything on the floor was to risk never seeing it again. Searching for sodden shoes buried in wet sand was a common chore.

Alarming creatures stalked the camp. Scorpions, tarantulas, huge centipedes and other desert-dwelling insects lived among their things. Roll down the blinds at night or unfold the mosquito net and something that had taken up residence in the day was sure to fall, fly or crawl out. More threatening were the malaria, dysentery, eye infections and skin diseases that were a constant concern. Safeguards against these and other illnesses included sleeping under mosquito nets, spraying the tents with insecticide, using anti-malaria cream, drinking chlorinated water and taking extra doses of salt.[4] And, of course, their old friends, bedbugs, were constant nocturnal companions. To combat this enemy the army had a crude but effective solution. Each month their bed frames were dipped into a large container filled with hot water and chemicals. And so the cycle would begin again: the first few nights free of the bugs, before the gradual increase culminating in another dowsing four weeks later.

Initially, however, the family was most troubled by the absence of letters from Rafał. Danusia wrote that it was sad not to hear from him, while Wanda complained on 1 February 1944 that two months had gone by and still there was no word. When letters finally arrived, Hanna wrote, there were 'many shrieks and much joy'. Coincidentally, the first we hear of Rafał's voice since his slightly delirious letters of 1940 was in letters dated 1 February 1944. This is the one received by Danusia:

Darling Danusia!

Thank you very much for the letter and the mementoes you sent me. Thank you also for the news which you conveyed so prettily from Mummy. I am afraid that I will not recognise you when we meet. For you will be Miss Danusia and not Little Danuśka. I am sending you a cheque for a pound, which you can exchange for local currency and I think that you won't spend it on ice cream or other treats but instead behave like an adult. Study hard, help your beloved Mother and try and smile at least once a day.

I hug you and kiss you, awaiting a letter from you.

Your Daddy

Wanda's letter was similar:

Darling Wanda!

I am waiting and waiting for a letter from you and can wait no longer. I have come to the conclusion that you have no stamps and so am sending you a cheque for a pound, which you can exchange. Please write a letter, saying what you have done with the money. As I know you are a grown-up girl I will send you a couple of pounds regularly so you have your own money for essential expenses. You can account for this money in your school reports, which I expect to be in order. Study, girl, as after the war you old Dad will need warm meals and the odd glass of beer.

Listen to your Mother and try and be helpful to her not only at home, as she is also working against her will.

For now, I hug you very very hard.

Your Daddy

These are typical of Rafał's letters to his daughters, as was the enclosure of money, often presented to the girls as a mark of their growing independence. Always expressly affectionate, they often reminded the girls of their responsibilities towards their mother and the importance of their schooling. If a little strict, this was offset by reassurance and guidance. Rafał reiterated repeatedly the need for his girls to view their experiences in a positive light. In March, for example, he wrote Danusia a particularly intimate letter, which blended patriotism with a special task:

It pleases me greatly that school is going well for you, and that you like the trips, for no school or books can do as much for the individual as actual observation and what one sees for himself. You're visiting countries which I have never seen and I expect you to tell me everything very precisely sometime. Look and see how people live, work, dress, pray; compare them with what you remember from home and you will convince yourself that you'll never see another country like Poland. I've been travelling the world for 30 years and I haven't found one either, which is why I miss it and you all. I finish with wishes for a happy return home.

In their replies something of the pain of separation and exile occasionally crept in, but in general little dampened the girls' spirits: their eagerness to recount progress at school reflected the pleasure they derived from Rafał reassuming his role as father. His approval, as well as the connection itself, meant a great deal to them. In May Danusia thanked him for a cheque, but hoped he did not think her ungrateful when she said that it was the words, 'which I so rarely receive', which pleased her more. In August she told her father, 'When I received the letter from the post office I cried so much that the tears rolled down my face but I was very pleased with the letter.'

Rafał's letters, peppered with brief but piquant detail, were always fatherly. In an otherwise brief missive he ticked off Danusia for writing 'fast if a little untidily': 'every letter slants in another direction'. In a note to Wanda he commented on how pleased he was by the improvements in her hand, though she had to take care her writing was not too small. He conveyed to the girls almost no news of, or allusion to, the military situation, despite the Eighth Army's progress. By now, on account of his age and long years of military service, Rafał had taken up service behind the front line. Following a brief period as a Supply Officer at the 6th Infantry Division Headquarters, he took command of the Polish II Corps salvage unit. Most frustrating is that his letters to Hanna, which might have been more forthcoming, are missing so we do not know how he felt about the famous Polish taking of Monte Cassino (January–May 1944) or their later role in the battle for Loreto, both accompanied by the great loss of Polish lives.

Wanda's and Danusia's letters told of their life in the camp, both tending to preface this with enquiries after the state of their dad's health. They repeatedly requested – sometimes with a hint of reproach – that Rafał send books. Their requests were reinforced with appended notes from

Hanna. 'I am waiting for the books from you,' wrote Wanda insistently in January, 'the promised textbooks: Mathematics, Latin, *Potop*,* History.' A couple of weeks later she pointedly noted that one of her friends had received a parcel of books including a copy of Sienkiewicz's *Pan Wołodyjowski*.

Danusia was a little more apologetic in her demands, seemingly less concerned that the absence of books was holding her back at school and less insistent her father fulfilled his obligations: 'I am sorry to bother you so about the books, but I really have nothing to read and really, really ask for some books if the circumstances allow.' This hunger for reading material was communal. By the end of February Wanda wrote that she had 'fallen into a fever of reading' and was racing through the Sienkiewicz oeuvre. Having devoured *In the Desert and the Jungle* and the first two parts of the great trilogy (*With Fire and Sword*, and *The Deluge*), she was now reading *Quo Vadis* and looked forward to *Fire in the Steppe* (*Pan Wołodyjowski*). 'Though forgive me', she wrote, reporting these enthusiasms, 'because I do not read alone but we gather together in a group in the Scout hut and there read aloud one after the other.' Aware of the efforts her father had made to supply these books, she was concerned he was annoyed that by sharing them she did not benefit fully from their educational value. Rafał, sociable and comradely, surely didn't object. More significant than Wanda's girlish concerns was how far Sienkiewicz's intoxicating diet of patriotism and adventure had captured the imagination of the camp.

Wanda's devotion to her Scouting duties saw her become a Scout leader, taking responsibility for twelve 'little girls'. Polish Scouts mixed with British and Hindu Scouts, taking part in jamborees and day trips, as well as sports competitions. Of the 'Sportman's Holiday' of 17 May, the girls reported their prowess (Wanda was a gymnast, Danusia a runner and long-jumper) and Polish successes. 'Naturally, the Poles won everything,' wrote Wanda.

One particularly memorable Scout trip took them to Mangho Pil, a religious site a little way outside the city. Here sacred crocodiles lived among Hindu temples. Wanda described her journey through 'huge mountains' in terms continuous with her memories of their old home life: 'I, like the former wanderer from Hruzdowa had to be first every-

---

* Sienkiewicz, *The Deluge*.

where, of course, and to the summit of the first and second [mountain] and on the return journey I was first back to the camp as well as the first to find herself at the communal supper and later at home.' As before, her independence of spirit seemed to blur into solitariness, the child who gets things done rather than lingers with friends. Her mother, though, wrote warmly of Wanda's maturity. 'She has grown and matured and the wise little girl tries to help me as much as she can.' Danusia's description of the day, fuller and more colourful, differed markedly:

> We have been on one outing to the sacred crocodiles, where we walked with the English Scouts as guides. It is 9 kilometres to the sacred crocodiles and we walked there. The oldest crocodile is 100 years old and walked gingerly. I saw how a Hindu prayed on a pile of ashes. He sat on a mat and a blanket which was folded into four pieces, on which lay five clear rocks.

Nana remembers how the mouths of the oldest crocs had to be held open with a stick when they needed feeding.[5]

Perhaps the most entertaining letter from this period also comes from Danusia. Sliding in and out of a grown-up manner, it contains a succession of delightfully metaphorical observations before ending on a curiously self-conscious note, evidence that the girl was beginning to embrace the role of spirited child so often ascribed to her by the adults around her. It begins on a strongly confident note, 'As usual I start my letter from health.' It goes on, possibly in response to Rafał's criticism of her handwriting, to imperiously 'assure' her father that she 'read fluently' and made 'very few mistakes in writing'. Since his last letter she could report she has 'enjoyed many entertainments'. Formalities out of the way, she rattled off a series of anecdotes. At the seaside she collected mussels, saw a crab, 'which nipped one lady on the foot', and an 'aquatic insect which was rainbow-coloured . . . just like an inflatable balloon in the shape of a snail'. One girl was bitten so badly her hand had to be bandaged up. The camp being so dry, she loved being by the sea and sat in the water the whole time like a 'zmokła kura', an idiomatic expression meaning wet hen, the equivalent of 'drowned rat'.

On a visit to the zoological gardens she saw lions, 'an enormous tortoise which was like a pillow', and 'huge palms' she had to 'crane' her neck to see, but she was disappointed that elephants were nowhere to be seen. 'There were so many kinds of birds there and even Polish storks, which moved around the pond and ate frogs. To greet us, they made such a noise that it rang in one's ears: they must have recognised us.' When storks migrate from Poland it is a sign that summer is coming to an end and the return to school is imminent. How fantastical it must have seemed to the girl to come upon these fellow Poles in their other home. In adult hands the 'Polish' storks might become a portentous symbol . . . Back at Scout camp she helped the older girls cook and took a hygiene course, but because their camp was in an orchard 'the little urchin Danka' preferred to sit 'in trees the whole day long'. When she got home, 'I was scratched as though a cat had got me.' This self-consciousness was again evident in another letter, written a month or so later, in which Danusia cheekily demanded Rafał 'instruct Mummy to buy me a pretty ring from India for Mummy says that I am still precocious'. She signed off 'your scatter-brain Danka'. The twelve-year-old girl was becoming aware of her charms though whether she would have been pleased to read that her mother thought her 'making such an urchin of herself at the moment that I simply can't control her' is another question.

Rafał rewarded Danusia on 24 April with a shorter though similarly entertaining letter. Saying the men, like him, had liked her letter greatly, he talked about spending his free time looking at monuments and walking in the mountains. The Italian spring, 'in all its beauty', was 'just like at home', and the nightingales sang all night, preventing everyone from sleeping. 'The day before yesterday I heard a cuckoo', but 'I didn't ask her about anything as she cuckooed twice and flew away'.

Easter and the 3 May celebrations elicited another delightful letter from Danusia. During the all-night vigil at St Patrick's Cathedral on Easter Saturday night, her duties as a Scout saw her form part of the 'honour guard at the tomb of Jesus'. She put in four shifts, two by day, two by night. Religious duties fulfilled, the Easter celebrations culminated in a meal in the large dining tent. Everyone gathered at tables laden with *swięcone* (baskets of blessed food) and decorated with painted eggs – Danusia, her creative streak finding a new outlet, had been busy, making no less than fourteen. For all but the most pious of the young, Easter's crowning glory was *Śmigus-Dyngus*. 'Wet Monday', which involves pouring water over people, comes as playful relief at the end of a long weekend of vigil and religious observance. The soakings are liked and loathed in equal measure by women and generally loved by young men keen on what can easily become a kind of aquatic kiss chase. Danusia – possibly beginning to appreciate this aspect of the celebrations – was thoroughly doused by a bunch of boys in one of the bathrooms. To her, however, fell the task of soaking her mother, until then 'quite dry': the boys, it can be supposed, were a little reluctant to tackle their headmistress. The British got the hang of things quickly enough, 'taking a bath of water and soaking whoever fell into their clutches'. A jolly good time it must have been. On Easter Tuesday Danusia played the ghost in a staging of *Kopciuszek*, the Polish version of the Cinderella fairy tale novelised by Józef Ignacy Kraszewski (1812–87), the other great Polish historical novelist.[6]

May 3 passed with the usual ceremonies commemorating the 1791 Constitution. Visiting dignitaries were honoured, the children paraded in traditional dress, the school and other buildings were decorated. Wanda felt her troop paraded well, keeping good time with the music. Both girls thought the most notable participants were the local military, including what Danusia described as 'an Indian orchestra in Scottish costume'. She was entranced by the baton-waving bandleader and the beautiful dagger decorated with 'an enormous ruby' carried by one bandsman. It was quite a mix of sound and style. Both girls, however, revealed their priorities in closing their letters by describing the grey, long-whiskered cat who had attached herself to their tent. Its four kittens, two greys, a ginger tabby and a milky angora, all had their mother's long whiskers. 'They are funny,' wrote Danusia, 'looking you in the eye and starting to wander.'

Rafał sent Wanda two tender letters to mark her sixteenth birthday. 'Above all,' he wrote, 'I want to send you, my "Little One" (the last time I'll write this) best wishes at having reached sixteen.' Noting that it was almost a year since he had seen her, he couldn't 'imagine' that she was 'now a young woman to look at'. Above all, he wrote to reassure her that her future would be bright, repeating advice he had given over the past few years: 'Learn what you can and look around you, my darling, and life will sort itself out if you are wise.' She should not worry about whether her schooling was adequate but instead remember that 'it's knowledge and not some class that assures a person their rightful place among people'. He sent 'my Little Miss' – a neat advance on Little One – an Egyptian silver necklace and a brooch, 'original products from by the Sphinx'. Wanda wrote to thank him, pleading that though 'you wrote that it was the last time you would write your little one but for you I am and always will be your little Wandeczka just as I have been until now'.

These touching letters see the father distantly trying to fathom what was happening to his daughter, grasping at ways of showing her that he respected the changes taking place in her, recognising they must reconfigure their relationship. Wanda, deploying the diminutive to devastating effect, writes that these changes are insignificant. Whether she wrote to reassure him or herself cannot be said, but it's clear she was upset by the suggestion that because she was no longer 'Little' but 'Miss' some distance had inexorably opened up between herself and her father. Whether her letter followed reassurance from her mother or reflected her own determination to preserve the old emotional regime, the words were an act of homage, reaffirming her father's tutelage over her. In the purest sense, these were love letters, guided by the language of courtly romance, and it is hard to imagine her father was anything but moved by her restoring the link he'd partially broken.

A fortnight later Rafał wrote in advance of Danusia's birthday. Not such a significant milestone – she was twelve – but still he wondered from afar at her ongoing transformation. 'Neither of us expected that a young lady would grow so quickly from an "Uzbek Poppy".' She too would receive a necklace, 'which one day will go with a pretty dress'.

Wanda, though, *was* getting older and in small ways was beginning to negotiate her relations with men. When Rafał wrote in April that she might receive letters from 'strange people', he assured her it was entirely her decision whether she replied. These were wounded Polish soldiers, mainly his friends, 'intelligent young people'. Both girls would write such letters, but Wanda's inevitably carried a more ambiguous charge. In June she reported receiving one from Pan Wiktor Szulc, which doesn't survive, and another from Second-Lieutenant Edmund Napieralski. She corresponded a little with Edmund. He wrote nice letters, descriptive and sensitive, which, in part, tried to establish if they had seen each other in Jakkobad. He could only recall Danusia, 'then still very young', who 'merrily flew through the Mess'. Joking about his own ugliness (he included a photograph), Napieralski wondered if she might send him a photograph so he could be absolutely sure of who she was. He also wondered whether she might consider addressing him less formally. Not: '"Dear Sir" but as I write to you, a little more lightly, it would give me enormous pleasure.'

Wanda was not yet ready to indulge the whims of young men and was perhaps a little alarmed by these requests. Somewhat indiscreetly, she told her father of them and her replies: 'I wrote that I will not send my photograph to anyone or show it to anyone except Daddy – as for "Dear Sir", I will write differently when I am twenty.' Rafał replied to the effect that Napieralski was a good chap, but 'what you have told me is very good and becoming on your part'. Though the young soldier would have squirmed with embarrassment had he learnt these modest requests were divulged to a senior officer, future letters indicate their nascent friendship survived her prim propriety.

With the worst of the fighting behind him by early summer, Rafał began to make reference to his military experiences in his letters to the girls. To Wanda (20 May 1944) he wrote that he'll not 'write about my work', but 'as you probably already know from the radio and the newspapers our

army covered our flags with glory at Monte Cassino hitherto considered unconquerable'. 'When we got there,' he wrote triumphantly, 'the Germans opened their mouths and kept them open for two hours.'

Evidence of the importance of Monte Cassino to Polish morale is found in a letter to Rafał from his cousin Tadeusz, then in France. 'All of us here are thinking of you in Italy as Heroes and after the taking of Cassino a new spirit has entered us, we step more proudly and look people directly in the eye and into the future.' On 10 July in another letter to Wanda, Rafał allowed himself to say a little more. 'As for us, we have finally caught up with the "Cockroaches" and keep beating the pants off them properly. You should see their faces when they get in our hands, and there are so many of them. Each of them trembles like jelly; there are no Germans, all Austrians and they say all they know, asked or not.' Rafał was even more explicit in a letter to Hanna. 'The roles have reversed and we are driving the Germans with machines, and they run on foot so it's hard to control them.' These few brief lines suggest the advance, with the major battles fought, had become a rounding-up exercise. The German forces were no longer putting up much resistance, their morale weakened by successive defeats, the reference to machines perhaps highlighting the contrast with the opening battles of the war when the Polish cavalry was confronted by German tanks. 'Anyway,' he wrote, apparently tired of talking of the war, 'you know from the newspapers and radio that we are advancing and are only halted for a few days.' More interesting was his visit with his men to the 'miraculous basilica of the Holy Mother of Loreto', the Santuario di Loreto. Wanda received the fullest account (dated 5 August):

Sometimes by accident I see many beautiful things and above all monuments from the Roman period. They really are wonderful. In the Church of Our Lady of Loreto there is a Polish chapel. Something miraculous. Our eagle in the stained-glass windows in Polish style, and most interestingly on the walls are two huge pictures showing Sobieski at Vienna in 1683 and Piłsudski on the Vistula in 1920. An amazing sight. I spent almost an hour visiting until I had so beaten it into my memory that I knew every detail of the pictures.

They had stumbled upon the Polish chapel, one of twelve in the church, which boasted a modern altar triptych by Gatti (1913–39).[7] The linkage made between Sobieski's victory against the Turks and Piłsudski's against

the Bolsheviks could hardly be clearer. Rafał paid for a Mass to be said
in Hanna's name and sent her some religious trinkets.

As the war progressed, the politicians began to focus on post-war reconstruction. The US, in particular, played a vanguardist role, arguing that
an internationally organised and funded effort would be required. With
the liberation of parts of Europe imminent it was clear that international
agencies were needed to cope with the chaos and humanitarian need left
in the wake of the fascist defeats and withdrawal. The advancing army
could not be expected to cope with the huge problems of governance and
supply its victories were creating. A particular problem was the Displaced
Persons, or the DPs, civilians who for various reasons were forced to leave
their homes during the war.[8] One official Allied estimate suggested that
by the middle of 1943, 21 million people in Europe had been displaced.
Some 8 million had been forcibly removed to Germany or Austria and
nearly 8 million were moved within their home country.[9] The Poles were
among the many thousands of refugees already dependent on relief:
millions more would be created by the Allied advance.

The search for a solution to this gigantic problem began with high-
level discussions commencing in the autumn of 1942. These led to a
meeting at the White House on 9 November 1943 during which agreement was reached to establish a new international authority. The United
Nations Relief and Rehabilitation Administration, or UNRRA, was to be
financed by those United Nations member states whose territory had not
been invaded, each contributing 1 per cent of national income: not less
than 10 per cent of the total was to be in currency, while the balance
could be paid in materials. In theory, the US and Great Britain were
responsible respectively for 72 and 13 per cent of the total, though in the
event the US contributed 85 per cent of the $4,000,000,000 the agency
eventually spent. Herbert Lehman, ex-Governor of New York, was named
UNRRA's first Director General. From the outset, as UNRRA employee
Marvin Klemmé recalled, UNRRA attracted criticism in the US from
right-wing antisemites owing to the number of Jewish and suspected
communist employees in its ranks and its Democrat Party associations.
Klemmé characterises the Americans who became involved as 'idealists
and super-internationalists', contrasting them with the more cynical and
calculating Europeans.[10]

Initially, UNRRA assumed that its role would be limited to the repatriation of civilian DPs; in the event, it became responsible for some of

the many thousands of freed POWs and demobilised soldiers. UNRRA supplied the essentials of life and though assisting in the repatriation of many thousands, it also found itself caring for DPs who refused to return home.[11] It became a holding operation, making the right noises about its continued commitment to repatriation, while political solutions were sought. A parallel development in the agency's role came with its recognition that many DPs, and Jews in particular, were enemy nationals who were victims of their own governments. In Council in June 1944 a US representative led the move to expand UNRRA's operations, allowing it to assist 'persons who have been obliged to leave their country or place of origin or former residence or who have been deported therefrom, by action of the enemy, because of race, religion, or activities in favour of the United Nations'.[12]

A decision of similar magnitude came in August 1945 when further Council meetings drew attention to a seeming contradiction in the Council's resolutions. Resolution 1 straightforwardly obligated UNNRA to assist DPs, while Resolution 57 provided for the assistance of DPs with the 'agreement of the country of which they are nationals'. According to UNRRA's official historian, the resolution of this contradiction led to sharp disagreement between the 'Slav nations' and the other members. The so-called Slav nations demanded that good DPs be distinguished from bad DPs. Good DPs wanted to return home and should be assisted; bad DPs did not and should not. The other members understood the situation differently, believing there were three classes, good DPs who wanted to return, good DPs who had legitimate reasons for not wishing to return, and a criminal element keen to exploit the situation. Given that a large proportion of the DPs who were refusing to return home were from Eastern Europe, the recognition that they might have legitimate reason not to return seemed a slur on the new Soviet-sponsored governments.

The 'Slav nations', dressing up their anger as the fear that the provision of care would delay repatriation, thereby delaying reconstruction – with which UNRRA was also heavily involved – were placated by the agreement that permission to provide care would be limited to six months. By the time of the Council meetings of 1946, the DP question was one of a number souring East–West relations. UNRRA, faced with demands to accelerate repatriation, fudged the issue, affirming its commitment to encourage repatriation while extending the length of time any individual could be in receipt of care. In short, it upheld the established principle that no individual would face forced repatriation.[13]

The Poles, a large proportion of whom were in Germany, were the biggest single group receiving UNRRA assistance in Europe between December 1945 and June 1947. The number receiving assistance declined fairly steadily during that time from 438,649 to 166,181. Other numerically significant national groups included Latvians, Ukrainians and Lithuanians, while the number of Jewish people in receipt of assistance steadily grew over the period to 167,531.[14] UNRRA's role in the Middle East followed a different pattern. In August 1945, 3,730 Greeks and 10,240 Yugoslavs were in receipt of relief, but by October 1946, thanks to successful repatriations, these figures had dropped to 111 and 741, respectively. By contrast, the number of Poles outside Europe financially supported by UNRRA in September 1946 numbered 30,004, falling only slightly to 27,007 by June 1947.[15] These fairly static figures, dramatically at odds with the overall trend, require some explanation. Why was it that by 1947 most Greeks and Yugoslavs had gone home but the Poles had not? The rationale, at once very simple and very complex, lay in the diplomacy and power politics that accompanied the Allied victory, all of which can be traced back to secretive Allied talks in late 1943.

As will be recalled, relations between the Soviet and Polish governments had been tense since they became Allies following the German invasion of the Soviet Union in 1941. The overriding question concerned Poland's eastern border. The Poles were determined that it would adhere as closely as possible to the pre-war border, as established by the Treaty of Riga and still recognised in international law. If small changes were required to take account of new conditions on the ground, they should be brought about by negotiation and formalised in an international peace treaty. The Soviet attitude was the obverse. They rejected the status quo ante and were determined to hold the territories gained – though since lost – in 1939. For the Western Allies, Soviet–Polish relations were a continual problem. The Poles, under immense pressure from the British not to antagonise Moscow, sought guarantees that under any post-war settlement the territorial integrity of the pre-war state would be respected. But as the war progressed it became increasingly clear that Moscow would be in a position to dictate the new shape of Eastern Europe once the fighting came to an end – the Allied decision not to mount a Balkan landing ensured the Red Army was the sole 'liberator' of Poland.

Everything changed in April 1943 when the Germans discovered the graves of the Polish officers at Katyń and announced the Soviet crime to the world. The Polish government-in-exile, determined not to become a pawn in the German propaganda machine, responded by demanding an International Red Cross investigation of the claims. The Soviets, ruthlessly opportunistic, accused the Poles of collaborating with the enemy and severed diplomatic relations with the government-in-exile. In terms of the international recognition the government needed in order to maintain its authority, this marked the beginning of the end for the old regime.

Diplomatic developments suggest these changed circumstances were all too apparent by the end of 1943. In the same month that the Ryżewscy were moved from Tehran to Karachi, the British Prime Minister Winston Churchill, the Soviet General Secretary Joseph Stalin and the US President Franklin D. Roosevelt met in the Iranian capital. Here the Big Three began to work out the shape of post-war Europe and Poland in particular. Without consulting the Polish government-in-exile, they decided that the so-called Curzon Line, rejected by both Poland and the Bolsheviks in 1920, would be Poland's eastern border. Poland would be compensated with more valuable and developed German lands in the west. The details of this agreement remained secret until rumours began to circulate in early 1944. At the same time, on 4 January 1944 the Soviet forces, driving back the German armies, crossed the pre-war Polish frontier into Volhynia (now part of Ukraine). Under mounting pressure to declare the government's position regarding the border question, Churchill reminded Parliament on 22 February that 'the British view in 1919 stands expressed in the so-called Curzon Line'. It was an ambiguous statement, which sidestepped clearly expressing their current view, though Churchill went on to say, following some doubtless sincere platitudes regarding his admiration for the 'heroic' Polish people, that he sympathised with 'the Russia standpoint'. Despite the promise of compensation in the West, Poles found it difficult to see Churchill and Roosevelt as having done anything but acquiesce in the Soviet annexation of sovereign Polish territory. As Anders later bitterly wrote, 'The rights of the Russians to the spoils given to them under the Ribbentrop–Molotov agreements of August and September 1939 were thus confirmed.'[16]

Churchill's thinking was further elucidated in private discussions with Anders in August and with Sikorski's successor as Polish Prime Minister Stanisław Mikołajczyk in October. A Polish secretary took minutes during the meeting with Anders and there is little reason to doubt that Churchill's words were recorded with reasonable accuracy. The Prime Minister told Anders: 'In concluding the treaty of alliance with Poland, Great Britain has never guaranteed her frontiers. She pledged and undertook the obligations for the existence of Poland as a free, independent, sovereign and great state, in order that her citizens might live happily with the opportunity for unfettered development, free from any alien interference.'[17] At first glance, Churchill's words appeared to reflect the complacencies of a Prime Minister of an island nation which rarely faced the territorial uncertainties so characteristic of Poland's history. The reality, however, was that Churchill's promise of a Poland free, independent, sovereign and great, but with significantly altered borders, was the best offer he could realistically make.

Anders, pointing out that further deportations, shooting and imprisonments were accompanying the Soviet advance,[18] was determined to impress upon the Prime Minister the fundamental malevolence the Soviets felt for the Poles. He insisted the Prime Minister understand that the 'Union of Polish Patriots', established at Lublin on 20 July and sponsored by Stalin, were traitors.[19] Churchill was none too keen on the Union but his diplomatic strategy was predicated on a faith in Stalin's goodwill and he would prove slow to recognise the depth of Stalin's betrayal over Poland. It seems likely that his readiness to trust in Stalin's stated commitment to free elections in Poland shortly after the end of the war was conditioned by his long-standing belief that it would not be desirable to see the restoration of Poland's pre-war eastern border. Continuing Polish insistence that this should be an Allied war aim infuriated Churchill, culminating in fierce private exchanges with Mikołajczyk. Churchill regarded the Polish proposition that the Western allies should eventually fight the Soviet Union with this end in mind as selfish as he found Polish pronouncements that they would fight on alone absurd. The Poles, Churchill lamented, were behaving without regard for the interests of Europe and the East–West alliance. When roused, he angrily reminded the Polish leadership of the failures of the interwar Polish governments and the simple fact that a free Poland was only conceivable thanks to the enormous sacrifices made by the Red Army.[20]

As Anders recorded in his memoir, Churchill's February announcement shocked the Poles, causing unrest in the ranks and when, in the summer of 1944, the liberation of Italy was complete, there was talk of the Poles refusing to continue service. Anders says their sense of duty overrode their sense of betrayal and discipline was maintained but there can be little doubt that from this moment the Poles, having enthusiastically joined the Allied cause as the representatives of their country, felt unsettled and newly anxious about the future.

The decline in authority of the Polish government-in-exile brought on by these developments underpinned the pessimism in the ranks and refugee camps. As the Soviets advanced into Poland, their sponsorship of the Union of Polish Patriots increased until it became clear that the Union would become a puppet government representing the interests of the Soviet Union. Anders may well have complained that these were traitors, but the facts on the ground in Poland were changing in ways that British and American political opinion had to adjust to. Doubtless, Churchill was sincere when he assured Anders that Poland would play a role in post-war peace discussions, but there was no guarantee that it would be represented by the London-based government-in-exile. While the Poles in Poland were certainly not sanguine about the imposition of a Soviet puppet government, concern about the *kresy* territories was for them a lower priority than for Anders' troops or the refugees. As Wanda's increasingly frequent epistolary references to the countryside around their home suggests, the refugees felt a deep attachment to an area that many Poles considered a backward sub-region, and one which had proven one of the sources of Poland's pre-war weakness.

The Ryżewski letters, silent about the war while the Poles were in action, began to refer to the political-military situation in the summer of 1944. A reluctance to confront the ramifications of the political situation runs through many of them. At their simplest, they expressed Danusia's 'wish' of 12 October that Rafał return to Poland so they could be together and that on the way he 'beat as many Germans as possible'. This demand, brutal and yet almost charming in its naïve simplicity, expressed the child's simple perception of what stood between her and their old life – the Germans – circumventing the anxieties agitating her parents. Rafał, writing to his wife twelve days later, could only admit rather than resolve the imponderables the Poles faced. 'Darling, today is the fifth anniversary of our mobilisation. In truth the end is not in sight, but constantly nearer than further. We don't have time here for wasting time with thinking and retain hope that everything will somehow end.' Hope rather than thought was the best he could do.

By December the strain was beginning to show. On 6 December he wrote Wanda an extraordinarily agitated letter, unprecedentedly frank in its readiness to address his concerns directly. Disturbed by her continued susceptibility to malaria, he sent his daughter a stark warning: 'You know that malaria itself isn't threatening, but its consequences if it isn't controlled can become a disaster for the rest of your life.' A later letter to Hanna shows he was worried about Wanda's fertility, suggesting that if their '"quacks"' could not help, Hanna should take her to see 'a Hindu artisan'. Either way, he urged that Wanda take all possible precautions and, in a rush of exhortation and agitation, he implored 'very much' that she think about these warnings, 'because you know how much it upsets my nerves – and in my condition getting worked up about things is very very bad'. Unprecedentedly needy, he urged that they organise a weekly letter-writing rota. His anxiety can only have been increased by the terrible news coming from Poland. The Warsaw Uprising, the doomed attempt by the Polish underground army to defeat the Nazi occupation (Hanna also alluded to it: 'What is happening with our people at home – for if it is as it seems it is bad'), had been brutally put down and Warsaw razed. This was quickly followed by the Red Army's entry into the city on 17 January. In particular, Rafał feared for his mother's safety: 'It worries me that at this moment Mamusia is in the fire and please God deliver her whole.'

By January, following the usual exchange of seasonal greetings, expressions of hope for the future, and *opłatek*, his letters became more composed and reflective. Though that new readiness to expose his fears to the girls as well as Hanna remained, on 18 January his more sanguine mood generated a particularly expansive letter, a stream of consciousness on the state of the world and his confused feelings about their agonising situation. Here he was, fighting an enemy who had inflicted untold damage on his people, alongside a similarly guilty ally who, it seemed, was turning Poland's liberation into conquest. The 'world is turning so strangely and making such zigzags', he wrote, 'that it's hard today to know anything and make projections for the future'. The moral certainties of the past were fast giving way and Rafał was unable to find a firm footing from which to evaluate the new circumstances: the 'border that once existed between evil and good is no longer there today'. 'Ideas', he speculated, warming to his theme, had been 'modernised' making them more 'appropriate to the moment'. That he was none too convinced that morality was so subjectively slippery seems clear and there was surely some irony in his suggestion that he knew, 'in the secrecy of my soul', that this resistance reflected 'premature old age and with it stubborn conservatism'. 'Like Socrates,' he concluded, 'I can only say that "I know that I don't know".'

Amid this uncertainty he felt one thing more strongly than ever: he wanted to be with his family. Never before had he confessed this so frankly and in terms that went beyond conventional endearments. Here again is the emotional neediness that was beginning to seep into his letters. 'I don't know why I want to be with you at all costs,' he wrote, 'I can't explain to myself what the cause of this is.' These yearnings, he explained, came in 'waves' but were not triggered by the content of their letters, nor did they require an external stimulus; they were a fixed aspect of his state of mind. Though not stated directly, the implication is that while all else fell apart, marital and fatherly love held firm. Drawing back from this theme, Rafał ironically commented on another possible explanation for the present troubles: 'Once upon a time astrology said that certain alignments between planets have a talent for influencing the psychic state of those on Earth.' If this were the case, he grimly concluded, 'then the system today is the most cursed of the cursed'. The word Rafał uses for system – in Polish *układ* – tends to refer to the prevailing political arrangements and rarely, if ever, has positive connotations.

On a more optimistic note, Rafał said his letters to Kuba in the US were achieving a kind of minor celebrity. Initially unsure whether they were getting through, and fearing they were being censored, he had heard that three at least had arrived safely. Kuba, though suffering some reversals in his business interests, remained well connected among Polish-Americans and had made copies for distribution at the local Polish club. When they arrived, Rafał wryly commented, they became that day's 'sensation'. Mindful of their future options, this unwitting chronicler was concerned his 'literature' did not 'create a bad impression' because 'these are the first steps in a new social area'.

The significance of these letters to Hanna should not be missed. The winter of 1944–5 marked a watershed in how the Ryżewscy thought about the war and their future. Until now, the reunion of the family and the return to Poland were interlinked, as Wanda's poems and many references in their letters show. Family life had been sustained by this promise, which at their micro level gave the war its purpose. Now the Ryżewscy openly contemplated the possibility that they would choose not return to Poland and that the war would end not with their restoration to the Motherland but with continuing odyssey. Though Rafał could still on occasion be found whistling in the dark about Poland's prospects, hereafter it was their survival as a family unit that had become miracle enough, Poland increasingly becoming something they could carry within themselves.

Consequently, on 1 February Rafał urged his wife try to get to Australia, New Zealand, or even Mexico, half-joking that a further ten thousand miles or so would make little difference. There was more serious intent at work here, for Rafał recognised that where they found themselves at the end of the hostilities, by creating facts on the ground, might prove vitally important to their prospects. Hanna, too, now realised a few thousand more miles were immaterial, in sharp contrast with her pre-occupation with distance in Tehran, when Polish prospects seemed greatest. She was made nervous when someone from UNRRA came to the camp asking questions about where they wanted to go after the war. Fearing a trap, she sought advice from her husband in March. Of particular note is her comment, 'I assume that there is a single-minded view, that there is no split and you know what to do in a particular case.'

It was a pertinent query. As yet, there was no serious split. The Polish refugees and soldiers were of one mind regarding their return to Poland when the war ended: they hoped to return but would not do so as a matter of course. They reserved the right to judge the political situation at home when the time came. As a report prepared in February for the Colonial Office about Polish attitudes in one of the African camps suggested, the authorities were also becoming appraised of the problem they would soon face. In the large Tegeru Camp at Arusha in the Tanganyika Territory, home to some 4,000 Poles, bad feeling was aroused by the visit of UNRRA representative S. K. Jacobs. His attempt to compose a register of the inmates did not provoke violence or indiscipline, but still it was abandoned owing to the strength of opposition. The 'principal cause of the trouble', the report explained, was that 'the refugees were asked to state to which place in pre-war Poland they wished to return, irrespective of whether that place was in the part of Poland claimed by Russia, or whether or not Poland would be controlled by the Government developing out of the Lublin Committee after the war. Polish refugees as a whole are anxious to get back to their own country, but a great majority of them seem to be bitterly opposed to both the Russian Government and the Lublin Committee, and may state openly that they will refuse to return to Poland if governed by Russia, or by Government under Russian control.'[21]

Their suspicions were confirmed in early 1945 when the Soviet Union unilaterally recognised a new Polish provisional government. At the Yalta conference of 4–11 February, one the three big meetings which shaped post-war Europe, Churchill and Roosevelt insisted that the representatives of the government-in-exile should be admitted to the provisional Polish government. Though the Prime Minister and the President were in no position to enforce such demands, Churchill relayed to Cabinet his faith that Stalin would adhere to the Yalta stipulation that there would be free elections in Poland. If this was the case, Churchill argued, Britain's obligations towards the Poles would cease. If, however, Stalin did not fulfil his side of the bargain, then Churchill made it crystal clear that members of the Polish armed forces, fighting under Allied Command, should be granted permission to settle in the British Empire. A fundamental difficulty arose regarding how this was to be conveyed to the Polish forces. How could they fortify their military commitment without suggesting a lack of faith in Stalin's undertakings?[22]

In response, General Anders struck a defiant note, angrily telling the Polish II Corps that with Yalta, 'the fundamental rights of our nation have today been obliterated'. However, Anders went on to emphasise the special need for continuing military discipline:

> Men, at this moment we are the only part of the Polish Nation which is able, and has the duty, loudly to voice its will, and just for this reason we must prove today by word and by deed that we are faithful to our oath of allegiance, true to our citizens' duty towards our country, and faithful to the last wish of our fallen comrades in arms, who fought and died for an independent, sovereign and truly free Poland.

The army, Anders made clear, must continue the fight, for it was now the only true representative of the will of the Polish nation.

> Our country, deprived of the rights of speech, looks towards us. It wishes to see us in the land of our ancestors – to that end we are striving and longing from the bottom of our hearts – but it does not want to see us as slaves of a foreign force: it wants to see us with our banners flying as forerunners of true freedom.

Despite the bitterness, London must have been relieved to note that the overriding message of Anders' speech was the virtue of patriotic duty. Less welcome was the next section of the address:

As such a return is impossible today, we must wait in closed and disci-
plined ranks for a favourable change of conditions. This change must come,
or otherwise all the terrible and bloody sacrifices of the whole world,
suffered throughout six years, will have been in vain. It is impossible to
imagine that humanity has suddenly become blind and had really lost the
consciousness of a mortal danger.[23]

Thus Anders fired the opening salvo in what would become a long
political struggle regarding the future of the Polish men under Western
Allied Command. Moreover, in identifying the Soviet system as a 'mortal
danger', Anders became the latest to articulate the idea that the Poles
had a special role to play in the defence of civilisation, if only as witnesses
to the West's capitulation.

Concerned Polish sympathisers brought reservations regarding Yalta
to the attention of the House of Commons and Churchill was called
upon to make a statement. Inevitably, the shape of the post-war settlement was somewhat bypassed and Churchill focused on the much easier
matter of the Poles in British care and under Allied Command in Western
Europe. Initially it seemed Churchill adhered to the official line, as established by the UN, that the Poles would eventually return to Poland.

> Finally, on this subject, His Majesty's Government recognised that the large
> forces of Polish troops, soldiers, sailors and airmen, now fighting gallantly,
> as they have fought during the whole war, under British command, owe
> allegiance to the Polish Government in London. We have every confidence
> that once the new Government, more fully representative of the will of
> the Polish people than either the present Government in London or the
> Provisional Administration in Poland, has been established, and recognised
> by the Great Powers, means will be found of overcoming these formal
> difficulties in the wider interest of Poland. Above all, His Majesty's
> Government are resolved that as many as possible of the Polish troops
> shall be enabled to return in due course to Poland, of their own free will,
> and under every safeguard, to play their part in the future life of their
> country.

Four points might be made about this passage. First, it is clear that
Churchill accepted that the only Poles the British could actively assist
were those in Allied uniforms. Second, in noting the allegiance of the
Polish forces – and we might add, the bulk of the refugees – to the govern-

ment-in-exile, Churchill recognised that the soldiers were fighting not simply for their country but according to a set of war aims dating back to the dark days of 1939–40. As Rafał's letters suggest, many Poles still had tremendous difficulty in coming to terms with the transformation that had come about with the German invasion of the Soviet Union. On the day Barbarossa was launched, the war became a different war, predicated on a new set of interests. Any number of Atlantic Charters could not change the fact that the Soviet Union believed that Eastern Europe lay in its sphere of influence and that there was very little the Western Allies, if they wished to defeat Germany, could do about this.

Third, equating the Polish government-in-exile with the emergent Lublin government confirmed its diminishing legitimacy in the eyes of the Great Powers. And the phrase 'Great Powers', so redolent of the diplomacy of the nineteenth century, affirmed another reality: the end of the war would be brought about by the Big Three, leaving them – and only them – with the capacity to determine Europe's future, which no amount of special pleading by the smaller powers could change. It is worth remembering that Poland was not alone in struggling to make its voice heard. At the same time General de Gaulle was tirelessly lobbying Whitehall on France's behalf, irritating any number of ministers and civil servants determined that the Free French forces, the French equivalent to Anders' Army, should make a visible contribution to the war effort and thereby bolster France's diplomatic position. Though just as defeated as Poland and with the added burden of a collaborationist government in the Vichy regime, France was greatly advantaged by its geography: in contrast to Poland, Germany's defeat would mean France's liberation. Fourth, Churchill's insistence that the Poles should be able to return of their own 'free will' and with every 'safeguard' deserves notice. On one level Churchill was simply stating the agreed position adopted by the United Nations, but in referring to safeguards he acknowledged British cognisance that Poles fighting in the West feared persecution from the new regime should they return.

The Prime Minister had not finished:

In any event, His Majesty's Government will never forget the debt they owe to the Polish troops who have served them so valiantly, and for all those who have fought under our command I earnestly hope it may be possible to offer the citizenship and freedom of the British Empire, if they so desire. I am not able to make a declaration on that subject to-day because

all matters affecting citizenship require to be discussed between this country
and the Dominions, and that takes time. But so far as we are concerned
we should think it an honour to have such faithful and valiant warriors
dwelling among us as if they were men of our own blood.[24]

These words, carried along by their Churchillian cadences, were heard
throughout the world, reaching attentive ears in Italy, Karachi, Kolhapur
and East Africa. Despite the caveats, this statement was effectively a declaration of intent and Poles quickly came to see it as 'Churchill's pledge'.
Indeed the Prime Minister was too experienced a politician to express
such aspirations in Parliament, knowing they would go into the official
record, without them marking a commitment that would be deployed
against any future government which took a contrary stance. Clement
Attlee, Churchill's successor, would later insist, though to no avail, the
words amounted to a 'hope' rather than a 'pledge'.[25]

On a personal level things were looking up for Rafał. In the New Year
he was made captain and wrote admitting how it pleased him far more
than he could have expected. Among his papers are a string of congratu-
latory notes from friends, family and fellow soldiers. Edward Bondar
heartily offered him a 'strong, legion-style handshake', his brother Stefan
'a hundred million congratulations', and Zych, perhaps a little ironically,
hoped he would 'jump even higher before demobilisation'. Hanna and
the girls were thrilled and hungered for further details, Rafał's promotion reinforcing the reassurance they drew from the continuing military
status of the Poles. 'We are very pleased that our army is staying an
army,' wrote Danusia in an undated letter. 'Please send us a photograph
with the new rank. I am very pleased that you are in the army because
it is good to have a Daddy in uniform.'

Echoing Danusia's optimism, Rafał's chipper letter on 24 March 1945,
written on the eve of the spring offensive, reflected his revived confidence in the future and the renewal of the military advance. As he
explained, he had spent the winter in an apartment, barely feeling the
cold, and something of his New Year musings must have reflected this
period of inactivity. His nerves were fine and, by his own admission,
unaffected – reusing his earlier phrase – by 'the political zigzags'. The
sense of security stemmed from the fact that 'we here in the army are
armed to the teeth: we are so eager and sure of our future that nothing
is fit to take away our courage'. This solidarity, enhanced by the release
of Polish POWs, which saw their numbers swell 'like yeast', meant

'optimism, not pessimism, is the epidemic among us'.[26] Was Rafał whistling in the dark? For many other Polish soldiers were much more pessimistic. Could it be that he envisioned Anders' Army leading a military liberation of Poland? The army certainly felt they could rely on themselves alone, Rafał implied, their strength and unity sufficient to determine their own future. Consequently, he wrote, they did not put great store by what was said in the press, recognising that 'in war speech is meant to heal that which one thinks about'. Buoyed up, he gave textbook Rafał advice: 'You there also remain calm and keep your chins up because whining wins nobody anything.' He might just as well have noted that letters from a serving soldier to his family are similarly intended to maintain morale. Nonetheless, he was right to tell them that they had nothing to fear from the UNRRA enquiries for it was necessary the agency clearly understood their point of view. 'If they do ask where you possibly want to go, it's clear: to Poland though not Soviet, and otherwise where I am.'

On 8 May, Victory in Europe or VE Day, Rafał wrote a momentous letter:

My Darlings!

I have not written for a long while and could not even on 1.5.45 send you the money you so need, but what I have lived through these last six weeks will explain to you fully. At first, the enormous preparation for the final struggle and everyone's tireless work did not allow anyone a moment, and then the fighting itself. We came out of the struggle on top . . . though we survived a couple of moments best not described. The Poles struck first (but that is as usual). The attack was monstrous. What was happening is impossible to describe. The Germans who remained alive had madness in their eyes even two days later. Then came the chase. I cannot describe these emotions accurately to you either. We had the satisfaction for 1939 we deserved. The difference being that we fought to the end and here the Germans are gathered like swine and marched to the rear. I even have to keep control of myself, for they became so meek and they slavishly look you in the eye and ask what is it you want from them. I once saw a German photograph of how they marched Polish prisoners of war – but they were prisoners of war and it was apparent they were. But what you see here arouses not hatred but simple disgust. I am writing this letter on the last day of the war (the so-called first war) that is, 8.5.45 at 15.00. I am sending you 5 one-pound cheques in this letter . . . and write only a little, as I am

preparing to write you a longer letter, my darling lass, once all of this
sinks in. I kiss you, your
    Rafał.

Perhaps this speaks for itself, but the syntax is sufficiently confused to
invite some comment. The reference to fighting to the end suggests criticism of the Polish performance in September 1939 – this time there would
be no surrender. The pathetic behaviour of German POWs captured
during the liberation of Bologna stirred Rafał's humanitarian instincts
and he steeled himself against their imploring looks and questions.
Defeated, the Germans were contemptible, showing nothing of the manly
dignity Rafał had perceived in photographs of captured Poles.

On the same day Rafał sent an exultant note to Danusia and Wanda.
His buoyant mood was unmistakable. He told of medals received, including
a 'gold cross', 'symbol of one of the greatest units in the Polish Army',
which was to be worn on his sleeve. He then commented on his appearance: 'I am completely healthy and suntanned like a black man, which
makes Indians grin when they see me.' Recalling their earlier days, he told
the girls of how the 'heat here is intense and brings Uzbekistan to mind,
only thankfully green and without tarantulas or other scorpions'.

Shortly afterwards, Rafał received a letter from Mary Ryżewska, one
of the elder Massachusetts Ryżewscy. She wrote of the negative coverage
Poland was receiving in the press, which she put down to the Communists,
finding preposterous the expectation that Poland could have sufficiently
industrialised in order to defend herself in only twenty years. 'But that's
enough,' she wrote, falling back on religious and nationalist platitudes,
'God's Mother is there and won't allow us to be harmed, let them do
what they like, but Poland has to be great, extending from sea to sea as
Mickiewicz said.'[27]

Captain Rafał Kornel Ryżewski had had a good war. He had survived,
enjoying promotion and witnessing the greatest Polish feats of the
struggle, his record noting that he saw action during the battles for Monte
Cassino, Ancona and Bologna, as well as on the Rivers Sangro, Rapido
and Senio, picking up a host of service medals along the way. His annual
appraisals, as issued for 1942, 1944 and 1945, describe a very intelligent,
well-educated man of high principle who not only commanded the respect
of his men but was greatly liked by them. In comments on his patriotism
and loyalty, Captain Ryżewski was thought a good Pole, a man who
demanded a lot, gave a lot, and got a lot back in return, inspiring his

men to reach the high standards he set. His only shortcoming, mentioned in all his reports, was a susceptibility to drink. Seemingly the problem was not alcoholism but a tendency, symptomatic of his sociability, joviality and high spirits, to get carried away. The nadir came in September 1942, shortly after the formation of Anders' Army, when following a particularly bad session he was placed under military arrest and imprisoned for three days. Though there is no evidence he misbehaved so badly again, it seems likely that incidents like this only endeared him to his men, as evidenced by surviving notes and gifts, including a home-made lighter. As the war came to a close, the appraisals hint that Rafał was beginning to chafe at military discipline and it seems fair to conclude that with his promotion to captain, his army career reached an appropriate peak.[28]

The war over, Hanna's preoccupation with her family's future was increasingly underpinned by a more sceptical outlook. Events were so momentous that she could not, as Rafał had advised, simply 'not bother with political affairs'; instead she wrote, as Lampedusa might have done, of how 'we are coming to the conclusion that nothing fundamental has changed about the world for centuries; everything is renewed only in another form'.[29] Her faith in God's mercy remained unchanged but it is possible to detect in these letters a weakening of her unconditional love of Poland. The hope of return was giving way to an acceptance of a long, if not permanent, exile. She had become adaptable and could accept anything but living under the Soviet system. 'We have got used to everything, only what is beyond us over the Caspian Sea we will never get used to and will always oppose. For the moment we are not going [to return to Poland] and have no intention to, and prefer to wait until a better time has dawned.'

Rafał, replying a week later (8 July), agreed: 'I write deliberately of meeting "somewhere" – because the situation is at the moment of a type that there is no discussion of a return to Poland. I don't want – for anything in the world – to go through the "Stalinist institute" or have it finish our children.' The Polish army, he again insisted, remained the guarantee of their continued and future security. Looking to the future, he felt that Canada, on account of its climate and 'other matters', looked like the best bet for the Ryżewscy if all else failed. However, 'as our affair is not yet lost and many signs in heaven and earth indicate that everything will turn around to our advantage, but not quickly, and therefore I wish you, darling, healthy and strong nerves'. A month or so later his views were unchanged. The mood remained 'distinctly anti-Soviet and doesn't permit a return to Poland'. Hanna, he insisted, had nothing to fear. She could rely on the fact that her husband was in the II Corps and, if the worst came to the worst, he wrote, 'I will do what my obligation indicates, and if you are to be found in the mountains of Tien Shan I will quickly find you on the other side of the barricade.'

That same day, the Foreign Office despatched a note to the Cabinet, selected embassies and friendly governments. It announced that as of 5 July 1945 the British government no longer recognised the Polish government-in-exile. In its place was the new Soviet-backed provisional government in Poland. All Polish government employees, maintained by the British, were to be dismissed forthwith and re-employed if necessary in purely adminis-trative roles. On 25 July, British embassies throughout the world were informed that the entire personnel of the Polish Mission abroad was to be relieved from duty with three months' salary on 31 July. Polish representa-tives would no longer enjoy diplomatic status, access to the diplomatic bag or cipher, or visa privileges, and should be discouraged from travelling to the UK. The British government pledged to maintain the Polish Mission's welfare responsibilities until such time as negotiations for its disposal were completed with Warsaw. In the meantime, essential welfare personnel would be re-employed by the British but it was essential that no one on British pay played any kind of political role. Henceforth, financial respon-sibility for Polish refugees passed from the former Polish government, funded by loans from the Treasury, to the Treasury itself. There would need to be economies.[30]

These moves reflected power realities in Poland itself, as confirmed at Potsdam (17 July–2 August 1945), the last of the major Big Three confer-ences. Poland was rewarded with German territories, the annexation of eastern Poland by the Soviet Union was rubber-stamped, and the expul-sion of Germans from Poland, Czechoslovakia and Hungary was approved. Free and democratic elections were to be held as soon as possible. 'With that,' as Norman Davies scathingly concludes, 'the Western Powers left Poland to its fate.'[31]

Out of the First World War emerged a series of ethnically diverse and deeply divided states, weakly buttressed by a liberal pluralism; the outcome of the Second World War was a series of relatively ethnically homogenous states. Poland's ethnic complexion was more changed than most. The majority of Poland's Jews had been murdered by the Nazis. Those surviving were to be found in camps as Displaced Persons, unwelcome in post-war Poland and frequently destined for the US or Israel. The Germans, including those living in the former German territories granted to Poland, faced expulsion and the 'national minorities' of the East found themselves not the inhabitants of independent nation-states but citizens of the Soviet Union. Little noticed in the West was the plight of the Ukrainians in eastern Poland, many of whom were violently expelled in the immediate post-war years. For the Poles this was vengeance for the massacres suffered at the hands of Ukrainians during the Nazi occupation; for both countries it left a legacy of enduring bitterness. Poland thereafter was overwhelmingly Catholic and Polish-speaking, forming one of the most homogenous and, as a consequence, conservative societies in Europe. There is a terrible irony in all this. World War Two had been caused by the vicious racial and nationalist ideologies which, though culminating in Nazism, had infected much political discourse outside Germany. The Allies fought the war to destroy fascism but created a Europe composed of states more ethnically uniform than had ever been the case in the continent's history.

As we shall see in the following chapter, the settling of Poland's borders, the expulsions, and the establishment of the Soviet sphere of influence in Eastern Europe did not entirely close this chapter of Polish history. The Polish armed forces under Allied Command and the Polish refugee camps provide an addendum to this main narrative, quickly becoming a new site for the ideological battles that shaped post-war Europe.

How were the two girls faring against this background of seismic political and historical change? If their story is picked up in late 1944, we find business as usual. Wanda is wishing her father a happy saint's day and hoping that the extended family will soon all meet again 'in our free beloved Homeland in our own warm corner'. She also sent 1000000000000000000000000 kisses. Rafał, much taken with Wanda's latest colour photo ('simply wonderful'), told his daughter it had pride of place by his bed. 'I have many questions on its account,' he teased, 'such as "where did you meet that beauty?"'

Danusia, too, seems to have been fairly oblivious to the new developments. Writing in the third person, she again mimicked the words of the adults around her, suggesting her dad 'probably won't recognise the Danka you saw in Tehran for she has grown into a young woman whose hair has settled down and sits quietly on the head of this whirlwind'. Hanna, often at her wits' end owing to Danusia's excessive energy, nonetheless affectionately told Rafał that Danusia was 'so similar to him'. Her developing adolescent self-consciousness coincided with a growing fascination for Hollywood, first clearly seen in a letter from around this time. 'Please explain to me why I am so attracted to art,' she wrote plaintively. 'I would like to be in America, playing various roles. More than once when I see a film and there are pretty actresses my heart breaks to be altogether with them and dance and play for them.'

Today, Nana remembers the effect the Hollywood movies brought by the Americans had on her. The lavish sets and fabulous costumes of MGM musicals all delivered in glorious Technicolor discombobulated the little girl living in the refugee camp. Esther Williams's remarkable synchronised swimming sequences, gaudy and brash in their blues and pinks,[32] and Carmen Miranda's extraordinary headdresses and Latin sensuality[33] are etched into her memory. Also remembered are the 'Road to . . .' movies, gag-fests starring Bing Crosby, Bob Hope and Dorothy Lamour, which took their audiences to Singapore (1940), Zanzibar (1941) and Morocco (1942), places made familiar to people owing to the war and benign thanks to these films. In one gently comic scene Hope and Crosby cross the Sahara on a camel, singing songs and passing helpfully placed signs pointing to Morocco. Finally, there were the films of 'darling' Shirley Temple, probably responsible for leaving more little girls dissatisfied with their lives than anyone else in history.

Wanda distanced herself from her sister's escapist fantasies, finding them a little ridiculous, but she, too, sought comfort in an idyllic alternative world and though her ambitions were less fanciful, in her imagined future, lived out on the landscape of childhood, she found common ground with her sister:

> I constantly think of living in the country because the countryside is one of the most beautiful and prettiest landscapes without regard to what kind it is, so I, truthfully speaking, would like to be an agronomist and remain for good in Korzyść. Danusia often talks with me on this subject: that she would like to be on the allotment and there found a theatre and on the river a bath-house and she would be a famous artist in the theatre, she says again that I would like to be a nun but I think neither agrees with me. As for this 'artist', I can say much for when she returns from school she immediately performs acrobatic exercises so much that she has bent the bamboo of the tent a little.

It is funny that Wanda is drawn into subjecting her sister's needling to consideration, not that she misses the opportunity to get her own back, mocking the 'artist'. However divergent Wanda's and Danusia's fantasies, both were mapped on to the same ideal landscape of their lost domain. Late at night, under the cover of darkness and curled up together, sensible Wanda and naughty Danusia through hushed whispers planned their futures, reaffirming their unique sorority.

By day, Danusia continued to wend her slightly eccentric way. In a letter written some months later she began to say a little more about herself. This time she told of her great liking for drawing, describing how when trying to draw herself in the mirror she had only got the hair right but in drawing class she had pulled off a wonderful eagle. This was now stored among the other pictures she was keeping to show her father. She had finished yet another malaria cure and was, her mother said, a little yellow and thin, but she insisted she went up for seconds at dinner. From her point of view the only notable news in the camp was the birth of two kittens. 'They are beginning to crawl and stand on their paws but when they walk it tires them for they shake as though they had malaria.'

Changing tack, it transpired there were other things she wanted to tell her father about. Going into confessional mode, she again wrote of her obsession with movie stars. 'I'm a little embarrassed but I will write about it. I am collecting little programmes and various magazines with actresses, but because it is so nice to have such and such an actress who performs in a film, I have about two thousand filling a box and I don't know how to take them with me when and if we go somewhere.' It's a strange confession, mingling concern that the collection could prove a burden with the possibility that her obsession might in itself be a problem. Was she hoping her father would say that there was nothing wrong with the collecting, strengthening her case for taking them with her, or was this a more serious unburdening, a half-recognition that she needed some release from her obsessive fantasy world? Either way, Danusia's identification with movie stars was a little self-aggrandising, a way of separating herself from the world around her, and this irritated Wanda, who also spilled the beans to their father. Ridiculing Danusia's wish to 'hang them above her bed like the men in the camps do', she reported that instead it 'turned out that she stuck them into her journal'. Had Hanna forbidden her from decorating her private space? Had the box been a secret, suddenly discovered? Too much should not be made of this adolescent furtiveness. Danusia was thirteen years old and transfixed by celebrity, proving as susceptible as any adolescent to the possibility of a different kind of life. In the same way Wanda's annoyance is equally predictable. Danusia and Wanda fitted classic psychological profiling: the sensible elder sibling, orientated towards the expectations of the adults around her, and the younger sibling, less conformist, less responsible and less obliging.

Sibling rivalries notwithstanding, the end of the war found the Ryżewscy in pretty good shape. In August Rafał was partway through major dental treatment: 'After it is all done I will have, to start with, 9 teeth up top and 12 on the bottom, and will also be able to carry them happily in my pocket.' He was living comfortably in a 'palace' comman-deered by the military. He had 'electric power, a bathtub, washing room, in one word comfort like a home, only I feel sorry at times that you over there keep living like Gypsies in tents'. His latest preoccupation was that the two girls should be learning English and though Wanda reassured her father that she was taking her English lessons seriously Rafał suggested to Hanna that if necessary she should hire a private tutor. Hanna gave him other things to think about: if he could see his older daughter now he 'would have to think of dowries and sons-in-law'. No such questions yet hovered over Danusia and, despite her daydreaming about Hollywood starlets, getting on at school remained the priority.

With the end of the war, the days of the Karachi camp were numbered. The authorities were determined that it should be shut down as soon as possible. Numbers dwindled as logistical barriers to travel were cleared away and the refugees were able to take up long available places else-where in India and in Africa. As 1945 wore on, the camp was depopu-lated and it became a shadow of its former self, very soon housing few more people than the administrators and staff like Hanna. The gong still summoned the hungry to the dining tent, but it now rang hollow, echoing through the empty camp. It brought not a throng of people but a host of cats, who sat up expectantly in the chairs. By September, Hanna, Danusia and Wanda were en route to Bombay and from there to Kolhapur, the penultimate stage in their journey.

At the Christian cemetery at Gora Qabristan, not far from Karachi's city centre, two rows of gravestones, simple and elegant, record Polish lives lost in the city during the Second World War. There are fifty-eight in all.

8

'Polish Indians': Valivade

Kolhapur airport is tiny, an ideal type lifted from a children's storybook or built in Lego. Though it's the monsoon season, the rains have been light, much to the disappointment of farmers, and a sprinkler washes the flower beds. The sun is bright, the weather beautifully warm, the landscape soft and green. It's immediately obvious that I've arrived in one of the most affluent areas of India. In the very south of the Maharashtra, Kolhapur state is blessed by an abundance of the most precious resource of all, water. Five rivers flow through the state, which means good soil, and a strong agricultural sector, now supplemented by a flourishing light industry. As I collect my bags and head for the rickshaw stand I notice the brackish smell I've brought with me from Mumbai. For a moment I feel nostalgic for the heaving, filthy metropolis I've left behind, but as the rickshaw wallah carries me into the city, I begin to rhapsodise about small-town Indian life. After the pressure of Mumbai, one need only walk a few steps down any street anywhere else to feel freed, elated by the sudden sense of openness. And this despite the drivers aggressively competing for road space with nonchalant pedestrians or donkeys huddled around foul heaps of food waste, or stray dogs trotting along on tiptoe. White-horned cattle do indeed amble peacefully through central streets, their haughty hip bones languorously signalling every step, though most beautiful are the gatherings of blackly purple water buffalo. Despite that Indian penchant for the car horn – trucks have signs on their tailgates asking that motorists sound their presence – little in Kolhapur disturbs the sense of well-being pervading the place.

Which is lucky, for having settled into my hotel, I went looking for the Mahavia Gardens with a hopeless set of directions. The gardens, where a memorial records the presence of the Poles in Kolhapur, seems a good place to begin getting to know this city. The evening rush is just

starting and it's raining. Rickshaws packed with mothers and children
trundle precariously past, the chatter from within audible to those on
foot, motorists impatiently overtake, flooring the accelerator of their
Marutis, pedestrians stroll oblivious to the constant threat from the traffic.
Fast-food sellers stare at me, inscrutable and intense, as I, with studied
casualness, repeatedly retrace my steps. The park is not where the park
is supposed to be, though I do find an intriguing and clearly very affluent
housing development, which could well have been transplanted from
provincial France. I collect some more directions, more decisive this time,
and head the opposite way.

The gardens are nicely laid out, pathways gracefully curving around
flower beds and slightly overgrown patches of grass. This place is of
the Raj, formal but not French, attractive if a little municipal.
Promenaders cluster quietly; in contrast to the streets the park feels
relatively empty. The absent hustle seems to reflect class and genera-
tional distinctions, though there are no formal restrictions on entry. A
large war memorial commemorates the dead of Kolhapur, lost to
various twentieth-century conflicts. It testifies to the feeling common
among older Indians that the Second World War was not the war of
the imperial powers but a war of humanity against inhumanity to
which they made a vital contribution. Nearby, in this memorial corner,
is the smaller Polish memorial erected in 1998. It's an elegant column,
a cross topped by a Polish eagle. The inscription simply records Polish
gratitude for the generosity and hospitality of the Kolhapur state and
its people. It is in Marathi, Polish and English, and it reads:

IN THE YEARS 1943–1948
THANKS TO THE HOSPITALITY
OF KOLHAPUR STATE
5000 POLISH REFUGEES
FOUND SHELTER IN
VALIVADE CAMP

DISPERSED
THROUGHOUT THE WORLD
WE REMEMBER INDIA
WITH HEARTFELT GRATITUDE

On the 50th anniversary
of our departure
Association of Poles in India
1998

Two men in black have appeared. They say nothing but stand and
watch me. Feeling obliged to explain myself I start a conversation and it
transpires they are the park guards – it seems that's all they want to tell
me. The three of us dutifully inspect the monument. The pressure to
appear purposeful prolongs my examination.

At the steps of the monument a group of elderly gentlemen have
gathered. Their suits have been worn for many years. I play the gauche
foreigner, which in these circumstances comes easily. Interrupting their
conversation I ask if they know about the monument. They do, though
they have a slightly awry view of what it represents. Something to do
with an aeroplane crash, which might be an obscure connection to General
Sikorski's fate – he died in a plane crash in July 1943. I clarify things a
little and when I tell them of my grandmother, a woman of their generation, there are smiles all round. 'Here? In Kolhapur?' Yes, here for two
years. The lively fellow with the best English takes control of the situation and tells me I must speak to the Colonel, he knows all about this.
I'm in luck: the Colonel is currently taking his walk.

Colonel Shankar Nanasaheb Nikam arrives moments later, accompanied by two friends. For me this is an incredibly fortuitous meeting.
Colonel Nikam greets me very warmly and before long is slapping me
on the back like an old comrade. Come, he says, beckoning me towards
his car; his largely silent friends elect to sit in the back. I learn later they
are Mr Bhosley, a retired industrialist born in 1930, and Mr Ghorpade,
born in 1918, a Cambridge-educated large landowner and evidently a
respected member of the community. Despite decades-old friendship,
these three old gentlemen treat each other with elegant courtesies.
Minutes later we've arrived at the Colonel's house in the middle of the
city and are sitting on his veranda.

Our conversation turns quickly to the Poles, about whom the Colonel
knows a great deal. As a young man he was in a peculiarly privileged
position. He's of a martial people, he explains. Like his father before him,
he had been in the British-Indian army. I'm shown a photograph of
himself as a young man among a group of Indian and British officers. I
ask why he is the only Indian not wearing Indian headwear. His father

always did, he explains, showing me another photograph. On account of his good English, his father entered the army as a non-commissioned officer, part of the crucial group of Indian soldiers who comprised the interface between the British officers and the sepoy rank-and-file. Colonel Nikam, however, standing on the shoulders of his father, trained as an officer and was treated as an absolute equal by the 'Britishers', hence his undifferentiated British dress. His old mates – I'm shown a photograph of his Company from the Second World War – included an Irishman, known for being less than deferential towards his superiors, and a cockney with an incomprehensible accent.

Colonel Nikam's attitude towards the former colonial power is complex. He is proud of his status within the British army, a reflection of his family's upward mobility, and he admires the 'Britishers' for their fairness and meritocratic outlook. The Americans he celebrates for, quite literally, changing the world. By entering the war, he says, Roosevelt consigned empire to the dustbin of history.

Colonel Nikam recalls that the Polish camp at Valivade, a settlement area a short distance from Kolhapur city, was at first a source of fascination to the local population. 'Though we thought of them as if in a zoo,' he jokes, 'we nonetheless assumed that as white people they must by a part of the ruling class.' As an officer, the Colonel was free to visit the camp and did so when on leave. He quickly realised the Poles did not share the same status as the 'Britishers' and, sixty years later, he wonders if they sympathised with the Indians as a fellow oppressed people. I say that there is evidence that the Poles sympathised with the nationalist movement and that when the Union Jack was lowered on British India on 15 August 1947 there were celebrations in the camp. In some respects the Poles went native, developing an affinity for the Indian people, some even wishing to stay on permanently.[1] It seems Polish–Indian relations were more informal than British–Indian relations. And, I say, many of the Poles who were at Valivade today identify as Polish Indians, regarding themselves as a particularly fortunate group within the Polish émigré community. The Polish Indians, now in their seventies and eighties, spent their formative years in Valivade, which left a deep impression and memories – almost without exception positive.

The Colonel confirms that those feelings were mutual. The Poles, he insists, were always treated respectfully, there was no local resentment – government reports don't quite bear this out – and the women, he pointedly observes, were never molested. I ask him if, as a young officer, a camp full of young women possessed a certain charm? Of course, he says, and he remembers talk in the town among 'educated people' about the possibility of marrying a Polish woman. Though Indian taboos and family expectations generally prevented this, the Poles were found appealing owing to their novelty, prettiness, the social status associated with their skin colour and the idea that it would be a progressive or modern thing to do. Two of the three marriages he remembers – and there were probably several more[2] – were unsuccessful. One ended the moment the Poles left, the bride choosing to leave India, the second couple divorced soon after, but the third remains strong to this day and Mr and Mrs Kuskihav still live in the city. The British looked askance at such relationships and restricted contact that could have led to cross-cultural romance.

Valivade was 'run like a concentration camp', says Colonel Nikam, 'but was not a concentration camp, but a home for them'. By this he simply means that it was efficient and largely self-contained, though dependent on the local community for supplies. A general store in the camp was run by a local Indian man, who ensured that essentials, including kerosene, were easily available. Poles were allowed out to town for shopping or, on a Sunday, to see a film at Mr Pardishi's cinema hall. Pardishi did well by catering to European tastes and was well known for importing foods as well as films. He was one of a number of local businessmen contracted by the authorities to supply the camp with essential items such as meat, bread, cloth, stationery and fuel.[3] Colonel Nikam was impressed by the cleanliness of the camp, the care and artistry which went into the flower beds, and the general good order of the place. It was 'a whole camp of women', he says, this being explanation enough. Most interestingly, he was aware of the class distinctions within the camp. You could see it on their faces, he explains, the strong sturdy lower-class women, generally simply dressed and used to hard physical work, and the slim, more refined women of the middle classes.

Such distinctions did little to diminish the fact that the Poles were comparatively well off and had greater surplus income than most of the Indians around them. Not only did they receive an allowance from the Polish government but their husbands and relatives in the army regularly sent money, their means reflecting salary and rank. This allowed them to order from Bombay merchants luxury items like dresses, shoes and handbags. Nana remembers their lives in India as comfortable. Her father regularly sent nice things and, as Rafał's letters show, each month he sent money orders, described by him, tongue firmly in cheek, as 'sacramental', 'a cash infusion . . . to wipe off your tears in these difficult times'.

Soon we move inside and the Colonel plies me with Indian whisky. We drink together, but he pours himself smaller glasses and in the morning I am certain someone has drilled a hole into my left temple. His wife, a silent woman as ancient as her husband, smiles kindly but largely stays out of view; the house is shared with their son Nitten, his wife Alpanna and their two children. The Colonel's approach is a little patriarchal but it is clear this is a happy family. I later observe quite how well it functions. While the Colonel gardens, listening to Indian classical music on his MP3 player, Nitten and his wife look after their expanding business interests from their small office. Nitten will later say, 'You must think my father rude, we're just very direct.' Nitten is modest and very articulate, occasionally moderating his father's reactionary attitudes or, with a hint of apology, explaining them. Alpanna seems a little amused by the old man and I'm convinced has more to say than she chooses to.

Following much talk about corrupt politicians, it's soon late and time for me to go. When the Nikams learn that I'm staying in an overpriced business hotel – at £20 a night, it's a steal – they insist I transfer to the Residency Club. Another legacy of the Raj and now a slightly scruffy social focus for the city's middle class, the club proves a very good move. When the following day I plan to go to Valivade, the club is on hand to help, summoning two teenage boys to accompany me, the younger speaking a little English, while the older drives the rickshaw.

Valivade, a name which has slipped out of use, is now known as Gandhinagar. A sizeable settlement near Kolhapur, the town long ago swallowed up the camp, which is now a neighbourhood called Koyne Colony and inhabited by Hindus, Muslims and Christians. Central Gandhinagar is busy and more makeshift than Kolhapur, the rows of shops and cafés more shack-like, more corrugated. We don't know where the former camp is and I can only observe the two boys as they seek directions, failing to assuage their anxiety about getting lost, taking too long, etc. We've asked perhaps half a dozen locals for guidance, only to find they generally don't have any idea of what it is we are talking about. Not surprisingly, few remember the Polish Indians. For me, the difficulties and slight delays merely bring more to stimulate ear and eye, and I readily entrust myself to the boys, only abandoning my passive role when an older man attempts to take control of our perambulations and has to be shaken off.

It eventually transpires that Koyne Colony is at the end of a long, narrow side street, down which we tuk-tuk briskly. It is immediately obvious that the colony is located somewhere quite distinct, adjacent to the town, but what once was a spacious oasis provided for the Poles is now embraced from every direction by suburban sprawl. Judging by the maps of the camp and the photographs I have seen, it is clear that the buildings have been significantly modified. The roofs are altered and the pathways lined with concrete, but nonetheless I'm struck at once by the sturdily attractive appearance of these rows of single-storey, whitewashed terraced cabins. The style is quite unlike that of the rest of the town. The buildings are laid out in a very orderly manner, separated by generous footpaths, and grouped around a series of central spaces. This is a planned and largely pedestrian settlement which, stripped of the dirt and with some fairly basic amenities added, and perhaps a touch of poetic licence, might be imagined as a holiday village. All the usual problems associated with poverty in the developing world are here, especially poor sanitation, but so many years later one cannot help but be impressed by the quality of the provision made for the Poles. Valivade was a very different prospect from the tent cities of Tehran and Karachi.

What I see around me confirms the positive impression I've gleaned of the camp from the records preserved in the India Office archives in London. Among those records are a series of reports outlining the provisioning of the camp. The first, dated 11 August 1943 and written by a Whitehall civil servant, is addressed to the engineer supervising the construction.[4] It details the number and cost of items required which had received official approval. Though little more than a list collated by a hard-pressed official, and with no further elaboration, it is a strangely moving testament to the scale of organisation and costs (in rupees) thought necessary to ensure a decent standard of living for even a relatively small number of people. As such, it is worth reproducing in full (the costs are pegged to the high rate of 1 shilling and 6 pence in 1926):

Initial grant for playground, swings, sand-boxes etc.: Rs. 5,000
Initial grant for establishing clubs and libraries: Rs. 10,000
Hospital equipment: Rs. 6,000
Small car for office: Rs. 3,000

Dental equipment: Rs. 3,000

Installation telephone: Rs. 9,558

2 lorries: Rs. 17,500

Farming equipment, including seeds: Rs. 5,000

Fire-fighting equipment: Rs. 5,000

Initial issue to each family quarter of broom, pans and brushes: Rs. 10,000

Charboy [bedstead] dipping tank: Rs. 1,000

Purchase of tools for sweepers and sanitary squad: Rs. 250

Purchase of miscellaneous items such as rope for laundry drying lines: Rs. 5,000

Digging trenches for night soil: Rs. 600

1,776 latrine pans: Rs. 7,992

3,360 chatties: Rs. 1,680

888 latrine seats: Rs. 5,328

Drainage from bathrooms: Rs. 300

10 sullage water troughs and 7 tanks for cleaning night chambers and pans: Rs. 10,600

150 metal drums: Rs. 2,400

Road making: Rs. 12,500

Water scheme: Rs. 100,000

Two large garages: Rs. 2,800

Three small ?: R. 3,600

60 boundary pillars: R. 300

Water tanks in each bathroom for laundry work: Rs. 13,500

Fencing of ballies and bamboos around bath water reservoir: Rs. 350

One bully trestle for pump at the river: Rs. 150

Furniture for schools including 600 desks: Rs. 7,200

600 benches: Rs. 4,200

Construction of additional brick work surrounding the fireplace in 1,344 family quarters: Rs. 4,368

Construction of fire-proof building for storing kerosene: Rs. 5,500

12 bathtubs: Rs. 144

2,980 buckets: Rs. 7,450

1,680 dippers: Rs. 945

3,360 7¾" Dia Sigrees [open grills] made out of second-hand iron plate: Rs. 4,200

5,200 Moonj [cane] beds with mosquito poles: Rs. 46,800

1,880 dressing tables, 3'6" with mirrors 18" by 14": Rs. 47,000

5,200 chairs: Rs. 25,675

1,680 tables 6' by 3'6": Rs. 25,200

762 bath boards: Rs. 3,048

1,880 side tables with top, bottom and centre shelves 2'6" by 2'6":
Rs. 15,040

1,680 kitchen tables 3' by 2': Rs. 13,440

12 wash-hand stands 3'6" by 2': Rs. 120

12 office chairs: Rs. 72

6 office tables 4' by 3': Rs. 90

2 kitchen tables 8' by 3': Rs. 40

2 meat safes 5' by 3'9": Rs. 260

6 stools: Rs. 18

25 dining tables 10' by 3': Rs. 600

50 benches 10' by 1' by 18" high: Rs. 600

6 crockery racks 6' by 1½' by 5': Rs. 180

12 commodes with pans: Rs. 150

Purchase of furniture for two officers' flats in the camp: Rs. 2,000

Purchase of iron grates for sigrees [open grills]: Rs. 3,360

Alteration to staff mess kitchen: Rs. 130

Construction of Police Outpost Buildings: Rs. 1,600

Purchase of 12 almirahs [cabinets]: Rs. 960

Purchase of furniture for matrons' quarters: Rs. 1,000

Sanitation dominates this list, with the supply of water and the disposal of waste accounting for a large proportion of the budget. Additional documents would almost certainly have been drawn up detailing how the 100,000 rupees were to be spent on the water supply. Other items, however, stand out more strongly still. It's hard to miss the provision made for chairs and desks for the schools or the fact that the list is headed with costings for the children's playground and a library. More telling still are the 47,000 rupees made available for dressing tables and mirrors. This luxury might seem frivolous, but the empathy it reflects carries its own poignancy. Around this time Hanna started to worry in letters that her looks had been ravaged and Nana remembers how the women in the camps, finally facing the prospect of reunion with their husbands, became more and more anxious about how desirable they were and the prospects of the marital bed. Rafał was good always to tell her not to worry, though his endearments ('my old woman') might not have helped.

Touching though this list may be, not least as evidence of goodwill – notwithstanding the disagreements between the British and Polish authorities regarding the extent of provision[5] – its meanings are not uncomplicated. If read as a manifestation of imperial practice rather than in the context of a refugee experience it reveals that Poles were the beneficiaries of the racial hierarchies that underpinned the Raj. As we have already seen, when discussions first began in October 1941 about the possibility of Poles going to India, the Secretary of State immediately raised questions about the difficulty of accommodating non-Asiatic refugees.[6] He was concerned about the safety of European children, particularly girls, arguing that they must always be supervised. Though not said explicitly, this suggests India posed particular sexual dangers and it is striking that Colonel Nikam said the women were not harassed, an allusion perhaps to the 'eve teasing' that can disfigure Indian life.[7] As the Viceroy clarified in December 1941, extra-special measures would need to be taken, not least because educating the children to the right standard posed a particular challenge. Though Catholic – the British tended to separate the small number of Jewish Polish children, sending them to camps in Palestine – they could not be expected to live in convent or mission schools intended for 'Anglo-Indians of humble origin'. Overall, the official understood,

> there are over a million Polish refugees in Russia and they are comparatively well to do middle class families. I feel therefore that I must endorse the majority view that if Polish children come to India they must be accommodated in camps, either specially constructed or formed by requisitioning existing buildings, in which schools would be set up.[8]

Alerted to these concerns, particularly those about the Indian climate, the Polish embassy in London was quick to allay British fears, reminding the Foreign Office that anything was preferable to Asiatic Russia.

An enterprise on this scale needed to be professionally run, requiring a large and varied staff. Members of the British administration took the most senior roles, local people fulfilled the most menial, and the Poles were drawn on for roles of the middling sort. Again it is the official list, this one drawn up on 13 August 1943, which most completely articulates the complexity of the task.[9] Reflected here is what was felt the minimum needed for 5,000 people, including a large number of children, to live adequately. It is not possible to say exactly which roles were taken by Indians, though where the job is described by its Indian name we can assume this was the case. Such roles were very poorly renumerated, again reflecting the racial hierarchies at work in the Raj and the caste system.[10] Though Colonel Nikam was right to see that within India the Poles did not have the same status as the British, they were treated as nominal equals, liable to be entrusted with positions of responsibility. Valivade was the Raj in microcosm, a place where roles were racially prescribed and status a symptom of skin colour and birth:

Liaison officer: Rs. 400
Accountant: Rs. 150
Stenographer: Rs. 125
Interpreter: Rs. 70
Chaprassi [messenger]: Rs. 20

Commandant's office:
Secretary: Rs. 220
Typist: Rs. 100
2 interpreters: Rs. 70 each
4 runners: Rs. 30 each

Stores and Account branch:
Officer-in-charge (trained accountant): Rs. 170
Storekeeper: Rs. 120
Cashier: Rs. 100
3 clerks: Rs. 80 each
Interpreter: Rs. 70

Registration branch:
Officer-in-charge: Rs. 100
2 clerks: Rs. 80 each

Chaplains:
2 priests: Rs. 150 each
2 sacristans: Rs. 60 each

Employment branch:
Officer-in-charge: Rs. 120

Assistant Officer-in-charge: Rs. 90

Tailors' superintendent: Rs. 90

Assistant tailors' superintendent: Rs. 60

Cobblers: Rs. 60

Carpenters: Rs. 60

Plumbers: Rs. 60

9 apprentices to above: Rs. 40 each

5 barbers: Rs. 40 each

Cultural uplift:

Officer-in-charge: Rs. 130

Assistant: Rs. 90

12 club matrons: Rs. 60 each

Artist: Rs. 60

Typist: Rs. 70

Translator: Rs. 70

Monthly grant for uplift expenses: Rs. 5,000

Controlling board:

3 auditors: Rs. 170 each

Camp guards:

Officer-in-charge: Rs. 120

Deputy: Rs. 100

5 wing superintendents: Rs. 85 each

50 guards: Rs. 60 each

6 firemen: Rs. 40 each

24 firemen: Rs. 30 each

Wings:

4 wing commanders: Rs. 120 each

8 assistant wing commanders: cost unspecified

Orphanage:

Superintendent of orphanage: Rs. 200

Assistants: Rs. 90

Allowances to matrons and their assistants, including kitchens, linen,
nursery and clothing: Rs. 750

Orphanage menial staff:

Head cook: Rs. 50

Assistant: Rs. 40

2 table servants: Rs. 30 each
9 cook's mates: Rs. 10 each
15 hamals [porters]: Rs. 18

Education:
Headmaster: Rs. 220
Assistant: Rs. 170
Clerk: Rs. 120
20 teachers: Rs. 120 each
Monthly grant for books and stationery: Rs. 1,000
2 porters: Rs. 30 each

Primary school:
Superintendent of schools: Rs. 220
Assistant: Rs. 120
Clerk: Rs. 80
4 Headmasters of wing school: Rs. 120 each
80 teachers: Rs. 100 each
Contingencies: Rs. 1,200
Rewards for children: Rs. 3,000
8 porters: Rs. 30 each

Medical (Laxmi Vilas Hospital):
Chief Medical Officer (non-Polish): Rs. 500
Matron (non-Polish): Rs. 300
10 qualified nurses: Rs. 100 each
Indian compounder: Rs. 35
Polish kitchen matron: Rs. 45
Indian cook: Rs. 40
4 Indian cook's mates: Rs. 10 each
6 hamals [porters]: Rs. 18 each
4 chowkidars [watchmen]: Rs. 9 each
5 lavatory sweepers: Rs. 20 each
3 female sweepers: Rs. 12 each
2 bhishtis [watermen]: Rs. 15 each
Electrician: Rs. 24
1 mali: Rs. 19
1 mali: Rs. 12
Laundry on contract: Rs. 75
Monthly grant for medicines: Rs. 1,000

Hospital contingencies: Rs. 400
Messing for 50 patients: Rs. 2,250

Camp dispensary and hospital for minor cases:
3 medical officers: Rs. 270 each
Public Health Inspector (non-Polish): Rs. 250
2 dental surgeons: Rs. 220 each
Head compounder (Polish): Rs. 130
2 compounders: Rs. 100 each
4 apprentices: Rs. 40 each
Matron: Rs. 150
12 qualified nurses: Rs. 100 each
1 home sister: Rs. 120
20 probationer nurses: Rs. 40 each
9 men for sanitary squad: Rs. 40 each
4 metranis [carers]: Rs. 12 each
4 laundry maids: Rs. 40 each
2 cooks: Rs. 75 each
8 cook's mates: Rs. 60 each
2 hamals [porters]: Rs. 18 each
Messing for 200 patients: Rs. 9,000
Monthly grant for medicines: Rs. 1,000
Hospital contingencies: Rs. 600
Dental drugs: Rs. 600

Menial establishment:
50 bhishtis [watermen]: Rs. 25 each
1 night soil maistry [worker]: Rs. 30
20 sweepers: Rs. 25
1 maistry for garbage, road sweeping: Rs. 20
18 sweepers: Rs. 270

And, on top of this, were the contingent costs (excluding allowances):

Lighting of roads: Rs. 500
Telephone charges: Rs. 22
Maintenance of ambulances and lorries (inclusive of drivers' wages):
Rs. 400
Municipal conservancy charges for removal of night soil and garbage:
Rs. 800

Water supply contract for pumping: Rs. 660

Upkeep office car: Rs. 120

Stationery and stamps for Commandant's Office: Rs. 100

Sanitary contingencies: Rs. 500

Alum and bleaching powder for water supply: Rs. 100

Expenses of charpoy [bedstead] dipping tank fuel and labour: Rs. 100

Miscellaneous and unforeseen: Rs. 1,500

These lists, even in this undigested form, are very revealing. The scope for young Poles to be trained as nurses reflected a wider provision for practical training. Courses were available in tailoring, mechanics, sewing, knitting, beekeeping, bookkeeping and typing. By 1946, some 420 people had graduated from vocational courses and 280 remained in training. At the same time there were 2,009 children at school. Most teenagers received a generalist education at the high school – one set of figures suggests a roll of 663 – though at the same time thirty-eight female students completed their secondary education at the commercial high school and a further seventy-five at the school of rural management, which had a three-hectare farm connected to it. Older boys and girls were sent to Catholic schools as far away as Karachi and Bombay, as well as nearby locations like Panchgani and Saugor.[11] On graduation, the boys might be sent to join the Polish armed forces. The lists also reveal the expectation that the Polish refugees would bring with them considerable professional skills, not least medical skills, and it might be recalled that the Indian government reserved the right to cherry-pick the Poles passing through Karachi.

The dry climate and buildings constructed from natural materials meant fire was a major hazard and the focus on firefighting was significant, as was the camp's overall concern with security. Most contentious, but in many ways most revealing, was the provision for 'cultural uplift'. The 5,000 rupees dedicated each month to this were intended to provide morally improving entertainments and activities. What had been practised informally in the *kolkhoz* and organised through the army in the Polish camps in the Soviet Union – the patriotic commemorations, the religious ceremony – came under highly politicised civilian control in Valivade. For the Polish authorities, 'cultural uplift' meant more than simply reviving Polish resourcefulness and self-reliance – though all recognised the need for this – it was also a weapon in the continuing ideological war for the hearts and minds of the

Polish people that had begun with the Soviet occupation of eastern Poland. As a consequence the theatre and the church, both generously endowed, were of central importance and the Poles resented British scrutiny of these accounts, demanding absolute autonomy where 'cultural uplift' was concerned.

Equally significant to the life of the camps was the Scout and Guide movement, which in 1946 boasted a thousand children enrolled in thirty-three packs.[12] Following their Soviet experience, many of the children were not only malnourished and prone to repeated illness, as we have seen with Wanda and Danusia, but were also listless, anxious, or withdrawn, displaying all the symptoms of psychological trauma. Through its provision of routine activities and the emphasis on healthy living, sociability, personal responsibility, practical education, and the disciplining of body and mind, the Scouting movement was believed to provide the perfect antidote for these suffering children. The regime of organised activity ranged from the preparation of ceremonial performances, through sport, camping, and, for some of the older children, trips by bicycle to distant sites of interest – Panhala, a hilltop town near Kolhapur with stunning views over the valley below, was one regular destination, while the strongest boys ventured as far as Goa, relishing the three-day journey. Surviving photographs of life in the camp, often produced for propaganda purposes, suggest an idyllic existence. Mothers look busy and industrious, whether in the classroom, the kitchen or the shop; children, some still with the blonde hair of the very young, are tanned and bright-eyed, thriving thanks to the largely outdoor life led by this semi-enclosed community. And from the child's perspective Valivade *was* almost perfect. There were no real dangers and much of the life of the camp revolved around them, in whom were invested the future hopes of this enclave of the Polish nation.

Such, of course, cannot tell the whole story. The post office, one of the hubs of camp life, brought bad news as well as good and as the Polish II Corps fought its way up through Italy letters arrived telling of yet more women widowed or yet another child orphaned. With the close of the war the search for missing relatives intensified. Letters arriving at the camp sometimes bore postmarks indicating long and complex journeys of forwardings that had carried them from destination to destination in search of their intended recipient. Some bore good news that might now be out of date or old bad news that shattered long-clung-to hopes. Good news, however, did begin to arrive written by or on behalf of released internees or POWs.

Another threat to the tranquillity of camp life brought by the cessation of hostilities came from the new Polish government. Claiming a limited sovereignty over the camp – rejected by the British and international law – it sought to influence the politics of the inmates. A propaganda war quickly broke out between Poland's new government and the former government-in-exile, which maintained its moral authority over its former charges, just as it did for the majority of the members of the Polish armed forces – in July 1946 Rafał would very deliberately refer in a letter to Hanna to 'our (London) authorities'. Former political functionaries continued to act unofficially, irritating the British and infuriating the new Polish government.

Standing in Koyne Colony, I have barely a moment to ponder these developments before I'm surrounded by excited teenagers and children, my unannounced appearance giving rise to an extraordinary welcome. It's impossible not to be instantly charmed by these dozen or so smiling faces and within minutes I'm being led from house to house, each of my inadvertent hosts keen that I meet their parents, uncles, aunts, grannies and younger siblings. Hustled into one house by the sheer force of their goodwill and many gentle hands, I'm sat down and presented with tea and biscuits. Tea in Maharashtra is infused in hot buffalo milk and presented in small espresso-sized servings. It is very sweet, apparently quite strongly caffeinated and rather comforting. I sip it knowing it is likely to upset my Western stomach ('you don't have the right bacteria', I've been told), but it's impossible to refuse when the ten people crammed into the tiny room wait so expectantly. I drink the tea, eat a biscuit and try to figure out who is related to whom. I think the answer is everybody to everybody for what I see before me is just a small part of an extended family. A toddler, a little boy, reaches for a biscuit but his hand is pulled away. I resist the urge to give him one, not sure if it is politeness to the guest which means he must not eat or that biscuits are rather expensive and not to be squandered.

The houses are sparsely furnished but very clean, with large collections of highly polished copper kitchenware, probably part of a dowry that will eventually be passed on to daughters entering marriage. I'm shown the Christian symbols with Marathi inscriptions which are discreetly painted on the walls and it's strange how inadvertently modish are the muted tones of this interior decoration. Kitschy pictures of Christ adorn the walls, which look Catholic but I'm assured these are a Protestant people. In back rooms elderly relatives lie wrapped in sheets, skinny limbs protruding, seemingly in permanent repose. Children defecate in the back alleyways close to running water, a bitch and her puppies tumble about, lads play football. The Christians, though poor, seem better off than most here and as ever in India it's striking how personally clean people are and humbling to contemplate the sheer physical effort that must go into keeping the strong colours of saris so bright. We tour the colony and I'm shown the quarters where the Muslims, Sindis and Gujaratis live, and the lumpy burial ground, where little more than a stray iron cross or two of recent vintage attest to its purpose. The further from the centre we go, the poorer the dwellings become and the more evident the sanitation problems.

One of my young guides is a Gujarati boy, perhaps of about fourteen. We exchange ironic politenesses. 'Hello, how are you?' I say. 'I'm fine and you?' he replies. He flushes red with delight, though it's clear he knows his triumph is a bit of a joke. His friends fall about laughing, whooping their congratulations. He introduces me to his parents, who are a little baffled by this visitor, and his sister, who hides her face when she sees my camera. Another girl, who wears a rather extravagant purple dress (probably donated by a charity), insists on me repeatedly taking her photo; a young man, perhaps twenty years old, implores that I visit again and I can only smile my refusal. I've discovered that he has recently finished his studies so I ask him if he has access to email. He quickly shakes his head and the question suddenly feels very insensitive, instantly creating distance between us. A young woman, who calls me uncle, asks me to lead them in prayer. I could dust off the 'Lord's Prayer' but, hypocrisy aside, and ungracious though it feels, this I also refuse. To be surrounded by kneeling Indians while I recite those words invokes too many uncomfortable colonial associations. My driver and his assistant are becoming restless and increasingly keen to get back to the Residency Club. Aware that I've momentarily disturbed the equilibrium of this place, and with a slightly guilty conscience, I submit to their wishes and make my farewells. The boys shake hands, the girls withdraw a little and volunteer a hesitant wave, and I clamber into the rickshaw.

Maintenance allowances at Valivade were paid each month in rupees as follows:

	Maintenance allowances	Dearness allowances	Pocket money	Total
Adults	35	8/12/-	10	53
Children 12+	35	5/-	5/-	45
Children 6–11	35	5/-	–	40
Children under 6	25	5/-	–	30

In November 1945 the following names are among the new entries in the Maintenance Allowance Lists for Kolhapur Camp:

3931 Ryżewska Anna F 42
3932 Ryżewska Danuta Ch 13
3933 Ryżewska Wanda F 17
3934 Ryżewska Olga F 38[13]

Hanna's contingent arrived in Valivade on 2 October 1945 and on the 15th she sent Rafał her first impressions. The sense of greater ease is immediately conveyed by her wry references to their journey to Valivade –

they 'toured a part of India along the River Indus' – and how the two girls were enjoying being on 'tropical holiday' before starting their new school in November. Wanda, she feared, might have to take an exam to secure her place in the already oversubscribed third year at the Gymnasium and though Danusia had to prepare to take the Gymnasium entrance exam in the spring she was more troubled by the state of her father's teeth: 'Will Daddy have his teeth in a glass?' she had been asking. As ever, books were needed – for algebra in particular – and Hanna was keen to get her hands on a copy of a history of Poland by Lewicki, which she heard had been published in London. Perhaps this was for work for she had been taken on as part of the teaching staff, though, she joked, 'I no longer rule.'

Though her initial judgements were cautious, it was immediately obvious that their new environment contrasted sharply with the desert camp at Karachi. 'Whether it is better than the previous ones were I don't know,' she wrote, 'only there is a lot of greenery here.' She was struck that the 'natives', 'mainly Indians', had learnt to speak some Polish and this does seem to have been one of Valivade's many remarkable characteristics. Most significant was that the 'actual organisation of the settlement is different, as everyone runs their own household individually, buying what they need to eat for themselves'. Though keen to stress that they liked their tents very much and remembered them fondly, Hanna was surely satisfied to report that their apartment, no. 136/5, comprised two rooms and a small kitchen and, within a week of their arrival, they had planted flower beds, which had already begun to show signs of life. Several years earlier a British official had written from Tehran hoping they 'could effect improvements in their Camp and in other institutions which will cause them to regard these as something more than indifferent staging posts in a painful Odyssey.'[14] Of all the Polish camps, such aspirations were most successfully achieved at Valivade. Indeed, so stark were the differing standards of living between the Poles and the local populations that Poles like Hanna, in regular receipt of both the camp allowances and cheques from her husband, could afford to take on help in the home. An Indian woman, remembered affectionately as 'Sonia', her husband and a local girl did jobs around the house, including keeping the fire buckets filled with water. The hierarchies in the home were clear and hard to break. Sonia would prepare their meals, but refuse to join them at the table, sitting on the floor waiting patiently until they were finished so she could clear away the plates. And when she accepted a share of the food she had prepared, she refused the meat, saying it was only for men – despite the fact that she was living in an all-female household – and would remain on the floor to eat, hiding her face with her sari. To the Poles, it seemed their generous instincts had disturbed Sonia, challenging her sense of what was correct behaviour, though we need to be very cautious before reaching any conclusions about Sonia's experience of these transactions.

Another encounter with Indian difference came during a trip into Kolhapur. There Hanna and Wanda witnessed an extraordinary scene, reported with all the enthusiasm of dazzled tourists: 'It's a typical Indian city,' Hanna explained and, preparing Rafał for the exoticism to follow, commented 'where no white people are to be seen'. In a public space they 'saw a dancer whirl with a harpoon, so that blood poured from his hands and back and when someone from the crowd of Indians cried out encouragement a madness took him in his whirling dance'. At the same time, they 'saw the sacred elephants', who 'bowed to us, scraping their foreheads with their trunks'.

Wanda's surviving notes to her father from this initial period at Valivade are brief. She also commented on the pressure on places at the school and the friendliness of the Indians and their spoken Polish. Wearily she wondered how many more times on their 'wanderings through the world we will change our temporary place of rest'. Danusia, she wrote, had taken as readily to the new camps as to the previous ones: 'I haven't gone out anywhere,' Wanda explained, 'but Danusia already knows every little corner.' Hanna too commented on this, saying that though Danusia had grown up a little and 'even got prettier' – so there was some hope! – she remained flighty (*wiaterek*), prying into everything going on in the camp. Nana admits causing her mother a lot of trouble, not least because her adventuring, be it bicycle racing, a trip into the jungle, or a dip in the lake, involved hanging out with boys which, however innocent, was beginning to ring alarm bells. Wanda, 'my dear dear sister', 'protected me', she says, on occasion taking 'a good clout on my behalf'. Can it be, as Nana remembers, that she really changed the marks of boys she liked in her mother's mark book? Not surprisingly there is no clue to the truth of this in her characteristically perfunctory greetings to her father. They did, however, boast the extraordinary news that she had managed to bring 'her cats', described as 'feral creatures', from Karachi, though so loudly and insistently did the mother meow she had to be left behind.

Animals, as well as boys, figure prominently in Nana's memories of Valivade. 'Tiger', the neighbourhood cat, was an adept thief, his greatest prize being a string of sausages once swiped from one of the teachers' homes. A friendly monkey was also tolerated, though a sharp eye was required if his dawn raids on the breakfast table were to be rebuffed. It could be so hot at night that Danusia and Wanda had recourse to the sheet kept in the kitchen by the water buckets. They would soak it and wrap it round themselves, enjoying the cold water against their clammy skin. On one hot night they discovered another of their house guests. The heat had drawn out the cobra living in the wall cavity and it too sought relief on the very same damp cloth. Sonia's husband took care of it, advising that in future they throw a cloth towards it and when it struck, sinking in its fangs, they should yank hard on the cloth, ripping out its poison sac. Not something they ever tried for themselves. Finally, there were the cockroaches. They got drunk on slightly fermented fruit juice and staggered around, colliding with each other.

All at 135/6 were keen to see Rafał's latest photo and were disappointed that the mail was too unreliable to allow them to send the silver cigarette case they had bought him for Christmas. Letters from Miecia to

Wanda suggested both she and their cousin Urszulka, both posted to Egypt, were planning on getting married. Danusia's 'mania' for actresses continued, her album of cuttings growing, and her latest obsession was to guess as quickly as possible the singer when listening to records. She complained that she was not given enough money to see the film shows or to buy photographs as often as she would like.

Rafał's letters from the autumn and early winter of 1945, addressed variously to 'My beloved Hanek!', 'My most beloved!' and 'My dearest!', carried a note of levity. For him the war continued, but now only with his teeth. His army, of which he was ironically possessive, was now based in 'wonderful' Italian parkland and he lived in its 'lovely' villa, with such comforts as electric light, central heating and a bathroom with hot and cold water. Despite the proximity of his men, he found the inactivity and the solitary life his seniority gave him boring (he uses the Russian word *skuczno*). Kuba, however, had grown greedy for accounts of his war experiences and so Rafał kept himself busy writing these – it is almost too tantalising to read that by October 1945 two eight-page letters taking the narrative to June 1941 had already been despatched and that on 1 December his fifth 'article' was in the post. Again, he urged the girls to write to Kuba 'a lot and lively as who knows if we might need him'. Another indication of Rafał's preoccupation with the future is suggested by his encouraging Hanna to make friends with the wives of certain of his men, women like Pani Szczepaniakowa and Pani Strachowska, and a relative of his corporal, Ms Prezęlewska.

As to the future, Rafał instructed them to sit tight, trusting no news until it actually resulted in action, for 'what thrills today, tomorrow turns out to be horrendous gossip, so based on this no horoscope can be written'. Politics, however, caused Rafał entertainment as well as concern. With the war over, he wrote, politics in Europe had entered the 'low season' and he described the 'Poles as having a lot of fun with the Italians who, under the influence of the propaganda, sigh for paradise' – 'Paradise', sometimes locked into scare-quotes, always signified the Soviet Union. A group of Italian POWs home from the Soviet Union were in such poor shape that a delegation of local communists quickly abandoned the planned welcome. In the next breath he implied that Italian enthusiasm for communism was a way of manipulating Anglo-American opinion, attracting from them more rather than less support. Either way, Rafał concluded, returning to a theme treated in earlier letters, 'higher feelings and values', like 'reverence, honour, the word etc.', were now treated with a 'very broad view'. His cynical assessment of the post-war situation was becoming fixed: the continuing chaos, he argued, ensured that "'the happy victory of democracy''', so trumpeted by the Allies, was an illusion. By contrast, he thought the political 'high season' had transferred to 'your territory', where 'the atmosphere electrifies from one day to the next'.

This is one of the few references in the Ryżewski correspondence to the momentous developments in India, though Nana remembers the anxiety generated by their few encounters with Gandhi's movement. On one occasion news reached Valivade that thousands of men were coming down from the mountains for a political rally. The Poles worried that they would be unable to defend themselves against looting or theft. The marauding mob they expected turned out to be anything but. Tired, dusty, half-naked and hungry, the men of the mountains greeted the Poles with traditional gestures of respect, touching their heads and bowing, before squatting on the ground and indicating they would like something to eat. The Poles did their best to oblige, learning something more about India.

The Italian autumn, Rafał wrote, gave way to winter in an instant: 'like at an order' the leaves fell and the country, so dazzling earlier in the year, turned grey. Only drab winter crops now grew and the fog hung thick, so thick that walking home Rafał once missed the town where he was stationed and only found his bearings seven kilometres later when he came upon a huge bridge. Should Hanna again have been worrying about his liver? Amid the gloom of winter, a distant glimpse of the Alps, snow-peaked and majestic, was reviving and when his ever-loyal men brought their captain a Christmas tree Rafał began to succumb to the seasonal spirit. The Ryżewski Christmas letters saw the *opłatek* shared; health, willpower, perseverance and courage wished for all; and cigarettes, in great shortage in Italy, requested, to be sent at intervals.

What, then, would determine the fate of the Polish Indians? First of all, they were not the most significant group of Poles to become the responsibility of the British or Allied governments. According to official figures produced in December 1945 there were Polish refugees in Sweden (15,100), Spain (256), Portugal (144), Greece (60), Holland (over 1,000), Italy (at least 7,000), South Africa (837), New Zealand (837, mostly orphans), Australia (250), Canada (500+), Southern Rhodesia (1,528), Northern Rhodesia (2,845), Tanganyika (6,408), Uganda (6,347), Kenya (408), India (5,032), Palestine (9,747), Egypt (80+), Iraq (an unknown but small number), Syria and Lebanon (938), and Iran (3,475).[15] The numbers in Syria and Lebanon rose constantly as the remaining Poles in Iran were finally moved out. In Britain itself, of the 282,264 'aliens' registered by March 1945, 21,744 were Polish, a number smaller than the Russian and German totals, but substantially more than the French and a little more than the Belgians.[16] All these figures, however, were dwarfed by the mass of Poles in uniform who had fought under Allied Command and were now universally thought the responsibility of the British. Facing questions in the House of Commons, Foreign Secretary Ernest Bevin admitted that only 30,000 had been repatriated to Poland, leaving 160,000 soldiers still in military camps awaiting their fate; 100,000 were overseas, a large proportion of whom, like Rafał, in Italy, and 60,000 in Britain.[17]

Ever since Churchill's famous 'pledge', the possibility that all these people might eventually be permitted to settle in Britain had shaped the debate and Polish expectations. Their legal position, however, was un-ambiguous. Under present law the Poles did not have a right to reside permanently in the UK and this position was clarified in November 1945 when the Home Office (Aliens Department) circulated a summary of the 1914 British Nationality and Status of Aliens Act. Naturalisation, which gave the right to permanent residence in the UK, required that at the point of application the individual had resided in HMG's dominions or been in the service of the Crown for not less than five of the last eight years. Moreover, any applicant must have been resident in the UK for the previous twelve months, they must be thought of good character and possess an adequate knowledge of the English language, and must intend either to reside in HMG's dominions or enter or continue in the service of the Crown. Polish servicemen were not in the service of the Crown, they could not fulfil the residency requirements and few had the requis-ite level of language proficiency. Legislation passed in 1943 had set the bar a bit lower in order to allow the naturalisation of certain categories of French citizens exiled by the war, but establishing whether a person met these conditions required close scrutiny of each individual case. The large numbers of Poles potentially seeking admission to the United Kingdom made this 1943 legislation unworkable. Naturalising Polish servicemen who were already in the UK owing to the exigencies of the war or those awaiting their fate elsewhere would demand new legisla-tion.[18]

Formulating new laws was stymied by uncertainty about the numbers involved. For a long time the British clung to the idea that a large percentage of the Poles would opt for repatriation. Bevin argued that Poland was where the Poles belonged, their duty being to help rebuild their nation; continued British cooperation with the Polish government was intended to bring this about. There were tensions, not least because the British refused to allow the Polish government to take control of the Polish camps – as already noted, following the de-recognition of the Polish government-in-exile its former authority and responsibilities were not passed to the new government. Determined to force some kind of resolution, the increasingly impatient Polish government insisted that the British work on the assumption that all Poles would return to Poland, demanding that those who were determined to refuse should be formally asked to opt out. With these choices established, it was likely that those who opted out would have their right to Polish citizenship withdrawn.[19] However, a complicating factor, enormously significant but easily overlooked, was the agreement reached on 6 July 1945 between the Polish provisional government and the Soviet government. This decreed that Polish refugees from former eastern Poland – those territories absorbed into the Soviet Union in 1939 – were considered Soviet rather than Polish citizens, a reversal of the agreements between Moscow and the government-in-exile that had preceded the evacuation. For many of the *kresy* refugees this meant going back would not mean a return to a Poland fast becoming a puppet state of the Soviet Union but to the Soviet Union itself. Their territorial origins rather than nationality would decide their fate.

At the beginning of 1946, the Chiefs of Staff presented the Cabinet with a remarkable memorandum. Signed by Lord Alanbrooke (Chief of the Imperial General Staff), Arthur Tedder (Chief of the Air Staff), and R. R. McGrigor (Vice-Chief of Naval Staff), the memo carried all the moral authority of the decided opinion of the military top brass. It toed the political line on the hope that members of the Polish forces would return to Poland, but its overall thrust was unmistakable:

We agree that the Foreign Secretary's statement should hold out a very discouraging alternative to return to Poland. On the other hand, we consider it most important that the former Prime Minister's pledge to those who have fought for us should be honoured. All the Services owe much to the Poles. Polish ships formed an integral part of the British Fleet. The Polish Corps in Italy under General Anders was a substantial reinforcement to the Allied Armies in that theatre; it fought gallantly and at the cost of heavy casualties; without it the series of offensives carried out from Cassino onwards could hardly have been possible. The Polish Air Force also made by far the greatest air contribution of all our European Allies. They have formed part and parcel of all R.A.F. operational commands and fought with us throughout the war, including taking a prominent part in the Battle of Britain.

We suggest, therefore, that although our policy of encouraging the maximum numbers to return necessitates our being as discouraging as honesty allows regarding the prospects of those who refuse to do so, we must in the end ensure the best possible terms for those who do refuse and who fought for us during much of the war.[20]

Such pressure when combined with an awareness of the significance of the July 1945 Polish–Soviet agreement soon began to tell. On 11 March 1946 Prime Minister Clement Attlee prepared a Note for Cabinet. 'We cannot tolerate very much longer either the grave political embarrassment, or the heavy financial commitment involved by our maintenance of these Forces under arms,' he wrote. 'The problem must be vigorously tackled, and all Ministers concerned must be ready to make a contribution towards the solution.' Now a matter of the 'utmost urgency', Attlee urged that 'specially early consideration' be given 'to the question of absorbing Polish troops into civil employment in the United Kingdom'.[21]

A little over a week later, on 20 March 1946, a government statement established what it considered to be the right 'treatment of repatriated members of the Polish Armed Forces', that is, Polish soldiers who returned to Poland. No punitive measures or reprisals should be directed against returning officers or soldiers unless they had served in the German army or were guilty of high treason or common criminality according to the Polish Penal Code of 1932. They should be placed on an equal footing with members of the Polish army formed in the USSR, with rank, length of service, decorations and military awards fully recognised. Their money should be transferred without prejudice to Polish bank accounts and any property brought into the country should be duty-free. All demobilised soldiers should have equal rights to land as the government's policy of land redistribution advanced. Finally, and this would have been of direct concern to many Poles in the PAF, any member 'originating from the provinces east of the Curzon Line will automatically be regarded by the Polish Government as Polish citizens if they are of Polish or Jewish race and will not be required to perform any act signifying that they wish to choose Polish citizenship'.[22] Though there was nothing unreasonable about these demands, the statement both failed to address the fundamental objections the soldiers had to the new Poland and served to confirm that the government recognised the legitimacy of their concerns. In effect, the British were admitting that safeguards, which they were in no position to enforce, were needed to protect returning Poles from persecution.

If intended as no more than a diplomatic gesture, this statement served to underscore the Churchillian commitment and a later memo, somewhat obliquely, also admitted its significance. Britain had effectively guaranteed the rights of those *kresy* Poles to Polish citizenship whereas UNRRA had not.[23] If the Polish government and the Soviet Union were not prepared to make the same guarantees, the logical corollary of this was that those affected Poles had become the responsibility of the new guarantor, namely the British government. The irony is clear: British efforts to persuade the Poles to return to Poland strengthened Britain's obligation to those same Poles.

At the same time Bevin issued a statement saying that although he believed the Poles had a duty to return to Poland for 'she requires the help of all her sons in the arduous task of reconstructing the country and making good the devastation caused by the war', he nonetheless reiterated their right to refuse repatriation. This carrot came with a stick. First, Bevin made it clear that the government could not offer the Poles any guarantee of where they would be settled, leaving it possible that they might be sent to any place within the empire and its dominions, and, second, it was certain the Polish Armed Forces (PAF) would not be maintained as a separate organisation or in any military capacity.[24] In 1946 various schemes of settlement were prospected, which might have taken groups of Poles to Chile, Australia, the Netherlands, Guatemala or the Dominican Republic. Each of these countries' governments sought to fill specific gaps in their workforce, toying with the idea of admitting a limited number of skilled workers. No country offered the Poles free entry and Santiago, in particular, made it explicit it was reluctant to take any Polish Jews.[25] Australia said no in November 1946, though it was prepared to take 400 orphans.[26] The Canadians, too, proved singularly ungenerous: refusing in August 1946, the High Commissioner for Canada wept crocodile tears when he explained that the Polish Indians were 'not admissible under the existing immigration regulations'.[27]

Some of the British decisions seem a little petty, such as the Treasury's refusal to finance the transfer of small numbers to the US or elsewhere to live with relatives because it was cheaper to keep them in India.[28] Less petty was their reluctance to settle the Poles permanently in Britain. An undated note by the Ministry of Labour and National Service laid out some of the difficulties. In short, the economic circumstances were uncertain and it was likely to be difficult to find jobs for the Poles, especially officer-class men who might expect certain conditions of work and remuneration. They had already encountered this problem with demobilised British soldiers, especially those without pre-war experience. Postwar reconstruction would bring jobs in construction, civil engineering, the building materials industries, coalmining, agriculture and iron production, as well as in nursing and domestic service (including public institutions like hospitals), but before decisions were made about who were to be so employed it would be necessary to hold discussions with the BEC and the TUC, as well as the employers' associations and the trade unions most likely to be affected.[29] In the event, the trade unions were hostile to the Poles, fearing not only that they would undercut pay, but also because they bought into Soviet propaganda that these particular Poles were right-wing fascists.

The fascist claim stuck for a number of reasons, not all of which were Soviet-inspired. First, some members of the Polish government-in-exile had been prominent in the right-wing Polish governments of the 1930s and did not have a good record on 'the Jewish question'. Reinforcing this anti-Jewish sentiment was a more generalised awareness among Poles in Britain that, to use Tony Kushner's words, 'Polish-Jewish soldiers were generally sympathetic to the Soviet cause'.[30] Second, concerns regarding the treatment of Polish Jews in Anders' Army, which had surfaced in the Soviet Union, dogged all the Polish forces under Allied Command. Public statements by the Polish political leadership consistently condemned anti-Jewish sentiment, but this public position was sometimes undermined. Particular embarrassment was caused by the antisemitic exile newspaper *Jestem Polakiem* ('I am a Pole'), backed by the *Catholic Herald*. The problem reached a head following the integration into the Polish forces in Britain of Poles serving in the German army who were captured in Tunisia in 1943. In early 1944 some 200 Jewish soldiers deserted the Polish army, citing antisemitic bullying and intimidation. Keen to avoid a damaging row and having some sympathy with the view expressed by some Poles that these Jewish soldiers were afraid to fight, the government had the deserters drafted into the Pioneer Corps.[31] Finally, among the Polish armed forces in Italy were Poles who had deserted from the *Wehrmacht*. Though the majority of these men had been forced into the German army, it was a stigma that was hard to shake off. In the event, many of these recruits to the II Corps, described by a Polish sociologist as 'usually young peasants between 17 and 21', were among those repatriated to Poland.[32]

All such reservations were relatively insignificant when faced with the demands of international law and, to use the favoured word of Whitehall civil servants, continued Polish 'recalcitrance' regarding repatriation. Although UNRRA eventually agreed to take financial responsibility for the Poles – which saw economies at Valivade – this was not a long-term solution given UNRRA's mandate to care only for refugees who wanted to be repatriated. Ultimately those who did not were the responsibility of the country of residence.[33] Following the non-cooperation of the Commonwealth nations, the collapse of various non-Commonwealth schemes of migration and the determined ruling of UNRRA, the government bowed to the inevitable. On 22 May 1946 it announced the creation of the Polish Resettlement Corps (PRC), which began recruiting in September. All remaining members of the Polish armed forces were eligible to join. Its purpose was to ease the settlement of Polish soldiers into the UK, housing them in disused military bases where they would be trained and gradually integrated into the workforce as a precursor to their integration into mainstream society. Members of the PAF were faced with a stark choice. They could either join the PRC, which though meaning a further period of institutional life in army camps would see them fed and clothed, or if they refused to join they would be left without entitlement to National Assistance. Few felt they had much choice but to enlist and the great majority opted for the PRC. On 22 March 1947 the Polish Resettlement Act received Royal Assent.

Following Bevin's announcement developments came quickly. Rafał found himself in the thick of it, in his role as quartermaster responsible for overseeing 'his' army's departure from Italy. Even now, a full year after the end of the war, his location remained a secret, though he told Hanna that he was 'stationed in a city which one "has to see once and then die"'. Surviving photographs show that he was indeed in Venice.

'Pretty it is,' he wrote, 'but dirty to the extent that even in Italy is unique.' In a string of impressionistic letters written mainly to Hanna between July and November 1946 he dispensed advice and speculated on his family's future. These are among his most lively and humorous letters, each darting from subject to subject, his syntax and clarity often losing out to his hurry and high spirits. Despite repeated references to the terrible weather in England, the prospect of having perpetual colds, 'a runny nose', and rheumatism, and his continued cynicism regarding the outcome of the war, these were optimistic letters, clearly excited by the imminence of the family reunion. At a briefing given by Anders himself, Rafał learned 'that all our emigrants will be delivered to England (from Palestine, Egypt, Africa and India)', the first time Rafał allowed Hanna such certainty.[34] 'Based on this I am convinced', he wrote, 'that after 8 years we will finally have a normal bed-sharing marriage.' 'But have no worries about it,' he joked – though quite where the stress of this joke lies is unclear – 'because every cloud has a silver lining.' Anticipating the move he was trying, as he had urged his daughters, to learn the '"fish-eaters' language"'. Progress was slow though smoothed along by beer.

Repeatedly Rafał advised Hanna to plan carefully what they would bring to the UK. Warm clothes were an absolute necessity, not only to protect them against the grim weather but also because prices in the UK were 'horrendously high'. They should bring sweaters, socks, stockings ('priceless'), raincoats, umbrellas and wellingtons. They were not to 'haul' all their possessions across the world, unless they were of very good quality. Kitchenware, in particular, he thought they should sell: 'In this respect I think Wanda has not forgotten the "paradise" practice and she can get rid of things elegantly', an allusion to Wanda's success in the marketplace before they left the Soviet Union. Rafał himself was also gathering clothing and other essentials, which he sent on to Valivade, including some 'very pretty and practical' garter belts. His perceptions of the UK, though jokey, brief and clichéd (bad food and bad weather are a recurring motif of these letters), nonetheless reveal something of what the soldiers were hearing from comrades already in the country.

We will have to go through different phases, very funny and practical, nevertheless hard and against our nature. First of all, the climate in which it rains 300 days a year or where there is fog and drizzle. We already have such news from there. Then ration cards, camps (well furnished) and corned beef for dessert. If not for the fact that we are supposed to meet there, my enthusiasm for the allies (aren't we lucky or what?) would have dropped to a minimum.

Despite this, he announced himself 'at peace with England itself' not least because in September he had been assured that his senior army position in Italy would guarantee him a similar position in England. This relieved him of his money worries though he was in no hurry to get to England itself. As the 'liquidator of the Polish emigrations and the Army in Italy', which brought him 'tremendous responsibility but a high position', he would be among the last to leave. Though he was enjoying the 'risk' brought by the uncertainty, which left him 'a whole lot younger and more entrepreneurial', he remained disillusioned, repeating his disapproval of the amoral opportunism unleashed by the power vacuum the end of the war created.

In the financial area as well as the moral one in the world there is panic and inflation. People have lost moral and ethical standards and all is stolen and conquered the American way regardless of the means. Millionaires are mushrooming and the prisons are full regardless of the social level and position. Because a naked person is not afraid of a robbery, therefore he can sleep peacefully and kiss our beloved daughters.

The swipe at the US was a little hypocritical, given his earlier hope that they might migrate to the States, but more significant was his sense of moral superiority. War had neither undermined Rafał's adventurism

nor his class identity. His disapproval of the criminality among people of
the higher social classes reflected a grim sense of their continuing obligation to set an example during difficult times, while he found vulgar
the exploitative materialism generated, presumably, by the black market.
The young man, encountered upright in his army uniform, had indeed
become a middle-aged man concerned with his dentures, gold caps and
dodgy hearing, but in his attitudes something of the minor gentry
remained. More than this, Rafał was an intelligent, educated man and
his prickliness surely reflected his understanding that the status he had
enjoyed as a civilian before the war and as an officer in the Polish II Corps
would end very soon. Like the experience of many of his fellow officers,
Rafał's journey to Britain would bring about a radical diminution in his
social status. Déclassé Poles would become one of the peculiar features
of post-war Britain.

This was all for the future, for now Rafał remained busier than he had
ever been, supervising the staged departure of thousands of men. Still,
he found time to attend to his personal matters. On 10 August 1946 Rafał
penned Hanna what are, perhaps, his sweetest surviving words:

> It so happens that I am writing this letter on the anniversary of the day
> when we first met. And it was anno domini 1922 in the Miświecki park
> when you, darling woman, had burnt your face with some acid and it
> made you terribly self-conscious. It is 24 years ago and it still stands before
> my eyes as if yesterday . . . I tell you this to also give myself pleasure rem-
> iniscing about the 'high and clouded' past.

These few words are strangely beguiling. Though conventionally
romantic they are not insincere for that, and the references to place and
Hanna's self-consciousness individualises the memory. As interesting is
how Rafał readily exposes the scaffolding of his emotional life and his
understanding that narrating their romantic past revivified it for the present,
strengthening bonds of affection stretched thin by distance, separation
and uncertainty.

After November 1946 nothing more is heard from Rafał until a letter
dated 13 February 1947. Addressed to Hanna, Wanda and Danuta, it is
headed 'Plasterdown Camp, nr Tavistock, Devon, England'.

In correspondence with the India Office, dated 30 May 1946, the Treasury
observed that having explored other options for the Valivade families the

'only conceivable destination for these people, insofar as they are dependants of members of the Polish Armed Forces, seems to be the United
Kingdom'. At first glance this seems a simple statement of government
policy but the 'insofar' caveat was a vital one. In the event, the process
was horribly drawn out by Whitehall's determination to establish precisely
who was eligible for resettlement in Britain. In theory, only those accepted
by members of the Polish armed forces as their dependants had entitlement; in practice, a series of exceptions emerged, notably those orphans
who as army cadets had come under the care of the PAF but were still
underage. The responsible civil servants made the case that the rightful
guardians of these boys and girls were the PAF, additionally arguing that
the cadets themselves 'were first rate material and if properly looked
after will make useful citizens'.[35] All of this much displeased the Polish
government.

Efforts to account for every prospective settler saw list after list,
each with slightly differing figures, pass back and forth between Delhi
and London. The Indian government, under enormous political pressure, became increasingly irritated by the delays, grumbling that they
found it difficult to 'appreciate unwillingness to remove from India
the relatively small number of Poles there (5,000) when H.M.G. apparently are planning to take some 150,000 Poles from Italy'.[36] At Valivade
itself people were becoming understandably restless and in November
1946, fifteen months after the end of the war, wives filed a petition
requesting that they be reunited with their husbands.[37] Questions were
asked in Parliament, the government insisting that the delays were
practical and did not reflect a soft-pedalling on their commitment to
reunite the Polish families.[38] Inevitably, the process became politicised.
When Major Kłoskowicz was sent to Valivade to settle the numbers
question once and for all, the Foreign Office soon after demanded his
removal on learning that he was undermining continuing efforts to
persuade some to repatriate.[39] Those Polish Indians ultimately not
categorised as legitimate dependants of the PAF were moved to Polish
camps in Africa. There were good reasons for this. Other refugee
groups like the Maltese and people from the Balkans kept a close eye
on the treatment of the Poles, keen to spot any transgression of the
rules that might be used to strengthen their own case to be granted
the right to settle in the UK. Nonetheless, the bureaucratic cruelty
which categorised as ineligible sons and married daughters over
twenty-one, brothers over twenty-one, and uncles and aunts of Polish

soldiers, is breathtaking. One set of figures, probably the most accurate, suggests that on the break-up of the camp 264 such individuals were refused leave to enter Britain, being separated from the 3,574 who were.[40] In all, 816 Polish Indians were denied entry to the UK and were eventually shipped to Kenya.[41]

Each dependant over sixteen granted access to Britain was given a bilingual copy of 'Form 223X'. This vital document secured their future:

> Temporary Certificate to be held by dependants of members of the Polish Forces or by members of civilian services attached to the Polish Forces, entering the United Kingdom.
>
> The present temporary certificate is issued in order to provide dependent members of the Polish Forces or members of civilian services attached to the Polish Forces with a document of identity to enable them to enter the United Kingdom. It is without prejudice to and in no way affects the national status of the holder. The temporary certificate remains valid so long as the holder remains in the United Kingdom and does not obtain a national passport. If the holder wishes to go abroad, application should be made for a fresh Certificate of Identity to:-
>
> H.M. Chief Inspector,
> Immigration Branch,
> Home Office,
> 10, Old Bailey,
> London, E.C.4.
>
> All persons of 16 and over require a separate certificate, but the particulars relating to children under 16 may be entered on a parent's certificate.[42]

In September 1947, more than two years after the close of the war, the Polish Indians began to leave India for Britain. They travelled by railway to Bombay from where they set sail, crossing the Indian Ocean, sailing up through the gulf of Oman, then the Suez Canal, the Mediterranean and the straits of Gibraltar, before heading north up through the Atlantic Ocean and entering the English Channel from which they finally docked at Southampton or Liverpool. Their departures were detailed in a report of 30 July 1948:[43]

1. MT *Empire Brent*, 6 September 1947, 969 persons, two special trains
2. MT *Empire Brent*, 8 November 1947, 972 persons, two special trains

3. SS *Ormonde*, 21 December 1947, 372 persons, one special train

4. HT *Empress of Scotland*, 29 January 1948, 257 persons, one special train

5. SS *Asturias*, 22 February 1948, 394 persons, one special train

The purpose of the report? To note that the charges for the train travel were being queried. The India Railway Board wrote back on 25 November 1948 saying the government had been correctly charged. The special rates for refugees travelling in reserved carriages had been cancelled on 15 November 1946.[44]

The Maintenance Allowance Lists kept by the administration at Valivade suggest many stories, each deserving its own book. What of the Masiulanis family, mostly deported from Belaka, near Vilnius, in June 1941? Antonina Masiulanis, aged eighty, was the camp's oldest resident. Despite her great age she survived deportation, the Soviet Union, Persia and Karachi, but sadly died at Valivade in 1946. She headed the camp's largest family, which included her son, Piotr, and daughter-in-law, Nadzieja, both fifty-four, their daughter Helena (twenty), Piotr's sisters Konstancja (forty), Pelagia (thirty-eight), and Jadwiga Materek, and Pelagia's children Ryszard (eight) and Halina (seven). Sadly, Nadzieja had been ill with tropical malaria since contracting the disease in Uzbekistan and died in 1945. The surviving family members arrived in the UK on 8 January 1947. Records relating to another large family, the Godlewscy, tell of tragedy. In August 1944 the lists show monies collected for Antoni (forty-seven), Janina (forty-one), and Irena (eleven), Witold (ten), Leon (eight), Ewa-Anna (one) and Halina-Danuta (one). The September 1944 lists show Irena's age amended to thirteen and Halina-Danuta's name crossed out. In April 1945 the age of Halina-Danuta's surviving twin sister was updated to two. How can this loss be balanced against the survival of Irena, Witold, and Leon, all tiny children at the time of deportation? The Godlewscy left for the UK on the 29 January sailing. Ewa's and Halina's births were not unique. Overall, thirty children were listed as aged one, suggesting they were conceived in the camps, perhaps in snatched moments in Tehran, when husbands were on leave, or under circumstances afterwards little talked about.

Hanna signed each month for their allowances until December 1947.[45] Nana recalls the moment their 'idyllic' existence at Valivade came to an end:

Our house help Sonia stood beside the truck awash with tears, four fire buckets dangling in her hands. Sonia had already been given everything we were not taking with us; the fire buckets had to stay in place until the last minute.

9

Britain: The 'hotel for the homeless'

It's a filthy wet January day and once again I'm driving down from London to Devon. I'm going to see Plaster Down, the Dartmoor site of the camp Rafał and his men were posted to in 1946 and the final Ryżewski reunion. Owing to this, and thanks to conversations with Nana, it has become a name freighted with mystique and significance. So it's with a surge of relief that I eventually negotiate the roundabouts at Hammersmith, hit the A4 and am soon racing along the M4. The feeling of uninhibited progress is great – speed cameras, roadworks and the occasional police car doing a teasing sixty-eight aside – and Britain seems to shrink beneath my wheels. Bristol passes in no time and soon I'm heading south on the M5, the landscape softening and the weather improving with every mile. As I skirt Exeter, I pull over, chuck the roof back, put on hat, gloves and coat, and smile. The weather front has been moving in the opposite direction and though it's still cold I have come upon the most glorious day. I head towards Moretonhampstead and up on to the moor, finding clear blue skies, bright sun and birdsong: a place of rapture.

I'm soon running along the B3212, slowing to avoid the sheep lolling at the side of the road or stopping just for the pleasure of looking and breathing. I halt more purposefully at Two Bridges for a hot pastie and a cup of tea from the post office – little rituals. The tea is served in a polystyrene cup as charmingly old-fashioned as the endearments the woman proprietor bestows on all comers, whether bloke down from London or local farmer. I chat about the weather with one old boy; he complains about kids stealing his fork and looks suspiciously at the car. I want to explain that it's an old banger disguised as a sports car. I spread out an OS map to locate my turning. It'll be Rundlestone, Merrivale (with its hotel and quarries), Barn Hill (fabulous viewpoint), then down the steep Pork Hill (amazing on a bicycle), rapidly passing Higher and Lower Longford (campsites), before grabbing the left at Moorshop (there is no shop there now) and on to the minor road for Horrabridge. There I'll be in the parish of Whitchurch, rapidly passing Pennycomequick, Underhill Cottage and Warren's Cross, before coming upon Plaster Down.

I set off, torn between the pleasure of the road and the knowledge that these bleak uplands come to an end all too soon. At Barn Hill I stop for the famous views: the moors stretch out east and south, Tavistock and the Tamar valley lies to the west with Brentor distantly in the north-west and Cornwall beyond. A few walkers jauntily set off down the slopes and retirees sit quietly in their cars; it's too early in the year for the ice-cream van. Back in the car and moments later I take the Horrabridge turning and suddenly I'm at Plaster Down. Below Pew Tor and surrounded by farmland, with the tiny village of Sampford Spiney to its east (spookily deserted church, llamas being farmed), this large flat piece of soggy open moorland boasts just a few scrubby bushes, some gorse, and the Grimstone and Sortridge leat. It is populated by Dartmoor ponies and frequented by dog walkers, women especially, who drive their shiny new estate cars the few miles from Tavistock or Horrabridge. I chat with a couple of vigorous old gentlewomen – white-haired, finely wrinkled, slim, quaintly well-spoken and terribly nice. They're just setting off into the squelch with a wet-nosed dog of similar vintage. The camp was originally for the Americans, they say, a field hospital, then the Ugandans came, fleeing Idi Amin. I felt sorry for them, one says, coming from Africa to Dartmoor and the rain. I mention that the Poles were here too and give a quick version of the story this book has been telling.[1] How wonderful, they say. I've stirred faint memories but their reaction is primarily that I've come to know from so many elderly people who learn I'm looking into my grandmother's history. One says that Britain always got on well with the Poles and I mention Churchill's 'pledge'. This seems to have been what they would expect of the great man. Are you doing some research? they ask. Have you tried the library or the internet? I have, I say, both. Good, they say. Have a good look around, they instruct, before issuing a brisk 'bye-bye'. Bye, I say. And off they stride.

Given Rafał's expectations, it had seemed appropriate to see Plaster Down in the rain, but this fine weather can be spun as fitting too, for in my pocket I have a copy of his only surviving letter written from here. It is sanguine, accepting and satisfied. What it is not, however, is overly impressed and the mildly begrudging tone might reflect this deeply self-reliant man's discomfort at being so dependent on the goodwill of another power and people.

For though post-war Britain did not dazzle this sceptical son of comfortably-off Poles – another Pole, not untypically, commented on how 'the English adore shoddiness'[2] – the major psychological hurdles to living in Britain had already been conquered. Since those exchanges between Rafał in Italy and Hanna in Karachi, their priorities had decisively shifted: the survival and reunion of the family would be their miracle. Not least, as Nana emphasises, because Rafał was determined his family would no longer live in camps. Here he would build the home where they might finally be a family.

As camps went, this one was decent, Rafał wrote, explaining that the brick-built accommodation was an improvement upon the 'miserable barrack' they were initially assigned on arrival. Many Poles in the PRC were lodged in former army camps where they were housed in Nissen huts, not necessarily an obvious improvement on their conditions in Italy. Having wangled the post of quartermaster, Rafał was on familiar ground, wryly pointing out that it was a role that 'had its good sides'. Responsible for the distribution of the camp goods, Captain Ryżewski was exactly where he liked to be: he had some authority, a little power of patronage and access to all camp business.

If camp life was pleasant enough, his view of the Poles in Britain was less easy. That creeping disillusionment, so evident in his Italy letters, encroached more and more on his sense of Polish prospects. The end of the war and diminution of purpose and military discipline saw the Poles, struggling to establish themselves in a new society, behave in ways he found morally compromising. 'Our people renounce everything,' he wrote obliquely, 'the end justifies the means – it's a war of everybody against everyone, protection, dirty tricks, denunciations, bribery, etc., one doesn't recognise good acquaintances.' Unduly condemnatory, perhaps, such attitudes saw Rafał place barriers between himself and this world, building a somewhat eccentric life for himself in England, buffered by his family and a tight-knit group of old army comrades.

West Devon itself pleased Rafał. 'I live 15 miles north of the town of Plymouth in the warmest part of England' and though 'appropriately wet' it was 'fairly nice'. This 'hilly' place comprised 'small forests in the valleys' and fields lying fallow, not unlike Wara, Hanna's birthplace. The land itself, he reckoned, in a curious echo of Soviet views of the *kresy*, belonged to 'Lords' – much of it was, and is, part of the Duchy of Cornwall. He found the style of farming odd, noting that 'one can encounter herds of stray horses, so-called ponies, and cattle that live and breed in the fields and there are no stables or pens'. The landscape itself seemed a 'desert' and he was a little baffled by the strong contrasts in west Devon. The evidence of long settlement and the relatively inhospitable environment testified to the peculiarity of the English. But he admired the 'very tidy and pretty small towns' and found the people kind, watching them watching their new neighbours 'with curiosity'. The Poles must have seemed rather strange to these country folk, Rafał thought. Did he see in these small farmers something of his social inferiors in the *kresy*?

Rafał described how significant the decision to join the Polish Resettlement Corps had seemed. Government impatience was all very well, but for these men it was 'equivalent to a final decision about one's future'. 'For the last two weeks,' Rafał told his wife and daughters, 'everybody, me included, has been walking around edgy, angry, undecided, every piece of gossip stirring excitement, panic, unsettlement – which impresses on one's health.' Though under far more benign circumstances, there are parallels here with the offer of Soviet citizenship made back in 1940. Once again, Poles faced the agonies of an uncertain future, of choices the consequences of which they could only half know. Rafał was right to think that those who had taken the opportunity to think things over for a month would come round, but he was equally correct to observe that the eventual adherence of the great majority of the men to the scheme was a remarkable outcome. The astronomical cost of living, and high rents in particular, he conjectured, drove the men into the safe-keeping of the state. He enlisted on 4 June 1947, telling Hanna and the girls that they need not worry for he had secured them space in this 'hotel for the homeless'.

Every new member of the Corps was subject to due bureaucratic process. A committee from the Ministry of Labour came to interview the men, one by one, trying to establish what type of work might suit them. Not surprisingly, Rafał's hope of returning to teaching was brushed to one side. Might not he work as a hotel interpreter? This time it was Rafał's turn to refuse politely but firmly. Better, he wrote, 'to live from hand to mouth on a leased farm' than on miserable wages in a miser-able job – the fate of many resettled Poles. And this prospect of farming again carries curious echoes of their former life. Działka, their *kresy* holding, was lost for ever, but Rafał's urge to root himself in the land remained strong. Farming, he thought, was 'almost non-existent here and needs people': an echo of the notion that the *kresy* had needed populating and developing. An old Polish mission could be revived in exile, restoring to England something the English – now an urban people, thought Rafał – had lost.

Evidence of a drainage system is the only sign of Plaster Down's previous incarnation as a military camp; so little remains, it's hard not to leave somewhat disappointed. Proust understood this experience better than anyone and the basic insight underpinning his great meditation in *À la recherche . . .* on places first constructed in the imagination has often occurred to me throughout this historical journey. Someone else put it more simply: 'What's the most evocative thing about Paris? The sign which says "Paris 100km".' Plaster Down, I have to concede, is just another patch of moorland, valued by dog walkers and the occasional excur-sionist but aesthetically insignificant. Nothing here tells of its previous busyness, of the men and women in fatigues, the nurses and doctors, the military-issue tents, the Land Rovers; the flashes of colour from the Stars and Stripes, the Union Jacks and the Polish Eagles; the camaraderie, the homesickness, the card games, the strong drink, the atmosphere in the mess, the high spirits, the news of triumphs and losses, and the eventual order to pack up for home. The smell, though, is good: earthy, animally, woody, damp.

Once enrolled in the Polish Resettlement Corps, the Polish II Corps was housed in dozens of camps scattered throughout Great Britain. There were particular concentrations in East Anglia, central England, the Home Counties, the north-west and the north-east, and a scattering in Wales and Scotland. Often taking over former military barracks and field hospitals, many of the camps occupied fairly isolated locations, and in this Plaster Down, the site of the former US Army 115th Field Hospital, was no exception.[3]

Finding employment for working-class Poles, particularly those with skills, proved relatively straightforward and by the end of 1948 some 70,000 of 120,000 had found jobs. The major obstacle was trade union hostility, particularly from the National Union of Miners and the Amalgamated Union of Engineering Workers. The NUM, characterised by a political culture saturated with memories of the 'hungry thirties' and pro-Soviet propaganda, was hostile to the Poles not only as 'landlords' and 'fascists' but also because they feared the newcomers' readiness to work would undermine their bargaining position. Knowing that some of these Poles had been forced into the *Wehrmacht* further strengthened such opposition. This defensiveness often manifested itself as straightforward xenophobia. With the end of the war graffiti demanding 'Poles go Home' and 'England for the English' had sprung up near Polish bases, and there were incidents of Poles being attacked by armed gangs and hospitalised. All this was accompanied by the growth of a deeply dispiriting anti-Polish racism. In the event, the trade unions used the Poles as a bargaining chip. In return for a five-day week, the promise that the Poles would be the first out in the event of job cuts and that the final decision to employ Poles would lie with the relevant local NUM branch, the Union agreed they might join their workforce as part of a wider deal on working conditions in January 1947. Six months later 2,288 Poles could be found employed as miners, though a further thousand are thought to have been denied available work owing to local branch decisions.

The AUEW played a similar game, finally acceding to Polish entry into their workforce in February 1949; the National Union of Agricultural Workers was also obstructive. To a degree, the Labour Party leadership's earlier insistence that the Poles opt for repatriation had licensed opposition, though once the government set about implementing the Polish

Resettlement Act, they placed the trade unions under a great deal of pressure to cooperate. As the government reminded the taxpayer, any Pole in the corps denied available work would remain a burden on the Exchequer. Strikingly, *Tribune*, the strongly socialist newspaper, was critical of the recalcitrant trade unions, naturally arguing that internationalist working-class solidarity must prevail over sectional self-interest. Some groups of workers were much less hostile and the hard-pressed members of the Transport and General Workers Union and the General and Municipal Workers' Unions encouraged Poles into their ranks, just as they absorbed Irish and, later, Afro-Caribbean migrant workers. By 1949, the Polish section had 6,000 members.[4]

Edward Wierzbicki's memoirs, sustained throughout by a feeling of moral outrage, recall an English hostility so great he emigrated to Australia in 1947:

> I knew I did not want to settle in England because I felt pretty bitter towards the country for the two-faced political attitude towards Poles and Poland. It was far from pleasant trying to explain to the indigenous population why I'd no intention of returning to my own country. The pro-Communist angling of the news did its bit as well. By a certain class of people we were hated and held in deep disregard. It seemed to me that at the time England was governed by pro-Communist sympathisers and workers' unions. Poles were accused of all manner of things probably because of their real contribution to the common victory. In such an atmosphere there was no chance for co-existence and therefore, in my search for a better future, it was necessary to find a more peaceful corner of the world. For many Poles Australia seemed the answer as it was in those days a large country virtually untouched. There was no established Polish society and so we looked in vain for advice. However there were among us energetic and unafraid-of-work pioneers so that today in both large and small towns throughout the length of Australia there are centres of Poles. We were the seed scattered on virgin soil which despite interference from the regime in Warsaw gave a magnificent yield.[5]

Rafał's reaction to the man from the Ministry was typical. Members of the 'intelligentsia' and officer class posed the British government particular problems. Highly educated and accustomed to occupying positions of considerable social and professional standing before the war, they could not be placed so easily. Their age could be a further complication; they were often physically unsuited to manual labour and had little aptitude for learning new languages. Whether the government's recognition of this group as a special case reflects an objectionable class-based bias or a laudable empathy is an open question. Either way, for highly decorated men only too ready to finger the Allies as Poland's betrayers, the possibility that they would be further demeaned was out of the question. Consequently, for the 20,000 or so who fell into this category, the compromise proposed came in the form of places on training schemes in areas such as deep-sea fishing, farming and forestry, mechanical, building and electrical trades and assorted skills such as tailoring, draughtsmanship, watch-repairing and so on. Turning professionals into skilled workers was not ideal but for some it was preferable to welfare dependency or digging coal or potatoes and for the economy as a whole it seemed an effective use of well-educated people.

The final piece of the resettlement policy fell into place in early 1948 when the government decided that in return for relinquishing their commissions, officers might receive a gratuity. Further amendment to the original settlement legislation allowed officers with their own means to set up businesses. Rather than being funnelled towards employment needs identified by the state, this telling concession allowed a small number of Poles to become entrepreneurs.* By February 1949, 8,369 had entered training schemes, including 2,869 who had relinquished their commissions. Not long after, Polish businesses began to proliferate, perhaps not in large numbers, but sufficient to suggest that this rather difficult part of the workforce, exceedingly conscious of its own dignity and a little belligerent, had been successfully absorbed into the economy. Among the 177 PRC men who took up farming was Rafał Ryżewski.[6] He was finally discharged, relinquishing his commission, on 3 June 1949, bringing to an end eight years of institutional life.

The SS *Empire Brent*, commissioned by the Ministry of Sea Transport, docked at Southampton on 26 September 1947. Officials were handed a passenger list comprising the 'names and descriptions of ALIEN passengers' on board. Number 727 was RYŻEWSKA Anna, aged forty-four, classified as Housewife; number 728 was RYŻEWSKA Wanda, aged nineteen, classified as Student; and number 729 was RYŻEWSKA

* In 1951 all restrictions on Polish employment were lifted.

Maria-Danuta, aged fifteen, classified as Student.[7] Hanna's 'Certificate of Identity', issued by the British authorities in India, was stamped by the Southampton immigration authorities that same day. An accompanying stamp told her she was 'permitted to land' on condition that she immediately registered with the police, did 'not take or change employment except with the consent of the Ministry of Labour and National Service' and agreed to leave 'not later than such dates as may be specified by the Secretary of State'. She was transferred to a transit camp at Uckfield, and her papers received a further stamp from the East Sussex Constabulary on 7 October 1947. Nana remembers the landing at Southampton as an anticlimax. Her father was not relieved of his duties and was not there to meet them off the ship. The disappointment was offset by giddiness when Gienek, her boyfriend, without a moment to lose, kissed her for the first time: 'A very clumsy but exciting event.'

We can only guess how Hanna felt at the moment her family was reunited – Nana says it was ecstatic – and finally there was no need for letters. It had been eight years since Rafał had been taken prisoner and over seven since Hanna and the girls were herded on to cattle trucks on that brutal night in April 1940.

Life at Plaster Down saw old patterns quickly re-established. Rafał gathered about him a gang of officers who had been through the war

together, Hanna again played hostess. Evenings were spent playing bridge, eating, drinking and reminiscing, Hanna doubtless on the receiving end of more gallantry than she quite needed. Younger soldiers held dances, sending trucks out to Tavistock to enlist female company, those same trucks taking them into town in subsequent weeks. This cannot have done much to endear them to local men, already taught by the newspapers to see Polish soldiers as advanced students in the dark arts of seduction. During the war women's magazines urged readers to resist those charming Poles, advising them to stick to the less immediately appealing native male.[8]

For Danusia and Wanda these young soldiers must have been a diverting presence, albeit one they were shielded from by the rank and standing of their parents. According to Nana, time spent cycling the lanes of the Dartmoor lowlands left the strongest impressions, though most memorable was the day Rafał took them for the first time to Haye Down. It was a glorious day and once dropped off in Tavistock the three of them walked the four miles to 'the Farm'. En route, Rafał explained his purchase. They did not have enough money to buy the plot on their own, so Stefan, Rafał's brother, was brought in on the deal, as were two Ryżewski cousins, including Ola's husband. Bronek Skalak, an official in the Polish government-in-exile (nominally functional), was a sleeping partner. Once a chicken farm, but now overgrown and unkempt, it was a place of great tranquillity, overlooked by the ancient granite church at Brentor. This land would be their Monte Cassino, he said, a place the family would conquer together, bringing it back into cultivation.

It is hard to contemplate that day without thinking of the excursions Danusia and Wanda used to take with their father to Działka. My own memories of doing the same walk from Tavistock to 'the Farm' cannot but shape how I think of theirs. The optimistic talk, the sense of mission, the pleasure taken in the exertion, the sense of physical freedom, the private world of parents and children, the hazy buzzing light of midsummer. How distant 1950 felt in 1980, yet now a further thirty years have passed. Was Tavistock in 1980 as like it was in 1950, as it now is like it was in 1980? In 1950, a father and his grown-up daughters no longer balanced on the same bicycle, but still they could take that walk, concerned only with the present and its practicalities. Choosing to walk those four miles today can only be a deliberate act of private commemoration.

Nana's recollections of life on 'the Farm' and her first few years in Britain are among her most vivid, crowded with detail and warm senti-ment. Perhaps inadvertently, she shows how her own coming of age was played out against the fading of her parents' generation, melan-cholic with memories of the 1920s and 1930s, and profoundly shaped by the comradeship of the army. Haye Down quickly established itself as the 'Officers' Club', with Rafał and Hanna collecting an eccentric crew of middle-aged Poles who gradually found places for themselves in a world made confusing not simply by language but also by peace. Britain in the late 1940s was a place of austerity and shortage, of stability and order. Attlee's government created a political consensus that, though buffeted by successive currency crises, a creaking industrial sector and deteriorating industrial relations, in time delivered a better standard of living and more educational opportunity than had ever before been the case. For this bunch of single-minded Poles, for whom World War One provided seminal experiences and whom World War Two found in their prime, post-war Britain, conservatively radical, seemed both strangely amenable and deeply alien. Old soldiers, including Dr Kramer, Colonel Surówka, the pilots Captain Adam Olszewski and Captain Edmund Erthracht, and officers Długoborski and Jasiński found temporary refuge on the Farm. Space was scarce and Olszewski improbably bought an old green double-decker bus, the No. 83 according to family lore, which became their Nissen hut.

Working as labourers for neighbouring farmers brought this strange collective a little extra money; farmers' wives were charmed by all the hand-kissing, their husbands perhaps appreciating having hard-working Poles on tap. Mundek Erthracht, prone to waving his injured little finger around – 'Battle of Britain, Battle of Britain!' – even managed to steal one farmer's wife, a Mrs Stone. Erthracht's first wife had been confined to a mental hospital after the war, suffering from post-traumatic stress. 'He's gained a stone', the men joked, slight evidence of a growing proficiency in the 'fish-eaters' language'. Nights continued in the mode established at Plaster Down. Hanna served up the food, Rafał poured the home brew and conversation turned to the war, boasting and the interminable discussion of tactics.

Though warmed by drink and comradeship, this was not an easy life. Money was scarce, water had to be drawn from the well and lighting was provided by paraffin lamps. It would be some years before running water and electricity found their way to the Farm. Hanna cooked on her 'diabolo', an ancient wood-fired range, which smoked terribly and demanded continuous attention; Rafał steered their old Massey Ferguson tractor across land strewn with granite, which had to be cleared by hand, generating little piles of heavy dense stone – a Sisyphean labour, says Nana. True to form, Rafał got on well with the local farmers, learning much from them, not least how to negotiate agricultural regulations – he discovered that by bringing disused land into cultivation he would earn the right to a small government subsidy. Together with Olszewski, he boosted their income by bringing Polish foods down from London importers in a military truck. At resettlement camps dotted throughout Devon, the most famous 'Little Poland' being at Newton Abbot, Rafał and Adam brought sausages and rye bread to men craving a taste of home.

In Tavistock itself, Rafał cut an odd figure. Known, unimaginatively but justifiably, as Mr Whisky, he could be seen in his army greatcoat and battledress, both stripped of all military insignia, and an ancient trilby, which he raised a fraction from his head with a slight bow when coming upon townswomen or acquaintances. If he made a good sale on market days, he'd join the other farmers at the Market Inn for a couple of shots, before wending his way home. Hanna was placated with a miniature bottle of Tia Maria, unbuttoned from his left breast pocket. From my heart, he'd say.

As in India, Hanna soon had vegetables growing, supplemented by a brood of chickens and some geese. Free-range *avant la lettre*, they ran wild, nesting in the undergrowth. Hanna knew where to look for eggs, although once in a while a particularly discreet hen would triumphantly lead her newly hatched chicks out into the yard. Legend has it that at some point a visit from the local constabulary put a stop to Hanna's cultivation of poppy seeds, meaning no more home-made poppy-seed cake.

Soon enough the Officers' Club began to break up. Dr Kramer got a post in a London hospital, presumably going to work for the new National Health Service; Stefan took a job at Southampton University, giving up the second-hand furniture shop he had established; Erthracht abandoned farming and departed with Mrs Stone, leaving behind their small, fully furnished cottage, which stood for many years in this state, strangely frozen in time – I remember peering in through the window. Colonel Surówka left for a place unknown, though one of the Polish resettlement camps seems likely; Olszewski, Długoborski and Jasiński, who kept bees and produced honey, finally moved out of the bus to a newly built bungalow in Wales, their new barracks. Other demobilised Poles from Plaster Down formed a small but notable presence in and around Tavistock. They married local girls and took jobs quarrying or working as farm labourers. Pan Szarlota opened a small shoe-repair business; Pan Frank got a job as a patisserie chef with the Queen's Head Hotel and, most successful of all, Edmund Kamiński began selling reclaimed building materials and was soon running a successful builders' merchant business: the family now has extensive business interests in the town (the latest generation boasting a commanding presence on Tavvy's rugby team).

Schooling for the girls took them to Stowell Park near Cheltenham in Gloucestershire. This old country house had been used by the American army during the war and the grounds were peppered with the inevitable Nissen huts, now converted into classrooms and dorms. Stowell was one of four secondary boarding schools established by the Government's Committee for the Education of Poles. Responsible for 8,244 Polish school-children of all ages, the committee's 1949 report explained why separate provision was needed:

It was impossible to send the incoming Polish children to British schools. They had lived in the Tower of Babel. Their native Polish was often imperfect and the scraps of tongues, ranging from Russian to Swahili, which they picked up during their transcontinental wanderings could hardly be regarded as suitable entrance qualifications for schools in the public education systems of England and Scotland.

It is salutary to note the committee's further concerns:

> To any observer it was patent that the ideals, content and methods of Polish education had been profoundly influenced by French models and, while all tribute must be paid to a system which believes so ardently in learning for its own sake, a certain rigidity of outlook and presentation, together with a preoccupation with examinations, tended to raise doubts in some minds as to whether such a vigorous mental discipline was altogether in the best interests of their pupils.

Nonetheless, the government backed the recommendation that a Polish secondary education sector be created, comprising two boys' and two girls' boarding schools.

Again, the Poles were prey to left-wing suspicions. The Polish girls' school at Dunalastair House, Perthshire – moved to Grendon Hall, near Aylesbury, in 1948 – attracted the criticism of labour MP Harry Hynd. Apart from advising that all Poles should return to Poland,[9] Hynd accused the government of maintaining an 'exclusive' girls' school at public expense. Investigations rejected claims that the school was 'snobbish' or 'undemocratic', finding instead students who had survived German and Soviet camps, including one nineteen-year-old girl who had been subject to Nazi medical experiments in Ravensbrück and another, aged eighteen, who had been forced to carry victims to the crematorium at Belsen.[10] Nana, too, remembers the older girls who had been rescued from German camps. She recalls them as distant and enigmatic – and allowed to smoke.

Going to boarding school, Nana explains, was the first time she was outside the realm of her mother's strict supervision and her vivid memories of this experience are at times redolent of an Ealing comedy. They begin with the moment of her arrival. Her uncle Stefan, at this point still in the RAF and based at Weston-super-Mare, commandeered a staff limousine and driver, and set off to Plaster Down to collect Rafał and the girls. Both men were in full uniform, should the headmistress be in any doubt as to their (sense of) importance. When the limo swept up to the house it brought the resident girls to the windows and Nana swears one girl, overwhelmed by the car and the uniforms, cried out, 'Princess Margaret has arrived!'

Danuta did well in geography, geometry, gymnastics and art, as well as exhibiting a penchant for history, but Latin grammar and dates left her baffled, despite the best efforts of Mr Brill. Much of her only surviving letter from Stowell Park, written in February 1948, breathlessly explains how, if she fails in any subject, she will punish herself by staying on over summer but then again she will not get a two (the fail mark) and so won't have to apply the punishment. It seems the girls were also developing a healthy attitude towards spiritual authority. 'When we returned from church we made a priest-snowman and pelted him with snowballs.' In Danka Pola, Danka Ryżewska found a soulmate, and together they wrote sketches and stories which lampooned the 'school oddities in very subtle ways'. For some unearthly reason, they once filled a bath with cold water and each girl was dared to take a turn and plunge in naked. Rules, of course, were there for the breaking. Food was smuggled out of the dining hall and parties were held after lights-out at 10 p.m. With the radio tuned to a music station, they were drawn out from under the sheets to dance whatever their state of undress. Pretty blonde Kama, who gyrated in her knickers, stockings and suspenders, transfixed the other girls. On one such night the girls were sure they caught sight of a shadowy figure outside in the moonlight.

There was much improving activity, too – not least visits to places of historical interest, which aimed to help them adjust to 'the British way of life' – though full assimilation was compromised by their continuing exposure to Polish national customs, song and dress. For most young Poles in Britain, Polish Saturday school was practically compulsory. Hoping to make of her girls 'fine ladies', Hanna booked piano lessons and on their first homecoming to Haye Down, Danusia and Wanda found their parents had somehow acquired an old piano. 'Wanda took to the piano with gusto,' writes Nana, 'but alas I had no time to practise as my mercurial character being quick and changeable had no time for persevering.' Instead, the money given for the music lessons was spent on 'trivia' when on excursions to Cheltenham.

During her last summer at school, Danusia took the option of spending a few weeks with an English family to polish up her English language skills. Consequently, she and her friend Zosia Truksa were assigned to a private school near Blackpool, another country house, where the only residents that summer were the formidable deputy headmistress, the music teacher Mr Hodges, and a Great Dane dog. They had the run of the building – so stocked with strange antiquities and mysterious rooms it seemed more museum than home – and they took trips into Blackpool, peeping at 'what the butler saw' on the Golden Mile. The deputy head, keen on vigorous physical exercise, routinely thrashed the girls at tennis and table tennis, building up their appetites for the long evening dinners. Mr Hodges gallantly advised the girls on the correct approach to the multi-staged journey through the cutlery at table, though the formality of such occasions was somewhat undermined by the presence of the dog, whose massive jaw rested on the table throughout, a patch of drool expanding as he waited for little titbits from his mistress.

Hanna and Rafał did not have the luxury of lapsing into peaceful retirement. Like many Polish settlers, money worries kept them hard at it until Rafał eventually scaled down their operations, selling off stock. His decision to take some temporary work in Coventry proved disastrous. Left alone on the farm, Hanna lapsed into depression and, according to Nana, had developed a persecution complex, which manifested itself in irrational terrors and, haunted by memories of the war, she feared long separations. Rafał returned home to pick up the pieces. In her confused state she put her hand too close to the chainsaw when he was cutting wood and lost three fingers.

During this period of separation, Hanna celebrated her fiftieth birthday. Rafał wrote her a typically jaunty letter, full of love and affection for his 'big' woman – a term of endearment difficult to capture in English. Though insisting that all was good in their lives together, the letter leaves the reader in no doubt that both ached for Poland, its landscapes and ways: 'I wish you, darling, with my whole heart, that you will live another half-hundred and in it a happy return under our sky, so that the two of us could once more travel to all those wonderful places which memory inhabits and will continue to inhabit.' Rafał was still cheerleading, echoing letters sent a decade earlier: '"Ears up" Big Mother, and the world will immediately show itself in its colours.'

A decade later Rafał's health had declined. He suffered a mild heart attack and shortly after was diagnosed with lung cancer, the product of many years' smoking. His last letters date from hospital stays in the spring and early summer of 1963. These focus on housekeeping, instructing Hanna on what food to buy and which bills to pay, and contain relentlessly upbeat reports on his condition. He was disappointed that she did not visit and it seems she had become a nervous traveller, even over fairly short distances. He joked about letting on that he was a captain, which brought extra attention from the nurses, and was amused by the organised activities laid on for patients, including lessons in painting, drawing and, he wryly noted, 'making "panama" hats' – a little unexpected in a respiratory clinic in Camborne, Cornwall. The operation had little effect and the cancer advanced quickly. Rafał died that September. 'I organised a modest refreshment for the mourners in a Tavistock café,' writes Nana. 'Mamusia was totally oblivious to what was going on around. I watched her as she tucked into a cake with a sort of enigmatic smile as though on a different planet. Was she with Tatuś in the days of joy and happiness?'

Hanna would live for another twenty years, more or less in isolation on the Farm. She grew more food than she could ever eat, kept chickens for eggs and meat, an Alsatian dog for protection, and the cat Kicia for company. One evening the local television news reported that the search was on for a dog that had been killing sheep. The aerial shot of the dog in action showed all too clearly that the culprit was Hanna's Reks. Reks had to be put down and this emergency was the strongest signal yet that Hanna was not coping well. Therapy was one possible solution and Wanda made arrangements for Hanna to come over to Canada. At the security checkpoint at the airport, she was paralysed by fear. A brief body search and routine check of hand luggage caused her to freeze on the spot, unable to move forward. She had stood in lines like this, been searched and asked to produce papers by people in uniform too many times before. Nana rapidly intervened, quickly explaining the situation to the security officers. The war. Russia. Siberia. Transports. Camps. Therapy. No English. They allowed the old woman in the print headscarf to go through without being searched.

Nana took Kicia home with her to Plymouth, but the cat promptly ran away. Hanna returned some months later. Staying with Wanda and Henio for those few months in Canada must have been a comfort, though no one can say whether therapy had any effect. Upon her return, Hanna found Kicia, alive but thin and bedraggled, in the Farm's generator shed. She had come home too.

On Rafał's death it transpired that the peculiarities of the Farm's purchase meant that Hanna did not have the right to continue living there. The Dickensian exactitudes of the legal wrangling can be passed over but suffice it to say Nana was adamant her mother would not again face eviction from her land. Sixteen years and three court appearances later, they were on the brink of final settlement, 'coerced', says Nana, into accepting an unfavourable agreement. That night she had a dream. 'I was in an art gallery, all the paintings were frozen over. Reaching the last one I started to crack the ice. It was Mamusia's portrait in profile. As I looked she turned her head. Looking sternly at me, she spoke. "You started, so you finish."' Her resolve renewed, Nana rejected the proposed settlement, creating pandemonium, 'wigs were scratched, gowns fluttered'. Her two and a half hours in the witness stand paid off. The judge finally ruled that Hanna Ryżewska should be granted the freehold, with the land unencumbered. 'Most interesting case,' were the judge's closing words, 'I wish I could have heard more.'

Hanna could have seen out her final years living in the corrugated-iron house she and Rafał had shared for the final fifteen years of their marriage, but Nana felt obliged to fulfil his old promise that one day there would be a new house on the Farm. With the court settlement reached and the finances in place, building began. Hanna paid close attention to certain details and I have vague memories of Nana exasperated at her mother's insistence that the kitchen floor tiles should extend under the kitchen cabinets. Those were happy days for Hanna who found in the builders' company a substitute Officers' Club. Few workmen ever ate so well.

Not long after, mother, now great-grandmother, and daughter, now grandmother, stood at the new front door. Danusia handed Hanna the keys. 'Tatuś's wish and promise fulfilled,' she said. 'It's yours.'

Although Hanna and Kicia enjoyed the comfort and security of the new house for only a few years, it is consoling to think that the old woman in the woods might finally have achieved some peace of mind and comfort. Whether or not the security provided by bricks and mortar eventually banished her fear, Nana insists her mother's six great-grandchildren were a tonic to her, final evidence of the permanency of her survival.

Hanna died at a quarter to four on Boxing Day 1983. I was eight years old and so remember this detail precisely. In the months before there had been talk of blood being found on her sheets and just before Christmas she had a massive stroke and had to be hospitalised. Wanda flew in from Canada and saw her mother shortly before she died; Danusia and her two daughters were present as she slipped away. *'Mam dobre dzieci'* ('I have good children') were her last words. She was buried with Rafał in Tavistock cemetery.

After finishing school, Wanda went to Portsmouth to study domestic science where she met a young Pole named Henryk Szumski, an electrical engineer. Henio, a man of great charm and wry humour, had been in the army and had fought at Monte Cassino. Wanda speaks fondly of those Portsmouth days, remembering them as the first time she did not feel burdened by a sense of responsibility, at ease with new friends and falling in love. In the 1950s she and Henio emigrated to Canada in search of better job prospects, where they have lived happily ever since, with two sons and now grown-up grandchildren.

After the summer spent with the drooling Great Dane, Nana returned to the Farm and took up a place at art school in Plymouth, living in lodgings. She met and married Michael or Miki Skalski, a Polish ex-army officer considerably older than her. They settled in Plymouth. It was not a good match, she says, leaving her parents bitterly disappointed. The only joy came from the two daughters bearing flower names, Jasmina and Narcyza, born in 1953 and 1954. Miki died in the 1960s. Nana remarried in the 1970s – this time picking a navy man. Arfer (the spelling a family idiosyncrasy) became grandfather to her six grandchildren.

On this note this story of deportation, displacement and settlement comes to an end. By some counts the balance sheet might weigh unbearably towards the negative, the account melancholic with loss. The loved ones, the possessions, the ways of life, the landscapes of youth and, until recently, the family members inaccessibly on the other side of the Iron Curtain. Nana name-checks the Ryżewscy among her immediate family lost to the war. The Nazis snatched her grandfather Józef Ryżewski and Rafał's youngest brother, Józef (Józio) off the street in Bielsko in 1939. They were never traced or seen again. Aunt Ola lost her baby son in Siberia. Aunt Marysia's daughter Jagusia was so traumatised by separation from her mother that when they were eventually reunited she needed lifelong care. Marysia was briefly reunited with Olek, though a sniper later shot him dead through the window of his office. Was this murderer a German, a Russian or Belorusian? It cannot be said. Władek and Kazik Ryżewski, Rafał's cousins, also came to Britain in 1946. Władek built a successful career as an engineer, but his brother had a nervous breakdown and never recovered. Hanna's fear was all too common among her generation of Polish settlers in the UK.[11]

The collapse of the Soviet Union allowed people to travel freely to parts of the *kresy* long out of bounds. Such journeys rarely give a satisfying sense of closure, often coldly confronting pilgrims with only the faintest traces of older ways of life. What though, did these pilgrims want to find? When Helena Tutak (*née* Masiulanis) returned to the place where she grew up, just over the Lithuanian border in Belarus, she found her childhood home still intact. 'It was very moving,' she says, 'but I didn't want to go in.'

If there can be closure, it is not generally detectable through these journeys back to the beginning, but in the photographs clumsily inserted at the end of the memoirs. These are amateurish, no more than family snapshots, badly lit and lacking in artistry. They show an old face and a frail body, often sitting a little bent in a chair, limbs limp and shrunken. This person, the subject and author of the memoir, is not the intended subject of the photograph. That is to be found in the sons and daughters, the grandchildren and the great-grandchildren that encircle them.

AFTERWORD

Poland Found?

Late into my research I spent a day at the Plymouth and West Devon Record Office. This small, friendly and efficient operation in the Cattedown area of the city mainly houses parish and local government records. I was there to leaf through some minute books in the hope that I might find some indication of local attitudes to the arrival of the Poles at Plaster Down. I found nothing. All historians have days like this and I insert an endnote in recognition of this unproductive labour.[1] The only mention of the camp referred to the possibility, following the departure of the Americans, of converting it into temporary social housing, rather than allowing vagrants in.

Opposite me sat a middle-aged couple down from Dorset, members of Britain's vast army of amateur genealogists who trace their ancestry as a hobby. This pair were leafing through city directories from the 1920s, trying to track down the home address of the woman's grandparents. Nana and Aunt Jasmina are now also playing this game and have constructed a family tree much more complicated than the impression given by the Ryżewski tale in this book. There are Ryżewscy, contemporaries of Hanna, Rafał, Wanda and Danusia, of whom you know nothing. And so it will remain. Like any historian, my task has not been to list all known facts, but rather to construct a narrative attempting to explain something.

Still, the question arises as to whether there is anything fundamentally different between my project and that pursued by the couple with the directories. I asked myself the same question when the two elderly women at Plaster Down enquired so matter-of-factly if I was doing family research: so commonplace has ancestry tracing become. The trend fuels a number of magazines and a successful TV programme, which takes celebrities on journeys into their family's past, asking 'Who do you think you are?' and often producing some surprising answers. As part of this very phenomenon, history documentaries on television are no longer complete without a staged visit to the archives, during which the archivist produces the correct dusty volumes, allowing the presenter immediately to fall upon the exact information he or she needs. The viewer is not troubled by the fact that the programme's researchers or historical advisers had spent hours if not days searching through files looking for a snippet of relevant evidence. It is the archivist who appears to hold the keys to the past, producing documents which straightforwardly provide the revelations sought, affirming that pleasant idea that historians are detectives uncovering truths. It is significant that as academic historians problematised the tweedy truth claims traditionally associated with their subject, evolving new French-cut research agendas and conceptual languages, a neo-empiricism propelled the fleece-jacketed amateur historians into the archives.

Academics are rightly curious about this turn to the past. Fascinated by the 'construction of memory' and the role of commemoration in the fashioning of identity, they have begun to historicise the family history boom, seeking to explain it as an historical phenomenon. This peculiar feature of our time seems to be related to the disruptions and dislocations caused by nineteenth- and twentieth-century developments. Apparently immemorial ways of life, shaped by custom and religious practice, and regimented by strict codes of conduct, were destroyed by urbanisation, industrialisation, secularisation and war, the last being modernity's great accelerator. New ways of living and experiencing the world evolved, rendering the past discontinuous with the present. No longer embedded in people's lived reality, the past became a felt absence to be recovered.[2]

Research into family history often begins with a decision to root out military records, to discover the role a grandfather or great-grandfather played at some important moment in the nation's history. For the British, on the whole at ease with their national history, particularly regarding the two world wars, such trips to the National Archives at Kew in London are minor rituals of affirmation. One can rightly be proud that the old boy did his bit, was mentioned in despatches, and perhaps picked up a medal or two. To find even a very modest record concerning an ancestor is pleasurable. It represents official recognition of service, the paper trail providing a new way of connecting with a deceased relative. I, too, experienced this thrill when I found Ryżewski names on the Maintenance Lists for Valivade. This was the first time I saw an official document containing their names and, in this case, Hanna's signature. There they are, I exclaimed, amid the studious hush of the Asian and African reading room in the British Library.

A question I keep asking myself is whether this book is an exercise in auto-exoticism, a way making myself 'other', an extended exercise in vanity. On rereading Miłosz's memoir *Native Realm* I am struck by how strongly he identified against the Poles of the heartlands, the ethnic nationalists, and found in *kresy* life a Poland he could celebrate for its diversity and cultural riches. Miłosz did not deny the class rigidities, poverty and ethnic tensions of the *kresy* of his youth, but still the idea of the *kresy* provided him with the basis of the argument he carried on throughout his life with the ethnically and religiously homogenous world of post-war Poland. In particular, Miłosz celebrated the extraordinary scholarship which came out of the Jewish shtetls, the commentaries on the Torah, which can now be found in university libraries throughout the world. He embraced this as a Polish cultural achievement. If only, the subtext ran, his fellow citizens could too.

Something of my own readiness to imagine myself 'other' stemmed from a similar unease with the mainstream society of my youth. It was hard to miss the intensity and depth of social and political conflict that characterised Thatcher's Britain, now obscured in popular memory by the New Labour boom years, themselves rapidly receding into the past. Britain in the 1980s was more divided than at any point since the 1920s, if not the 1840s. And British people of a certain age and political inclination are left uneasy with the way in which Blair's children are fed a triumphalist version of this decade, with Tory commentators and their New Labour inheritors unabashed as they deploy dubious languages of inevitability, with the unemployed, impoverished and marginalised portrayed as the collateral damage of a necessary disruption.[3]

In his fifteenth year Rafał joined the Legionnaires, in mine I watched the Poll Tax riots on the television news. An absurd comparison in many respects, for I was fortunate enough to grow up in less interesting times. Nonetheless, I was gripped by this politics and though convinced I knew what I was against, felt strangely dissociated from what I fancied was the squalor of 1980s Britain. Roy Foster, the Irish historian, has written about the tendency of those Englishmen and women who were repelled by the materialism and industrial misery of nineteenth-century Britain to identify with an idealised Ireland. Their counterparts were the charismatic and charming Irishmen and women who flourished in Britain, particularly as writers and journalists. Versions of Foster's 'Marginal Men and Micks on the Make' can be found in all societies.[4] Ireland, however, was not my vantage point, my ideal place from which I could survey Thatcher's Britain. Until reflecting on this, I'd forgotten how imbalanced my hyphenated identity was and how I felt ashamed of Ireland: the bloody carnage of 'the North', Granny's anti-English bitterness, and the occasional expressions of a kind of fatalistic respect for the Provisional IRA that surfaced around me. I could feel an antagonism for Thatcher's Britain, but Ireland did not provide me a comforting lens through which to observe it.

Poland, less knowable, was more appealing. This was not because I naïvely hankered after Soviet communism but because Poland seemed locked into a noble struggle with a far greater foe. The enigmatic charm of the Polish Pope and the compelling unity of *Solidarność*, under the bushily moustached leadership of Lech Wałęsa, happily merged with family lore. Given my rejectionism, it is paradoxical that the positive images of John Paul II and *Solidarność* were promoted in the West as grist to its Cold War mill. Poland, by contrast with Ireland, appeared to provide a relatively uncomplicated counterpoint to Britain.

At one level, this quest to 'find Poland' reflects my realisation that Poland's history is thornier than I might once have supposed. And though I've grown attached to the title of this book, I'm also increasingly aware of both the presumption in the verb *and* my realisation that the story is of a family taking *leave* of Poland. For what has been jostling for space on these pages with my 'finding' is Rafał's, Hanna's, Wanda's and Danusia's 'leaving'. This contradiction struck me most forcefully when Nana explained how after her first husband died she decided to become a fully naturalised citizen of the United Kingdom (a move which in earlier years risked ostracisation by the Polish community),[5] thinking this was something she should do for her daughters, ending any uncertainty in their status. At the same time she stopped going to the Polish Club in Plymouth, decisively placing what illusions she may have harboured about a possible return to Poland to one side. By hanging on to 'finding', I signal the situatedness of myself in relation to my subject while also tentatively suggesting that by reflecting on her past Nana has allowed herself to look for Poland again. It's strange, she says, that just recently letters have started to come from forgotten distant relatives.

Poland, no more than any country, cannot be *found* and then inscribed onto the pages of a single book. My training as an Irish historian meant

I was not so naïve as to suppose that I would find in Poland the moral high ground on which to stand. Nonetheless, I underestimated quite the complexity of the problems of interpretation posed by the history of Poland during the Second World War, of which this story of displaced people is only a tiny fragment. And what follows may feel an abrupt and unwarranted intervention, but haunting any examination of the Polish experience during the Second World War is the fate of Poland's Jews. It is a subject of such moral presence that it threatens to subsume all other questions. Before I take leave of this book (which cannot be but something of a heroic narrative, an effect reinforced rather than diminished by the melancholia of exile) I must give what recognition I am able to the fact that there can be no ethically defensible history of Poland that does not duly acknowledge that 'it is as tragically Jewish as it is triumphantly Christian'.[6] And if the defeat of 1945 was redeemed in 1989 – the story of a people coming out of the Soviet darkness and into the light of democratic freedom and European integration – Poland's history cannot be shown as a unidirectional moral tale of triumph over adversity. As Dorota Glowacka observes, the Poles have not yet mourned the deaths of 'their' Jews or admitted the gaping hole this absence leaves in their life and culture.[7]

The dislocations and disconnections that have seen the British craze for tracing ancestry were experienced on an apocalyptic scale in Poland. Poland lost a higher proportion of its population than any other nation during the Second World War and, though it emerged victorious and boasting a record free of formal collaboration with fascism, the outcome was also a defeat. Poland's Jews were the greatest victims of the onslaught and no amount of special pleading can equate the treatment of Polish Catholics and Polish Jews. Books on the 'forgotten holocaust' or the 'Polish Holocaust' remind us that the Nazi occupation of Poland was brutal and murderous to a degree largely unknown in Western Europe and that immoral acts were committed by individuals from all groups party to the conflict, including Jews.[8] Nonetheless, it is inescapable that the 2 million or more Catholic Poles murdered by the Soviets and the Nazis represent a much smaller proportion than the 3 million Jewish Poles who were sent to the gas chambers or met their deaths in other ways. The great majority of Polish Jews died during the Second World War, while the great majority of Catholic Poles survived. In any debate conducted at the bar of international public opinion and shaped by a sense of competing victimhoods, Poles who insist on the equivalence of their suffering to that of the Jews are likely to seem morally suspect even to sympathetic observers.

I've written a book about people I love, but no sophistry can convince that 'Siberia' equals 'Auschwitz', mindful though I am that the first victims of Auschwitz were members of the Polish Catholic elite and, in the words of Christopher R. Browning, that the Nazi intention for the ethnic Poles was 'denationalization' or a 'cultural genocide' aimed at reducing the nation to a slave labour force.[9] Polish Catholic life continues in Poland whereas Polish Jewish life was almost fully obliterated by Nazism, marking a break with the past unmatched in its comprehensiveness or the brutality that brought it about. The Nazis differentiated between Polish Jews and Polish Catholics or 'Slavs' and, to understand what happened in the Second World War, so must we.

Admitting that 'Siberia' or the brutally murderous German occupation, as experienced by Catholic Poles, was qualitatively distinct from the Nazi genocide of the Jews is only a part of the challenge the war poses Polish national memory. Of the numerous appalling things that happened during 1939–45 in Poland, some were perpetrated by Polish Catholics against Polish Jews. Polish behaviours covered the whole moral spectrum from good to evil. Some Poles were extraordinarily brave, hiding Jews for days, weeks, months or even years, saving them from the death camps and other forms of genocidal violence. Others, such as informers or the notorious *szmalcownicy*, who blackmailed Jews in hiding, threatening to betray them to the Gestapo, behaved despicably. Most appalling was the infamous mass murder, which occurred in a small north-eastern town called Jedwabne, where on one terrible day in July 1941 Catholic townsmen were largely responsible for the murder of hundreds of their Jewish neighbours, incinerating them alive in a barn. Most people, however, were neither exceptionally good nor horrifically evil, though whether they should be described en masse as 'witnesses', 'indifferent' or 'bystanders', notions common to writing on Poland and the Holocaust and freighted with ethical implication, remains an open question.[10]

The Poles were not genocidal antisemites and no serious historian claims that 'the Poles' collectively collaborated in the Holocaust.[11] Nonetheless, slippages of language, common in the US, can create very unfair impressions. Auschwitz or Treblinka were not Polish death camps but Nazi death camps in Poland. And before calling Poland a place of death, a thought might be spared for the 40 million people who live there and the fact that with very few exceptions those deaths were inflicted not by Polish citizens but by Germans. Commentators who are quick to criticise Poles for generalising about Jews must ensure they are not similarly at fault regarding the Poles. Always writing *some* Poles or *some* Jews awkwardly burdens a text but such discipline is necessary when evidence that seems significant is far from comprehensive or complete. Nor should we be unmoved when some Poles routinely remind their critics of the death sentence facing any Pole and their relatives caught helping Jews, a rule which did not apply with the same severity elsewhere. That the Nazis thought this precaution necessary speaks volumes and the simple observation that a sizeable proportion of the 2.5 million non-Jewish Polish deaths was brought about through shootings and summary execution indicates the extent of the day-to-day terror. And despite this, our interlocutor will exclaim, there are more Poles than members of any other national group memorialised as Righteous Among the Nations at the Yad Vashem Institute in Israel (6,066 of 22,211 in 2008); this can only ever be a fraction of the Poles who helped Polish Jews. Moreover, we will be reminded, the action of a single informer could cause many deaths whereas the protection of a single person required the cooperation of many people.

Be that as it may, in recent times criticism directed at the Poles often reflects less 'their' actions during the war, than 'their' later failure to bear true witness to the Holocaust. Few now doubt that this owed much to the way in which the Soviet Union fashioned the memory of the war and, in particular, the Holocaust. Not only was the war celebrated as a victory against capitalism but, as Richard Ned Lebow observes, 'By identifying Jews murdered in the East not as Jews but as citizens of their home countries, then totting up the war's victims by nationality, Communist regimes could argue that the Holocaust was a non-event, which freed East Europeans of any need to consider their share of responsibility for genocide.'[12] Since then, the unfulfilled expectation that the Poles should be recognised equally as 'victims' has obscured in popular Polish memory the exceptional nature of the industrial murder of 'their' Jews, which occurred in their midst. And the sense of grievance sustained by this non-recognition has sometimes weakened the resolve of even decent people to oppose resolutely present-day anti-Jewish attitudes.

New ways of giving expression to Polishness are needed, which, free of communist distortions, can recognise that during the critical period of the war some Poles situated certain of their fellow citizens outside their 'universe of obligation'. As Poles evolve new ways of collectively articulating painful memories, which do not rely on the simplification of their own record or the relativising of the suffering of others, they become better placed to deal with some of the uglier aspects of their present. This is not a call for self-flagellation but for the casting off of the defensive self-pity that denies Poles ownership of their past and, therefore, their present. When they collectively look that past squarely in the eye they possess it and achieve authentic self-representation. When they do not, representing Poland becomes the prerogative of those who will.

Since the late 1980s, a more critically engaged and open public debate about the Second World War in Poland has developed. Much of this has comprised a relatively subdued and largely constructive discussion among scholars and intellectuals, often driven by émigrés determined to open up dialogue between Poles and Jews in the Diaspora.[13] The rarefied and generally constructive atmosphere of these exchanges was disturbed in 2001 by the publication of *Neighbours* by Jan T. Gross, a brief and highly readable account of the Jedwabne massacre that brought to popular notice Polish involvement in a crime until then attributed to the Nazis.[14]

'Event Jedwabne' was a seismic moment in Polish public life, generating intense and highly politicised debate.[15] The book's great importance stemmed from the collective character of the crime it described and it was evident that, post-communism, a shift had taken place in Polish attitudes. Jedwabne could not simply be written off as an aberration, leaving intact the prevailing Polish World War Two narrative of patient suffering and heroic martyrdom, familiar tropes from the book of Polish nationalism. Instead, Jedwabne polarised opinion between 'the defenders of Polish honour and the confessors of Polish shame', generating an anguished but overdue bout of national self-scrutiny that soon transcended the particularities of the Jedwabne case.[16] Debate in early-twenty-first century Poland has carried echoes of debates that have taken place in Western European countries since the 1960s and, in all cases, whatever the degree of guilt or collaboration, speaking openly of how the people of Nazi-occupied nations became implicated in the Holocaust has been a painful process.[17] The peculiarities of history have made it the turn of the former Warsaw Pact and Soviet republics to reckon with the particularities of their Second World Wars. This is only possible when people begin to see beyond the legacy of political oppression, the cultures of victimhood, deep-seated poverty and the mental dislocations caused by political transition.

Jedwabne, like the investigations of the Katyń murders and similar if less noticed Polish–Ukrainian dialogue, has at times proved cathartic, allowing some Poles to think less defensively about their history. Gross accelerated an ongoing process and there is much evidence that some Poles have developed a new interest in the Jewish and non-ethnically Polish dimension of the nation's history. In particular, attention is now being paid to the physical remains of Jewish life in Poland, with numerous restoration projects seeking to overcome the appalling neglect of Jewish heritage that characterised the communist period. Students are studying Jewish history and culture at university. Some Poles have discovered that they are of Jewish descent, grandparents revealing that they covered up their identities, Polonising names in order to make life easier in the post-war years. Small numbers are even converting, convinced that through their historical exposure to Jewish culture and history they too are Jewish, while others still suggest they can have a Jewish dimension to their lives without being Jews, and that this makes them truer Poles. Such developments suggest how increased political freedom is freeing up ways of being Polish, which reflect more fully the complexities of Poland's past.[18]

Surveys conducted shortly after the collapse of communism suggested that Poles had an exaggerated sense of the number of Jews living in their country;[19] antisemitic graffiti of football supporters is not yet a thing of the past; and for some Poles, blaming 'the Jews' for everyday problems (prices going up and so forth) is a reflex made more dangerous by its linkage to the pernicious myth that 'the Jews' dominated the communist repressive apparatus. Above all, right-wing nationalists, riveted to the old heroic narratives of the martyr nation with its hereditary enemies within and without, remain powerfully present in Polish society and politics.[20] Nonetheless, Poles of goodwill are now better placed to contest such myths and behaviours, but continued vigilance is needed if this new spirit of openness, generally resistant to the construction of coercive new orthodoxies yet liberated from the full weight of national tradition, is to shape new Polish historical discourses both within and without the academy.

I'm writing this on Easter Sunday 2009 and the The World at One (BBC Radio 4) happens to be a special from Warsaw, marking twenty years since the legalisation of Solidarność. Focused on the Polish economy, it précised Polish history, dwelling on the Polish victory against communism. A number of people were interviewed, including the Minister of Finance, a professor of ethics, a father and son team, a Solidarność activist turned successful architect, an investment banker, a middle-class shopper, and a factory worker from industrial Łódź. Only a priest and a farmer were missing. Among the subjects surveyed was the relationship between the communist legacy and political corruption (the son more hard-nosed than his father about the need to purge former communists from positions of power), the 'global victory against communism' led by *Solidarność*, and 'the credit crunch' and why Poland was economically better placed than most. That unmistakable strain of Polish patriotism was evident in almost all the speakers, so too was the distinct lack of reticence. It was stirring stuff, though I felt moved less by what was being said than by the timbre of the voices, the accents, the rapid speech, the mix of joviality and seriousness. I felt similarly moved when speaking to Helena Tutak, who with a calm dignity related a little of her family history. This response must be traceable back to those summer holidays with the 'old woman in the woods'. If my Dartmoory Poland is to take its place as a reference point alongside Fellini's Rome, Godard's Paris and Joyce's Dublin, then just as I accept I will never have a love affair with Claudia Cardinale, dance to a jukebox in *that* café, or remake English literature, so too must my Poland of sentiment also be a Poland of mature reflection.

I revere the survivors of the deportations and confronting readers with something of the complexity of Polish history does not turn victims into perpetrators or imply crude notions of collective guilt or responsibility. Instead, it reminds us that history is an interrogation room and, though some corners will always be shaded by darkness, false confessions or denials have a tendency to come to light eventually. And if Poland's coming to terms with the complexities of its past is a necessary part of its transition to liberal democracy, let me add that Britain (or, indeed, the United States) does not necessarily provide firm ground from which to pronounce on how we should handle our pasts. We are entranced by the empire, particularly the Indian Raj, and we coyly experience an occasional neo-imperial spasm, sure that 'they' were fortunate to have 'us' as their colonial masters rather than our more unsavoury fellow empire-builders; we celebrate the continuity of our institutions and liberties, conveniently forgetting Ireland and, most recently, our tolerance of a sectarian regime in Northern Ireland between 1920 and 1972; we celebrate the abolition of slavery, but fail to recognise, as we wonder at great eighteenth-century houses maintained by our subscriptions to the National Trust or English Heritage, the extent to which that old prosperity was based on the slave trade; we marvel at the Victorians and make of their suffering poor a Dickensian picturesque.

Whether British or Polish or Irish, history does not provide a comfort blanket any more than it does a way of predicting the future. What history does provide is evidence – more plentiful than any one person can know and more immediately affecting than abstract knowledge – of the need to keep questioning ourselves, developing our ability to think critically and enhancing our capacity to duly recognise the ideas of others. If we are to find firmer ground from which to observe this complexity, it might be secured through our vigilant adherence to the principle that a single perspective never embodied the totality of anything truly important.

Acknowledgements

I have been helped in many different ways by many people. In the UK, Danuta Pniewska talked to me, lent me books and introduced me to many members of Koło Polaków z Indii (Assocation of Poles in India). Without her enthusiasm for the project, I would never have had the opportunity to talk to Halina Szafrańska, Jan Siedlecki, Ludmiła Jakutowicz, Henry Bobotek, Halina Gnyra, Stanisław Harasymow, Janina and Bozena Pająk and many others. I have very fond memories of the association's gathering at Nałęczów in June 2006. Much of what they told me about their experiences did not make it into the book, but everything they told me shaped my thinking. The same goes for the letters and memoirs kindly sent to me by Jan Bednarz, Franciszek Herzog, Mrs K. Kosiba, Halina Szopińska, Mrs T. Babicz, Andrew Brzezina, Mrs I. Rybka and Michael Kulik. On my travels I repeatedly benefitted from the generosity of perfect strangers. In Omsk, Marina Zyrianova showed me around, and in Pavlodar, Feruza Nuralievna helped arrange the trip to Gresnovka and accompanied me to translate. In Karachi, thanks to introductions from Ian Talbot and Sarah Ansari, I enjoyed the extraordinary hospitality of Rafiq Safi Munshey and Nausheen Ahmad. Sahin Naqui and Iqbal Abbasi helped me find the Country Club and Maleeha Naqui showed me something of the city. In Kolhapur, a chance meeting saw Col. Shankar rao Nikam and Mrs Malati Nikam, and their son and daughter-in-law Nitten and Alpanna Nikam, take me under their wing for the entirety of my stay in their city. Nitten and his friend Ujjwal Nageshkar helped me understand something of their city's culture: the visit at dusk to the cremation site was an unusual privilege. In Poland, Magdalena Kubit-Szczuka and Wiesław Szczuka helped facilitate the trip to Belarus, ensuring that I had the scissors needed to cut the red tape I might face. Olga Apolaika at the Belarus Tour Service was very helpful and one can only hope that in time it will become easier to visit her beautiful country. Patrycja Płowy undertook the formidable task of transcribing the Ryżewski letters and Jaime Ashworth, deploying his exceptional grasp of the Polish language, translated them. Jaime is among the friends and colleagues at the University of Southampton who have taken an interest in this project. In particular, I am grateful to Mark Cornwall, my head of department throughout the period of research and writing, and to the School of Humanities, for supporting this rather unorthodox project. Julia Eichenberg of Trinity College, Dublin, was also helpful, as were my friends Naoko Takahatake, Magdalena Szałowska and Louise Tillin. Books also rely on agents, editors and publishers. Roy Foster, my former DPhil supervisor, introduced me to Clare Alexander, who agreed to act as my agent, and she successfully persuaded Dan Franklin at Jonathan Cape to commission the book. Few authors can have been so fortunate in their agent and editor and to Clare, and Dan and his team I offer my heartfelt thanks. It is not possible to detail the innumerable ways in which Julia has helped this project along. I could say that her readiness to read drafts, check translations and correct Polish spellings and my grammar has been beyond the call of duty except that she would say that duty has nothing to do with it. The feeling is reciprocated. Not everyone named here will agree with everything I've written and any errors are, of course, my own but I hope that the sincerity of purpose will be evident to all. My greatest debt is recorded in the dedication and foreword.

M.K.
London, December 2009

Notes

1 Trains

1 Czesław Miłosz, *Native Realm. A search for self-definition* (London, 1968), p. 16.

2 Life in the Wild Lands

1 Antony Polonsky, *Politics in Independent Poland* (Oxford, 1972), p. 30. • 2 Gustav Herling, *A World Apart* (London, 1951, 1986), pp. 117–18. • 3 Milan Kundera, *Immortality* (London, 1991), pp. 3–4. • 4 Manuscript in author's possession, p. 17. • 5 Eva Hoffman, *Shtetl. The History of a Small Town and an Extinguished World* (London, 1997), pp. 193–4. • 6 Daniel Stone, 'Jews and the Urban Question in Late Eighteenth Century Poland', *Slavic Review* 50, no. 3 (Fall 1991), 533. • 7 Ezra Mendelsohn, 'Interwar Poland: good or bad for the Jews?' in Chimen Abramsley, Maciej Jachimcyk, & Antony Polonsky (eds), *The Jews in Poland* (Oxford, 1986), pp. 136–8. • 8 Hoffman, *Shtetl*, p. 169. See also, Miłosz, *Native Realm*, pp. 91–107. • 9 One of the most notorious statements by a Polish politician in the interwar period came when the new prime minister of May 1936 stated: 'Economic struggle – by all means, but without causing harm.' The phrase is Michał Głowiński's in his *The Black Seasons* (pub. in Polish, 1999; English translation: Illinois, 2001), p. 155. • 10 Norman Davies, *God's Playground*, vol. II, 2nd ed. (Oxford, 2006), p. 192; William W. Hagen, 'Before the "Final Solution": Towards a Comparative Analysis of Political Anti-Semitism in Interwar Germany and Poland', *The Journal of Modern History*, vol. 68, no. 2 (Jun. 1996), p. 377. • 11 Hoffman's phrase in *Shtetl*, p. 192. Useful starting points for further exploration of this subject include essays in Yisrael Gutman, Ezra Mendelsohn, Jehuda Reinharz and Chone Shmeruk (eds.), *The Jews of Poland Between Two World Wars* (Hanover and London, 1989), especially essay by Emanuel Melzer; and Antony Polonsky (ed.), *Studies from Polin. From Shtetl to Socialism* (London and Washington, 1993). • 12 Wojciech Roskowski, *Landowners in Poland 1918–1939* (New York, 1991), pp. 13, 19, 21. • 13 Miłosz, *Native Realm*, p. 29. He explores the same theme in his marvellous autobiographical novel *The Issa Valley*, first published in Poland in 1955 and in English translation in 1978. • 14 Paul Robert Magocsi, *Historical Atlas of Central Europe. From the early fifth century to the*

present (London, 2002), pp. 97–9. • **15** Timothy Snyder, *The Reconstruction of Nations. Poland, Ukraine, Lithuania, Belarus, 1569–1999* (Yale, 2003), pp. 17–26 • **16** M. K. Dziewanowski, *Joseph Piłsudski. A European Federalist, 1918–1922* (Stanford, 1969), pp. 18–19. • **17** Czesław Miłosz, *The Captive Mind* (1953, Harmondsworth, 1980), p. 143. • **18** Miłosz, *The Issa Valley*, p. 61. • **19** Quoted in Diarmaid MacCullough, *Reformation. Europe's House Divided 1490–1700* (London, 2003), p. 192. • **20** Snyder, *Reconstruction of Nations*, pp. 19–20 • **21** Ibid. pp. 19–20. • **22** Quoted in Geoff Cubitt (ed.), *Imagining Nations* (Manchester, 1998), p. 75. • **23** For a sympathetic account of the plight of the Polish monarchy and its attempts to preserve some measure of Polish autonomy, see Adam Zamoyski, *The Last King of Poland* (London, 1992). • **24** This is traced in Brian Porter, *When Nationalism Began to Hate: Imagining Modern Politics in Nineteenth-Century Poland* (Oxford, 2000). • **25** For a nuanced discussion which suggests that the rise of economically and culturally assertive Ukrainian, Lithuanian, Jewish and Belorussian identities posed a greater challenge to Polish (and Russian) influence in the East than Russification, see Theodore R. Weeks, 'Defining Us and Them: Poles and Russians in the "Western Provinces", 1863–1914', *Slavic Review* 53, no. 1 (Spring 1994), pp. 26–40. • **26** Snyder, op. cit., pp. 33–44, 122–32. • **27** Weeks, 'Defining Us and Them', p. 29. • **28** Henryk Sienkiewicz (trans. Samuel A. Binion, 1898), *With Fire and Sword*, Vol. 1 (repr. Amsterdam, 2002), p. 75. • **29** Ibid., pp. 147–51. • **30** Porter, op. cit., p. 223. • **31** Ibid. • **32** Dziewanowski, op. cit., pp. 41–2. • **33** Miłosz, *Native Realm*, p. 51. • **34** Polonsky, *Politics in Independent Poland*, pp. 62–3. • **35** Dziewanowski, op. cit., p. 49. • **36** Ibid., p. 52. • **37** Ibid., pp. 92–139. • **38** Snyder. op. cit., pp. 62–3. • **39** Norman Davies, 'The Missing Revolutionary War. The Polish Campaign and the Retreat from Revolution in Soviet Russia, 1919–21', in *Soviet Studies*, vol. xxvii, no. 2 (April 1975), pp. 178–95. • **40** Letters from Emil Ryżewski, 1 August 1919, 1 December 1919 and 10 March 1920. • **41** Snyder, op. cit., pp. 64–5. • **42** This was particularly the case regarding the recovery to the Catholic Church of churches forcibly converted by the Russians to Orthodoxy in 1875. Poles found it hard to believe why this produced such resistance, wrongly believing former Catholics – or people descended from Catholic families – would happily shrug off Orthodoxy. Not so, and the fate of former Catholic churches became another point of contention between the Polish government and the national minorities. See Konrad Sadkowski, 'From Ethnic Borderland to Catholic Fatherland: The Church, Christian Orthodoxy, and State Administration in the Chelm Region, 1918–1939', *Slavic Review* 57, no. 4 (Winter 1998), pp. 813–39. • **43** Tadeusz Piotrowski, *Poland's Holocaust: ethnic strife, collaboration with occupying forces and genocide in the Second Republic, 1918–1947* (Jefferson, 1998), p. 146. • **44** Ibid. • **45** Kulik MS, p. 12. • **46** Ibid., pp. 139–40, 152–3. • **47** Piotrowski, op. cit., p. 146. • **48** Edmund I. Zawacki, 'The Utopianism of Stefan Żeromski', *Slavonic and East European Review. American Series*, vol. 2, no. 1 (March 1943), pp. 96–113. • **49** Eric Hobsbawm, *Interesting Times. A Twentieth-Century Life* (London, 2002), pp. 135–6. • **50** Shimon Redlich, *Together and Apart in Brzezany. Poles, Jews, and Ukrainians, 1919–1945* (Bloomington, In., 2002). All detail on Brzezany is drawn from this important history-memoir. •

51 Quoted in J. G. Alexander, 'The Legacy of Three Crises: Parliament and Ethnic Issues in Prewar Poland', in *Slavic Review*, vol. 27, no. 4, 1968, pp. 564–80 (p. 577 for statistics). • **52** See sympathetic discussion in Snyder, op. cit., p. 70.

3 *Deportation*

1 Parts of the first section of this chapter are derived from *Stalin's Ethnic Cleansing in Eastern Poland. Tales of the Deported 1940–1946* (London, 2000), a collection of 148 separate testimonies, assembled by the Association of the Families of the Borderland Settlers, and amounting in all to 800 pages. Points taken from specific testimonies located in this collection are indicated in the footnotes as *Stalin's Ethnic Cleansing*. • **2** *Stalin's Ethnic Cleansing*, p. 183. • **3** Wesley Adamczyk, *When God Looked the Other Way. An Odyssey of War, Exile and Redemption* (Chicago, paperback 2006), pp. 26–7. • **4** Kulik, MS 2.10. • **5** Quoted in Jan T. Gross, *Revolution from Abroad. The Soviet Occupation of Poland's Western Ukraine and Western Belorussia* (Princeton, 1992, 2002), p. 212. • **6** *Stalin's Ethnic Cleansing*, p. 51. • **7** Ibid., p. 202. • **8** Gross, op. cit., p. 210. • **9** *Stalin's Ethnic Cleansing*, p. 526. • **10** Gross, op. cit., p. 214. • **11** Anna M. Cienciala, Natalia S. Lebedeva and Wojciech Materski, *Katyn. A Crime Without Punishment* (New Haven and London, 2007), p. 173. • **12** Gross, op. cit., pp. 194–5. • **13** Natalia Lebedeva, 'The Deportation of the Polish Population to the USSR, 1939–41', *Journal of Communist and Transition Politics*, 16, nos. 1–2 (March–June 2000), p. 18. • **14** Gross, op. cit., p. xiv. • **15** Anne Applebaum, *Gulag. A History* (London, 2003), p. 517. • **16** Herling, *A World Apart*. For a fuller summary of these general characteristics, see Applebaum, op. cit., pp. 22–4. • **17** Cienciala, Lebedeva and Materski, op. cit., p. 174. • **18** Keith Sword, *Deportation and Exile, Poles in the Soviet Union, 1939–48* (London, 1994, repr. 1996), p. 23. • **19** Adamczyk, op. cit., p. 35 • **20** Gross, op. cit., p. 160. • **21** Manuscript in author's possession. • **22** Pawel Korzec and Jean-Charles Szurek, 'Jews and Poles under Soviet Occupation (1939–1941): Conflicting Interests' in Antony Polonsky (ed.), *Studies from Polin*, pp. 400–1. • **23** Cienciala, Lebedeva, and Materski, op. cit., pp. 432–3. • **24** Ibid., p. 55. • **25** Ibid., p. 65. • **26** Terry Martin, *The Affirmative Action Empire. Nations and Nationalism in the Soviet Union, 1923–1939* (Cornell, 2001), p. 4. • **27** Ibid., p. 6. • **28** Ibid., p. 167. • **29** Ibid., p. 36. • **30** Ibid., pp. 40, 49. • **31** Kate Brown, *A Biography of No Place: From Ethnic Borderland to Soviet Heartland* (Cambridge, MA, 2009) p. 108. • **32** Martin, op. cit., p. 315. • **33** Ibid., p. 322; Brown, op. cit., p. 107. • **34** Martin, op. cit., pp. 320–1. • **35** Ibid., p. 329. • **36** Ibid., pp. 325–6. • **37** Ibid., p.329. • **38** Brown, op. cit., p. 123. • **39** Ibid., p. 125. • **40** Ibid., p. 128. • **41** Ibid., pp. 38–47. • **42** Ibid., p. 49. • **43** Martin, op. cit., p. 330. • **44** Ibid., p. 332. • **45** Gross, op. cit., p. 17. • **46** Ibid., pp. 33–4. • **47** Ibid., p. 148. • **48** Adamczyk, op. cit., p. 23. • **49** Gross, op. cit., pp. 46–8. • **50** Ibid., pp. 35–45. • **51** Ibid., p. 57. • **52** On the revolution in schooling and the rebellions, see Gross, op. cit., pp. 126–40. • **53** Cienciala, Lebedeva, and Materski, op. cit., p. 136. • **54** Lebedeva, 'Deportation', p. 40. • **55** Cienciala, Lebedeva and Materski, op. cit., pp. 149–52.

• **56** Ibid., p. 153. • **57** The debate is discussed in ibid., pp. 136–48. • **58** Lebedeva, 'Deportation', p. 37. • **59** Cienciala, Lebedeva and Materski, op. cit., p. 77. • **60** Miłosz, *Native Realm*.

4 In 'Siberia': Life in Kazakhstan

1 Sword, *Deportation and Exile*, pp. 24–5. • **2** Lynne Viola, *The Unknown Gulag. The Lost World of Stalin's Special Settlements* (Oxford, 2007), pp. 22, 115. • **3** Ibid., p. 96. • **4** Ibid., p. 75. • **5** Ibid., p. 99. • **6** This process as summarised in the following paragraph, can be followed in Viola, op. cit., pp. 115–131. • **7** Ibid., p. 101. • **8** Ibid., p. 5; Martin, *Affirmative Action Empire*. • **9** Viola, op. cit., pp. 160–5. • **10** For a detailed discussion of a wide range of evidence see Katherine Jolluck, *Exile and Identity. Polish Women in the Soviet Union during World War II* (Pittsburg, 2002), pp. 45–86. • **11** Ibid., p. 123. • **12** Quotations in ibid., pp. 137–9. • **13** Central Omsk, a Siberian city on the Irtysh to the north of Pavlodar, is now dominated by a new Orthodox basilica. It was consecrated in 2007 in a ceremony of great civic and religious pomp and circumstance, further cementing the alliance between church and state that characterises contemporary Russia. • **14** I am grateful to the Hoover Institute Archive, University of Stanford, for supplying me with a copy of Wanda's 1941 deposition. • **15** Gross, *Revolution from Abroad*, p. 47. • **16** Full report is reproduced in Oleg V. Khlevniuk, *The History of the Gulag. From Collectivisation to the Great Terror* (Yale, 2004), pp. 282–286. The report further suggests that the capacity of the Poles to meet these excessive norms were resented by the other collective farmers. The report's authors indicated the contempt they felt for the indolent wives of these farmers. They also drew attention to the sympathy the Poles had attracted from Trotskyists. • **17** Jolluck, op. cit., p. 46. • **18** I've changed the name. • **19** Herling, *A World Apart*; Applebaum, op. cit., pp. 284–292. • **20** Jolluck, op. cit., pp. 164–75. • **21** Cienciala, Lebedeva and Materski, op. cit., pp. 114, 171, 174. • **22** Khlevnink, op. cit., p.284 • **23** Quoted in Jolluck, op. cit., p. 63. • **24** Ibid., p. 119. • **25** Ibid., p. 144. • **26** Ibid., p. 227. • **27** Ibid., p. 220–244.

5 Leaving the Soviet Union

1 Sword, *Deportation and Exile*, p. 29. • **2** Ibid., pp. 29–30. • **3** Lebedeva, 'Deportation', p. 16. • **4** Sword, op. cit., p. 40; Herling, *A World Apart*, p. 178; Applebaum, *Gulag*, pp. 402–3. • **5** Sword, op., cit., p. 32. • **6** Ibid., pp. 35–6. • **7** Herling, op. cit., pp. 190–209. • **8** Sword, op. cit., p. 57. • **9** Władysław Anders, *An Army in Exile. The Story of the Second Polish Corps* (Nashville, 1981), pp. 63–4. • **10** Ibid., p. 94. • **11** Sword, op. cit., pp. 62–5. • **12** Ibid., pp. 61–2. • **13** This description of the Soviet war effort draws on the remarkable analysis in Richard Overy, *Why the Allies Won* (London, 1995, 2006). Quote at p. 122. • **14** This account is from Tadeusz Piotrowski (ed.), *The Polish Deportees of World War II. Recollections of Removal to the Soviet Union and Dispersal Throughout the World* (Jefferson, 2004), pp. 77–80. •

15 Herling, op. cit., p. 51. • **16** Sword, op. cit., p. 45. • **17** The following examples can be examined in more detail in Piotrowski (ed.), *Polish Deportees*, pp. 80–96. • **18** For a peculiar illustration of the importance of 'Rota' to Poles during World War Two see Meta Maclean, *The Singing Ship. An Odyssey of Evacuee Children* (Sydney, 1941), pp. 186–94, translation, p. 193: 'Never we'll leave the land we love / Her tongue relinquish never! / Polish in nation, blood and kings, / Piast's line shall live for ever. / We shall resist the foeman's rod – / This by the help of God! / Spirit of Poland, our heart's blood / We'll give for thy defending / Until the German menace dies, / All its oppression ending! / Strongholds remain where we have stood – / This by the help of God! / Children of Poland, freed from scorn / Poles to the end remaining, / Armed by tradition, we shall fight, / True liberty regaining. / The Bugle of God unsheathes the sword! / This by the help of God.' • **19** FO to IO, 30 March 1942 (IOR: L/PJ/8/413/365). These files are held by the British Library and form part of the India Office Records (IOR). They reproduce much that is also to be found in the Foreign Office, Colonial Office, Dominion Office and War Office files held at the National Archives (NA), Kew. • **20** Hodge to Patrick, 19 September 1941 (BL IOR: L/PJ/8/412/298). In the original, Hodge refers to Mohammadans, as was often the case at the time. • **21** Hodge, 'Proposed scheme for the organisation of the transfer of Polish families from Russia to India' (IOR: L/PJ/8/412/296–7). • **22** Anon., *My Name Is Million. The Experience of an Englishwoman in Poland* was published by Faber and Faber in 1940. The author is entranced by Poland, uneasy with Britain's tardiness in actually intervening militarily in Poland, and provides a touching if somewhat mawkish narrative until page 262, when she hits the reader with a long paragraph peddling every antisemitic generalisation associated with memories of the Soviet invasion and occupation. • **23** Patrick to Hodge, 21 October 1941 (IOR: L/PJ/8/412/282). • **24** 15 October 1941 (IOR: L/PJ/8/412/287). • **25** IOR: L/PJ/8/412/285. • **26** For example, telegram from the Polish embassy to the Foreign Office, 3 Febuary 1942 (IOR: L/PJ/8/412/259). • **27** 1 November 1941 (IOR: L/PJ/8/412/281). • **28** IOR: L/PJ/8/412/254. • **29** FO to IO, 30 March, 1942 (IOR: L/PJ/8/413/365). • **30** FO to Tehran, 1 April 1942 (IOR: L/PJ/8/413/354). • **31** Sword, op. cit., pp. 63, 65, 71. • **32** Ibid., p. 68. • **33** FO, WO, CO, IO and DO meeting, 31 March 1942 (IOR: L/PJ/8/413/356). • **34** Tehran to FO, 7 April 1942 (IOR: L/PJ/8/413/346). • **35** FO to Tehran, 11 April 1942 and Tehran to FO, 19 April 1942 (IOR: L/PJ/8/413/345, 337). • **36** Sword, op. cit., pp. 74–8. • **37** Eden to Amery, 6 June 1942 (IOR: L/PJ/8/412/232). • **38** IOR: L/PJ/8/412/228. • **39** Cairo to FO, 8 June 1942 (IOR: L/PJ/8/412/326). • **40** Tehran to FO, 16 June 1942; FO to DO, 22 June 1942 (IOR: L/PJ/8/412/320, 321). • **41** Cairo to FO, 22 June 1942 (IOR: L/PJ/8/412/319). • **42** FO to Cairo, 29 June 1942 (IOR: L/PJ/8/412/316). • **43** Cairo to FO, 26 June 1942 (IOR: L/PJ/8/412/318). • **44** Sword, op. cit., pp. 77–9. • **45** For Kot see 'Introduction' in Norman Davies and Antony Polonsky (eds), *Jews in Eastern Poland and the USSR, 1939–46* (Basingstoke, 1991), p. 43 and for Anders see his memoir *An Army in Exile*, p. 96. • **46** 'Introduction' in Davies and Polonsky (eds), op. cit., pp. 41–2. This introduction is unusual because it implicitly undermines a contribution in the same volume which the editors commissioned, namely Ryszard Terlecki's crude apologia for Anders' Army. • **47** For a view highly sceptical as to the good intentions of the Polish government and army leadership see David Engel, *In the Shadow of Auschwitz. The Polish Government-in-Exile and the Jews, 1939–1942* (North Carolina, 1987), pp. 132–47. See also Yisrael Gutman, 'Jews in Anders' Army in the Soviet Union', *Yad Vashem Studies* 12 (1977) and Shimon Redlich, 'Jews in Anders' Army in the Soviet Union, 1941–1942', *Soviet Jewish Affairs* 2 (1971). • **48** The phrase is common to much of the literature. • **49** Useful discussions of this complex and highly politicised subject can be found in Robert Cherry and Annamaria Orla-Bukowska, *Rethinking Poles and Jews. Troubled Past, Brighter Future* (Lanham, 2007), especially Helene Sinnreich, 'Polish and Jewish Historiography of Jewish–Polish Relations during World War II', pp. 99–108. • **50** Eva Hoffman, *Shtetl*, p. 210. • **51** The debate is summarised in a long footnote in Samuel D. Kassow, *Who Will Write Our History?* (London, 2009, orig. pub. 2007), pp. 476–7. • **52** The most nuanced analysis I have read of this phenomenon – nuances which would have been lost on many Polish soldiers – is Pawel Korzec and Jean-Charles Szurek, 'Jews and Poles under Soviet Occupation (1939–1941): Conflicting Interests' in Antony Polonsky (ed.), *Studies from Polin*, pp. 399–402. See also 'Introduction' in Davies and Polonsky (eds), op. cit., pp. 12–22. • **53** 'Introduction' in Davies and Polonsky (eds), op. cit., pp. 16, 22–5. • **54** Jolluck, *Exile and Identity*, p. 200. • **55** Ibid., pp. 189–201. The depositions were made in 1942–4 following evacuation from the Soviet Union and are now held at the Hoover Institution Archives at Stanford University. • **56** Herling wrote that the Jewish deportees of June 1940 'became the most bitter enemies of Soviet communism, more uncompromising in their hatred than old Russian prisoners and even the other foreigners. They exaggerated their hatred, as once they had exaggerated their love for it, with unequalled passion.' (*A World Apart*, p. 168). • **57** Engel, op. cit., p. 146. • **58** Ryszard Terlecki, 'The Jewish Issue in the Polish Army, 1941–44', in Davies and Polonsky (eds), op. cit., p. 165; Jan E. Zamojski, 'The Social History of Polish Exile (1939–1945). The Exile State and the Clandestine State: Society, Problems and Reflections' in Martin Conway and José Gotovitch (eds), *Europe in Exile. European Exile Communities in Britain 1940–5* (Oxford, 2001), pp. 209–10. • **59** Engel, op. cit., p. 144. • **60** Terlecki, op. cit., p. 167; Benjamin Meirtchak, *Jewish Military Casualties in the Polish Armies in World War II* (Tel Aviv, 1995), p. 133. • **61** Piotrowski (ed.), *Polish Deportees*, p. 90. • **62** A later letter from Rafał to Hanna (26 July 1946) suggests this story is true. • **63** Wesley Adamczyk, *When God Looked the Other Way*, p. 122. • **64** Ibid., pp. 132–3. • **65** Sword, op. cit., p. 81.

6 'We live in a state of tension': A Year in Persia

1 A note on usage: from 1935 Persia was officially known as Iran, though in popular usage it took a long time for the new name to stick. The government succumbed to pressure in 1949 and conceded that official use might be made of both Persia and Iran. I use Persia in this chapter because this reflects general usage at the time and is often how the country is remembered. • **2** Adamczyk, *When God Looked the Other Way*, p. 133. • **3** Piotrowski (ed.), *Polish Deportees*, p. 100. • **4** Jan Bednarz, 'The Life Story of a Very Ordinary Man', handwritten manuscript in author's possession, p. 41. • **5** Adamczyk, op. cit., p. 137. • **6** Piotrowski, (ed.) *Polish Deportees*, p. 102. • **7** Anders, *An Army in Exile*, p. 127. • **8** Piotrowski (ed.), *Polish Deportees*, pp. 99, 103; Bednarz, p. 42. • **9** Bednarz, p. 42. • **10** *Stalin's Ethnic Cleansing*, p. 100; also p. 213. • **11** Ibid., p. 44. • **12** Piotrowski (ed.,), *Polish Deportees*, p. 100. • **13** Ibid., p. 104. • **14** Ibid., p. 101. • **15** Reader Bullard, *Letters from Tehran: A British Ambassador in World War II Persia* (London, 1991), p. 223. • **16** Peter Avery, Gavin Hambly and Charles Melville (eds), *The Cambridge History of Iran. Vol. 7. From Nair Shah to the Islamic Republic* (Cambridge, 1991), pp. 436–7. • **17** The following extracts come from letters written on 4 and 22 April 1942. See Bullard, op. cit., pp. 128–9, 132–3. • **18** Herling, *A World Apart*, pp. 21–2. • **19** Bertha Bracey, 'Europe's Displaced Persons and the Problem of Relocation', *International Affairs*, vol. 20, no. 2 (April 1944), p. 229. • **20** IOR: L/PJ/8/413/188, 192, 194–5, 273–6, 285–8. • **21** Quoted in Sword, *Deportation and Exile*, p. 85. • **22** Letter from Treasury to Dr L. Grosfeld, Polish Minister of Finance, 4 May 1944 (IOR: L/PJ/8/413/123): 'It shows us that less than half the money is spent on food, clothing, rents and pocket-money, whereas [the rest is spent on] salaries, Polish supervising personnel in camps and medical and educational expenses. It is said that the total of Polish staffs in Persia is 21% of the number of refugees and that in the hospital the staff totals 86% of the number of patients. I think you know that we would not wish in any way to be harsh or ungenerous, but if there is substance in the above, I am sure you will appreciate the big danger involved of inflation or exhaustion of goods in short supply, quite apart from the consequent irritation to the native inhabitants concerned.' • **23** Government of India to IO, 16 October 1942 (IOR: L/PJ/8/412/149). • **24** IOR: L/PJ/8/414/141–144. • **25** According to the *Times of India*, 17 September 2006. • **26** IOR: L/PJ/8/414/100. • **27** *Stalin's Ethnic Cleansing*, p. 72. • **28** IOR: L/PJ/8/414/89. • **29** IOR: L/PJ/8/414/112. • **30** IOR: L/PJ/8/413/219. • **31** IOR: L/PJ/8/413/211. • **32** IOR: L/PJ/8/413/183, 187. • **33** Anders, op. cit., p. 127. • **34** Piotrowski (ed.), op. cit., p. 105. • **35** Ibid., p. 112; for landscape see also *Stalin's Ethnic Cleansing*, p. 76. • **36** Piotrowski (ed.), op. cit., p. 115. • **37** Ibid., pp. 106–7. • **38** A particular concern was the fate of Jan Lipiński, the brother of Lieutenant Zygmunt Lipiński, one of the famous Polish airmen who escaped to France at the moment of Poland's defeat and later fought in the Battle of Britain. Both his wife Janina and his mother were looking for him, and Hanna wanted Rafał to provide evidence of Zygmunt's and Jan's service so the women could demonstrate that they were of a military family. • **39** Piotrowski (ed.), op. cit., p. 109. • **40** *Niepojęta* is difficult to translate. As here, it is often used in a religious sense and means impossible-to-grasp, unimaginable, ineffable perhaps. • **41** The angel bespeaks an eastern influence; Father Christmas delivered presents in Warsaw. • **42** IOR: L/PJ/8/413/179, 25 September 1943. • **43** Sword, op. cit., p. 85. • **44** Bracey, op. cit., p. 230. • **45** IOR: L/PJ/8/413/132.

7 Karachi

1 Marvellous footage of its maiden voyage, including shots of its Polish-designed interior, can be seen at www.youtube.com/watch?v=Rdk-QoGcvWy or found under the title 'M/S Piłsudski i M/S Batory'. • **2** Meta Maclean, *The Singing Ship: An Odyssey of Evacuee Children* (Sydney, 1941). • **3** In June 1944 Wanda mentions that the great heat of May has given way to the strong winds of June. Anuradha Battacharjee notes that statistics from May 1945 indicate there were more cases of eye infection (451) caused by dust and the glare of the sun than there were malaria (203): see Anuradha Battacharjee, 'History of Polish Refugees in India between 1942–1948', PhD, 2006, University of Pune. • **4** Battacharjee, op. cit. • **5** When I was in Karachi there were seven small bombs and my friends thought it too dangerous to visit Mangho Pil. • **6** The author of over two hundred novels, he is best known for his epic cycle of twenty-nine novels on Polish history *Dzieje Polski*. • **7** www.santuarioloreto.it/eng/visitaguidata/vg_interno_07.htm • **8** The official definitions are in George Woodbridge, *UNRRA The History of the United Nations Relief and Rehabilitation Administration II* (New York, 1950), p. 471; see also Marvin Klemmé, *The Inside Story of UNRRA. An Experience in Internationalism. A first hand report on the displaced people of Europe* (New York, 1949), p. 114. • **9** Woodbridge, op. cit. p. 469. • **10** Klemmé, op. cit., pp. 1–9. • **11** Woodbridge, op. cit., p. 473. • **12** Ibid., p. 481. • **13** Ibid. pp. 486–7, 490–1. • **14** Woodbridge, *UNRRA III*, p. 423. • **15** Woodbridge, *UNRRA II*, p. 498. There was also a sizeable UNRRA operation in China, assisting some 15,500 Europeans, though this was dwarfed by the numbers of Chinese passing through Chinese transit centres run by the Chinese National Relief and Rehabilitation Administration. • **16** Anders, *Army in Exile*, p. 193. • **17** Ibid., p. 210. • **18** For detail see Sword, *Deportation and Exile*, pp. 143–173. • **19** Anders, op. cit., pp. 211–3. • **20** A full account of these exchanges can be found in Martin Gilbert, *Winston S. Churchill, Vol. VII. Road to Victory 1941–1945* (London, 1986), pp. 673–6, 681–4, 687–8, 1011–1016. • **21** IOR/L/PJ/8/413/69, 17 February 1945. • **22** War Cabinet, 21 February 1945 (NA: CAB/65/51/23). • **23** Anders, op. cit., pp. 276–8. Churchill's House of Commons statement (28 February 1945) was extracted in a report prepared by the India Office for the Indian Government – see IOR/L/PJ/8/414/450. • **24** Katherine Knox and Tony Kushner, *Refugees in an Age of Genocide: Global, National and Local Perspectives During the Twentieth Century* (London, 1999), p. 222. • **25** Some 21,750 released Polish POWs joined the Polish forces before July 1945, some 21,000 enlisted after. The political significance of this is discussed in the following chapter. • **26** In an earlier letter (22 January 1945), Mary had been impressed by Rafał's continued youthfulness (he sent her a photograph). Her Romek, though younger, had aged less well, but then he 'poor guy . . . took a wife unsuitable for him'. • **27** Records released by the Ministry of Defence, RAF Northolt, reference P/10756. • **28** The theme of Giuseppe Tomasi di Lampedusa, *Il Gattopardo* (*The Leopard*),

(1958). • **29** IOR/L/PJ/8/414/ 495, 492, 485. • **30** Norman Davies, *God's Playground II*, p. 364. • **31** http:// www.youtube.com/watch?v=ESklBgoxMt8 • **32** http://www.youtube.com/ watch?v=FBE90a3ODK0

8 'Polish Indians': Valivade

1 Battacharjee, 'Polish Refugees in India', pp. 293–6. • **2** Ibid., p. 294. • **3** Ibid., pp. 260–1. • **4** IOR/L/AG/40/1/169. • **5** Battacharjee, op. cit., pp. 262–4. • **6** Secretatry of State for India to Viceroy, 18 October 1941 (IOR/L/PJ/413/285). • **7** Viceroy to S of S for India, 1 November 1941 (IOR/L/PJ/415/281). • **8** Viceroy's Camp to Amery, 23 December 1941 (IOR/L/PJ/412/254). • **9** IOR/L/AG/40/1/169. • **10** The relationship between caste and Raj has come under very complex scrutiny from historians and cannot be summarised here, but suffice it to say that some historians see the *particulars* of the caste system under the Raj are now viewed as a creation of the Raj rather than an unchanging aspect of Indian life. • **11** Figures from *Memorial Album of the Polish Settlement of Valivade* (pub. India, 2nd ed., 1946); Battacharjee, op. cit., p. 277. • **12** *Memorial Album.* • **13** IOR/L/AG/40/1/171. • **14** Tehran to Cairo, 14 February 1944 (IOR/L/PJ/413/154). • **15** IOR/L/PJ/8/414/368. • **16** IOR/L/PJ/8/414/375. • **17** IOR/L/PJ/8/414/282. • **18** IOR/L/PJ/8/414/376. • **19** Discussed by the Inter-Departmental Committee on Disposal of Non-Repatriable Members of the Polish Armed Forces, FO, 21 December 1945 (IOR/L/PJ/8/414/348). • **20** NA: CAB 129/6. • **21** Ibid. • **22** IOR/L/PJ/8/414/319. • **23** File copy of 'Memorandum on the removal of Polish refugees from India' (IOR/l/PJ/8/414/233). • **24** IOR/L/PJ/8/414/318, 26 March 1946. • **25** IOR/L/PJ/8/414/302, 9 April 1946. • **26** IOR/L/PJ/8/415/570, 26 November 1946. • **27** IOR/L/PJ/8/414/126, 15 August 1946. • **28** Treasury to IO, 13 December 1945 (IOR/L/PJ/414/386). • **29** Note by Ministry of Labour and National Service, n/d (IOR/L/PJ/414/378). • **30** Tony Kushner, *The Persistence of Prejudice. Antisemitism in British society during the Second World War* (Manchester 1989), pp. 126, 140–1. • **31** Bernard Wasserstein, *Britain and the Jews of Europe 1939–1945*, 2nd ed. (London, 1999), pp. 108–16. • **32** Jerzy Zubrzycki, *Polish Immigrants in Britain. A Study of Adjustment* (The Hague, 1956), p. 56. • **33** IOR/L/PJ/8/414/196, 193; IOR/L/P&J/8/415/587. • **34** By this time Rafał, we can be sure, was as unconvinced as the British government was annoyed by parts of Anders' Italian speech. 'We shall go from Italian soil', the General prophesied, 'through the British Isles and tomorrow along the unknown road to Poland. We shall go to the Poland for which we fought and which no Polish heart can imagine without Lvov and Vilna . . . Our march towards a free and independent Poland goes on' (NA: CAB/128/5). • **35** IOR/L/PJ/8/415/551, 469, 466, 467, 406. • **36** IOR/L/AG/50/1/117. • **37** IOR/L/PJ/8/415/569. • **38** IOR/L/PJ/8/415/239. • **39** FO to WO, 21 January 1948 (IOR/L/P&J/8/415/32). • **40** IOR/L/PJ/8/415/174. • **41** IOR/L/PJ/8/417/97. • **42** IOR/L/PJ/8/415/208. • **43** IOR/L/PJ/8/417/28. • **44** IOR/L/PJ/8/417/24. • **45** IOR/L/AG/40/1/175.

9 Britain: The 'hotel for the homeless'

1 Plaster Down was periodically used as an army camp since at least the 1880s, which has often been a source of controversy among local people. *The Times*, 29 April 1886, 25 October 1950, 15 August 1962. • **2** J. Potocki, *A Severed Branch* (Warsaw, 1960) quoted in Jerzy Zubrzycki, *Soldiers and Peasants: the Sociology of Polish Migration* (London, 1988), p. 158. • **3** Keith Sword with Norman Davies and Jan Ciechanowski, *The Formation of the Polish Community in Great Britain* (London, 1989), p. 250. • **4** Sword, op. cit., pp. 257–63; Zubrzycki, *Polish Immigrants in Britain*, p. 99; Zamoyski, *The Forgotten Few. The Polish Air Force in the Second World War* (London, 1995), pp. 206–9. • **5** *Stalin's Ethnic Cleansing*, pp. 644–5. • **6** Sword, op. cit., pp. 265–6. • **7** Incoming Passenger Lists, 1878–1960 can be found at www.ancestry.co.uk. • **8** Adam Zamoyski discusses British responses to the amorous reputation of the Polish airmen in *The Forgotten Few*, pp. 173–180. 'They were not a bunch of Don Juans,' he writes, 'and many of them had sweethearts back in Poland whom they still hoped to marry. But, being Poles, they were peacocks, and highly flirtatious.' • **9** *The Times*, 13 April 1947. • **10** Sword, op. cit., pp. 279–81. • **11** Evidence from 1950 suggests the incidence of mental illness among Polish settlers was significantly above the norm (4.42 per 1,000 as opposed to 0.82 per 1,000); more fragmentary evidence suggests the same of the Polish suicide rate. These trends were attributed to 'cultural isolation, war-time frustration and occupation and social degradation'. See Zubrzycki, *Polish Immigrants in Britain*, pp. 186–8. Also, Elizabeth Stadulis, 'Resettlement of Displaced Persons in the United Kingdom' in *Population Studies*, vol. 3 (March 1952), pp. 229–30.

Afterword – Poland Found?

1 Plymouth and West Devon Record Office: Tavistock Rural District Council Minutes, call number 1690/13; Sampford Spiney Parish Council Minute Book, 1051/1; Whitchuch Commoners Association, 1250; Plaster Down Parish Council Minutes, 1251. • **2** The academic literature on the 'memory boom' is now huge. Pierre Nora set much of the agenda in a seminal article: 'Between History and Memory: *Les Lieux de Mémoire*', in *Representations*, 26 (1989). Pioneering general treatments include Raphael Samuel, *Theatres of Memory. Vol. 1: past and present in contemporary culture* (London, 1994) and David Lowenthal, *The past is a foreign country* (Cambridge, 1985). • **3** Exhibit A: Norman Tebbit during the discussions on the twenty-fifth anniversary of the 1984 Miners' Strike. • **4** Roy Foster, *Paddy and Mr Punch* (London, 1991). • **5** Zubrzycki, *Polish Immigrants in Britain*, pp. 162–4. • **6** Aspects of this discussion are informed by essays from Dorota Glowacka and Joanna Zylinska (eds), *Imaginary Neighbours. Mediating Polish–Jewish Relations after the Holocaust* (Lincoln and London, 2007), p. 125. • **7** Glowacka, 'Forgiving, Witnessing, and "Polish Shame"', in ibid., p. 256. • **8** Richard C. Lukes, *The* *forgotten holocaust: the Poles under German occupation, 1939–1944* (Lexington, 1986) and Tadeusz Piotrowski, *Poland's Holocaust*. • **9** Interview, March 1997, available at www.yadvashem.org. Summarising German intentions, Browning writes: 'Central Poland was to be a vast reservoir of cheap Polish labour – deprived of its present and potential leadership through extensive executions, denationalised by the systematic repression of Polish culture, raided for what the Nazis considered its most valuable biological elements by a process of selection and "Germanization" (*Eindeutschung*) or "re-Germanization" (*Wiedereindeutschung*), and forced to work on German terms by means of a deliberately depressed standard of living.' See Christopher R. Browning, *The Origins of the Final Solution* (Lincoln, 2004), p. 106. • **10** On this and much more, see Donald Bloxham and Tony Kushner, *The Holocaust: critical historical approaches* (Manchester, 2005). • **11** For example, see Yisrael Gutman, 'Polish Antisemitism Between the Wars: An Overview' in Yisrael Gutman, Ezra Mendelsohn, Jehuda Reinharz and Chone Shmeruk (eds), *The Jews of Poland Between Two World Wars*, p. 107. • **12** Richard Ned Lebow, 'The Memory of Politics in Postwar Europe' in Richard Ned Lebow, Wulf Kansteiner and Claudio Fogu (eds), *The Politics of Memory in Postwar Europe* (Durham and London, 2006), p. 14. • **13** Jan Błoński's essay 'Poor Poles Look at the Ghetto', in *Polin* 2 (1987), published in Polish in 1986, began the modern debate and key pre-*Neighbours* studies in English include Antony Polonsky, *My Brother's Keeper? Recent Polish Debates on the Holocaust* (London, 1990); Carol Rittner and John R. Roth (eds), *Memory Offended: The Auschwitz Convent Controversy* (New York, 1991); and Michael Steinlauf, *Bondage to the Dead: Poland and the Memory of the Holocaust* (Syracuse, 1997). • **14** Jan T. Gross, *Neighbours. The Destruction of the Jewish Community in Jedwabne, Poland* (Princeton and Oxford, 2001). The Catholic intellectual monthly *Więź* translated into English some of the most important initial responses to *Neighbours* under the uncompromising title *Thou Shalt Not Kill. Poles on Jedwabne*. Available at http://wiez.free.ngo.pl/jedwabne/main.html • **15** The phrase is Joanna Zylinska's, drawing on the work of Milchman and Rosenberg. See her '"Who is My Neighbor?": Ethics under Duress' in Dorota Glowacka and Joanna Zylinska (eds), op. cit., p. 280. • **16** Dorota Glowacka, 'Forgiving, Witnessing, and "Polish Shame"' in ibid., p. 255. • **17** The literature on this subject is now huge. A notable recent addition is Neil Gregor, *Haunted City. Nuremberg and the Nazi Past* (New Haven, 2008). • **18** For the complexities of this phenomenon see the brilliant essay by Erica Lehrer, 'Bearing False Witness? "Vicarious" Jewish Identity and the Politics of Affinity' in Glowacka and Zylinska (eds), op. cit., pp. 84–109. • **19** Noted in Marita Grimwood, 'Imagined Topographies. Visions of Poland in Writings by Descendants of Survivors', in ibid., p. 137. • **20** For an excellent treatment see Annamaria Orla-Bukowska, 'New Threads on an Old Loom. National Memory and Social Identity in Postwar and Post-Communist Poland', in Lebow, Kansteiner and Fogu (eds), *Politics of Memory*, pp. 177–209.

Bibliography

Manuscript sources:

British Library, London

India Office Records: Public and Judicial Dept., 1792–1955 (IOR/L/PJ)
– Evacuation of Polish women and children from Russia to India, Sept. 1941–Apr. 1946 (IOR/L/PJ/8/412)
– Disposal of Poles evacuated from Russia to Persia and India, Mar. 1942–Nov. 1946 (IOR/L/PJ/8/413)
– Polish refugees in India and question of their removal, Jul. 1945–Nov. 1946 (IOR/L/PJ/8/414)
– Polish refugees in India and their removal, Nov. 1946–Nov. 1949 (IOR/L/PJ/8/415)
– Polish refugees in India and their removal, Sept. 1947–Feb. 1948 (IOR/L/PJ/8/416)
– Polish refugees in India and their removal, Feb. 1948–Jun. 1950 (IOR/L/PJ/8/417)
– Appointment of liaison officer with Polish refugees in India, Jul.–Oct. 1946 (IOR/L/PJ/8/418)

India Office Records: Accountant General's Records, c1601–1974 (IOR/L/AG)
– Polish Refugee Camp files, mainly of the Government of India (IOR/L/AG/40/1/167–182)

Hoover Institute, University of Stanford

Records of the Polish Ministry of Information and Documentation
– Testimony of Rafał Ryżewski and Wanda Ryżewska.

The National Archive, Kew

Records of the Cabinet Office
- Minute 2: Poland: Discussion on the future Government of Poland, 21 Feb. 1945 (CAB 65/51/23)
- Cabinet Conclusions, Jan. 1 – Jun. 27, 1946 (CAB 128/5)
- Cabinet Memorandum, Jan.1 – Feb. 11, 1946 (CAB 129/6)
- Cabinet Memorandum, Mar. 8 – Apr. 10, 1946 (CAB 129/8)

The Plymouth and West Devon Record Office

Plasterdown Parish Council Minutes (1251)
Sampford Spiney Parish Council Minute Book (1051/1)
Tavistock Rural District Council Minutes (1690/13)
Whitchuch Commoners Association (1250)

Manuscript sources in possession of the author

Jan Bednarz, 'The Life Story of a Very Ordinary Man' (unpublished autobiography)
Franciszek Herzog, 'The Herzog Family Chronicle' (unpublished family history)
K. Kosiba, 'My Journey from Poland to England in 1939' (unpublished autobiography)
The Ryżewski Papers

RAF Northolt (Ministry of Defence)

Records of the Polish Armed Forces
- Army record of Rafał Ryżewski (P/10756)

Printed Sources:

Collections of Published Testimony:

Association of the Poles in India 1942–1948, *Poles in India 1942–1948. Second World War Story* (London, 2009)
Association of the Families of the Borderland Settlers, *Stalin's Ethnic Cleansing in Eastern Poland. Tales of the Deported 1940–1946* (London, 2000)
Tadeusz Piotrowski (ed.), *The Polish Deportees of World War II.*

Recollections of Removal to the Soviet Union and Dispersal throughout the World (Jefferson, 2004)

Books, articles and essays:

Adamczyk, Wesley, *When God Looked the Other Way. An Odyssey of War, Exile and Redemption* (Chicago, 2006)

Alexander, J. G., 'The Legacy of Three Crises: Parliament and Ethnic Issues in Prewar Poland', in *Slavic Review*, vol. 27, no. 4 (1968)

Anon., *My Name Is Million. The Experience of an Englishwoman in Poland* (London, 1940)

Anders, Władysław, *An Army in Exile. The Story of the Second Polish Corps* (Nashville, 1981)

Applebaum, Anne, *Gulag. A History* (London, 2003)

Avery, Peter, Hambly, Gavin & Melville, Charles (eds), *The Cambridge History of Iran. Vol. 7. From Nair Shah to the Islamic Republic* (Cambridge, 1991)

Błoński, Jan, 'Poor Poles Look at the Ghetto', in *Polin* 2 (1987)

Bracey, Bertha, 'Europe's Displaced Persons and the Problem of Relocation', *International Affairs*, vol. 20, no. 2 (Apr. 1944)

Brown, Kate, *A Biography of No Place: From Ethnic Borderland to Soviet Heartland* (Cambridge, MA, 2004)

Browning, Christopher R., *The Origins of the Final Solution* (Lincoln, 2004)

Bullard, Reader, *Letters from Tehran: A British Ambassador in World War II Persia* (London, 1991)

Cherry, Robert & Orla-Bukowska, Annamaria (eds), *Rethinking Poles and Jews. Troubled Past, Brighter Future* (Lanham, 2007)

Cienciala, Anna M., Lebedeva, Natalia S. and Materski, Wojciech, *Katyn. A Crime Without Punishment* (New Haven and London, 2007)

Cubitt, Geoff (ed.), *Imagining Nations* (Manchester, 1998)

Davies, Norman, *God's Playground. Vol. II.* (Oxford, 2006)

Davies, Norman & Polonsky, Antony (eds), *Jews in Eastern Poland and the USSR, 1939–46* (Basingstoke, 1991)

Davies, Norman, 'The Missing Revolutionary War. The Polish Campaign and the Retreat from Revolution in Soviet Russia, 1919–21', in *Soviet Studies*, vol. xxvii, no. 2 (April 1975)

Dziewanowski, M. K., *Joseph Piłsudski. A European Federalist, 1918–1922* (Stanford, 1969)

Engel, David, *In the Shadow of Auschwitz. The Polish Government-in-Exile and the Jews, 1939–1942* (North Carolina, 1987)

Foster, R. F., *Paddy and Mr Punch* (London, 1991)

Glowacka, Dorota, 'Forgiving, Witnessing, and "Polish Shame"' in Dorota Glowacka & Joanna Zylinska (eds), *Imaginary Neighbours. Mediating Polish–Jewish Relations after the Holocaust* (Lincoln and London, 2007)

Głowiński, Michał, *The Black Seasons* (Illinois, 2001)

Gregor, Neil, *Haunted City. Nuremberg and the Nazi Past* (Hew Haven, 2008)

Grimwood, Marita, 'Imagined Topographies. Visions of Poland in Writings by Descendents of Survivors', in Glowacka & Zylinska (eds), *Imaginary Neighbours. Mediating Polish–Jewish Relations after the Holocaust* (Lincoln and London, 2007)

Gross, Jan T., *Neighbours. The Destruction of the Jewish Community in Jedwabne, Poland* (Princeton and Oxford, 2001)

Gross, Jan T., *Revolution from Abroad. The Soviet Occupation of Poland's Western Ukraine and Western Belorussia* (Princeton, 1992, 2002)

Gutman, Yisrael, 'Jews in Anders' Army in the Soviet Union', *Yad Vashem Studies* 12 (1977)

Gutman, Yisrael, 'Polish Antisemitism Between the Wars: An Overview' in Yisrael Gutman, Ezra Mendelsohn, Jehuda Reinharz, and Chone Shmeruk (eds), *The Jews of Poland Between Two World Wars* (Hanover and London, 1989)

Hagen, William W., 'Before the "Final Solution": Towards a Comparative Analysis of Political Anti-Semitism in Interwar Germany and Poland', *The Journal of Modern History*, vol. 68, no. 2 (Jun. 1996)

Herling, Gustav, *A World Apart* (London, 1951, 1986)

Hobsbawm, Eric, *Interesting Times. A Twentieth-Century Life* (London, 2002)

Hoffman, Eva, *Shtetl. The History of a Small Town and an Extinguished World* (London, 1997)

Jolluck, Katherine, *Exile and Identity. Polish Women in the Soviet Union during World War II* (Pittsburg, 2002)

Kassow, Samuel D., *Who Will Write Our History?* (London, 2007)

Khlevniuk, Oleg V., *The History of the Gulag. From Collectivisation to the Great Terror* (Yale, 2004)

Klemmé, Marvin, *The Inside Story of UNRRA. An Experience in Internationalism. A first hand report on the displaced people of Europe* (New York, 1949)

Knox, Katherine & Kushner, Tony, *Refugees in an Age of Genocide: Global, National and Local Perspectives During the Twentieth Century* (London, 1999)

Korzec, Paweł & Szurek, Jean-Charles, 'Jews and Poles under Soviet Occupation (1939–1941): Conflicting Interests' in Antony Polonsky (ed.), *Studies from Polin. From Shtetl to Socialism* (London, 1993)

Kundera, Milan, *Immortality* (London, 1991)

Kushner, Tony, *The Persistence of Prejudice. Antisemitism in British society during the Second World War* (Manchester, 1989)

Lebedeva, Natalia, 'The Deportation of the Polish Population to the USSR, 1939–41', *Journal of Communist and Transition Politics*, 16, nos. 1–2 (March–June, 2000)

Lebow, Richard Ned, 'The Memory of Politics in Postwar Europe' in Richard Ned Lebow, Wulf Kansteiner & Claudio Fogu (eds), *The Politics of Memory in Postwar Europe* (Durham and London, 2006)

Lehrer, Erica, 'Bearing False Witness? "Vicarious" Jewish Identity and the Politics of Affinity' in Glowacka & Zylinska (eds), *Imaginary Neighbours. Mediating Polish–Jewish Relations after the Holocaust* (Lincoln and London, 2007)

Lowenthal, David, *The Past is a Foreign Country* (Cambridge, 1985)

Lukes, Richard C., *The Forgotten Holocaust: The Poles under German Occupation, 1939–1944* (Lexington, 1986)

Maclean, Meta, *The Singing Ship. An Odyssey of Evacuee Children* (Sydney, 1941)

MacCullough, Diarmaid, *Reformation. Europe's House Divided 1490–1700* (London, 2003)

Magocsi, Paul Robert, *Historical Atlas of Central Europe. From the early fifth century to the present* (London, 2002)

Martin, Terry, *The Affirmative Action Empire. Nations and Nationalism in the Soviet Union, 1923–1939* (Cornell, 2001)

Meirtchak, Benjamin, *Jewish Military Casualties in the Polish Armies in World War II* (Tel Aviv, 1995)

Mendelsohn, Ezra, 'Interwar Poland: Good or Bad for the Jews?' in Chimen Abramsley, Maciej Jachimcyk, & Antony Polonsky (eds), *The Jews in Poland* (Oxford, 1986)

Miłosz, Czesław, *Native Realm. A Search for Self-Definition* (London, 1968)

Miłosz, Czesław, *The Captive Mind* (1953, Harmondsworth, 1980)

Nora, Pierre, 'Between History and Memory: *Les Lieux de Mémoire*', in *Representations*, 26 (1989)

Orla-Bukowska, Annamaria, 'New Threads on an Old Loom. National Memory and Social Identity in Postwar and Post-Communist Poland', in Lebow, Kansteiner & Fogu (eds), *The Politics of Memory in Postwar Europe* (Durham and London, 2006)

Overy, Richard, *Why the Allies Won* (London, 1995, 2006)

Piotrowski, Tadeusz, *Poland's Holocaust: Ethnic Strife, Collaboration with Occupying Forces and Genocide in the Second Republic, 1918–1947* (Jefferson, 1998)

Antony Polonsky, *My Brother's Keeper? Recent Polish Debates on the Holocaust* (London, 1990)

Polonsky, Antony, *Politics in Independent Poland* (Oxford, 1972)

Polonsky, Antony (ed.), *Studies from Polin. From Shtetl to Socialism* (London & Washington, 1993)

Porter, Brian, *When Nationalism Began to Hate: Imagining Modern Politics in Nineteenth-Century Poland* (Oxford, 2000)

Redlich, Shimon, 'Jews in Anders' Army in the Soviet Union, *1941–1942*', *Soviet Jewish Affairs* 2 (1971)

Redlich, Shimon, *Together and Apart in Brzezany. Poles, Jews, and Ukrainians, 1919–1945* (Bloomington, In., 2002)

Rittner, Carol & Roth, John R. (eds), *Memory Offended: The Auschwitz Convent Controversy* (New York, 1991)

Roskowski, Wojciech, *Landowners in Poland 1918–1939* (New York, 1991)

Sadkowski, Konrad, 'From Ethnic Borderland to Catholic Fatherland: The Church, Christian Orthodoxy, and State Administration in the Chełm Region, 1918–1939', *Slavic Review* 57, no. 4 (Winter 1998)

Samuel, Raphael, *Theatres of Memory. Vol. 1: Past and Present in Contemporary Culture* (London, 1994)

Sienkiewicz, Henryk, *With Fire and Sword. Volume 1* (Amsterdam, 2002)

Sinnreich, Helene, 'Polish and Jewish Historiography of Jewish–Polish Relations during World War II' in Robert Cherry & Annamaria Orla-Bukowska (eds), *Rethinking Poles and Jews. Troubled Past, Brighter Future* (Lanham, 2007)

Snyder, Timothy, *The Reconstruction of Nations. Poland, Ukraine, Lithuania, Belarus 1569–1999* (New Haven & London, 2003)

Stadulis, Elizabeth, 'Resettlement of Displaced Persons in the United Kingdom' in *Population Studies*, vol, 3 (Mar. 1952)

Steinlauf, Michael, *Bondage to the Dead: Poland and the Memory of the Holocaust* (Syracuse, 1997)

Stone, Daniel, 'Jews and the Urban Question in Late Eighteenth-Century Poland', *Slavic Review* 50, no. 3 (Fall 1991)

Sword, Keith, *Deportation and Exile: Poles in the Soviet Union, 1939–48* (Basingstoke, 1994)

Sword, Keith, with Davies, Norman & Ciechanowski, Jan, *The Formation of the Polish Community in Great Britain* (London, 1989)

Terlecki, Ryszard, 'The Jewish Issue in the Polish Army, 1941–44', in Norman Davies & Polonsky, Antony (eds), *Jews in Eastern Poland and the USSR, 1939–46* (Basingstoke, 1991)

Viola, Lynne, *The Unknown Gulag. The Lost World of Stalin's Special Settlements* (Oxford, 2007)

Wasserstein, Bernard, *Britain and the Jews of Europe 1939–1945.* (London, 1999)

Weeks, Theodore R., 'Defining Us and Them: Poles and Russians in the "Western Provinces," 1863–1914', *Slavic Review* 53, no. 1 (Spring 1994)

Woodbridge, George, *UNRRA. The History of the United Nations Relief and Rehabilitation Administration II* (New York, 1950)

Zamojski, Jan E., 'The Social History of Polish Exile (1939–1945). The Exile State and the Clandestine State: Society, Problems and Reflections' in Martin Conway & José Gotovitch (eds), *Europe in Exile. European Exile Communities in Britain 1940–5* (Oxford, 2001)

Zamoyski, Adam, *The Forgotten Few. The Polish Air Force in the Second World War* (London, 1995)

Zamoyski, Adam, *The Last King of Poland* (London, 1992)

Zawacki, Edmund I., 'The Utopianism of Stefan Żeromski', *Slavonic and East European Review. American Series*, vol. 2, no. 1 (Mar., 1943)

Zubrzycki, Jerzy, *Polish Immigrants in Britain. A Study of Adjustment* (The Hague, 1956)

Zylinska, Joanna, '"Who is My Neighbor?": Ethics under Duress' in Dorota Glowacka & Joanna Zylinska (eds), *Imaginary Neighbors. Mediating Polish–Jewish Relations after the Holocaust* (Lincoln and London, 2007)

Unpublished PhD Thesis:

Battacharjee, Anuradha, 'History of Polish Refugees in India between 1942–1948', PhD 2006, University of Pune, India

Index